3|11

The International Encyclopedia of Gambling

The International Encyclopedia of Gambling

VOLUME I

William N. Thompson

Santa Barbara, California • Denver, Colorado • Oxford, England

Library of Congress Cataloging-in-Publication Data

Thompson, William Norman.
  The international encyclopedia of gambling / William N. Thompson.
    p. cm.
  Includes bibliographical references and index.
  ISBN 978-1-59884-225-8 (alk. paper) — ISBN 978-1-59884-226-5 (ebook) 1. Gambling—
Encyclopedias. 2. Gambling—Social aspects. I. Title.
  GV1301.T474 2010
  306.4'8203—dc22   2009048274

14 13 12 11 10 1 2 3 4 5

This book is also available on the World Wide Web as an eBook.
Visit www.abc-clio.com for details.

ABC-CLIO, LLC
130 Cremona Drive, P.O. Box 1911
Santa Barbara, California 93116-1911
This book is printed on acid-free paper ∞

Contents

Section Two: Games, 239

Section Three: Biographies of Leading Figures in Gambling, 289

Volume 2

Section Four: Venues and Places, 355

Acknowledgments

The editor is grateful for help received from many people and many organizations in compiling this encyclopedia.

As mentioned in the acknowledgments in the first *Gambling in America* edition in 2001, this work is vitally dependent upon libraries and librarians, especially those with the special collections unit of the Lied Library at the University of Nevada, Las Vegas. Special thanks go to the University of Nevada, Las Vegas, for providing released time and a sabbatical year grant that enabled much of the travel and research that has contributed to this volume. Of particular note was the editor's sabbatical as visiting scholar at the Osaka University of Commerce (OU of C) in Japan, under the sponsorship of its president Ichiro Tanioka, who is Japan's leading gambling scholar. OU of C scholars H. C. Yang and Kotaro Fugimoto were wonderful in assisting the research effort and in hosting tours of Korea and Korean casinos.

Many others assisted in contributing to various entries, and their names are listed in the text either as coauthors or as research helpers.

The greatest value of participation in gambling, according to the editor, is social interactions with others. Readers of this encyclopedia should be able to sense that among all gambling venues, the editor has a decided preference for destination resort casinos. Traveling to more than 500 casinos on five continents as well as Oceana have permitted the editor to engage in interactions with the true authorities on world gambling—the frontline managers and employees of casinos and other gambling facilities. The editor is very thankful for information they freely shared with him—information that has found its way into many of the entries of this book.

Last, this writing endeavor would not have been possible without the active helpful participation of the staff of ABC-CLIO, particularly Kim Kennedy White and Holly Heinzer. The editor is most grateful for the assistance and help he has always received from his traveling partner in life for more than 45 years, Kay Thompson.

Thank you all.

Preface

"Molly and Tenbrooks" ("The Horse Race")

Run O Molly run, run O Molly run
Tenbrooks gonna beat you to the bright shinin' sun.
To the bright shinin' sun O Lord to the bright shinin' sun

Tenbrooks was a big bay horse he wore that shaggy mane
He run all around Memphis he beat the Memphis train
Beat the Memphis train O Lord beat the Memphis train

See that train a-comin' it's comin' round the curve
See old Tenbrooks runnin' he's strainin' every nerve
Strainin' every nerve O Lord strainin' every nerve

Out in California where Molly done as she pleased
Come back to old Kentucky got beat with all ease
Beat with all ease O Lord beat with all ease

The women all a-laughin' the child'n all a cryin'
The men all a-hollerin' old Tenbrooks a-flyin'
Old Tenbrooks a-flyin' O Lord old Tenbrooks a-flyin'

Kyper Kyper you're not A-ridin' right
Molly's beatin' old Tenbrooks clear out sight
Clear out of sight O Lord clear out of sight

Kyper Kyper Kyper my son
Give old Tenbrooks the bridle let old Tenbrooks run
Let old Tenbrooks run O Lord let old Tenbrooks run

Go and catch old Tenbrooks and hitch him in the shade
We're gonna bury old Molly in a coffin ready made
Coffin ready made O Lord coffin ready made

Introduction

This edition of *The International Encyclopedia of Gambling* represents an expansion and updating of ABC-CLIO's 2001 book *Gambling in America: An Encyclopedia of History, Issues, and Society* by the same editor. In addition to updated versions of most entries from that volume, these volumes contain entries on all major gambling venues in the world—not just those of the Western Hemisphere—as well as biographies of leading gambling figures and descriptions of world events. As the editor considered a new edition, he realized that a comprehensive overview of organized gambling activity could no longer be confined to single countries and continents. As the European Union has torn down barriers for gaming investments by entrepreneurs as well as players, so too has the World Trade Organization made the gaming enterprise like almost all other enterprises—global in scope. As never before, activities in one venue are now more related to activities in all venues. The opening of China to casino gambling with the political annexation of Macau has had a global impact. The Chinese regime broke the monopoly of one organization over the casinos of Macau and awarded franchise licenses to two American concerns, tying the activity of casinos in Las Vegas and Asia closer together than ever before. Moreover, the availability of Internet gambling in homes across the globe, often without any respect for national boundaries, makes it necessary for any contemporary encyclopedia of gambling to be international in scope.

As Table 1 indicates, the growth of legalized casino gambling over the past few decades has been global, with most new national venues being located outside of the Americas.

As in the 2001 volume, here the editor tends to use the term *gambling* throughout the text in the entries as well as in the encyclopedia title, unless another term is used in previously published material. Leaders in the gambling industry today like to use the word *gaming* instead of *gambling*. Generally, they do so for public relations purposes, believing that the word *gaming* has a more pleasant tonal sound and that it can be associated with the types of play in which every person has participated: softball, jacks, hopscotch, Monopoly, or checkers. The word *gaming* is also associated with

TABLE 1. Number of Casinos per Country

Country	1986	1996	2005
Africa	20	30	29
Asia*	12	19	21
Europe	20	32	43
North America**	17	19	29
South America	8	9	10
Total	77	109	132

*includes the Middle East
**includes Central America and the Caribbean

recreational hunting and fishing. For historical reasons and because the word *gambling* is tied to the word *gamble* instead of the much less identifying word *game,* the editor finds the word gambling to be more appropriate for use in this encyclopedia.

The editor must make this observation. Today, opponents of legalized gambling almost invariably use the word *gambling* instead of *gaming.* Proponents use the word *gaming.* In this encyclopedia, the use of the term *gambling* is not intended to suggest to the reader that the editor is either a proponent or an opponent of legalized gambling activity. In truth, he has both supported and opposed various campaigns for legalization of gambling. He purports to have done so—hopefully—with a consistency that is discussed in the text (see especially Economics and Gambling; and Economic Impacts of Gambling). The same economic rationale that can be used in some instances to oppose gambling can in other cases support the cause of increased legalization of gambling. It is the same as saying that in some cases a cost-benefit analysis will lead to a conclusion that we should build a bridge, and at other times the same cost-benefit analysis methodology will lead to a conclusion that we should not build a bridge.

It is the editor's true desire to present concepts as well as ideas about gambling in a neutral and nonbiased way. There is no doubt that in some places individual or selected commentary may imply favoritism or animosity toward gambling activity. Be that as it may. The editor has striven for objectivity, realizing that at different times the entries may be utilized by both opponents and supporters of gambling.

It is the editor's belief and contention that the words *gambling* and *gaming* are essentially synonymous. For the most part, the words have been used to mean the same thing in the law, although debates over usage persist. Other words that have been applied to the gambling phenomenon include *betting, wagering,* and *risk taking.* Again, although the words may carry different connotations for some readers, they all have the same common core elements in their definitions.

The most comprehensive dictionary of gambling is *The Dictionary of Gambling and Gaming,* written by the late professor Thomas Clark of the University of Nevada, Las Vegas (Clark 1987). Most definitions of gambling cited by Clark find three elements that are essential to the activity: consideration, chance, and reward. The first, consideration, is the money put up—or staked. It represents something of value. The second is chance. A game involves at least some degree of chance—a randomly occurring risk that may or may not be calculated. The third element is reward. A reward is something of value that may be in excess of the value of the consideration. Clark defined *gambling* as "of or pertaining to risking of money or something of value on the outcome of a chance event such as a card or dice game" (Clark 1987, 88). He defined *gaming* as "the playing at games of chance for stakes." *Game* is short for gambling game and in verb form it is defined as "to stake a wager on the outcome of an event, as at cards or dice; to gamble." All the definitions encompass notions of risk taking, although Clark chose not to offer a definition of *risk*. Additionally, Clark defined the verb *to bet* as "to wager or stake, usually between two parties, on the outcome of an event" (16–17).

The activities Clark utilized in refined definitions include casino games and horse racing events. *Wager* is also defined as "a stake placed on the outcome of an event, such as a horse race or hand of a card game or roll of the dice" (Clark 1987, 246).

Again, it is not the purpose here to make very specific legal distinctions among the terms used most often to describe participation in the games of chance focused upon in these volumes. Instead the text will examine specific aspects of individual games and discuss the notions of skill and luck in their play. Whether the games involve races, lotteries, bingo, slot machines, cards, dice, or other casino play, the terms may be used interchangeably. The term *gambling,* the editor repeats, will be the preferred term.

Gambling is a risk-taking activity, but this encyclopedia will not be devoted to a comprehensive discussion of all risk-taking activities. Instead, attention is given to risk-taking activities involving games of that produce some chance outcomes, the placing of stakes on the outcomes, and the awarding of prizes for those who have put their money (consideration) on the outcomes that actually occur.

This encyclopedia is not about risky activities such as mountain climbing, sky diving, deep sea diving, surfing, ski jumping, or high-speed automobile racing. It is not concerned with business activities and businesspeople, who are sometimes described in macho terms as the ones who "swim with the sharks." A discussion of investments and trading on securities markets is included in order to make distinctions from (or to point out some similarities with) activities that are more universally described as gambling activities.

Much of the business world devotes attention toward minimizing risky activities. These risky activities may have been a part of the human condition before modern developments occurred. Spencer Johnson penned *Who Moved My Cheese,* an interesting book that describes the contrast between the modern world and the world of nature—the book comes down on the side of the latter—as a guide for behavior (Johnson 1998). The premise of the book is that two human beings from the civilized world discover that their "cheese" is disappearing. That is, they discover that what is of value to them is disappearing. So too do two mice. All had lived in comfort, having all that their hearts could possibly desire. One day, however, the stash of cheese upon which they all feasted disappears completely. Perhaps it was depleted by their excessive consumption, perhaps a stock market crashed, or other "investors" found it.

To briefly recap Johnson's discussion, the reaction of the humans and the mice to the loss of the cheese is quite different. The two little mice were initially stunned, but they soon rushed back out into the cruel world (the "real world") and once again engaged in the risky activity of hunting down "new cheese." The humans reacted differently. After looking at each other in stunned astonishment, they held a discussion (they could think, and they were civilized). They came up with the same thought at almost the same time and expressed it out loud: "Who moved my cheese?" Their subsequent thoughts and activity were ones of complete denial. They thought that they were entitled to the cheese. They wanted reparations of various kinds for having had it taken from them. When one suggested they engage in a new search, the other howled about the risk that they faced if they ventured out into the "real world."

Eventually the two humans split up, and one yielded to his inner feelings and began a new quest for cheese. Perhaps Johnson's story illustrates a deep-seated feeling within our genetic makeup that leads us on a quest for a prize, even if that quest involves dangers and unknown factors. Yet society may work against this natural force. Before we can undertake risk, we humans often have to first brush aside societal tendencies that tell us to stay in place. For other animals the impulse is much closer to their surface behaviors. Perhaps people have an inner impulse to gamble—to reach out and accept a fate that awaits them if they "let the dice roll." But then, they may feel the forces of society constraining their impulses.

As a species we have a dichotomous history: We took the risk of hunting, but our civilizing tendencies also urged us to abandon the hunt and settle in one place—to stop searching, to avoid risk and chance. Abt, Smith, and Christiansen (1985) begin their book on gambling by suggesting that the first gamblers were Adam and Eve in the Garden of Eden (1). They took a risk and as a result either won or lost something, but afterwards with a newfound knowledge they developed conventions and rules and regulations over their activities.

Over time the games played by people became less and less related to "the hunt" and more and more contrived exercises with artificial rules. The games were controlled by laws of society. As governments became increasingly formal organizations, the laws of games became more formal as well. Although almost every society ever recognized by anthropologists has had some sort of gambling activity associated with its games, organized societies also have had rules that either prohibited gambling or limited gambling to specific occasions and specific games. Those rules in a general sense provide the essence of the content for the entries found in this encyclopedia.

The fight for change was brought to the American people as the basic theme for Barack Obama's successful 2008 presidential campaign. The fight for change engenders the notions of the characters of Spencer Johnson, but it also brings to mind the mythical character of Sisyphus, who kept up the fight by pushing a rock up a mountain, time and time again, even after the rock would slip out of his hands and roll back down the mountain side. The book *Over the Top: Solutions to the Sisyphus Dilemmas of Life* (Bloomington, IN: First Books, 2003, with Bradley Kenny) examines the activity of Sisyphus. If Sisyphus walked among us today, he would be a likely candidate to buy a Powerball ticket twice a week. Maybe the chance of a big lottery win would represent an example of looking at the mountain in a new way. It would be somewhat akin to the solution of blasting a tunnel through the granite so that the struggle could be eased by a lateral pushing exercise vis-à-vis a vertical one. The editor is certain that Sisyphus would have participated in modern gambling activity. So too as the modern human race struggles against mountains of depressions and recessions—figuratively and literally—the modern human race takes notice of its condition and gambles.

The editor also recognizes that this is not the first encyclopedia of gambling. One would have to go back many years to find the first such effort in this field. But more recently, John Scarne's *New Complete Guide to Gambling* in 1986 stands out. Even more recently, in 1990, Carl Sifakis prepared a very comprehensive *Encyclopedia of Gambling.* He covered more than games, featuring discussions of properties and personalities as well. Rather than trying to become a rival for that excellent volume, the editor recommends it highly. The Sifakis encyclopedia covers gambling throughout the world and also offers the kind of detail on games that is also found in Scarne's work. This encyclopedia complements Sifakis's work by providing more detailed analyses of gambling laws and operations and venues throughout the world, as well as providing updated information on many topics that are found in both encyclopedias.

The items in the encyclopedia are arranged alphabetically in categories. Following the table of contents, acknowledgments, this introduction, and a chronology is a collection of entries on (I.) General Topics. Next come entries on (II.) Games, followed by (III.) Biographies of Leading Figures in Gambling and (IV.) Venues and Places. Additional sections include (V.) Annotated Bibliography, (VI.) Leading Law Cases on Gambling, (VII.) A Glossary of Gambling Terms, and (VIII.) Selected Essays on Gambling.

References

Abt, Vicki, James F. Smith, and Eugene Martin Christiansen. 1985. *The Business of Risk: Commercial Gambling in Mainstream America.* Lawrence: University Press of Kansas.

Clark, Thomas L. 1997. *The Dictionary of Gambling and Gaming.* Cold Spring, NY: Lexik House Publishers.

Johnson, Spencer. 1998. *Who Moved My Cheese.* New York: G. P. Putnam

Scarne, John. 1986. *Scarne's New Complete Guide to Gambling.* Fireside Edition. New York: Simon and Schuster.

Sifakis, Carl. 1990. *Encyclopedia of Gambling.* New York: Facts on File.

Thompson, William N., and Bradley L. Kenny. 2003. *Over the Top: Solutions to the Sisyphus Dilemmas of Life.* Bloomington, IN: First Books.

1780s–1830s: Lotteries become an economic tool for financing civic projects in the new states. They help build the new capital city on the Potomac as well as buildings for many colleges, including Harvard, Yale, Columbia, Rutgers, and Dartmouth, and even some churches. From 1790 to 1830, 21 state governments issue licenses for nearly 200 games.

1810: Former president Thomas Jefferson says he never gambles on lotteries, and he issues a letter very critical of lotteries and gambling.

1812: The first steamboat, Robert Fulton's *New Orleans,* operates on the Mississippi River. The boat inaugurates an era of riverboat gambling in the West. Within a decade more than 60 riverboats are operating with gamblers on board.

1815: New Orleans licenses casino gaming enterprises in the city. New Orleans was already a wide-open "sin city" when it became part of the United States with the 1803 Louisiana Purchase. Legislation and licensing are seen as a means to control the widespread gambling and generate moneys for municipal improvements.

1826: Jefferson supports the use of lotteries as a means for persons to dispose of their property in a respectable manner so that they can pay their bills. He calls lotteries a tax "laid on the willing only." His own lottery for sale of goods at Monticello is unsuccessful.

1827: John Davis opens the first complete casino in the United States in New Orleans, at the corner of Orleans and Bourbon Streets. The high-class establishment caters to aristocratic tastes, and although it is open only until 1835, it serves as a model for modern Las Vegas– and Atlantic City–type casinos.

1828: The first Canadian horse racetrack opens in Montreal.

1832: The high point of early lottery play, with 420 lottery games in eight states. Scandals plague many of the games, however, leading to a reaction prohibiting lotteries and other gambling.

1833: The Jacksonian era ushers in a mood of general governmental reform. Reformers call for a cessation of gambling. Pennsylvania and Maryland are the first to prohibit lotteries, and most other states follow suit. Between 1833 and 1840, 12 states ban lotteries. By the time of the Civil War all legal lotteries have halted.

1834: Cockfighting is banned in England.

1835: New Orleans declares casinos to be illegal. John Davis's house closes, but lower-class gambling dens continue to operate illegally. The antigambling reform movement moves up the Mississippi River, where a vigilante committee torches the gambling haunts of Vicksburg, Mississippi, and lynches five gamblers.

1836: The first stakes horse race in North America is held in Quebec.

1848 and following years: The gold strike in California marks a new trend: mining camp gambling halls. Eastern reform and western opportunities redistribute much of gambling sin activity in the 1840s, lasting for 100 years or more. Although opportunity brings prospectors west, reform pushes gamblers in the same direction, with gamblers drawn by the opportunity to strike gold in the gambling dens themselves. San Francisco becomes a gambling center.

1855: Reformers close down open gambling in San Francisco.

1860: Riverboat gambling reaches its apex, with 557 boats operating on the eve of the Civil War. It is estimated that 99 percent of the games on the boats cheat players.

Player-banked games are banned in California.

1864: The Travers Stakes horse race is run for the first time at Saratoga, New York, the first stakes race in the United States.

1865: The totalizator is invented in France. It permits horse race bets to be pooled and odds calculated as bets are being made. The device allows for the creation of the pari-mutuel system of betting. This makes it much easier to tax horse race betting and also to collect funds for race purses. The totalizator was not used in North American tracks until 1933, but the pari-mutuel system is now in place at every major track in North America.

1867: The inaugural running of the Belmont Stakes takes place in Belmont, New York.

1868: Gambling activity gains a new momentum as the Louisiana Lottery begins a three-decade reign of abuse and corruption. Initially started in order to bring needed revenues to a war-torn, bankrupt state, the lottery is soon overcome by private entrepreneurs who sustain it by bribing state officials. The lottery enjoys great success, as tickets are sold through the mail across the continent.

1873: The inaugural running of the Preakness Stakes takes place at Pimlico racetrack in Baltimore.

1875: The first Kentucky Derby is run on 17 May at Churchill Downs in Louisville. It is won by Aristides.

1876: Congress bans the use of mails for lottery advertising.

1877: Congress actually adjourns so that members can attend horse racing events at Pimlico racetrack in Baltimore.

1886: The first dog "coursing" events are held in the United States in Kansas.

1887: Charles Fey invents the slot machine in San Francisco. This first machine accepts and pays nickels. Soon similar devices are found throughout the city, and since patents on the concept of a gambling machine are not granted by the government at this time, other manufacturers open the door for imitation.

1890: Congress bans the sale of lottery tickets through the mail. This significantly restricts the Louisiana Lottery. Lottery advertising in newspapers is also prohibited. Two years later the Louisiana Lottery is voted out of existence, yet its operators seek to keep it operating, using foreign ports for ticket delivery.

1891: The Broadmoor Casino Resort opens in Colorado Springs, Colorado. This casino brings a new elegance to western gaming. As many as 15,000 players visit the establishment each day. The casino fails to make money from gambling, however, as people gamble among themselves rather than playing house-banked games. The casino is destroyed by fire in 1897.

The first organized regulation of horse race courses begins with licensing of jockeys and trainers by a private board of control in New York State. The growth in popularity of race betting requires the establishment of integrity in racing.

1892: An antigambling movement takes hold in Canada as Parliament bans most forms of gambling by means of revisions to the Criminal Code.

1894: The Jockey Club of New York is established. It helps develop national standards for horse racing.

1895: Congress bans the transportation of lottery tickets in interstate or foreign commerce. When the act is upheld by the courts, the Louisiana Lottery operations finally end.

1900: The total prohibition on gambling in Canada begins its century of unraveling as small raffles are permitted in an amendment to the Criminal Code.

1902: Belgium law decrees all casinos illegal, commencing a century of paradoxes that sees tolerated, regulated, and taxed casinos, albeit illegal ones.

1906: Kentucky becomes the first state to establish a government-run state racing commission. At the same time, other states begin to ban horse racing.

1907: The Arizona and New Mexico territorial governments outlaw all gambling as part of their quest for statehood.

French law permits casinos with player-banked and skill games. Casinos must be at least 100 kilometers away from Paris.

1910: The era of antigambling reform seems nearly complete in the United States. Nevada closes its casinos, and legalized gambling in the United States, with the exception of a few horse racetracks, is dormant.

In Canada the Criminal Code is again amended, this time to allow betting at racing tracks.

1915: Horse racing begins in Cuba.

1916: Horse race betting is permitted in Puerto Rico.

1919: Italy closes casinos, only to begin a process of selective licensing in 1927.

The Black Sox scandal hits professional baseball. Gamblers, including Arnold Rothstein, bribe Chicago White Sox players, who purposely lose the World Series.

Casino gambling begins along with jai alai in Marianao, Cuba.

1920s: Dog racing is popularized as 60 tracks open throughout the United States, the first in Emeryville, California.

1922: The Canadian Criminal Code is amended to ban the use of dice in any gambling activity. Some casinos simulate dice games by placing dice configurations within roulette wheels or on slot machine reels.

Costa Rican law defines legal and illegal casino gambling.

1925: Limited gambling activity is permitted at fairs in Canada.

1928: The first casino in Chile opens at Vina del Mar.

1929: A racetrack is opened at Agua Caliente near Tijuana, Mexico. A casino also has government approval.

1930: Ireland authorizes its Irish Sweepstakes lottery to benefit hospitals.

1931: The state of Nevada legalizes wide-open casino gambling. At first, gambling is confined to small saloons and taverns and is regulated by cities and counties. Casino taxes consist of set fees on each table or machine game. Taxes are shared between local and state governments.

1933: The first totalizator is used at a U.S. horse racetrack in Arlington Park, Illinois. Soon legal horse race betting returns to several Depression-bankrupt (or near bankrupt) states, including California, Michigan, and Ohio as a means of gaining revenues.

After 60 years Germany again allows casinos as Baden-Baden reopens. Austria also allows casinos.

Casinos are closed in Cuba.

1934: Casinos gain legal status in Macao, and soon the Portuguese enclave becomes the gambling center of Asia.

1935: New horse race betting legislation is approved in Illinois, Louisiana, Florida, New Hampshire, West Virginia, Ohio, Michigan, Massachusetts, Rhode Island, and Delaware.

1937: Bill Harrah opens his first gambling hall in Reno, beginning one of the largest casino empires. In 1971 his casino interests become the first to be publicly traded on open stock exchanges.

1938: The casino in Tijuana, Mexico, is closed by the new national government headed by Lazaro Cardenas.

1940: New York legalizes pari-mutuel horse race betting.

1940s and 1950s: Casinos reopen in Cuba under the control of dictator Juan Batista.

1941: The Las Vegas Strip begins its legacy as the world's primary casino gambling location. The El Rancho Vegas is the first casino on the Strip and is soon joined by the Last Frontier and the Desert Inn. These new-style casinos offer hotel accommodations and recreational amenities to tourists.

1944: Argentina closes all private casinos. Many reopen as part of a government corporate monopoly.

1945: Casinos in Panama are placed under government ownership.

The state government of Nevada begins to license casinos for the first time. In addition to set fees on games, the casinos begin to pay a tax on the amount of money they win from players. Nevada casino activity increases as World War II ends, but operators of illegal gaming establishments throughout the country face a new wave of reform. Reform is triggered with the end of World War II as public resources and public concern turn to domestic problems. Gamblers shift operations to Las Vegas.

1946: Brazil closes its casinos. They remain closed for the remainder of the 20th century.

Gangster Benjamin ("Bugsy") Siegel, financed by organized crime figure Meyer Lansky, opens the Flamingo Casino on the Las Vegas Strip. The casino features a showroom with Hollywood entertainment.

1947: Siegel is murdered at his girlfriend's Hollywood home. The murder sensationalizes the Strip and firms up Las Vegas's reputation as a risky, naughty place where Main Street Americans can rub shoulders with notorious mobsters.

The Idaho legislature passes a slot machine law that permits licensing and taxing of machines. A few years later the voters decide to outlaw machines once again.

1948: Congress permits casino gambling in Puerto Rico as part of Operation Bootstrap.

The first postwar casinos open in Germany.

1949: The voters of Idaho decide to ban all slot machines. No other state completely bans a form of gambling again until 1999.

Congress passes the Gambling Ship Act of 1949, which prohibits U.S. flag ships from operating gambling casinos.

1950: The U.S. Senate investigates organized crime and gambling casinos. Tennessee senator Estes Kefauver leads a committee that fingers Las Vegas as a "den of evil" controlled by "the Mob." Ironically, while the Senate committee is seeking a crackdown on casinos within the United States, Congress authorizes the expenditure of U.S. taxpayer funds to open a casino in Travemunde, Germany, under the provisions of the Marshall Fund for business recovery in Western Europe after World War II.

1951: The Johnson Act is passed, banning the transportation of gambling machines in interstate commerce unless they are moving to jurisdictions where they are legal.

1955: Nevada creates the Gaming Control Board under the direction of the State Tax Commission. A process of professionalizing gaming regulation begins as an effort to convince federal authorities that the state can run honest crime-free casinos.

1955–1962: The McClelland Committees of the U.S. Congress investigate organized crime activity, including gambling activity.

1956: Great Britain authorizes its Premium Bond lottery.

Ireland institutes a gaming and lottery act permitting charity games but banning most others.

1959: The Nevada Gaming Commission is created to oversee the decisions of the Gaming Control Board. Gaming regulation is removed from the State Tax Commission.

1959–1961: Fidel Castro closes down the casinos in Cuba. He closes down a lottery as well.

1960: Dictator Jean-Claude "Papa Doc" Duvalier authorizes casinos in Haiti. They are run by mobsters who have left Cuba.

The Betting and Gaming Act is passed in Great Britain. Betting shops take bookies off the street but unanticipated are the hundreds of "charity" casinos that open.

1961: In response to the McClelland investigations, Congress passes the Wire Act, the Travel Act, and the Waging Paraphernalia Act in order to combat illegal gambling.

1962: Congress amends the Johnson Act of 1951 to include all gambling devices.

Mathematics professor Edward Thorpe writes *Beat the Dealer,* which describes the card counting system for blackjack play. Almost instantly, blackjack becomes the most popular casino table game in Las Vegas.

1963–1964: The legislature of New Hampshire authorizes a state-run sweepstakes game, which becomes the first government lottery in the United States since the closing of the Louisiana Lottery. The state sells its first lottery ticket in 1964.

1964: The voters of Arkansas defeat a measure that would have allowed casino gambling in Hot Springs, a location of much illegal gambling in recent years.

1965–1967: The President's Commission on Law Enforcement and the Administration of Justice meets. Small attention is given to gambling.

1966: Billionaire Howard Hughes moves to Las Vegas and begins to purchase Nevada casinos from owners with suspicious connections to organized crime. This helps to improve the city's image. Hughes has a flamboyant image but also a reputation as an entrepreneur with integrity.

Jay Sarno opens Caesars Palace in Las Vegas. This is the first "themed" casino on the Las Vegas Strip. He follows this with the opening of the Circus Circus Casino in 1970.

1967: Casinos open in Korea but only for foreign gamers.

Alberta permits charity casinos at the two-week Edmonton Exhibition. This is the first authorized casino gambling in Canada.

New York begins a lottery, but it fails to meet state officials' budget expectations. Similar to the New Hampshire games, the lottery's monthly draw game proves to be too slow. Few other jurisdictions take notice of the lottery.

1968: The federal government initiates actions to prohibit Howard Hughes from purchasing any more Las Vegas casinos (specifically the Landmark) on antitrust grounds. Hughes is angered and initiates a plan to win federal approval by allegedly bribing presidential candidates Richard Nixon and Hubert Humphrey (see Michael Drosnin's *Citizen Hughes* [1985]). Kennedy family confidant Larry O'Brien is on Hughes's staff at time.

A new Gaming Act in Great Britain imposes strict regulation upon casinos.

1969: Nevada permits ownership of casinos by public corporations. This action is prompted by the industry's need to maintain and upgrade facilities and by a continuing need to improve the state's image.

The World Series of Poker is established at Binion's Horseshoe Casino in Las Vegas.

Kirk Kerkorian opens the International Hotel and Casino in Las Vegas. With 1,512 rooms, it is the largest hotel in the world. He soon sells it to Hilton Corporation, and he builds the MGM Grand with 2,084 rooms. It becomes the largest hotel in the world. He sells it to Bally's.

New Jersey authorizes a lottery. In 1970, the state begins sales of weekly lottery tickets using mass marketing techniques. The New Jersey operation is successful from the beginning, and other states realize that large revenues can be realized from lotteries if ticket prices are low and games occur regularly. Lotteries begin to spread quickly.

The Canadian Criminal Code is amended to permit lottery schemes to be operated by governments and charitable organizations. Soon many of the provinces have lotteries, and the door is wide open for the charities and governments to offer casino games.

Malaysia licenses the Genting Highlands casino, and for many years it is the largest casino in the world.

1970: The Yukon Territory permits the Klondike Visitor's Association to conduct casino games from mid-spring through the summer at Diamond Tooth Gerties in Dawson City.

Loto Quebec, an agency of the Quebec provincial government, initiates the first lottery gaming in Canada.

Congress passes the Organized Crime Control Act. Among other provisions it authorizes a study of gambling activity. The study does not begin until 1975.

New York City creates the Knapp Commission to investigate police corruption, much of it tied to illegal gambling operations.

Don Laughlin opens the first casino in Laughlin, Nevada.

Genting Highlands resort and casino opens in Malaysia. With a gambling floor of 200,000 square feet, for several decades it is the largest casino in the world.

1970s and 1980s: Casinos with unauthorized games begin operation in Costa Rica despite law defining legal and illegal casino gambling.

1971: New York authorizes off-track betting. New York City creates a public corporation to conduct the operations within its boundaries.

1972: Richard Nixon orders a break-in of Larry O'Brien's office in the Watergate Building in Washington, D.C. It is suggested that Nixon wants to find out what information O'Brien has about alleged bribery by Howard Hughes in 1968. O'Brien is the national Democratic Party chairman.

1973: Following disastrous forest fires, the Tasmanian government authorizes casinos as a means of gaining revenues to deal with the calamity. The Tasmanian casinos are the first allowed in Australia.

1974: New Jersey voters defeat a proposal for local-option casinos, which would be operated by the state government.

Massachusetts becomes the first North American jurisdiction to have an instant lottery game. This becomes the most popular lottery game of the decade, and all other lotteries begin to sell instant games.

Maryland authorizes the creation of an interest-only lottery program like one used in England. The player buys a no-interest bond and may cash it in at full purchase price at any time. As long as the player holds the bond, however, he or she is illegible to win lottery prizes, which are awarded in lieu of interest payments. The system is never implemented.

Casino gambling is authorized in the Netherlands. A government corporation wins the right to run all casinos.

1975: The Western Canada Lottery Corporation initiates the first intergovernmental lottery anywhere. The provinces of Manitoba, Saskatchewan, Alberta, and British Columbia operate these games together. British Columbia later drops out of the joint operation in order to have its own lottery games.

New Jersey starts the first "numbers game," with players selecting their own three-digit numbers. The game is offered with hopes that it will drive the popular illegal numbers games out of business. Other lotteries adopt the numbers game as well, often adding a four-digit number game. There is little evidence that illegal games do stop.

1975–1976: The Commission on the Review of the National Policy toward Gambling meets and issues a report affirming the notion that gambling activity and its legalization and control are a matter for the jurisdictions of state governments. The Commission concludes, however, that casinos should be located in remote areas far removed from metropolitan populations.

1976: New Jersey voters authorize casino gambling for Atlantic City by a margin of 56 percent to 44 percent.

The Atlantic Lottery Corporation is formed by action of the provinces of Newfoundland, Prince Edward's Island, New Brunswick, and Nova Scotia. Lotteries are begun in these four provinces, thereby bringing the games into each Canadian province.

1977: The New Jersey legislature creates a regulatory structure for casino gaming.

Sol Kerzner opens his first Sun City casino in the South African homeland of Bophuthatswana.

1978: Casino gaming begins in Atlantic City with the opening of Resorts International on Memorial Day weekend.

The Interstate Horse Racing Act is passed, providing standards for operating off-track betting as well as inter-track betting.

1979: Sam's Town Casino opens on Boulder Highway in Las Vegas, ushering in an era of casinos that cater to local residents of the gambling community.

High-stakes bingo games begin on the Seminole Indian reservation in Hollywood, Florida, signaling a new period of Native American gambling. In subsequent federal court litigation the Indians retain the right to conduct games unregulated by the state.

Scandal rocks the Pennsylvania lottery as its numbers game is rigged. Although the culprits—who were paid by the government—go to prison, the state continues all its lottery games without interruption.

The province of Ontario initiates the world's first lotto game, called Lottario. The game requires players to select six numbers, and all play is entered into an online computer network. A jackpot prize is given to any player who picks all six numbers. If there is no winner, more prize money is added to the next drawing. Jackpots in North American lotto games have grown to exceed $250 million.

Casino gambling is authorized by the corrupt regime of General Lucas Garcia in Guatemala. The casinos are closed after a Christian Fundamentalist, General Rios Montt, overthrows Lucas Garcia in 1982.

Luxembourg authorizes casino gambling.

1981: The New York legislature rejects measures to authorize casino gambling after a major attack on gambling by state attorney general Robert Abrams.

Charity blackjack games are given formal authorization in North Dakota. The success of the games leads the charities to successfully campaign against state lotteries. North Dakota is the only state to vote against lotteries until Alabama joins it in 1999.

1984: Arkansas voters defeat casinos a second time.

California voters authorize a state lottery.

Donald Trump opens Harrah's Trump Plaza, the first of his three Atlantic City casinos.

1985: The Canadian national government agrees to place responsibility for the administration of all gambling laws with the provinces in exchange for a $100 million payment to offset the cost of the Calgary Winter Olympics of 1988.

The President's Commission on Organized Crime meets but fails to issue a report on gambling, as it now considers gambling to be, for the most part, a legitimate industry.

1986: Congress passes the Money Laundering Control Act, requiring casinos to record many large gambling transactions.

The Megabucks slot machine network is introduced in Nevada, allowing very large jackpot prizes.

Donald Trump opens his second casino, Trump Castle, in Atlantic City.

1987: The U.S. Supreme Court upholds the rights of Indian tribes to offer unregulated gambling enterprises as long as operations do not violate state criminal policy. The case *California v. Cabazon Band of Mission Indians* determines that any regulation of noncriminal matters must come from the federal government or be specifically authorized by Congress.

One century after its invention, slot machine gaming becomes the number-one form of gambling in U.S. casinos.

1988: The Indian Gaming Regulatory Act is passed by Congress in response to the *Cabazon* decision. The act provides for federal and tribal regulation of bingo games and for mutually negotiated Indian–state government schemes for the regulation of casinos on reservations.

The voters of South Dakota authorize limited ($5) stakes casino games of blackjack, poker, and slot machines in casinos in the historic town of Deadwood.

1989: Stephen Wynn of the Mirage Corporation opens the Mirage, the first new Las Vegas Strip casino in over a decade.

Donald Trump opens the Taj Mahal in Atlantic City, the third of his three casinos.

The South Dakota legislature passes enabling laws, and limited casino gambling begins in Deadwood. A state lottery also begins operation of video lottery terminals throughout South Dakota.

The Iowa state legislature approves riverboat casino gaming with limited ($5) stakes betting on navigable waters in the state. Boats begin operations in 1990.

The state of Oregon starts the first sports game–based lottery in the United States. Proceeds of the gambling are allocated to support college athletics in Oregon.

The Manitoba Lottery Foundation, a government-owned entity, opens the first year-round permanent casino facility in Canada. The Crystal Casino is located in the classic Fort Garry Hotel in Winnipeg.

The jackpot prize in the Pennsylvania lotto game exceeds $115 million. It is won, and shared, by several lucky ticket holders.

1990: New legislation permits casinos in Denmark

New Zealand authorizes casinos.

Alaska voters defeat a proposal for local option casino gambling. Ohio voters refuse to authorize casino gaming.

Riverboat casinos begin operation in Iowa. Riverboat casinos are also approved by the Illinois state legislature.

The voters of Colorado approve limited casino gaming for the historic mountain towns of Blackhawk, Cripple Creek, and Central City.

West Virginia permits slot machines to operate at racetracks. The "racino" begins. This action is later imitated by other states and by many Canadian provinces during the 1990s.

1991: Riverboat casinos are approved by the Mississippi legislature. It is determined that the boats may be permanently docked. Casino boats begin operation in Illinois, and limited casinos start in Colorado.

Oregon and Colorado introduce keno as a lottery game.

1992: The Atlantic Provinces—New Brunswick, Prince Edward's Island, Nova Scotia, and Newfoundland—authorize video lottery terminals for locations throughout their territories.

The Louisiana legislature approves riverboat casinos and one land-based casino in New Orleans. Missouri voters also approve riverboat casinos. Colorado voters refuse to expand casinos to additional towns.

Congress prohibits the spread of sports betting beyond the four states currently authorizing it: Nevada, Oregon, Montana, and Delaware. New Jersey is given one year to approve sports betting for an Atlantic City casino but declines to do so.

Congress passes an act allowing U.S. flag ships to have casino gambling.

Rhode Island and Louisiana permit slot machines to operate at racetracks.

1993: The Ontario government approves a casino for the city of Windsor. The casino is to be government-owned but privately operated. The provincial government selects a consortium of Las Vegas casino companies, including Caesars Palace, Circus Circus, and the Hilton, to operate the casino. The province of Quebec opens a government-owned and -operated casino in Montreal at the site of the French Pavilion of the Montreal World's Fair. Quebec also approves gaming sites at Charlevoix and Hull.

The Nova Scotia government removes video gaming machines from all locations that are accessible to young people.

The Indiana legislature approves boat casinos. Five boats are authorized for Lake Michigan ports, five for ports on the Ohio River, and one for an interior lake. Riverboat and gulf shore casino gambling is also permitted in Mississippi.

Georgia establishes a lottery and devotes revenues to university scholarships for all high school graduates with B averages or better. The scholarship program is very popular and becomes a model for other states desiring to win approval for gambling enterprises.

Kirk Kerkorian opens the new MGM Grand, with 5,009 rooms, making it the largest hotel in the world.

1994: Florida voters defeat a proposal for limited casino gambling, which would have authorized about 50 major casinos in various locations around the state. Colorado again defeats efforts to expand casino gambling. Riverboat casinos begin operation in Louisiana and Missouri.

Congress passes the Money Laundering and Suppression Act.

The government of the province of Nova Scotia authorizes casino gambling.

A new national lottery begins in the United Kingdom.

1995: A temporary casino opens in New Orleans. It is operated by a group including Harrah's Casinos and the Jazzville Corporation. Riverboat gambling begins in Indiana.

Provincially owned casinos open in Halifax and Sydney, Nova Scotia, and also in Regina, Saskatchewan.

The voters of the Virgin Islands approve casinos.

Costa Rica changes its laws to permit most forms of casino games.

Delaware and Iowa permit slot machines to operate at racetracks.

1996: The new government of South Africa authorizes the establishment of 40 casinos.

The New Orleans casino project closes and declares bankruptcy. The casino reopens in 2000.

The U.S. Supreme Court rules part of the Indian Gaming Regulatory Act of 1988 unconstitutional. The Court determines that the act's provision allowing tribes to sue states over compact negotiations violates the 11th Amendment.

Congress passes a law setting up a nine-person commission to study the social and economic impacts of gambling on U.S. society.

Congress gives blanket approval to "cruises to nowhere" that leave from state ports and go into international waters for gambling purposes unless states specifically prohibit the cruises.

In November, the voters of several states speak out on gambling, but they give mixed messages. Michigan voters approve a law that authorizes three major casinos for the city of Detroit. Ohio and Arkansas voters defeat casinos; West Virginia approves machine gaming for racetracks, and Nebraska voters say no to track machines. Colorado also says no to new casino towns. Washington state voters defeat slot machines for Native American casinos, but Arizona voters mandate the governor to sign compacts for new Native American casinos.

Two historical casinos on the Las Vegas Strip—the Hacienda and the Sands—are imploded to make way for newer and bigger gambling halls. Three new casinos open up in Las Vegas: the Monte Carlo, the Orleans, and the Stratosphere. The Stratosphere boasts of having the tallest free-standing tower on the North American continent.

Casino Niagara opens in Niagara Falls, Ontario, in December. It is owned and operated by the Ontario Casino Corporation, a government corporation. The Ontario government also permits a native casino to open in Rama near Orilla.

The Saskatchewan government opens Casino Regina.

1997: Major casino expansions take place in Las Vegas. These include the opening of the New York, New York resort casino and expansions of the Rio, Harrah's, Caesars, and Luxor.

The National Gambling Study Commission begins operations.

1998: California voters pass Proposition 5, designed to allow Native American tribes to have unlimited casino gambling. The tribes of the state invest over $70 million in the campaign for Proposition 5, and Nevada casinos spend $26 million in opposition. It is the most expensive referendum campaign in history.

New Mexico permits slot machines to operate at racetracks.

The Palestine Authority opens a casino at Jericho on the Israeli border.

1999: The Ontario government abandons a plan for 44 charity casinos in all parts of the province and instead authorizes four new "charity" casinos in Thunder Bay, Sault Ste. Marie, Point Edward, and Brantford. A Native casino also operates near Port Erie. Gambling machines are authorized for provincial racetracks.

The Canadian ban on the use of dice in any gambling activity ends as Ontario casinos seek to compete with new Detroit casinos.

The voters of Alabama defeat a lottery. This is only the second state to have voters say no to lotteries.

The Supreme Court orders that the slot machines of South Carolina be shut down. On June 30, 2000, over thirty thousand machines stop. It is the first major shutdown of a form of statewide gambling since Idaho voters closed down machines in 1949.

Expansion in Las Vegas continues with the opening of the Bellagio, Mandalay Bay, Venetian, and Paris casinos.

The National Gambling Study Commission issues its report.

The Supreme Court of California rules Proposition 5 to be unconstitutional.

Belgium reverses a near century-old decree that casinos are illegal, and authorizes slot machine gambling and gambling in Brussels.

The Kang Won Land casino opens in Korea and admits Koreans as customers.

2000: The new Chinese authorities in Macau grant three licenses to run casinos. They are given to Sheldon Adelson, Steve Wynn, and Stanley Ho.

Kirk Kerkorian's MGM Corporation purchases the Mirage Corporation and all its properties—including the Golden Nuggets of Las Vegas and Laughlin, the Mirage, and the Bellagio.

The new Aladdin Casino opens in Las Vegas.

A casino opens in the Virgin Islands, the first since casinos were approved by voters in 1995.

California voters approve Proposition 1A, which allows Native American casinos, with some regulations and limits. The ban on player-banked games in California is lifted.

2001: New York State authorizes slot machines for racetracks as well as casinos for Native American lands.

Sweden authorizes the establishment of government-run casinos.

2003: Voters in Maine approve slot machines for racetracks.

North Dakota legislature approves state participation in the multistate Powerball lottery.

2004: Sheldon Adelson opens the Sands Macau casino.

Pennsylvania authorizes slot machine gambling for fourteen casinos, seven attached to racetracks

Oklahoma voters authorize compacts for Native American casinos.

2005: The MGM-Mirage corporation purchases Mandalay (formerly Circus Circus) Resorts. Harrah's purchases the Caesars Entertainment group of casinos.

Voters in South Florida approve slot machines for racetracks.

2006: Congress passes the Unlawful Internet Gambling Enforcement Act.

Steve Wynn opens the Wynn Macau resort.

Russia passes legislation confining casinos to four remote areas of the country.

2007: A referee for games played in the National Basketball Association pleads guilty to betting on games in which he participated.

The Venetian Macau opens, operated by Sheldon Adelson's Sands Corporation.

Kansas passes a law permitting "government-owned" but privately operated casinos.

2008: Maryland voters approve a plan to put 15,000 slot machines at racetracks and other venues. Massachusetts bans dog racing.

2009: Voters in Ohio approve four casinos to be located in Cincinnati, Cleveland, Columbus, and Toledo.

Section One
GENERAL TOPICS

CARDS, PLAYING

Many gambling games utilize playing cards. Although games can be traced to prehistoric times, the use of cards did not become prevalent until the invention of paper in China about 2,000 years ago. It is likely that the Chinese and the Koreans were the first to use card-like objects for gambling. Systematic decks or series of cards can be traced to Hindustan (northern India), dating to about 800 CE. The Chinese and Koreans probably had cards during the same era, and Europeans developed card games in the Middle Ages, aided especially by the development of the printing arts. Cards were present in Italy in 1279. The nature of today's deck of cards was gradually established over the 15th and 16th centuries.

The sailors on Columbus's first voyage to the New World played cards on board the *Pinta, Niña,* and *Santa Maria.* Except for graphics, cards have not changed much since those times. The modern deck is made up of the same 52 cards divided into 4 groups, or suits, of 13 cards each. Two suits are red in color. In the French system, they were named *couer* ("hearts") in honor of the clergy and *carreau* ("diamonds") in honor of the merchants. There are two black suits, which were named swords or *pique* ("spades") in honor of the nobility and *trefle* ("clubs") to represent the peasants. In each suit, there are cards numbered from 1 (an ace) to 10, and there are also three picture cards—the jack, queen, and king.

In the American colonies, there were many card players, and printers such as Benjamin Franklin were happy to supply them with cards. Cards were so popular that when the British found they needed more revenue to support their administrative activities in the colonies, they decided to tax playing cards. Franklin quickly became a tax protester, then a tax rebel, and finally a revolutionary demanding independence for the colonies. The British would have been best advised to leave the card industry alone when they were choosing items to tax.

The wide proliferation of cards led to an ever-expanding number of games and a great variety of rules for those games. Confusion reigned supreme over gaming until Englishman Edmund Hoyle (1672–1769) began composing a series of books on the manner of playing games. In his early career, Hoyle was a barrister. He was also a gambling instructor. When he was over 70 years old, he wrote *A Short Treatise on the Game of Whist.* He also published books on the games of brag, quadrille, and piquet, along with guides on the dice game of backgammon and also chess. By the time he died at the age of 97, he was considered the authority on card games, and whenever a dispute arose over the rules of a game, someone would inevitably introduce the solution with the words, "according to Hoyle." In the 20th century, several game rulebooks incorporated his other works and honored him in their titles (e.g., *The New Complete Hoyle* [Morehead, Frey, and Mott-Smith 1964] and *According to Hoyle* [Gaminara 1996]).

The 20th century saw the introduction of many new games such as poker and blackjack that had not been played during Hoyle's life. Nonetheless, he remains one of the greatest card experts of all time.

References

Gaminara, William. 1996. *According to Hoyle.* London: Nick Hern Books.

Morehead, Albert H., Richard L. Frey, and Geoffrey Mott-Smith. 1964. *The New Complete Hoyle.* Garden City, NY: Doubleday.

Scarne, John. 1986. *Scarne's New Complete Guide to Gambling.* New York: Simon and Schuster, 625–636.

Sifakis, Carl. 1990. *Encyclopedia of Gambling.* New York: Facts on File, 56–57.

CASH TRANSACTION REPORTS AND MONEY LAUNDERING

Gambling enterprises, both legal and illegal, have long been considered to be integrally involved with criminal elements in various ways. In recent decades, concerns have revolved around the use of casino organizations as banking institutions that could aid criminals in what is called money laundering. The Bank Secrecy Act of 1970, with amendments; the Money Laundering Act of 1986; and the Money Laundering Suppression Act of 1994 address the problem of money laundering.

Money laundering involves various activities. One example of money laundering is simply exchanging one set of cash bills for another set of cash bills. Many criminal enterprises rely upon patronage of ordinary people at the street level—purchasers of drugs, illegal bettors, or customers of prostitutes. Such people pay for products and services with small denomination bills—ones, fives, tens, and twenties. As a result, criminal enterprises have very large quantities of paper money. It is difficult to carry the money, and it is especially hard to transport the money outside of the country in order to put it into secret bank accounts in other countries. When a bank or a casino willingly changes many small bills for a few large bills, they may be laundering money for criminal elements.

Laundering also occurs when financial institutions convert cash deposits into different forms—traveler's checks, cashier's checks, or money orders. The institutions may also assist inadvertently by initiating a series of wire transfers of money to foreign bank accounts or to other people's accounts in a series of transactions that make it difficult for law enforcement to identify the true source of the money.

Casinos are also vulnerable for use by criminals who simply wish to establish a legitimate source for their funds so that they may use them openly. Theoretically, it would be very easy for a criminal to come to a casino, change cash into casino chips, wager with a confederate at roulette (one playing black, the other red), and then claim all the chips they end up with as income—keeping a record only of their wins and not of their losses. If a casino would cooperate in such a ruse, the gamblers may be very happy to let the casino have its 5 percent edge in the game (both players would of course lose when the roulette ball fell into the zero or double zero slot of the wheel).

In the case above, the gamblers are content to pay income tax on their winnings, freeing them from the fear of being subject to investigation from the Internal Revenue Service. The situation is even better in Canadian and European casinos, where no income tax is imposed upon winnings. All the gambler needs is a verification that the money was won at the casino. That casinos might participate in laundering money was suggested in an interview with the manager of a large European casino. When asked, he quietly said, "[I suppose] that is a service we provide." He would be pleased to have the player's action, because the casino could not lose. Today, however, casinos in the United States can lose by laundering criminal money: they can be fined or closed down if they are caught playing such games.

In 1970, Congress enacted the Bank Secrecy Act. Initially, the act applied to traditional bank-type institutions only. Banks were required to report to the U.S. Treasury Department any single-day transactions that involved more than $10,000 in cash. The bank was required to be vigilant and to track smaller transactions to make sure that a single party was not violating the law through multiple transactions. In 1985, Treasury Department regulations extended the provisions of the act to the casino industry. Casinos with over $1 million in annual revenues had to abide by the reporting procedures and other requirements. In 1986, the Money Laundering

Control Act criminalized violations of the procedures. The act specified a very large number of criminal activities that generated money that would likely be laundered. If any person attempted to launder any such money through a bank or casino, that person would be committing a criminal offense. Anyone knowingly assisting such a person in moving that money would also be guilty of a criminal action. In 1994, the Money Laundering Suppression Act extended the provisions of the acts to Native American casinos.

Banks and other financial institutions, Native American casinos, and commercial casinos in all states except Nevada make reports to the U.S. Treasury Department. The state of Nevada made a plea to Treasury officials to allow state casino regulators to implement the requirements. Accordingly, Nevada gaming agents spend over 20,000 hours a year collecting reports, checking records, visiting casino cages, and investigating complaints regarding cash transactions. Nevada authorities have also levied much higher fines for violations of the procedures than have been levied elsewhere. One casino had to pay fines in excess of $1.5 million for multiple infractions discovered by state agents.

Casinos must track all gamblers to ensure that none is exchanging more than $10,000 a day without making a full report involving positive identification of the gambler. Reports must be given to authorities within 15 days of the transaction. Casinos must also keep records of every transaction over $3,000 so they can later assess whether a single-day transaction of $10,000 has been made. The requirements apply to cash brought into the casino for any reason—to buy chips, to deposit money for later play, to make cash wagers. The procedures also apply to money coming out of the casino—as prizes, withdrawals from deposits, or cashed checks. Nevada casinos are also required to report events involving suspicious activities by players or by employees.

The money laundering laws, as amended, require all casino organizations to conduct special training for all employees to ensure that they are familiar with the reporting and recording requirements. They also must have an accounting plan in place to conduct the required activity.

References

Burbank, Jeff. 2000. *License to Steal: Nevada's Gaming Control System in the Megaresort Age.* Reno: University of Nevada Press, 35–103.

Cabot, Anthony N. 1999. *Federal Gambling Law.* Las Vegas: Trace, 247–281.

CASINO

A casino is a singular location where gambling games are played. The word *casino* can be modified with many adjectives that narrow its scope. In this encyclopedia, attention is focused upon government-recognized or legal casinos, those that are authorized by law and that share their revenues with public treasuries through commission fees or taxation. Casinos considered here also have permanence. They are places where games are played on a regular basis, as distinguished from places that offer only occasional gambling events, such as Las Vegas Nights. A casino operation is also one in which the house establishment is an active participant in the games. It participates as a player (e.g., in house-banked games) or it conducts player-banked games by furnishing house dealers and using house equipment. Again, a casino is more than a mere place where independent players can conduct their own games, as they did, for instance, on Mississippi riverboats in the 19th century.

A person studying gambling casinos must be wary of other uses of the word *casino.* In a generic sense, the word *casino* means "a small house" (from the Italian *casa,* meaning "house," and *ino,* meaning "small") or room in a house that is "used for social amusement" (according to the 10th edition of *Merriam Webster's Collegiate Dictionary*). From other dictionaries, we can find casinos identified as "Italian summer villas," "brothels," and "social clubs." The word also means "dancehall." The large casino on the Southern California resort island of Catalina is a movie house. Inquiries were made in Santiago, Chile, in search of a regulatory authority for gambling "casinos." They led a researcher in circles from one government office to another. At the end of the journey, the researcher found himself in offices outside a large cafeteria for government employees.

Indeed, he had found the "national casino."

In order to distinguish gambling casinos from other casinos, the Spanish (of Spain) call their casinos *casinos de juegos,* meaning "casinos of games." In Germany, the gambling casinos are called *Spielbanken* ("play banks"). (Perhaps too many had been getting requests from visitors from Italy for certain nongambling services.)

A real casino should have some distinction from places that merely have a side room for games within a larger establishment devoted to other activities. The Las Vegas Supermarket casino is really a supermarket with machine gambling; in smaller stores with machines, the machines can provide the dominant flow of revenue for the establishment. The gambling area that is a casino is a focal point for social activity wherever it is located.

The first gambling casinos appeared in ancient times, probably across the vast Eurasian land mass. The historical record of Asian gambling halls of the distant past is rather incomplete. It is known, however, that Greeks and Romans of the privileged classes traveled to beach resorts or resorts that were adjacent to natural spas and mineral waters with health-giving powers. Today's casino resorts at Spa, Bad Aachen, and Trier were also Roman gambling centers. Roman authorities actually taxed the wagering activity of these resorts. During the Middle Ages, gambling flourished at these same places and also at houses for overnight stays along the roads used by commercial travelers and the privileged elite.

In the 1600s, Venice became one of the first sites for a government-authorized casino. In 1626, the government gave permission for the Il Ridotto (the Redoubt) to have games, provided it paid a tax on its winnings. Part of the rationale for granting what was at first a monopoly casino franchise was that the government was having a hard time controlling many private operators. It was hoped that they would lose their patrons to the "legal" house. The Il Ridotto then did what many "high-roller" houses do now—it protected the privacy of the players. Indeed, the players all wore carnival masks as they made their wagers. Unfortunately, this practice allowed many cheats to ply their trades without fear of easy discovery. In the early 18th century, the Spa casino in present-day Belgium reopened, as did casinos at Bad Ems, Wiesbaden, Bad Kissingen, and Baden-Baden. Organized play at various houses near the Palais Royal in Paris also flourished. The 19th century saw a great proliferation of casinos across Europe. The most prominent developers of the century were the Blanc brothers, Louis and François. They started games at the Palais Royal and then moved to Bad Homburg, where they managed the house until the Prussian government banned gambling in the 1850s. The Blancs followed opportunity and accepted an invitation to take over a failing facility in Monaco, which they developed into what is even today the world's most famous casino, the one at Monte Carlo.

The entry on European casinos provides a look at why European gambling failed to maintain a leadership role in world gambling into the 20th century. The 1900s instead saw the central interest in casino gambling shift to the Western Hemisphere and especially the United States. Illegal gambling houses in cities and resorts such as Richard Canfield's first attracted attention, and then Nevada came on the scene, where Las Vegas has dominated the world casino scene for more than 50 years.

European halls remain, and many newer major casinos have been established in a large number of the countries around the world. However, the model—the yardstick—for analyzing all casinos in the world today is found in Las Vegas. (It may be that this editor has a parochial bias toward the "hometown" that he has adopted, along with 90 percent of the other local residents!)

There is a wide variety of casinos in Las Vegas. They cover just about all the types of casinos found on the world scene, save the exclusive private membership casinos of England and some European jurisdictions. The Las Vegas casinos must all be open to the public, and no admission charges are permitted at the doors to the gambling rooms— indeed, if you could find such doors they would be open *all* the time. There are several categories of casinos in Las Vegas. First, there is the major resort hotel casino that caters to patrons from all over the world. Some of these properties include the Bellagio, Mandalay Bay, Caesars Palace, Flamingo Hilton, Mirage, and the MGM Grand. Second, some resort hotels seek convention business from business personnel. Two such major properties are the Venetian and the Las Vegas Hilton. A third category consists of other Strip casinos that market more to a middle-class crowd seeking a reasonably priced (even low-cost) resort vacation with all the trappings of gambling and Las Vegas sights. The Imperial Palace, Ballys, Riviera,

and Sahara fill this bill, as well as the Excalibur and the Circus Circus, two establishments that have made a success out of niche marketing to vacationers who want to bring their children with them. (See the section "The Family That Gambles Together" in Selected Essays.) Fourth, there are several smaller downtown casinos, including the Union Plaza and Lady Luck, that appeal to a drive-in audience from California and Arizona, and they keep the customers coming back with low-cost facilities. Fifth, the California Hotel focuses its marketing efforts on Asian-Americans, especially those living in Hawaii.

On the edge of the city and in the suburbs there is a genre of casinos that seek the patronage of local residents. They have very large gambling floors, but not many hotel rooms (they have to meet a minimum requirement of 200 or 300 rooms). They emphasize machine gambling and bingo. They offer good food at low prices, as well as movie theaters, bowling alleys, dance floors, and even ice rinks; anything that will keep the people coming back. Many rely on construction workers and senior citizens to keep them going. They actually run buses to senior living centers. Then there are smaller slot joints and a very wide array of bars and taverns that rely on the money from machine gambling (they are allowed 15 machines) in order to be profitable. Convenience stores, liquor stores, drug stores, restaurants, and even grocery stores also have machines, although it would be somewhat of a stretch to call these places casinos. They do, however, come close to matching the atmosphere of some of the casinos in the small dealing; 69 percent found it a boring job; 70 percent disliked the lifestyle of their job; and 68 percent felt they were less happy than workers in other jobs. Unfortunately, the money from tips in good casinos makes their overall compensation packages quite lucrative, and few find the initiative to give up their jobs for better jobs that might require, at least at first, a reduction of their income.

The tip system varies from casino to casino. Only a rare casino in Nevada will let dealers keep their individual tips. In almost all casinos, tips are pooled. In some places, for instance the Mirage, the pool consists of every dealer of every game for the entire day. In other places, such as Caesars, the tip pool goes to dealers on particular pits of games for their particular shift on one day. The different methods of tip distribution can cause wide differences in compensation, as certain games and pits attract better (more affluent) players, as do certain shifts and days of play. An example of the differentials was offered when a billionaire gambler from Australia made two visits to Las Vegas. On each occasion, he made a $100,000 tip for the blackjack dealers—actually, he played $50,000 for the dealer. He won both times. At Caesars, each blackjack dealer for the shift was given $300 in tips as a result. When the exercise was repeated at the Mirage, all dealers of all games for the day received a cut, and the individual result was a $110 tip.

In many international jurisdictions, casino dealers are unionized. Many dealers with unions have gone on strike. This has happened in Winnipeg and Windsor, Canada; in Spa, Belgium; and in casinos in southern France. This is not the case, however, in Las Vegas. When the leading union, the Culinary Union, organized all the other nonmanagement workers in the casinos and the hotels, they agreed that they would leave dealers alone. Most Nevada casinos have firmly established the notion that they need direct control over workers in order to maintain tight security at the casinos. Dealers are subject to drug and lie detector tests, at least at the hiring stage.

Supervisory personnel in the casinos—pit bosses and casino managers—have general responsibilities for monitoring the flow of the games and the flow of money in and out of the games. They also are the key casino employees with the responsibility for ensuring that the top players receive complimentary services. They work with hosts to make sure that good players get free rooms, free transportation, free meals, show tickets, and other "services" that may be appropriate—that is, from a casino economics standpoint. The pit boss is responsible for making sure that the high-roller player is actually making the wagers that he or she is obligated to make in order to qualify for the free services.

Change personnel for slot players are not as prevalent as they were in the past. Much of their job function has been automated. Where they do exist, they are usually the lowest of the low among regular casino employees. Shills, persons paid to sit at tables and essentially pretend they are playing, are the really lowest, but they are not regular employees. Change persons are still very much needed, however, as the majority of the casino wins (even on the Strip) are from machine gamblers, and without change persons the players lose most of the human contact that a casino can give them. Change persons and other slot personnel are necessary as ambassadors to the group that is collectively the best-playing group in the casino.

The work situation in casinos varies from jurisdiction to jurisdiction. In Las Vegas, with competition from many new properties, good treatment of dealers and others is essential if the casino is to be successful. Labor is in such demand that firings without cause have become much more rare. Enlightened management is also learning a corollary to the golden rule of good customer service: "Treat your employees the way you would like your employees to treat the customer."

References

American Gaming Association. "Industry Information." http://www.americangaming.org/Industry?factsheets?general_info_detail.cfv?id=28, accessed March 18, 2009.

American Gaming Association. 1996. *Economic Impacts of Casino Gaming in the United States.* Las Vegas: Arthur Andersen.

Bureau of Labor Statistics. "Casino Hotels." http://www.bls.gov/oes/current/naics5_721120.htm, accessed March 18, 2009.

Christiansen, Eugene Martin. 1998. "Gambling and the American Economy." In *Gambling: Socioeconomic Impacts and Public Policy* (special volume of *The Annals of the American Academy of Political and Social Science*), edited by James H. Frey, 36–52. Thousand Oaks, CA: Sage.

Frey, James H., and Donald E. Carns, 1987. "The Work Environment of Gambling Casinos." *Anthropology of Work Review* 8, no. 4 (December): 38–42.

Thompson, William N., and Michele Comeau. 1992. *Casino Customer Service = The WIN WIN Game.* New York: Gaming and Wagering Business, 170–174.

CASINO NIGHTS (LAS VEGAS NIGHTS)

Casino Nights are also called Las Vegas Nights, Monte Carlo Nights, Millionaire Nights, and other such names in various states and provinces. Although rules for operations of the games vary, the basic elements of Casino Nights are the same in the more than 25 states and provinces that permit the events. Nearly $2 billion goes from gamblers to various causes as a result of these events each year. Data are very sparse on Casino Nights, because many are governed entirely by local regulations, with perhaps only a general permissive statute on the state books. Very few states keep records on games revenues.

The existence of Charity Nights gambling and similar gambling events has been considered to be "permitted" casino gambling for the purposes of negotiating Class III casino gambling compacts for Native American casinos in many states. These states include Arizona, Connecticut, Michigan, Minnesota, Montana, New Mexico, New York, North Dakota, and Washington.

A (CASINO) NIGHT ON THE TOWN

The following account is based upon the editor's visit to an El Paso, Texas, charity Casino Night on January 15, 2000.

It would have been the 71st birthday of legendary civil rights leader Dr. Martin Luther King Jr. Members of the El Paso chapter of Alpha Phi Alpha, a predominantly African American social fraternity, were celebrating. They were serving as volunteer dealers and croupiers at the North East El Paso Optimist Club's Casino Night. The players were a multiracial group that would have made Dr. King proud. There were whites (some affluent, but mostly working class), Latinos (Hispanics from Mexico and the United States), Native Americans, and African Americans. They were of all age groups, although most seemed to be over 50, or even 60. There were also at least a dozen children, preteens and youngsters in their early teens, in the Optimist Hall.

The 12 Alpha Phi Alpha volunteers were selling their services as dealers and were loaning their equipment—tables, cards, chuck-a-luck cage—to the Optimist Club in order to raise money for college scholarships for young African Americans. They charged $700 to run six blackjack tables, one poker table, a craps table, and a poker table. The North East Optimist Club cleared another $2,000 or more for its work with youth. Pictures of Scout troops, Little League sports teams, summer camps, and fishing trips were in a case on the wall. At least one of the players, a 13 year old, was in his Scout uniform. A six- or seven-year-old girl was sitting next to her mother, and both were playing blackjack hands. The mother seemed to know the Optimist sponsors of the game.

The approximately 100 players had paid $20 each to enter the gambling hall. They began to gather at 6:00 p.m., and gambling started at 7:30 p.m. They were given a beef brisket meal that would have cost $6.95 down the street at the Village Inn. The meal was put together by Optimist volunteers (members and spouses) at one-third that cost. The persons entering the hall were also given $10,000 in casino cash in addition to their meal. The "cash" could be exchanged for chips, the smallest value of which was $1,000. In other words, the players were sold single lowest-value chips at a cost of approximately $15 for ten ($20 minus the cost of the meal), or $1.50 each. The players were also permitted to purchase additional chips at a cost of $5 for $10,000, or 50 cents each. One man was observed writing a $50 check for $100,000 in casino money, or 1,000 "$1,000" chips. Later in the evening—the gambling went beyond 10:00 p.m.—an Optimist volunteer was giving bonus chips to anyone spending more than $100 (real money) for extra chips.

During the gambling session, Optimist members were drawing numbered ticket stubs for door prizes. The biggest prize was a round-trip air ticket to Las Vegas, Nevada. Other prizes were for meals at local restaurants and free bowling games and movie tickets. At the end of the gambling session, the players gathered for an auction of prizes. The money they won at gambling could now be offered in bids for their prizes. The biggest prize was a television set, probably carrying a retail value of $300. Other prizes included four automobile tires of similar retail value, as well as smaller appliances, tool sets, and various kitchen dishes. Organizers of the event indicated that merchants had donated the prizes or sold them to the Optimists for

(Continued on next page)

A (CASINO) NIGHT ON THE TOWN, *Continued*

cost. They could also discount the full retail value from business revenues for taxation purposes.

The players were gambling by any definition of the term. They were advancing something of value—real money—in order to make wagers at games of chance. As a result of the play at the games of chance, they were able to claim prizes that had values greatly in excess of the money they had individually wagered. They also had participated in raffles that involved buying a ticket, having numbers drawn by chance methods, and winning prizes of greater value than the cost of tickets.

The games were played in the same manner as they would be played in a Las Vegas casino, albeit hands were dealt more slowly, and the dealers advised players on the game rules as well as expectations for certain kinds of play. (They generally advised players to assume that cards to be dealt at blackjack would likely be ten-value cards—something that is true 31 percent of the time.) The blackjack cards were dealt in the same sequence as in Las Vegas, and players were allowed to split and double down. The dealer hit on 16 and held on 17. A four-deck shoe was used. The craps rules were identical to casino craps, and the three-dice game of chuck-a-luck was played as it used to be played when it was popular in Las Vegas several decades ago. All these games were clearly house-banked gambling games. In the poker game, the dealer competed with the players on an even odds basis, as his hand was but one of the several played, and the best hand won the pot played by all the players. The dealer contributed to the pot the same as the players did.

The Alpha Phi Alpha fraternity ran about one game a month through the year in El Paso and also in nearby New Mexico. They would often have 10 blackjack tables, as well as poker, chuck-a-luck, craps, and roulette—for a service cost of $1,000. In the summer, they ran their own game and drew over 300 players. Their biggest month was May, when they ran games for high school graduation classes. The president of the fraternity indicated that 20 years ago they had a lawyer go closely over all the rules in Texas to assure that everything being done was legal. He certainly agreed that the games were casino games and that they were gambling games. The event was clearly advertised in the El Paso newspaper as a Casino Night. Some may question whether it was legal in all aspects, but there can be no doubt that the state of Texas permitted the gambling games at the event. They were publicly advertised, and the public was invited in. An armed law enforcement officer from the police force of the city of El Paso was present at the event from the beginning to the end. Auxiliary police personnel were also present at all times. A former El Paso city councilman was prominently present, smiling and shaking hands with players and dealers. The Alpha Phi Alpha's president indicated that there was no local or state license or fee for the event.

The auction at the end of the session added an extra element to the gambling that is not present in other casinos. The players would have to assess their relative wealth vis-à-vis other players in order to decide how to bid. It is quite likely that only the tires and television carried money values higher than the money values of the amounts wagered by most individual players. At the end of Las Vegas games, winners and losers are clearly identified, and players need not go through another gambling session in order to find out if they are winners.

CHEATING SCHEMES

Cheating at games is part of the history of gambling enterprise. Over time the terms *gambler* and *riverboat gambler* have rightly or wrongly become closely associated with dishonesty. Jewish courts would not recognize the testimony of a gambler because his veracity was always suspect. *The Gamblers*, in the Time-Life series on the Old West, asserts that 99 percent of riverboat gamblers cheated at one time or another (Time-Life, Inc. 1978, 61). Graphics of Old West poker games invariably show pistols on the table, reminders to one and all that cheating was frowned upon.

Carnival games and private games are most susceptible to cheating, as there is inadequate outside supervision. Licensing authorities for casinos, however, usually mandate that surveillance systems be installed and activated during play. Security rooms have monitors, and personnel watch play as monitors record action. Videotapes typically are kept for a period of time (a week or a month) in case any question arises over the integrity of the games. The racing industry has state racing authorities who are always present at tracks to make sure that the racing is legitimate, to the extent that they can.

Customer service begins with the "win-win" game: winners talk and losers walk. That is an essential ingredient for the marketing and advertising of gambling meccas such as Las Vegas. Typically, winners love to tell of their Vegas triumphs, whereas losers tout the wonderful weather and bargain rates for slop food at the buffets or for their rooms. Everyone wins, and only the winners talk about gambling. This situation fails when players feel they are cheated or exploited. For the latter reason, it is in the self-interest of casinos to minimize and mitigate the volume and effects of compulsive gambling. But they must also make sure that the games are honest. A loser who feels that the games were not honest will be very willing to tell the world about it, whereas other losers are quite content knowing that no one else knows the results of their gambling activity.

Indeed, the games in Las Vegas are honest. There could be no Las Vegas if the games were not honest. Certainly, the gambling city would not be able to attract 40 million visitors each year. But gambling games have always attracted persons who would want them to be something other than honest. Cheating has been perpetrated by parties running the games, and also by players.

There are many forms of cheating. In the less-than-honorable (and usually unregulated) establishments, the instruments of gambling have been manipulated so that they do not give honest results. Dice are sometimes weighted and shaved so that certain numbers will fall. Shaved dice have been found in Egyptian tombs dating back thousands of years. Crooked dice can also be weighted to influence the way they fall. Metal pieces have been put into dice, and tables have been magnetized to affect falls as well. One reason that dice are of a clear plastic is so that they can be seen through. A clear die will also reveal if the numbering on the cube is correct.

Card decks can also be altered. Extra aces can be slipped into a game. More likely, however, is that a cheater can mis-shuffle and misdeal, taking cards from the bottom of the deck or middle of the deck in order to help or hurt a particular player. Quick hands can result in the placement of cards where the dealer can retrieve them at will and deal them without discovery—of course, then there are those pistols at the table. Other cheaters at card games can become adept at peeking at cards about to be dealt, or they can have confederates peeking over the shoulders of their opponents and sending them signals. It has often been said that if you have been at a private poker game for an hour and you are still wondering who the patsy (victim) is, it is you.

Roulette wheels have been magnetized to stop at certain numbers. Bias wheels have also been constructed not to cycle evenly. Dealers or others can also use techniques—from friction to electric stoppers—to cause the wheel to end its spin on certain numbers. The big wheel (wheel of fortune) is quite exposed and vulnerable to being nudged by a foot, hand, or one's hindquarters.

The Ping-Pong balls used in devices producing numbers for bingo games and lotteries can also be manipulated. In one case, balls were weighted down with lead paint so that other balls would be selected—hence, producing certain numbers for the prizes. Although that case was detected, one can certainly wonder if such cheating had not occurred many times before and since.

Number randomizers in modern machine-driven games—slot machines, keno games, computerized bingo games—can be manipulated if one can get access to them. State casino regulators carry devices that can quickly check if the chip in a slot machine or keno machine is identical to the one that has been registered to assure fully random play. One of the agents of the Nevada Gaming Control Board who was given the responsibility for inspecting the chips at the factory saw his opportunity, however, to be a dishonest person. He took a chip and reprogrammed it to distribute numbers in a certain sequence if a machine was played with a certain pattern of multiple coins on consecutive plays. He enlisted confederates to play the machines. Fortunately for the regulators, when his friends won the big prizes, they refused to identify themselves (as big winners must do for tax purposes), and their behavior revealed that they were not playing honestly. Of course, one thing led to another and then another, and the scheme was found out. Unfortunately, the culprit had probably gotten away with his cheating for some time before he was caught.

Ironically, the same regulator had broken another case in which American Coin, a major slot route company, was revealed to have programmed its poker machines to not allow royal flushes if a player put in maximum coins for a play. The discovery resulted in the company immediately losing its license. Before a criminal trial of company officials took place, an employee who was to be a key witness was murdered. This happened in the 1990s, and Las Vegas residents shuddered at the realization that the old days had not gone away entirely.

Regular casino chips are also subject to counterfeiting. As a chip can represent up to $100 in value (or more), casinos must be very vigilant against this possibility. Special companies make chips that can be observed by detectors that can verify their legitimacy. Slugs have always been used in slot machines. Modern machines have comparators, which can detect the size, weight, and metal composition of coins or slot tokens to make sure they are proper. Nonetheless, because a token may cost only 20 cents to make, but might represent $1 (or as much as $500), thieving persons will always seek to find a perfect (or workable) match for a machine.

Throughout history, many ways have been used to manipulate slot machines. The handles of old mechanical machines could be pulled with a certain rhythm, and reels could be stopped by design. After a cheater began giving lessons on how to do this, machine companies quickly retrofitted the machines with new handles.

Other simple, silly-sounding schemes were used to compromise machines. A hole would be drilled into a coin, and a string attached to it. The coin would then be dropped into the machine, and after play was activated, the coin would be pulled back out to be played over and over again. Slot cheats would also use spoon-like devices to reach up into the machine from the hopper tray in order to make coins flow. Other schemes involved groups that would distract casino security agents as they opened a machine or drilled holes in the machine in order to affect the spinning of the reels.

Probably the most prevalent type of cheating still going on in casinos is past posting. Quite simply, a player will make his bet after the play has stopped—after the dice have been rolled, or the cards dealt, or the dice rolled. When a dealer is trying to work a busy table, he can be naturally or purposely distracted as the cheater slips the extra chip on the winning number. If done very quickly, past

posting can go undetected. A suspicious dealer or games supervisor can quickly ask officials in the security room to review their videotapes to check what happened.

Much of the gambling cheating at casinos involves collusion between dishonest dealers and dishonest players. The simple technique of paying off a loser will work if there are no supervision and no camera checks. Dealers and players may also work together by using false caps that are placed over chips. A player will play a stack of white chips ($1) covered by a cap that makes them look like black chips ($100 value). The dealer will pay off bets as if the higher amount was bet, and the cameras may not catch the deception.

Another kind of cheating is not cheating of the game, but rather cheating of government authorities. Unauthorized or unlicensed owners will seek to get their share of the profits by "skimming." Legitimate owners may also try to skim profits in order to avoid their taxation obligations. One way they do this is to give credit to certain players who then simply fail to pay off their debts. Another quite ingenious means of skimming at one casino involved the use of miscalibrated scales that displayed the wrong value of coins when they were weighed. A thousand dollars in coins was weighed and declared to be $800, and the owners put the extra $200 in their pockets, while they paid taxes on only $800 in profits.

There are as many techniques for surveillance of cheating as there are techniques for cheating; nonetheless, cheating will continue as long as some see an opportunity. Casinos work together and trade photographs, names, and descriptions of known cheaters and then ban then from the casinos. The state of Nevada also keeps a black book list of excluded persons.

In horse racing, cheating can be as simple as collusion among jockeys to have a certain horse win. In other situations, ringers are used. A good horse is slipped into a race disguised as a horse with a bad record so that the payoff odds are much better. Horses may be drugged for better performances as well. Horsemen may have their steed run slowly in a few races to establish it as a loser. Then when it gets long odds, they bet heavily on it and have it run at its full potential. There is the story of a horse owner who told his jockey to hold back during a race. The jockey did so and the horse finished fifth, out of the wagering and the prize money. The owner then asked the jockey if the horse had anything left in him at the end of the race, and if the jockey thought he could have beaten the four horses in front of him. "Sure," said the jockey. "The horse had much left in him, and had I turned him loose around the corner, we could have sprinted by the four horses." The owner thanked him for the good ride and indicated they would run against the same field in a few weeks, and he was sure the horse could win. The jockey then revealed the truth. "Sir, I'm sure we can beat the four horses that were ahead of us, but we are going to have a lot of trouble with several of the horses that were behind us." The trouble with cheating is that there is often more than one cheater.

References

Burbank, Jeff. 2000. *License to Steal. Nevada's Gaming Control System in the Megaresort Age.* Reno: University of Nevada Press.

Farrell, Ronald A., and Carole Case. 1995. *The Black Book and the Mob: The Untold Story of the Control of Nevada's Casinos.* Madison: University of Wisconsin Press.

Scarne, John. 1986. *Scarne's New Complete Guide to Gambling.* New York: Simon and Schuster, 74–78, 420–428.

Sifakis, Carl. 1990. *Encyclopedia of Gambling.* New York: Facts on File, 59–62.

Thompson, William N. 1997. *Legalized Gambling: A Reference Handbook.* 2nd ed. Santa Barbara, CA: ABC-CLIO.

Time-Life, Inc. 1978. *The Gamblers. The Old West Series.* Alexandria, VA: Time-Life Books.

CHIPS, GAMBLING

Gambling chips are used in games to represent money being wagered by players. Here the word is used generically and also includes references to gambling checks, tokens, jetons, and plaques. Chips are used to make play more convenient, as well as more routine and more secure.

From the earliest times, it has been felt necessary to have objects that represented wealth wagered, rather than having the actual wealth put forth in the games. Native Americans had very good control over excessive gambling, in that the players in a game would have to physically place the thing being wagered into an area near the game. If they were betting a horse and a saddle, the horse and saddle would be brought to the game. With these rules of engagement, the players would never wager more than they possessed, nor would they incur a debt because of their gambling. The development of money currencies simplified gambling activity considerably.

One of the latent functions of the use of chips in games has been to help the player "pretend" that the game is just a game and not about the risking of real wealth. This self-delusion has led many players into wagering amounts way beyond their means. The introduction of markers and the use of personal checks in exchange for chips has led many players into serious debt as a result of gambling. One casino executive applauded the value that chips have given to casinos and game operators, saying that the "guy who invented the chip was a genius" (Sifakis, 65). No one knows who that guy was.

The earliest use of chips in games may have been in ancient Egypt. In the western world, chips have been used for many centuries. European (French-style) chips were found in 18th-century casinos such as Bad Ems and Wiesbaden. They were engraved in mother-of-pearl and later made of bone or ivory. In 19th-century games in the United States, chips were made from other materials. Ivory was used until it became too scarce and too expensive. In the 1880s, clay chips with a shellac finish were developed. A great advance in chip technology came in the 1950s when plastic became a major component of the chips. Mixed materials were sometimes used, with clay and plastic compositions surrounding metal centers for the chips. The 1980s saw the development of multicolored chips of very distinctive appearance

that could not only be picked out by the trained eyes of dealers and pit bosses but could also be electronically read to assure their genuine character.

The first gambling chips in the United States did not have indications of value marked upon them. They could be used interchangeably for low-stakes and high-stakes games, merely by designating their value at the start of a game. These "plain" chips were especially popular in early illegal casinos because they could not be used as evidence if there was a police raid. Legitimate casinos soon found a need to control the flow of chips, however, and they did so by distinctively marking the chips with values and also with casino logos. Today, the only unmarked chips are those of different colors that are used by different players at U.S. roulette games in order to indicate which bet belongs to which player.

European (French-style) chips are different from basic U.S. casino chips in two ways. The European chip (called a jeton) is usually of a plastic composition that has a rounded surface and an oval or round shape. The chips cannot be placed on top of one another but must be spread out to determine their value and to count them. Europeans also use squared plaques for higher denominations—as do some U.S. casinos with substantial play from high rollers. The U.S. chip is invariably circular but has a flat surface. Although European chips of different values vary in size, all U.S. chips are the same size, with the exception of plaques and some very high-value chips that are larger circles. The U.S. chip can be easily stacked and moved about. Side color markings allow casino personnel and cameras to see their values and check for authenticity. Most of the U.S. chips are the same size as an old silver dollar. Games in the United States move faster than those in Europe, and the stacking chips facilitate game speed.

The value chips in U.S. casinos today are referred to by their colors. A $1 chip is white, a $5 chip is red, a $25 chip is green, a $100 chip is black, and a pink chip is worth $500. The notion that a high roller is a "blue chipper" or that a solid value stock on Wall Street is a "blue-chip stock" is apparently a term left over from another day.

U.S. slot machines began using tokens instead of actual coins when the silver dollar started to go out of circulation in the 1960s. The earliest machines used tokens as a way of hiding the fact that they were gambling machines, but law enforcement authorities did not fall for the ruse for long. Federal laws regarding the use of tokens other than official coinage for value transactions were modified so that casinos could have machines accept the tokens. Today, many casinos outside of Nevada accept only tokens for slot play—in machines with coin acceptors. The token-accepting devices have sophisticated mechanisms with comparators that can assess the token shape, size, weight, and metal composition to assure its honesty, for the most part. Slugs or counterfeit tokens and coins are still a problem. The problem is lessened somewhat by the fact that most of the machines have dollar bill acceptors that are gradually replacing coin-in usage for slots and video slots. The players should now have that ultimate reality check each time they put a 20 or 50 dollar bill into a machine. They should know they are playing "real money." Once the bill is in, however, the player starts hitting a button and playing not money but "credits"—the newest gimmick to separate the player from reality.

References

Herz, Howard, and Kregg Herz. 1995. *A Collector's Guide to Nevada Gaming Checks and Chips*. Racine, WI: Whitman Products.

Sifakis, Carl. 1990. *Encyclopedia of Gambling*. New York: Facts on File, 65.

Spencer, Donald D. 1994. *Casino Chip Collecting*. Ormond Beach, FL: Camelot Publishing.

Chuck-a-Luck. *See* Craps and Other Dice Games (in Games section).

COCKFIGHTING

Cockfights are banned throughout most of the world, including Canada and the United States, with the exception of Oklahoma. No European, African, or continental Asian country allows the sport; the only Pacific jurisdictions that permit cockfighting are the Philippines and Guam. Most of the "action" is found in Latin America and the Caribbean, including Puerto Rico, Mexico, Panama, Honduras, the Dominican Republic, Aruba, Guadeloupe, Martinique, and Haiti. Although banned almost everywhere, the fights are also found in many clandestine locations throughout North America.

A bird owner readies a cock for a fight inside the Casino Del Caribe, Cartagena, Colombia.

Cockfighting dates back to the ancient world. Greeks and Romans bred birds especially for fighting purposes. J. Philip Jones's history of gaming tells of a Greek commander who was inspired by two fighting birds on his way to a victorious battle against the Persians in the fifth century BCE. In thanks for his triumph, he declared that there would be cockfighting everywhere in a celebration recognizing the victory (Jones, 97). The activity spread throughout Europe.

At first the birds fought on tabletops, but later enclosed pens were used. The Romans brought fighting birds to England, and cockfighting developed into a popular activity there during the 17th century. In the American colonies, the cockfight was a regular side attraction at horse race meetings.

As birds are raised, they are closely watched for signs that they could become fighters. The training process is as elaborate as that used for race horses or dogs. Each "cockmaster" directs the bird in rituals and practice fights using leather guards over their spurs. Before they are engaged in contests, the spur covers may be removed and the birds allowed to attack other chickens in order to keep their instincts intact. They are isolated so they can rest and fast before the match to assure that they are fresh and ready for battle.

Betting at the cockfight is usually conducted privately on a one-on-one basis among the players. There are also bookies who will cover the action of many bettors. The heaviest betting is between the owners of the birds, with the loser losing not only money but also his prize fighter. The vicious nature of the fight to the death causes animal rights groups to vigorously oppose the sport. It was banned in England in 1834 and in most U.S. jurisdictions not long afterwards. Clifford Gertz offers a poignant description of the emotions surrounding participation in the cockfight in his essay, "Deep Play: Notes on the Balinese Cockfight."

References

Gertz, Clifford. 1972. "Deep Play: Notes on the Balinese Cockfight." *Daedalus* 10 (Winter): 1–37.

Jones, J. Philip. 1973. *Gambling: Yesterday, and Today, a Complete History.* Devon, England: David and Charles, 97–100.

COMMISSION ON THE REVIEW OF NATIONAL POLICY TOWARD GAMBLING (1974–1976)

The 1970 Organized Crime Control Act authorized the president and Congress to appoint a commission to examine gambling in the United States. The commission was charged with conducting a "comprehensive legal and factual study of gambling" in the United States and all its subdivisions and was instructed to "formulate and propose such changes" in policies and practices as it might "deem appropriate." At its conclusion, the commission included four U.S. senators (Democrats John McClellan of Arkansas and Howard Cannon of Nevada and Republicans Hugh Scott of Pennsylvania and Bob Taft of Ohio) and four members of the House (Democrats James Hanley of New York and Gladys Spellman of Maryland and Republicans Charles Wiggins of California and Sam Steiger of Arizona). Seven "citizen" members included commission chairman Charles Morin, a Washington, D.C., attorney; state attorney general Robert List of Nevada; Ethel Allen, a city council member in Philadelphia; Philip Cohen,

director of the National Legal Data Center; prosecutor James Coleman of Monmouth County, New Jersey; Joseph Gimma, a New York banker; and professor of economics Charles Phillips of Washington and Lee University. Former federal prosecutor James Ritchie served as the executive director of the commission, which had a life of almost three years. The first meetings were held in January 1974, and its final report was presented on October 15, 1976.

The commission staff of nearly 30 professionals, 20 student assistants, and 26 consultants prepared several dozen research studies. Additionally, the Survey Research Center of the University of Michigan was engaged to conduct the first national survey of gambling behavior. It also conducted a gaming survey of the Nevada population. The commission also held 43 days of public hearings in Washington, D.C., as well as in several other cities, including Las Vegas. Testimony was received from 275 law enforcement personnel; persons involved with gambling enterprises, both legal and illegal; and persons representing the general public.

The report presented conclusions suggesting a much more relaxed view of gambling than had been found in earlier federal investigations. Indeed, the commission seemed to be urging the federal government to remove itself from the regulatory process almost entirely. A certain mixed message was given—a recognition that gambling has a downside, but a frustration that legislation seeking to totally outlaw gambling is simply unenforceable. Hence citizens and governments were urged, for the most part, to "roll with the punches."

The sense of the commission's feelings is presented in Chairman Morin's foreword to the final report: "[We] should carefully reflect on the significance of the fact that a pastime indulged in by two-thirds of the American people, and approved of by perhaps 80 percent of the population, contributes more than any other single enterprise to police corruption . . . and to the well-being of the Nation's criminals. . . . Most Americans gamble because they like to, and they see nothing wrong with it." He then highlights a statement from the report: "Contradictory gambling policies and lack of resources combine to make effective gambling law enforcement an impossible task." He adds, "Not 'difficult'—not 'frustrating' not even 'almost impossible'— but impossible. And why not? How can any law which prohibits what 80 percent of the people approve of be enforced?" (Commission on the Review of the National Policy toward Gambling, Foreword).

The commission made a firm recommendation that gambling policy be a matter that is determined by the states.

Indeed, it urged that Congress enact a statute "that would insure the states' continued power to regulate gambling" (Commission on the Review of the National Policy toward Gambling). Moreover, the federal government was asked to take care that its regulations and taxing powers not interfere with states' rights in this area. The commission urged that player winnings from gambling activities not be subject to federal income taxes and that the federal wagering tax and slot machine tax be removed. State authorities were asked to devote law enforcement energies against persons operating gambling enterprises at a "higher" level and to relax enforcement against "low-level" gambling offenses. Prohibitions against public social gambling should be removed. If a state had a substantial amount of illegal gambling, however, the federal government should be authorized to use electronic surveillance techniques not authorized before, and judges were urged to give longer prison terms and more substantial fines to convicted offenders.

The report suggested that states use considerable caution before legalizing casinos. If they did legalize casinos, the state regulatory law should provide a series of player protection provisions. Moreover, casinos should be private— not government—enterprises. Casinos should not be built in "urban areas where lower income people reside" (Commission on the Review of the National Policy toward Gambling). The commission recommended that racetracks and off-track betting facilities lower the take-out rate on wagers (the amount the track removes from its betting pool). If the bettors were able to keep more of their wagers at legal betting facilities, they would be less inclined to turn to illegal operators when placing bets. The states should also determine if players were allowed to make wagers on out-of-state races. The commission felt that state lotteries were often unfair to players and that full information about true odds for the games should be presented to the public. Advertisements by the lotteries should also be more honest and accurate. States were discouraged from allowing wagers on single-event sports games, especially on games involving amateur teams. The commission recommended that states not have sports betting without a referendum vote of the citizens.

Reference

Commission on the Review of the National Policy toward Gambling. 1976. *Gambling in America: Final Report.* Washington, DC: Government Printing Office.

Commission to Investigate Allegations of Police Corruption and the City's Anti-Corruption Procedures. *See* The Knapp Commission.

Compulsive Gambling. *See* Problem Gambling.

CREDIT AND DEBTS

In 1990, this editor visited the Casino Copanti in San Pedro Sula, Honduras. The casino owners were an American, Eddie Cellini, and his sons. Members of Cellini's family had previously worked in casinos in Havana, Cuba, and Lagos, Nigeria. While speaking with a manager, the editor observed a player approach the cage and (it seemed) purchase a full tray of tokens. He thought nothing about it until the same man returned 10 minutes later and purchased another full tray of tokens. He commented to the manager that the man appeared to be a "high roller." The manager laughed and said, "No, he is buying tokens to loan to the players." He went on to add that the tokens were sold at a discount to certain individuals. Those individuals would then know which players they could loan them to with a good expectation of being paid back. The individuals made their own loan and collection arrangements with the players. The casino management endorsed the practices. They had learned several things when they first opened up and made loans directly to the local players. They learned that they were the "ugly Americans" when they tried to collect repayments from players who had been losers. Often the players would say, "I gave you your money back at the tables." Then they would suggest that the casino's request for repayment was an affront to their "manhood" and dignity. When the casino owners went to court to collect the debts, they found judges who were quite reluctant to support the cause of the foreigners from the casino who were now seeking to "exploit" the local players. The casino's solution was simple—let the locals borrow from each other. After asking if this might represent casino support for loan sharking, the editor was assured that the loan agents were respected local businessmen and that the casino had never heard of a complaint that their collection procedures were anything but fair.

The Jaragua Casino of Santo Domingo loaned chips to players directly. They had two sets of chips; the set of chips that were loaned to players had white stripes across them. The casino manager reported that they had had problems with players borrowing funds to gamble and then cashing in the chips and not repaying the loans on time. Credit players could only win the striped chips. The players could not cash these until their debts were fully paid.

Gambling credit and indebtedness pose many issues for the gambling industry. There are simple business decisions, such as, can the person borrowing money from the establishment be trusted to pay it back? There are also legal questions. For instance, can an establishment go to court to force repayment of a gambling debt? Moral issues confront the industry when casinos may offer loans to players who are not in control of their play (e.g., compulsive gamblers). Other questions concern the use of credit card machines and automated teller machines (ATMs) in gambling places. There is also concern expressed in gambling jurisdictions about the presence of "loan sharks" representing organized crime interests.

Without credit, many large gambling casinos would not be able to sustain ample profits to support their operations in a viable manner. Perhaps as much as one-half of the table play at Las Vegas Strip casinos is credit play. High rollers appreciate being able to set up accounts with casinos upon which they can draw; they also like to be able to draw upon credit allotments as well. As with credit card machines or an ATM, this ability permits the player to come to the casino without having to carry large sums of money. Also, winnings can be placed back into accounts instead of being converted into cash that would have to be carried out of the casino on one's person. This latter situation remains a major problem for casino ATMs, as they allow only withdrawals but no deposits.

By establishing accounts with a casino, a high roller can begin to establish a record of play activity. This enables the casino to award the good player with complimentaries such as free transportation (air flights), free hotel rooms, meals, beverages, and show tickets. Additionally, by engaging in straight credit play, the player and the casino can avoid the necessity of reporting large cash transactions as required by the Bank Secrecy Act of 1970. This may give the player an added sense of anonymity.

In jurisdictions where gambling credit is permitted (as in Nevada and New Jersey), there are usually detailed rules surrounding the loans. In Nevada, regulations require casinos to check the credit history of players seeking loans. They must also look at the previous loans given to the player to be sure that they were repaid. They must also check with other casinos regarding the player's activity. Casinos are required to check identifications when players cash checks. In actuality, a credit loan from a Nevada casino is like a bank counter check. The credit instrument is called a marker, and it contains information about player bank account numbers and authorizes loan repayments for the accounts. It also acknowledges that the loan was made entirely within the state of Nevada and that the player is willing to be sued in court, including Nevada courts, for repayment if necessary. The player also agrees to pay the cost of collection.

In the "old days," casinos may have resorted to ugly tactics to retrieve money owed by players. Nowadays such tactics as threatened physical harm or embarrassments bordering on blackmail are hardly ever used. If they were used and discovered, casinos would be severely disciplined. Most players truly want to repay loans. One major consideration many have is that they will not be able to return to the casino to play again with VIP (very important person) treatment unless they repay the loans. If they are temporarily without sufficient funds, casinos will give them a "long leash"—that is, adequate time to get the necessary resources. Casinos will also discount loan amounts to encourage quick repayment.

Discounts may be as much as 25 percent of the value of the loan. Of course, the casino would have a record that the debtor actually lost the money while playing in the casino. Casino loans that are repaid in a reasonable time do not carry any interest. This factor distinguishes casino loans from those received from loan sharks. Typically, the loan shark requires a repayment with 10 percent interest per week. If the person cannot make the total repayment, then only the 10 percent is accepted (that is mandatory), and the full loan plus the 10 percent interest carries over until the next week. Casinos in Nevada may use collection agencies that are bonded and licensed; in New Jersey, casino organizations do all the collection activities themselves.

The casinos must make a bona fide effort to collect all debts. Otherwise, they will be assessed taxes as if they had collected the debt in full. New Jersey limits the amount of "bad debt" that can be deducted from their casino win for taxation purposes.

Most North American jurisdictions follow the edict of the Statute of Anne (1710), which became part of the common law of England. The statute holds that debts incurred because of gambling represent contracts that are unenforceable by courts of the realm. Before 1983, Nevada also followed the Statute of Anne. Because the Nevada law would apply anywhere as long as it pertained to a Nevada debt, the casinos could not collect debts from out of state, even if the debtor's state permitted collection of gambling debts through the courts. In 1982, a federal tax court ruled that uncollected Nevada debts could no longer be subtracted from casino wins for tax purposes. Although the decision was overruled by other courts, Nevada was stimulated into action for change. Also, with the advent of New Jersey casinos and the fact that New Jersey courts allowed collection of gambling debts, Nevada casinos found themselves at a disadvantage. Players with debts in both states were paying off the New Jersey debts and ignoring the Nevada debts when they did not have sufficient funds to cover both. In 1983, Nevada repealed the Statute of Anne, and now gambling debts may be collected through courts in Nevada as well as New Jersey.

Even with the Statute of Anne repealed, both states found that other states' courts would still refuse to order repayment of the loans. Hence, casino operators in Nevada and New Jersey have adopted another method for collection. In Nevada, casinos take their cases only to Nevada courts. There, the facts support them; the courts give judgments in favor of the casino against the debtors. The court ruling is then entered into the courts of the debtor's home state. Those courts then will issue orders supporting the Nevada court rulings and will not consider the gambling issue. Fortunately for the casinos, debt matters do not have to go to court very often.

A gambling debt is, in effect, the result of a contract between the casino and a player. When a player is taken to court to repay the debt, he or she may offer several defenses regarding the contract, perhaps making a case that the gambling activity in question is illegal. If proven, that would make the contract for a loan illegal and unenforceable. The gambling debtor may also claim that the debt is excessive and that the casino should not have allowed him or her to incur such a large debt. Puerto Rican courts have entertained such defenses and have actually reduced the amount of the debt ordered to be repaid.

If the player is too young to gamble, age is a complete defense against compulsory repayment of the loan. In a reverse case, a 19-year-old was denied a $1 million jackpot he "won" at Caesars Palace in Las Vegas. Even though Caesars was in a sense indebted to the player to pay the amount, the casino did not do so. The gaming control board and the courts voided the casino's obligation to pay the jackpot because the player was too young to gamble.

Some have argued that debts from gambling should not have to be repaid if the player was intoxicated. Courts have heard such cases, although they have not ruled in favor of such a debtor. A special defense heard in many cases today is that the player was a compulsive gambler. In such situations, the player must have proof that the casino knew of the compulsive condition prior to the debt. There have also been third-party suits from family members or victims of embezzlement seeking recovery of moneys gambled by compulsive gamblers. There have been some out-of-court settlements in these cases, but as of yet, no major decisions have disallowed collection of debt or given recovery because of compulsive gambling. Efforts continue, however, to bring such cases to court.

References

Cabot, Anthony N., ed. 1989. *Casino Credit and Collection Law.* Las Vegas: International Association of Gaming Attorneys.

Lionel, Sawyer and Collins. 1995. *Nevada Gaming Law.* 2nd ed. Las Vegas, NV: Lionel, Sawyer and Collins.

Thompson, William N. 1991. "Machismo: Manifestations of a Cultural Value in the Latin American Casino." *Journal of Gambling Studies* 7 (Spring): 143–164.

CRIME AND GAMBLING

The crime issue has been and will continue to be an essential issue in debates over the legalization of gambling. Opponents of gambling make almost shrill statements about how organized crime infiltrates communities when they legalize gambling. They also suggest that various forms of street crimes—robberies, auto theft, prostitution—come with gambling, as do embezzlement, forgery, and various forms of larceny caused by desperate problem gamblers.

On the other hand, proponents of gambling contend that the evidence of any connections between crime and gambling is rather weak. They contend that the stories of Mob involvement with gambling are a part of the past, not the present, and that even then the involvement was more exaggerated than real. Most cases of increased street crime are passed off as owing to an increased volume of people traffic in casino communities. Moreover, proponents of legalized gambling even argue that because gambling may lead to job growth in gambling communities, crime may actually go down, because employed people are less inclined to be drawn to criminal activities than are people without jobs. They also suggest that by legalizing gambling, society can fight the effects of illegal gambling.

OPPORTUNITIES FOR CRIME

Criminologists have identified opportunity as a factor in explaining much criminal activity. The kinds of crimes that are purportedly found in association with gambling indicate the efficacy of "opportunity" theories of crime. For instance, the several types of crimes that might be associated with the presence of casinos include inside activity concerning casino owners and business associates and employees, crimes tied to the playing of the games, and crimes involving patrons. Organized crime elements may try to draw profits off the gaming enterprise through schemes of hidden ownership or through insiders who steal from the casino winnings. Managers may steal from the profit pools to avoid taxes or to cheat their partners.

Organized crime figures may become suppliers for goods and services, extracting unreasonable costs for their products. Crime families have been the providers of gambling junket tours for players and, in New Jersey, for various sources of labor in the construction trades. Organized crime figures also may become involved in providing loans to desperate players, and the existence of the casinos may facilitate laundering of money for cartels that traffic in illegal activities such as prostitution and the drug trade.

Another set of crimes attends the actual games that are played. Wherever a game is offered with a money prize, someone will try to manipulate the game through cheating schemes. Cheating may involve marked cards, crooked dice, and uneven roulette wheels. Schemes may involve teams of players or individual players and casino employees. Cheating is also associated with race betting and even with lotteries. In some cases, the gambling organization may attempt to cheat players.

The greatest concern about crime and gambling involves activities of casino patrons. On the one hand, they present criminals with opportunities. Players who win money or carry money to casinos may be easy marks for forceful robberies as well those by pickpockets. Hotel rooms in casino properties are also targets. Players are targeted by prostitutes and also by other persons selling illicit goods, such as drugs. On the other hand, desperate players may be drawn to crimes in order to secure money for play or to pay gambling debts. Their crimes involve robberies and other larcenies, as well as white-collar crime activity—embezzlements, forgeries, and so on.

STUDIES OF CRIME AND GAMBLING

The issue of crime and gambling has been well studied for generations. Virgil Peterson, director of the Chicago Crime Commission, issued a scathing attack on gambling in his book *Gambling: Should It Be Legalized?* (1951). He makes the following assertions:

> "Legalized gambling has always been attractive to the criminal and racketeering elements."

> "Criminals, gangsters, and swindlers have been the proprietors of gambling establishments."

> "Many people find it necessary to steal or embezzle to continue gambling activity."

> "The kidnapper, the armed robber, the burglar and the thief engage in crime to secure money for play."

In a 1965 article that seemed prophetic, considering future events in New Jersey, Peterson wrote, "The underworld inevitably gains a foothold under any licensing system. If state authorities establish the vast policing system rigid supervision requires, the underworld merely provides itself with fronts who obtain the licenses, with actual ownership remaining in its own hands; and it receives a major share of the profits."

Other stories of the relationships between organized crime and gambling are plentiful. While Peterson was gathering information for his book, the Senate Committee on Organized Crime was holding hearings under the leadership of Estes Kefauver in 1950 and 1951. The committee was specific in identifying gambling as a major activity of organized crime.

In the 1960s, Ovid Demaris and Ed Reid wrote *The Green Felt Jungle,* a shocking account of the Mob in Las Vegas. Demaris continued the saga with his *Boardwalk Jungle,* an early account of casinos in New Jersey. His story was built upon *The Company That Bought the Boardwalk* (1980), Gigi Mahon's journalistic account of crime involvement in Atlantic City's first casino. The role of organized crime was tangential to the activities of the first company that won a casino license in New Jersey and persisted with involvement in labor unions that served companies constructing the casino facilities.

The issue of organized crime and gambling has lost much of its punch over the past 30 years, however, as major corporations have emerged as the most important players in the gambling industry. Nonetheless, gaming control agents and other law enforcement agencies from the local, state, and federal levels must remain vigilant lest organized crime elements return to the gambling scene. In reality, they have never completely left the scene. In the 1990s, they were still found seeking inroads to the management of casino operations in one San Diego County Native American casino. They actually infiltrated the operations of the White Earth Reservation casino in Minnesota, and the tribal leader was indicted for wrongdoing in connection with his Mob ties. In another instance, slot machine operations in restaurants and bars in Louisiana were compromised by organized crime elements and indictments ensued. As the 20th century ended, organized crime interests maintained ties with several Internet gambling enterprises operating in other countries.

The major concern over gambling has, however, turned toward ambient crime—personal crime that appears in the atmosphere around gambling establishments. In September 1995, L. Scott Harshbarger, Massachusetts state attorney general, commented to the U.S. House Judiciary Committee that "one of the noted consequences of casino gambling has been the marked rise in street crime. Across the nation, police departments in cities that have casino gambling have recorded surges in arrests due to casino-related crime. In many cases, towns that had a decreasing crime rate or a low crime rate have seen a sharp and steady growth of crime once gambling has taken root" (quoted in Worshop 1996, 785). Although there were many statements from law enforcement officials that echoed Harshbarger's thoughts, there were also those who disputed the claims.

EMPIRICAL STUDIES

Much of the data for the studies mentioned above was anecdotal or came from personal testimony of law enforcement personnel. Other entries into the literature have been based upon similar kinds of evidence. Such studies may be interesting, but they have only a limited value. Anecdotes may not always be precise or accurate.

More solid data have come from analyses of criminal statistics. George Sternlieb and James Hughes's study of Atlantic City revealed that crime increased rapidly in the community after the introduction of casinos in 1978. Pick-pocketing activity increased eighty-fold, larceny increased over five times, and robberies tripled, as did assaults. Simon Hakim and Andrew J. Buck found that the levels of all types of crime were higher in the years after casinos began operations. The "greatest post-casino crime increase was observed for violent crimes and auto thefts and the least for burglaries." As one moved farther from Atlantic City in spatial distance, rates of crime leveled off, although Joseph Friedman, Simon Hakim, and J. Weinblatt found that increases in crime extended outward at least 30 miles to suburban areas and to areas along highways that extended toward New York and Philadelphia.

Similarly a study of Windsor, Ontario, found some crime rates increasing after a casino opened in May 1994. Overall, previous decreases in rates of crime citywide seemed to come to an end, whereas rates in areas around the casino increased measurably. The downtown area near the casino saw more assaults, assaults upon police officers, and other violent crimes. Particularly noticeable were increases in general thefts, motor vehicle thefts, liquor offenses, and driving offenses.

Not all the evidence points in the same direction. Several riverboat communities in Iowa, Illinois, and Mississippi saw decreases in crime rates following the establishment of casinos. A study by Ronald George Ochrym and Clifton Park compared gaming communities with other tourist destinations that did not have casinos. They found that rates of crime were quite similar. Crime statistics soared following the introduction of casinos in Atlantic City, but so too did crime in Orlando, Florida, following the opening of Disney World. If the casinos themselves are responsible for more crime, gaming proponents suggest that Mickey Mouse also must cause crime.

Casino proponent Jeremy D. Margolis, a former assistant U.S. attorney, discounts the link to crime as well. In a December 1997 study for the American Gaming Association, he summarized the literature of crime and gambling studies by finding that Las Vegas, Nevada, had a lower crime rate than other tourist destinations, and that the crime rate in Atlantic City, New Jersey, had been falling. So too were crime rates in Joliet, Illinois (a casino community), and in Baton Rouge, Louisiana, since casino gaming had begun.

A study by Thompson, Gazel, and Rickman (1996) found a mixed pattern of crime and gambling associations in Wisconsin. Crime rates for major crimes and arrest rates for minor crimes in all 76 counties from 1980 to 1995 were analyzed. The analysis compared counties with casinos to other counties. The authors considered all crime data prior to l992 to be data from counties without casinos. Utilizing a technique called linear regression, they looked at the incidence of crime in 14 counties with casinos for 1992, 1993, and 1994 as data from casino counties, whereas 1992, 1993, and 1994 data from other counties was considered noncasino county data.

They found that the introduction of casinos did impact the incidence of serious crimes. For each 1 percent increase in the numbers of major crimes statewide, the number of major crimes in the casino counties increased an additional 6.7 percent, a significant jump. Reduced to simple language, the existence of nearby casinos explained a major crime increase of 6.7 percent above what would otherwise be experienced in the absence of casinos. As there were approximately 10,000 major crimes in these counties in 1991, it was suggested that casinos brought an additional 670 major crimes for each of three years after casinos came. The largest share of casino-related crimes were burglaries.

An analysis of Part II (minor) crimes found that the number of arrests in counties with nearby casinos was 12.2 percent higher than elsewhere. Relationships could be demonstrated for arrests for assaults, stolen property, driving while intoxicated, and drug possession.

Assaults increased 37.8 percent more in these counties than in the state as a whole, and arrests for stolen property increased 28.1 percent. Drunk driving arrests increased 13.9 percent, and drug possession arrests increased 21.9 percent. Although the percentage increase was not as great as for some other categories, the most significant relationship linking the presence of crime and casinos was driving while intoxicated.

Although the general comments and anecdotal evidence suggest ties between casinos and forgery, fraud, and embezzlement, no strong links were found in the data. No relationships were established with embezzlement arrests although this does not mean they might not exist at a future time. This kind of crime, when it is linked to gambling, takes time to develop since it is associated with problem or pathological gambling. First, the cycle of pathological gambling itself takes time to develop. Second, as the cycle is developing, the pathological gambler typically uses all possible legal means to get funds for gambling. Only in the later desperate stages does the gambler usually turn to illegal means for funds.

The presence of additional crime also imposes additional costs on society. Using standard criminal justice costs for arrests, court actions, probation, and jail time, as well as property losses, the authors concluded that the additional 5,277 serious crimes per year cost the public $16.71 million, and the additional 17,100 arrests for minor crimes cost society $34.20 million each year. The data suggest that casinos may be responsible, directly or indirectly, for nearly $51 million each year in societal costs resulting from crime.

A confirmation of the link between crime and casino gambling was provided by Earl Grinols in a study of statistics in all 3,165 counties of the United States between 1977 and 2000. He found that 12.5 percent of the crimes committed in counties with casinos would not have occurred in their absence.

POLITICAL CRIMES AND GAMBLING

Gambling interests (and potential gambling interests) have money. Often their profit margins may be very large, especially in monopoly or semimonopoly situations. The interests are willing to spend their money to advance their causes. The very open bribery of Louisiana legislators in the late 19th century by operators of the state's lottery led to the reforms that ended that lottery and precluded the reestablishment of any state lottery until 1964. Gambling interests will still invest large sums of money in politics. Often their targets are referenda campaigns. The California Proposition 5 campaign of November 1998 was the most expensive ballot initiative campaign in U.S. history. Nevada casino interests put $26 million into the campaign, and tribal gambling interests in California invested

nearly $70 million. Prior to 1998, a 1994 campaign to legalize casinos in Florida that drew almost $18 million from the casino industry had been the most expensive referenda campaign in history.

Casinos and other gambling enterprises also invest large sums of money in lobbying campaigns and public persuasion campaigns. This is the political process in the United States, one that thrives on the clash of interests and the clash of issues. It is a Madisonian system in which rival interests protect their turf by making their positions known and by commandeering the facts that will help them persuade policymakers that they are on the correct side when the issues rise to decision points on the public agenda.

Some of the interests might go too far. After all, the potential benefits can be extraordinary. In some jurisdictions, forces desiring casino licenses or contracts with government-controlled gambling operations have crossed the line. A former governor of Louisiana, Edwin Edwards, was a leader in the effort to get casinos and gambling machines into his state. Rumors about bags of money being brought into state offices filled the air from the beginning—but those were just rumors. Federal Justice Department officials gathered the facts, however, and Edwards was indicted more than once for taking bribes. The new century began with the former governor on criminal trial; since then he has been convicted and incarcerated. Officials in Missouri were charged with the same kind of wrongdoing, and several resigned during the 1990s. One Las Vegas gambling interest withdrew from pursuing casino activity in Missouri because of the exposure of political activities considered inappropriate. Another company remained an active Missouri player but only after removing key company officials. In the

1980s, both Atlantic City and Las Vegas were rocked by FBI sting operations, which involved undercover agents offering bribes to influential public figures in exchange for their intervention in the casino licensing process. The Atlantic City operation—called ABSCAM (a code name based on *Arab* and *scam*)—resulted in the resignation of U.S. Senator Harrison Williams (D-New Jersey). Several local officials in Nevada also saw their political careers end when they were exposed for taking bribe offers.

Lines between acceptable—even honorable—political activity and unacceptable—or even illegal—activity can be blurred. Incentives remain, however, for continued activity—even intense activity. Citizens, political leaders, law enforcement officials, and industry operatives must always be on watch for wrongdoing; if they are not, the industry will suffer in the long run.

LEGALIZATION AS A SUBSTITUTE FOR ILLEGAL GAMBLING

Advocates of legalizing gambling suggest that there is a certain quantity of illegal gambling existing in any society and that the process of legalization will serve to eliminate the illegal gaming and channel all gambling activity into a properly regulated and taxed enterprise. As with the evidence related to other topics, the research here is also mixed. Nevada certainly had a large amount of illegal gambling before "wide-open" casino gambling was legalized in 1931. Since 1931, there has been very little evidence of illegal casino gambling games in Nevada. Illegal operators simply obtained licenses from the state government.

Similarly, David Dixon found that illegal bookmaking was effectively replaced by legal betting when Great Britain passed legislation in 1960 permitting betting shops. Opposite results have been found elsewhere, however. An examination of casinos in Holland by William Thompson and J. Kent Pinney found that legalization in 1975 seemed only to promote an expansion of illegal casinos that had operated before laws were passed for government-operated casinos (Thompson and Pinney 1990). Clearly the illegal operators were not permitted to win licenses. Also, the government placed many restrictions on its own casinos—they had to be located (at first) outside cities and they could not advertise, give complimentary services, or operate around the clock. Illegal casinos found new places to advertise—at the doors of the legal casinos when they closed at 2:00 a.m. David Dixon also found that when Australia established its government-operated betting parlors, illegal sports and race betting underwent a major expansion (Dixon 1990).

References

Demaris, Ovid. 1986. *Boardwalk Jungle: How Greed, Corruption and the Mafia Turned Atlantic City into the Boardwalk Jungle.* New York: Bantam Books.

Dixon, David. 1990. *From Prohibition to Regulation: Bookmaking, Anti Gambling and the Law.* Oxford, UK: Clarendon Press.

Dombrink, John D. 1981. "Outlaw Businessmen: Organized Crime and the Legalization of Casino Gambling." Ph.D. diss., University of California, Berkeley.

Friedman, Joseph, Simon Hakim, and J. Weinblatt. 1989. "Casino Gambling as a 'Growth Pole' Strategy and Its Effects on Crime." *Journal of Regional Science* 29 (November): 615–624.

Grinols, E. L. 2000. "Casino Gambling Causes Crime." *Policy Forum* 13, no. 2.

Hakim, Simon, and Andrew J. Buck. 1989. "Do Casinos Enhance Crime?" *Journal of Criminal Justice* 17 no. 5: 409–416.

Miller, William J., and Martin D. Schwartz. 1998. "Casino Gambling and Street Crime." In *Gambling: Socioeconomic Impacts and Public Policy* (special volume of *The Annals of the American Academy of Political and Social Science*), edited by James H. Frey, 124–137. Thousand Oaks, CA: Sage.

Ochrym, Ronald George, and Clifton Park. 1990. "Street Crime, Tourism and Casinos: An Empirical Comparison." *Journal of Gambling Studies* 6 (Summer): 127–138.

Peterson, Virgil W. 1951. *Gambling: Should It Be Legalized?* Springfield, IL: Charles C. Thomas.

Peterson, Virgil W. 1965. "A Look at Legalized Gambling." *Christian Century* 82 (May 26): 667.

Reid, Ed, and Ovid Demaris. 1963. *The Green Felt Jungle.* New York: Trident Press. Reprint, 1994. New York: Pocket Books.

Sternlieb, George, and James W. Hughes. 1983. *The Atlantic City Gamble: A Twentieth Century Fund Report.* Cambridge: Harvard University Press.

Thompson, William N., Ricardo Gazel, and Dan Rickman. 1996. *Casinos and Crime: What's the Connection?* Mequon, WI: Wisconsin Policy Research Institute.

Thompson, William N., and J. Kent Pinney. 1990. "The Mismarketing of Dutch Casinos." *Journal of Gambling Behavior* 6 (Fall): 205–221.

Worshop, Richard L. 1996. "Gambling Under Attack," *CQ Researcher* 6 (33): 771–791.

See also California; Cash Transaction Reports and Money Laundering; Cheating Schemes; Problem Gambling.

CRUISE SHIPS

There are several categories of shipboard casino gambling. Gambling on riverboats or other vessels within the waters of a specific jurisdiction is discussed under the entries covering the various jurisdictions (e.g., Illinois). The two categories discussed in this entry include ocean (or high seas) cruises and what have come to be known as "cruises to nowhere."

VOYAGES ON THE HIGH SEAS

The shipboard cruises encompass destination vacation activities for passengers. Typically, the cruises last several days or even weeks. The ships are luxurious, the cruises are expensive, and the amenities aboard the ships are many—food, dancing, sports activities. Casino gambling has been an activity on more and more of the cruises. The leader among the cruise companies with casinos aboard their ships is Carnival Cruise Lines, which operates more than 40 ships that offer casino games. Carnival has a gambling staff exceeding 1,000 individuals for its ships. The ships offer slot machines linked among several vessels, permitting mega-jackpots. Other major cruise lines with casinos include Holland American Line, Norwegian Cruise Line, Princess Cruises, and Royal Caribbean International.

These ships must operate their games on the high seas, and their voyages are essentially international. They stop at several seaport cities on their venture—at least two of which are in different jurisdictions (countries). While in port, no casino gambling is allowed.

The ship lines listed above are not U.S. companies. Indeed, very few U.S. ships have casino gaming, and very few have luxury cruises either. In 1949, the U.S. Congress passed very strict prohibitions banning gambling on U.S. flag vessels no matter where they were operating, whether in territorial or international waters. The ban affected vessels registered as U.S. and also those principally owned by U.S. citizens. Although the point of the law was clearly to regulate the type of gambling ship offering "cruises to nowhere," the effect was general. Even though the law was meant to apply to ships that were used "principally" for gambling (a rather vague term), U.S. ships ceased to have casinos on their voyages.

The Johnson Act of 1951 made possession of gambling machines illegal except under certain circumstances (e.g., they were legal in the jurisdiction where they were located). This law gave an emphasis to the notion that U.S. ships could not have machine gambling and come into any U.S. port where state law prohibited the machines (which included every port city in the United States in 1951). Foreign vessels could stop the use of the machines in these ports and not be in violation of the 1951 law, as they were still under foreign or international jurisdiction to some degree while in port.

By 1990, the cruise ship industry was flourishing. More than 80 cruise ships utilized U.S. ports. All but two flew foreign flags. Moreover, the general state of U.S. shipbuilding and U.S. companies

operating sailing vessels was one of deterioration. In 1991, the U.S. attorney general ruled that a ship was not a "gambling ship" if it provided for overnight accommodations and/or landed in a foreign port on its cruise. This ruling led to renewed interest among U.S. shipping to offering gambling on cruises. As a result, Congress passed the Cruise Ship Competitiveness Act on March 9, 1992, in order to establish "equal competition" for U.S. ships. Now the U.S. flagships can have gambling on their cruises while in international waters.

The international cruise ships are, for the most part, not subject to the regulation of any jurisdiction regarding their gambling activities. There are few limitations on licensing of casino managers or employees and few guidelines on surveillance and player disputes. Nonetheless, the major cruise ship companies have considerable internal regulations. Most have definite limits on the amounts of money that can be wagered, as they do not wish to take opportunities for spending money on other amenities away from the passengers, who may have to remain on the ship for several days after their gambling venture has ended. Because Carnival Cruise Lines and other ship casino companies (Casinos Austria runs several of the casinos) have land-based operations in other jurisdictions (Carnival is in Louisiana and Ontario), they do not want to have their licenses there jeopardized by any unacceptable practices within their shipboard casinos.

There is one ship on the high seas that has been subjected to the direct regulation of a state. Nevada requires its casino license holders to secure permission of the Nevada Gaming Commission and the Gaming Control Board if they are operating gambling operations outside of the state. Prior to 1993, the permission had to come from the state authorities before out-of-state operations could begin. Accordingly, in 1989 Caesars Palace applied for approval to manage the casino on board the *Crystal Harmony,* an exclusive Japanese-owned ship flying the flag of the Bahamas. The approval was granted under the condition that Caesars establish a fund for the Nevada gaming authorities so that the state could conduct background investigations of the ship owners, operators, and crew. Internal auditing controls also had to meet state standards, with independent accountants conducting regular reviews of the books. Nevada agents were given full access to the casino's records, as well as to the facilities. Caesars absorbed all the costs of regulation. The *Crystal Harmony* was the first and only international ship to have a casino regulated by the jurisdiction of a state of the United States.

CRUISES TO NOWHERE

The 1949 act banning gambling on U.S. flagships resulted from a controversy lasting several decades in California and other coastal states. Starting in the 1920s, floating barges appeared in the waters off of San Francisco and Los Angeles, as well as off the Florida coast. The ships anchored in international waters—three miles off the coasts. They had brightly lighted decks that could be seen from shore and beyond. Each day and evening they would provide boat taxi service for customers from nearby docks. The ships had entertainers, food, drinks (it was Prohibition time), and gambling. They operated through the 1930s without much opposition from law enforcement. When Earl Warren became attorney general of California, however, he decided to crack down. Raids were conducted, but the

issue of what was definitely legal or illegal remained in dispute until U.S. Senator William Knowland of California persuaded his congressional colleagues to pass legislation in 1949. The law now had teeth and was enforced until there was pressure for change in the 1990s.

Even before the passage of the 1992 Cruise Ship Competitiveness Act, vessels began to test the resolve of states and the federal government regarding coastal gambling operations. The actions of one company seemed to be the catalyst for the legalization of riverboat and coastal casinos in Mississippi in 1990. After the 1992 legislation passed, the states were given the opportunity to opt out of the Johnson Act prohibition on machines in their waters. Hence, they could allow boats to have cruises out to international waters for gambling even if the boats did not stop at foreign ports. In 1996, the U.S. Congress acted again. This time Congress gave blanket approval for the cruises to international waters—"cruises to nowhere"—unless the state (of debarkation and reentry) specifically prohibited the gambling ships. The state could only prohibit them if the ship did not make port in another jurisdiction. The ship's gambling operations would not be subject to any jurisdiction unless the state took specific action for regulation.

Since the 1996 law was passed, a large number of ships have begun operations off of Florida and also in the northeast. The state of California specifically passed a ban on the ships. More than 22 ships operate off of Florida, generating collective revenues of well over $200 million a year. Ships also have used South Carolina ports. Several ships attempted to gain docking rights in New York City, but local officials, including Mayor Rudolph Giuliani, fought the efforts and demanded that the boats go out to at least 12 miles off the coast before they could have gambling. After many months of negotiations, the city agreed to establish a gambling regulatory board for the ships through passage of an ordinance. One major vessel, the *Liberty I,* agreed to follow the local regulations.

In several states, including South Carolina and Florida, opponents of the boats have sought legislation against them, but so far their efforts have been to no avail. Even California has accepted the reality of regular gambling cruises for local residents. On April 15, 2000, the *Enchanted Sun* began voyages out of San Diego. The ship goes out three miles and hugs the coast until it reaches Rosarito Beach, south of Tijuana, Mexico. It hits the dock, briefly drops anchor, and then returns. The ship is at sea for less than eight hours. On each trip, more than 400 passengers enjoy a meal, entertainment, drinks, and gambling. Commercial success of such operations is not guaranteed. Passengers have to pay a cruise fee of $68, and as with other ships, there is always the problem of rough seas. An interesting twist to the *Enchanted Sun* casino is the fact that the California Viejas Band of Native Americans is an operating partner in the venture on the high seas.

Coauthored by Anthony N. Cabot
and Robert Faiss

References

Cabot, Anthony N., and Robert Faiss. 1999. "High Seas." In *International Casino Law,* 3rd ed. Edited by Anthony N. Cabot, William N. Thompson, Andrew Tottenham, and Carl Braunlich, 605–612. Reno: Institute for the Study of Gambling, University of Nevada, Reno.

Doocey, Paul. 1997. "A Mixed Forecast." *International Gaming and Wagering Business* 18, no. 12 (December): 1, 18–40.

Lionel, Sawyer and Collins. 1995. *Nevada Gaming Law.* 2nd ed. Las Vegas: Lionel, Sawyer, and Collins.

Cruises to Nowhere. *See* Cruise Ships.

DEMOGRAPHIC CATEGORIES OF PLAYERS

GAMBLING AND ETHNICITY

Players in the African American Community

African American players are not distinguishable by quality of play from most other players. However, particular cultural, historical, and situational factors may be related to certain gambling behavior in some circumstances. Minority groups and lower-income individuals who live in poorer communities have often been targeted by gambling entrepreneurs as being a valuable potential market. Government lotteries have been faulted for directing marketing campaigns at minority communities with advertisements suggesting that gambling is "the way out" of the ghetto. Also when states such as Illinois purposely located casino facilities in areas needing economic development, they caused casinos to be very near minority communities. As a result, African Americans and others living close to the casinos had a much higher level of participation in gambling than did other people.

Historically, the African American community, especially in urban settings, has embraced the numbers game. The games, which were first operated by members of the community (and later taken over by white organized crime groups), served many functions for the community. First, the numbers game provided employment for residents. Local people were given jobs as salespersons and numbers runners. They managed groups of runners, and they were also the entrepreneurs, or owners, of the games.

Second, the numbers game was functional in that it provided a mechanism for capital accumulation in the community. Historically (and even today), financial institutions such as banks redlined urban minority communities and refused to make loans to residents or businesses in the designated districts. In turn, members of the minority community would not patronize the banks—to do so would involve the inconvenience of traveling some distance and meeting with persons who discriminated against them. The numbers entrepreneurs took money from their profits and made investments in the local area and also made loans to local businesspeople, a practice that stimulated business activity. In addition, the entrepreneurs provided many charity gifts at a time before there was a well-developed welfare system in place.

Third, the numbers game provided a savings function for people who did not have bank accounts. Each week—or day—they would "invest" a small amount, maybe just a dime or a dollar, on a number. They acted much like a person in the suburbs putting a few dollars away in a Christmas Club account at a branch bank. By playing a number over and over, the resident generally could be assured of having an occasional win. That win could represent a time for a major purchase and a celebration. The numbers game also contributed to community solidarity, as residents would share their dreams with each other.

Colin Powell wrote about the functional value of the numbers game in the New York City community where he grew up: "The secret dream of these tenement dwellers had always been to own their own homes. My father also dreamed about numbers. He bought numbers books at the newsstands to work out winning combinations" (Powell 1995, 301). Powell describes how every day his father would confer with Powell's Aunt Beryl, and together they would buy a number. One Saturday night, Aunt Beryl dreamed of a number. The next day in church the first hymn had that number in it. "This, surely, was God taking Luther Powell by the hand and leading him to the Promised Land. Pop and Aunt Beryl managed to scrape up $25 to put on the number" (303). They hit the three-digit number, and the payout equaled three-years' pay. "And that's how the Powells managed to buy 183–68 Elmira Avenue in the . . . boroughs of Queens" (303). The numbers represented the Powells' "way out." Colin Powell was just entering college, and perhaps the pressure of having to help his family out an extra bit was lifted from his shoulders, enabling him to pursue his education and career goals in a more focused way.

The gambling establishment knows the value of games to poor people and to persons such as Colin Powell's father and aunt. Very few African Americans have become leading entrepreneurs on the legitimate side of commercial gambling, however. Very few casinos are predominantly owned or controlled by African Americans, and few of the casino executives are minorities. Prior to the 1960s, most of the major casinos on the Strip would not let African Americans play at their tables or stay in their hotel rooms. For a short time, a casino called the Moulin Rouge in the northern part of Las Vegas became the venue for African American players, from low rollers to high rollers. It was also the place where leading black entertainers would stay, even though they were performing on the Strip. The barriers of discrimination were broken down in the early 1960s when James Macmillan, a young local dentist from the minority community, became head of the Las Vegas branch of the National Association for the Advancement of Colored People. He refused to acquiesce to the policies of "going along to get along." He threatened a major protest parade that seemed to have all the news elements in it that would make it a national story for a media looking for civil rights protest stories. The casinos agreed to integrate almost overnight. By the time federal legislation on public accommodations was passed in 1964, Las Vegas was fully integrated in that sense.

Employment was something else and still is. Prior to the 1970s, there was overt employment discrimination in Las Vegas, but a court decree accepted by the industry opened doors for general employment. Nonetheless, many jobs are still secured through a process called "juice," or "who you know." The bulk of entry-level jobs in hotels are now held by Hispanic Americans, who are very adept at using family connections to make sure their friends know about job openings and have the right introductions to those making hiring decisions. African Americans are still not represented in the industry to the extent that their numbers would suggest they should be, given that they make up approximately 10 percent of the population of Las Vegas.

New casino projects in other urban centers such as Detroit and New Orleans carry very specific obligations for hiring target percentages of minorities and women. Groups applying for licenses also are encouraged to enlist local minority members among their ownership ranks. The extent to which the local policies for minority participation are successful remains to be assessed after the casinos enjoy their first years of operation.

Asian Players

Asians and Asian Americans have a reputation of being very active gamblers. They enjoy playing in groups and sharing the excitement of winning or even coming close to having a win. Observers in Great Britain have noted that play from the Asian sector of the population essentially keeps the casinos in business. Although this is not the case in most U.S. jurisdictions, the play of the Asian high roller is critical for the profits of many of the casinos on the Las Vegas Strip. Moreover, in urban communities on the West Coast of the United States and Canada, Asian play is often a majority of the play. People who have studied gambling sense that there are cultural values that make gambling a part of Asian community life. Numerology and a mystique about fate and luck propel people into gaming. There is also a great desire to participate in games of all sorts, so the drift to gambling games is not unusual.

Asians may be susceptible to developing gambling problems. Their subcommunities may encourage some play that might be considered reckless and harmful. One facet of this is that most of the Asian players have strong families, and they are also tied to family businesses, which have cash flows that can be utilized for daily gambling. When the play begins, the player may feel that he or she can risk everything on the game because the player has a safety net that other Americans may not have. No matter whether the player loses all or wins, a member of the extended family will always have a place for him or her to stay. Thus homelessness is not the problem that it is for some other compulsive gamblers. Moreover, someone in the family structure will have a job for a player who is broke. Such a tight family structure, which is a positive force in other situations, tends to present barriers for programs of recovery, as there is a notion of "shame" attached to any social problems. To go outside the family for help, especially to persons outside of the ethnic group, may be considered an embarrassment to the entire group.

Asian gamblers are discussed further in "The 'Best' Gamblers in the World" in the Selected Essays.

Latino and Hispanic American Players

There are many separate Latino and Latin American communities throughout the Western Hemisphere. Generalizations can never be totally accurate. Nonetheless, at the risk of making ethnic behavioral associations that certainly will not apply to all people, the editor authored an essay on gambling in Latin America (see "Machismo and the Latin American Casino" in the Selected Essays). His study was the result of personal visits to casinos in 14 Caribbean and Latin American jurisdictions. During the visits, he discovered a casino that held cockfights, another that banned women players unless they had written permission from their husbands (or former husbands), and another that used local loan agents (perhaps "sharks") because local players would not pay back debts to "foreign" owners. Many of these situations seemed to be a manifestation of the cultural value of machismo in many aspects of daily life and certainly in the daily life of gambling operations.

GAMBLING AND AGE

There appears to be a correlation between age and gambling behavior. Gambling activity occurs among all age groups, but it seems to increase with age through the adult years until the 60s, when a decline starts. Nonetheless, at both ends of the age spectrum there are factors that suggest excessive gambling may be a major concern for society.

Youth Gambling

The childhood years are devoted to much play activity, and it is through such play that basic social values can be learned: competitiveness and striving for goals, camaraderie and team involvement, adherence to rules and notions of fair play, acceptance of defeats and a sense of renewed efforts, gracefulness in enjoying victory. Certainly an emphasis on playing games, and encouragement for playing one or another kind of game, can cause children to want to participate in games and contests in which the reward—the goal—is money. Gambling has to have a natural draw for persons who are compelled to engage in fantasy play as part of their socialization. And indeed, when children are given the opportunity to gamble, they do so.

Studies by Goodman, and Arcuri, Lister, and Smith indicate that young people may be very involved in gambling. For instance, one study found that 75 percent of young people in the United States had purchased lottery tickets by the time they were seniors in high school. Another found that 77 percent of high school students had gambled at some time. A survey in Atlantic City found that more than 60 percent of high school students had played slot machines in casinos. In most cases, parents were aware of this activity.

The surveys suggest that youthful gambling and gambling problems occurred before young people turned to alcohol or drug use. Early gambling was associated with parental gambling and parental problem gambling. In later adolescence, gambling was associated with peer group acceptance. The studies suggest that young people craved acceptance and saw gambling as a means toward that goal. Those who persisted at gaming tended to do it alone, however, in order to escape either a bad home environment or their failure to participate in social activities with their peers. The availability of gambling in the community was related to youth participation, even though in most of the surveys the young people were gambling illegally.

Youthful gamblers will play whatever game is available, but because they must be wary of being excluded from a facility because of age, they gravitate toward the hidden-away slot machine areas of casinos. They also participate in sports betting, usually making their wagers with a bookie or with an intermediary who is not concerned with the fact that they are young—only that the gambling costs will be paid.

Youthful gamblers exhibited the same or even higher rates of pathological gambling as the adults who were surveyed. A survey for the recent National Gambling Impact Study Commission suggests that as many as 6 percent of teenagers have characteristics of pathological gamblers, a percentage several times higher than that for adults. The issue of youth gambling is important because many surveys of pathological gamblers find that they started their gambling activity while they were teenagers, due to an exposure to the activity and in part due to parental support of their participation. Henry Lesieur's book *The Chase* portrays an early "big win" as a critical time in the development of a compulsive gambling career. Psychologically, young people are less able to handle the emotional rush coming with that early win than are adults who are seasoned in life's many ups and downs. As a result of the research information gathered, the National Gambling Impact Study Commission urged that youth not be exposed to gambling opportunities.

Senior Gambling

The great expansion of gambling opportunities has also attracted many senior citizens to situations that may not be socially beneficial. Senior gambling has not been extensively studied, but there is an indication that in areas where casinos are available, seniors do play in large numbers. Overall their gambling participation rates are not as high as those of other adults, but the rates are growing. A 1975 survey found that 38 percent of the elderly (over 65) had gambled during the previous 12 months; a 1998 survey found that 80 percent had done so. Gambling is a growing recreation among the elderly because, in contrast with the past, they now collectively have better health and more resources. Of course they also have more time available for gambling than do other adults. In Las Vegas, the locals-oriented casinos target seniors as players to fill the casinos during daytime hours and soft weeknights as well as the down-seasons when tourists are not as plentiful. The casinos feature special buffet meals at low costs, they offer their regular players bargains through "slot clubs," and they even offer a regular bus service into senior neighborhoods (Sun City–type communities) and senior housing developments.

One study from Las Vegas finds that elderly men gambled less than younger men did, but the opposite was the case for elderly women. For the latter, the gambling opportunity was seen mostly as a social event and a chance to escape the boredom of daily life, often spent in an apartment-type setting. Among men, those who rented apartments gambled much more than did homeowners.

As with youth, seniors have their games of choice. In the casino, they are ardent video-poker machine players as well as bingo players.

GAMBLING AND GENDER

Traditionally, gambling has been a male-dominated activity. The same can be said of sports and other competitive games, and even ventures into the business world. But gradually, women are participating in gambling activities at higher and higher levels. This reflects the growing importance of women in the workforce and also that more and more women are financially independent. On the downside of the equation is that many women find themselves in abusive situations and turn to gambling as an escape mechanism, much as they have also turned to alcohol and drugs. As gambling is more available in communities across the country, it is becoming an addiction of choice for many escape-prone women.

In the recent past, women played bingo more than men did, as it was a social event and a very acceptable activity. Most played for excitement rather than escape. The casinos that first welcomed women found that they preferred machine play to table play. This is still the case, as the bravado of the tables fits male traits more closely. Women may sense that the action at the tables is too fast or too competitive and that players are too serious about the competitive nature of the games. These psychological barriers persist, but they are falling to a large extent. Nonetheless, today the favorite game for the woman player in the Las Vegas casino is a slot machine, or its major variation, the video poker machine. And of course, as is discussed in the entry on slot machines, this is a device that can get gamblers into trouble rather quickly. Indeed, one person who counsels women problem gamblers in Las Vegas indicated that 95 percent of his clients were playing the video poker machines. Nonetheless, problem gambling is still a greater problem among the male gender. A national survey for the National Gambling Impact Study Commission found that the rate of problem and pathological gamblers among men was double that of women.

References

Arcuri, Alan F., David Lister, and Franklin O. Smith. 1985. "Shaping Adolescent Gambling Behavior." *Adolescence* 20 (Winter): 935–938.

Goodman, Robert. 1995. *The Luck Business: The Devastating Consequences and Broken Promises of America's Gambling Explosion.* New York: Free Press, 43–44.

Lesieur, Henry R. 1984. *The Chase: Career of the Compulsive Gambler.* Cambridge, MA: Schenkman Publishing.

Moehring, Eugene. 1989. *Resort City in the Sunset: Las Vegas 1930–1970.* Reno: University of Nevada Press.

Mok, Waiman P., and Joseph Habra. 1991. "Age and Gambling Behavior: A Declining and Shifting Pattern of Participation." *Journal of Gambling Studies* 7, no. 4 (Winter): 313–336.

National Gambling Impact Study Commission [NGISC]. 1999. *Final Report.* Washington, DC: NGISC, 7–30.

Stinchfield, Randy, and Ken C. Winters. 1998. "Gambling and Problem Gambling among Youths." In *Gambling: Socioeconomic Impacts and Public Policy* (special volume of *The Annals of the American Academy of Political and Social Science*), edited by James H. Frey, 172–185. Thousand Oaks, CA: Sage.

Strachan, Mary Lou, and Robert Custer. 1989. "The Female Compulsive Gambler in Las Vegas." Paper presented at the 4th International Conference on Compulsive Gambling, October 19, Las Vegas.

See also Japan and Pachinko Parlors; Lotteries; Slot Machines and Machine Gambling; in Selected Essays: The "Best" Gamblers in the World, The Family That Gambles Together, Machismo and the Latin American Casino.

Dice. *See* Craps and Other Dice Games (in Games section).

DOG RACING

Dog racing began in the United States in 1919 with the opening of a greyhound track in Emeryville, California. Although gambling on dog races is permissible under the law in 18 states, today there are tracks in only 15 states. Since 1919, there have been tracks in more then 40 states at one time or another, although in most cases betting on races was not formally sanctioned by the law. Currently in the Western Hemisphere there are also tracks in the U.S. dependency of Guam, in Mexico (two states), and in Panama. Previously there were tracks in Puerto Rico, Haiti, the Dominican Republic, Barbados, and Montreal, Canada. The 49 operating tracks in the United States employ 30,000 people and generate approximately 13 percent of the pari-mutuel betting in the United States. In 1998, the tracks won $494 million (including off-track and inter-track wagering, and after prizes given to players). Wagering totals have remained stable, increasing an average of 1 percent a year since 1982. All legal wagering at dog tracks today is through pari-mutuel betting systems. Systems operate both on track and

Starting gate on a dog-racing track in Wisconsin.

through off-track or inter-track parlors (Christiansen 1999).

Today racing is confined essentially to one breed of dog, the greyhound. Evidence of the domesticated greyhound is found in Egyptian carvings that have been dated back to 2800 BCE. Early Greek civilizations probably named the dog Greekhound, and a corruption of that word yielded its present name. Others suggest that the dog has a grey tone in its face and on its head as it ages—almost a human-like quality. The Egyptians may have used the greyhound for hunting hares and gazelles, but the first recorded evidence of this activity came from the Roman era. The Romans also began the sport of "coursing." Hares would be placed in a large field, and the dogs would compete to see which one could run the poor animal down the fastest. In England, coursing events were formalized. As early as 1576, meetings were held in which two greyhounds would race across a field to reach a trapped animal in a fixed spot.

Dogs were bred for the events. A certain breed of greyhound resulted from a cross and recross with English bulldogs. A resulting dog named King Cob excelled, and today all the racing greyhounds worldwide can show lineage back to this one dog. In 1836, the Waterloo Cup competition began, and by 1858, a National Coursing Association was established in England to govern the events.

Coursing began in the United States with an event in Kansas in 1886. Animal rights activists stifled growth in the competition, however, as they protested the killing of jackrabbits that were used in the events. Their protests led dog enthusiasts to seek out alternative, nonanimal lures or bait. Owen Patrick Smith answered their call. He experimented with stuffed jackrabbits that he mounted on motorcycles. By 1920, he had received a patent for an artificial mechanical lure that he used in Salt Lake City. Finally he contrived a mechanical rabbit that could be run around a track in front of a pack of greyhounds. He put his device into use at the country's first dog track, which he called the Blue Star Amusement, located in Emeryville, California, near the present-day Oakland Bay Bridge. Smith's first venture was not successful, but he did better as he took the idea of greyhound track racing to other locations. In 1921, tracks opened in Tulsa, Oklahoma; East St. Louis, Illinois; and Hialeah, Florida. A track that opened in Chicago in 1922 proved to be successful. In 1925, there were seven tracks; by 1930, there were more than 60 tracks in the United States. In 1926, Smith founded the International Greyhound Racing Association, which works with the American Kennel Club to register dogs and regulate racing. Owen Smith lived long enough to see his sport flourishing, but he died in 1927, before he could reap major profits from its success.

Coursing activity waned with the introduction of dog track racing; however, coursing is still found in the United States and elsewhere, but no live lures are used. Events are governed by the American Sighthound Field Association and the American Kennel Club.

Although dog racing was here to stay after the 1920s, in many places it did not stay long. Of the tracks that opened before 1930, only four can be counted among the active tracks today. To be profitable, the tracks allowed bookies to come in and set up shop next to the racing areas. They gave a healthy fee to the track for the right to do business, but they also had to bribe the local sheriff in many places, as the betting was not legal. As political tides would turn, the sheriff would be persuaded to ban events. Opponents also seized upon opportunities to discredit the sport with revelations that mobsters, such as Al Capone, were involved in track operations. He reportedly owned an interest in the Hawthorne (dog) racetrack in Chicago. The political forces of opposition would sometimes be directed by horse track interests who did not enjoy the competition. A Miami track initiated the innovative use of night racing in order to placate the horsemen, and other dog tracks imitated the practice. Pari-mutuel racing was initiated with greyhound events in Montreal in 1928, and when Florida legalized the betting system for its horse tracks, the dog track owners sought and won legislative approval for pari-mutuel betting as well.

Dog tracks struggled through the Depression years and the early 1940s as the nation's attention was consumed by economic and war matters. But racing survived. According to Thomas Walsh (1991, 8–9), in the early 1940s, a Massachusetts operator actually used monkeys as jockeys, mounting them on the greyhounds' backs. He had his monkeys tour throughout the East as a serious effort to make the races more interesting. The experiment was novel and drew some spectator interest, but it proved not to be at all functional. Racing was closed down in the later war years but was revived after peace resumed, and in 1946, an American Greyhound Track Owners Association started operations. Today this organization joins with the National Greyhound Association in setting forth the rules for all races. The latter organization registers all dogs and maintains records. Dogs must be tattooed (on their ears), and breeding is regulated. Artificial insemination is permissible, whereas it is banned for horse breeding. A National Greyhound Hall of Fame opened in 1973 in Abilene, Kansas.

Dog races have the same kind of officials—secretaries, paddock judges, patrol judges, and so on—that are found at horse tracks. Ownership and training functions are also similar. Of course there is no jockey, and exercise workers are not significant at the kennels. The structure of betting is very similar to that on horse racetracks. Newborn greyhounds are given about 60 days of general freedom before their training begins. Then they are tattooed, registered, and started in walking and running exercises. When the greyhound is 14 months old, it is either sold to a racing kennel or placed there by the owner. Dogs start racing several months after training begins. Both male and female greyhounds run, but the males tend to have longer careers—up to five years. The dogs race from 5/16th mile to 7/16th mile. The dogs have a grading system that is used by racing secretaries to create well-matched races. Dogs will race every two to three days during the peak of their careers. Some stakes races have prizes running into the hundreds of thousands of dollars; however, as with horse racing, dog ownership is often not a good business venture. It is an activity tied to excitement, and many owners are in the game to be in the game, not to reap financial rewards.

A severe problem facing the dog racing industry has been the discarding of dogs that do not win. They are generally not put to pasture, sold as pets, or put to stud; they are killed. Over 8,000 dogs were killed during one five-year period in the 1970s. In response to the issue, an organization called Retired Greyhounds as Pets (REGAP) was formed in 1982 by Ron Walsek, an employee at a racetrack, to facilitate the adoption of the animals. Today there are 100 groups associated with REGAP. They have brought about over 15,000 adoptions. The adoption costs are very low—less than $50. The animals are extremely gentle, well mannered, intelligent, and affectionate. Thousands of people are finding that they are wonderful pets around children and in the home (Walsh 1991, 121).

References

Branigan, Cynthia A. 1997. *The Reign of the Greyhound.* New York: Howell Book House, Simon and Schuster.

Christiansen, Eugene Martin. 1999. "The 1998 Gross Annual Wager." *International Gaming and Wagering Business* (August): 20ff.

Walsh, Thomas. 1991. *Greyhound Racing for Fun and Profit.* Deerfield Beach, FL: Liberty Publishing.

See also Horse Racing.

Dominos. *See* Pai Gow and Games with Dominos (in Games section).

Draw Poker. *See* Poker (in Games section).

ECONOMIC IMPACTS OF GAMBLING

Does gambling help the economy? This question has been asked over and over for a long time. Economic scholars such as Paul Samuelson have suggested that since gambling produces no tangible product or required service, it is merely a "sterile" transfer of money. Therefore the energies (and all costs) expended in the activity represent unneeded costs to society. Further, he points out that gambling activity creates "inequality and instability of incomes."

On the other hand, myriad economic impact studies have concluded otherwise, indicating that gambling produces jobs, purchasing activity, profits, and tax revenues. Quite often, these studies have been designed by, or sponsored by, representatives of the gambling industry. For instance, the Midwest Hospitality Advisors, on behalf of Sodak Gaming Suppliers, Inc., conducted an impact study of Native American casino gaming. Sodak had an exclusive arrangement to distribute International Gaming Technologies (IGT) slot machines to Native American gaming facilities in the United States. The report was "based upon information obtained from direct interviews with each of the Indian gaming operations in the state, as well as figures provided by various state agencies pertaining to issues such as unemployment compensation and human services."

Their study found that Minnesota Native American casinos had 4,700 slot machines and 260 blackjack tables in 1991. Employment of 5,700 people generated $78.227 million in wages, which in turn yielded $11.8 million in social security and Medicare payments, $4.7 million in federal withholding, and $1.76 million in state income taxes. The casinos spent over $40 million annually on purchases of goods from in-state suppliers. Net revenues for the tribes were devoted to community grants as well as to payments to members and to health care, housing, and infrastructure. The report indicated that as many as 90 percent of the gamers in individual casinos

were from outside Minnesota; however, there was no indication of the overall residency of all the state's gamblers.

The American Gaming Association (AGA) ignored the question of where the money comes from as it reported that "gaming is a significant contributor to economic growth and diversification within each of the states where it operates." An AGA survey talked of the jobs, tax revenues, and purchasing of casino properties in 1998: a total of 325,000 jobs, $2.5 billion in state and local taxes, construction and purchasing leading to 450,000 more jobs, and $58 million in charitable contributions for employees of casinos. Their report indicated that the "typical casino customer" had a significantly higher income than the average American, with 73 percent setting budgets before they gamble (there was no indication about how many of these players *kept* their budgets), making them a "disciplined" group. The report made no attempt to see if the players were local residents or not.

Likewise, another study sponsored by IGT and conducted by Northwestern University economist Michael Evans found that "on balance, all of the state and local economies that have permitted casino gaming have improved their economic performance." Evans found that in 1995, casinos had employed 337,000 people directly, with 328,000 additional jobs "generated by the expenditures in casino gambling." State and local taxes from casinos amounted to $2 billion in 1995, and casinos yielded $5.9 billion in federal taxes. Yet Evans did not consider that the money for gambling came from anywhere specifically, nor that the money could have been spent elsewhere if it were not spent in casino operations, nor that if spent elsewhere, it would also generate jobs and taxes. The studies by industry-sponsored groups also neglected the notion that there could be economic costs as a result of externalities to casino operations—namely as a result of the increased presence of compulsive gambling behaviors and some criminal activity. Evans brushed aside the possibilities with a comment that "the sociological issues that are sometimes associated with gaming, such as the rise in pathological gamblers who 'bet the rent money' at the casinos, are outside the scope of this study. Nonetheless, it seems appropriate to remark at this juncture that occasional and anecdotal evidence does not prove anything."

Whatever is produced by a gambling enterprise does not come out of thin air; it comes from somewhere, and that "where" must be identified in order to assess the economic impact of gambling operations. The impact studies commissioned by the gambling industry fall short.

So what is the impact of gambling activity upon an economy? This is not really a difficult question to answer, although the answer must contain many facets and will vary according to the kind of gambling in question as well as the location of the gambling activity. Although the question for specific gambling activity is complex, the model necessary for finding the answers to the question is actually quite simple. It is an input-output model. Two basic questions are asked: (1) Where does the money come from? and (2) Where does the money go? The model can be represented by a graphic display of a bathtub.

Water comes into a bathtub, and water runs out of a bathtub. If the water comes in at a higher rate than it leaves the tub, the water level rises; if the water comes in at a slower rate than it leaves, the water level is lowered. An economy attracts money from gambling activities. An economy discards money because of gambling activity. Money comes and money goes out. If, as a result of the presence of a legalized gambling activity, more money comes into an economy than leaves the economy, there is a positive monetary effect because of the gambling activity. The level of wealth in the economy rises. If more money leaves than comes in, however, then there is a negative impact from the presence of casino gambling. Several factors must be considered in what will be called the "Bathtub Gambling Economics Model." The source of the money that is gambled by players and lost to gambling enterprises must be recognized, and how the gambling enterprise spends the money it wins from players must be considered.

FACTORS IN THE BATHTUB GAMBLING ECONOMICS MODEL

- **Tourist players:** Are players persons from outside the local economic region (defined geographically)—and are they persons who would not otherwise be spending money in the region if gambling activities were absent? Tourist spending brings dollars into the bathtub unless they otherwise would have spent the money in the region.

- **Local players:** Are the players from the local regional economic area? If so, does the presence of gambling activities in the region preclude their travel outside the region in order to participate in gambling activities elsewhere? If

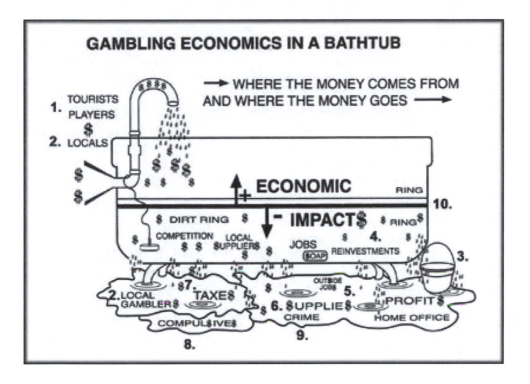

they are locals who would not otherwise be spending money outside the region, their gambling money cannot be considered money added to the bathtub.

- **Additional player questions:** Are the players affluent or people of little means? Are the players persons who are enjoying gambling recreation in a controlled manner, or are they playing out of control and subject to pathologies and compulsions?

- **Profits:** Are the profits from the operations staying within the economic region, are they going to owners (whether commercial, tribal, or governments) who reside outside the economic region, or are they reinvested by the owners in projects that are outside of the region?

- **Reinvestments:** Are profits reinvested within the economic region? Are gambling facilities expanded with the use of profit moneys? Are facilities allowed to be expanded?

- **Jobs:** Are the employees of the gambling operations persons who live within the economic region? Are the casino executives of the companies who operate (or own) the facilities local residents?

- **Supplies:** Does the gambling facility purchase its nonlabor supplies—gambling equipment (machines, dice, lottery and bingo paper), furniture, food, hotel supplies—from within the economic region?

- **Taxes:** Does the facility pay taxes? Are profits leading to excessive federal income taxes? Are gambling taxes moderate or severe? Do the gambling taxes leave the economic region? Does the government return a portion of the gambling taxes to the region? How expensive are infrastructure and regulatory efforts that are required because of the presence of gambling that would not otherwise be required? Do the gambling taxes represent a transfer of funds between different economic strata of society?

- **Pathological gambling compulsive or problem gambling:** How much pathological gambling is generated because of the presence of the gambling facility in the economic region? What percentage of local residents have become pathological gamblers? What does this cost the society—in lost work, in social services, in criminal justice costs?

- **Crime:** In addition to costs caused by pathological gamblers, how much other crime is generated by gamblers because of the presence of a gambling facility? How much of this crime occurs within the economic region, and what is the cost of this crime for the people who live in the economic region?

- **The construction factor:** If a gambling facility is a large capital investment, the infusion of construction money will represent a positive contribution to the economic region at an initial point. The investors must be reimbursed for the construction financing with repayments and interest over time, however. The long-range extractions of money from a region will more than balance the temporary infusions of

money into a region. An application of the model must recognize that the incomes eventually produce outgoes. The examples that follow therefore ignore the construction factor—although more refined examples may see it as positive for initial years and negative thereafter.

SOME DESCRIPTIVE APPLICATIONS OF THE MODEL

The Las Vegas Bathtub Model

The Las Vegas economy has witnessed phenomenal growth in the recent decades. This has occurred even in the face of competition from around the nation and world, as more and more locations have casinos and casino gambling products. As the 21st century began, the Las Vegas economy was strong because the overwhelming amount of gambling money (as much as 90 percent) brought to the casinos came from visitors. According to 1999 information from the Las Vegas Convention and Visitors Authority, visitors stay in Las Vegas an average of four days, spending much money outside of the casino areas. Las Vegas has money leakage as well. State taxes are very low, however, and much of the profits remains, as owners are local. Or if not local, they see great advantages in reinvesting profits in expanded facilities in Las Vegas. The costs of crime associated with gambling and compulsive gambling are probably major; however, many of these costs are transferred to other economies, as most problem players return to homes located in other economic areas. Las Vegas is not a manufacturing or an agricultural region, so most of the purchases (except for gambling supplies) result in leakage to other economies. Gambling locations in Las Vegas such as bars, 7-11 stores, and grocery stores represent very faulty bathtubs—bathtubs with great leakage, as the players are all local residents, and the stores are most often owned by out-of-town interests.

Other Jurisdictions in the United States

Atlantic City's casino bathtub functions appropriately, as most of the gamblers are from outside the local area. Players are mostly "day trippers," however, who do not spend moneys outside the casinos. Most purchases, as with those in Las Vegas, result in leakage for the economy. Like those in Las Vegas, state gaming taxes are reasonably low. Other taxes, however, are high.

Most other U.S. jurisdictions do not have well-functioning bathtubs, because most offer gambling products, for the most part, to local players. Native American casinos may help local economies because they do not pay gambling excise taxes or federal income taxes on gambling wins, as they are wholly owned by tribal governments who keep profits (which are in the form of tribal taxes) in the local economies.

Two Empirical Applications of the Model

Illinois Riverboats In 1995, the editor participated with Ricardo Gazel in gathering research on the economic impact of casino gambling in the state of Illinois. Illinois had licensed 10 riverboat operations in 10 locations of the state. The locations were picked because they were on navigable waters and also because the locations had suffered economic declines. We interviewed 785 players at five of the locations. We also gathered information about the general revenue production of the casinos and the spending patterns of the casinos—wages, supplies, taxes, and residual profits. The casinos were owned by corporations; most of them were based outside of the state, and none of them were based in the particular casino communities.

The focus of our attention was the local areas within 35 miles of the casino sites. The data were analyzed collectively, that is, for all the local areas together.

In 1995, the casinos generated revenues of just over $1.3 billion. Our survey indicated that 57.9 percent of the revenues came from the local area, from persons who lived within 35 miles of the casinos. From our survey we determined, however, that 30 percent of these local gamblers would have gambled in another casino location if a casino had not been available close to their home. Therefore, in a sense, their gambling revenue represented an influx of money to the area. That is, the casino attracted money that would otherwise leave the area. We considered part of the local gambling money to be nonlocal money, in other words, visitor revenue. On the other side of the coin, as a result of our survey, we considered that 22 percent of the visitors' spending was really local money. Many of the nonlocal gamblers indicated that they would have come to the area and spent money (lodging, food, etc.) even if there were no casino in the area.

By interpolating the income for one casino from the total data collected, we envisioned a casino with $130 million in revenue. The share of these revenues that came from within the 35-mile economic area (after adjustments for the 30 percent retained from other casino jurisdictions) equaled $60 million. In other words, we can represent this as local money lost to the casino. The question then is, how much of the money from the casino revenues of $130 million was retained in the 35-mile area (see Table 1).

The direct economic impact was negative $8.367 million; that is, $60 million of revenues came from the local 35-mile area, but only $51,632,200 of the spending was locally retained. A direct economic loss for the area of $8,367,800 may be multiplied by approximately two, as the money lost would otherwise have been able to circulate two times before leaving the area economy. The direct and indirect economic losses due to the presence of the gambling casino therefore equaled $16,735,600.

Added to these economic losses are additional losses due to externalities of social maladies. For each local area, there will be an increase in problem and pathological gambling, and there will also be an increase in crime due to the introduction of casino gambling. The presence of casino gambling, according to one national study by Grinols and Omorov, added to the other social burdens of society, such as taxes and per-adult costs of $19.63 due to extra criminal activity and criminal justice system costs due to related crime. The National Gambling Impact Study Commission found that the introduction of gambling to a local area *doubled* the amount of problem and pathological gambling. Our studies of costs due to compulsive gambling find adults having to pay an extra $56.70 each because of extra pathological gamblers (0.9 percent of the population) and an extra $44.10 each because of extra problem gamblers (2 percent of the

TABLE 1. Economic Impact of Illinois Casinos

Casino Expenses	$ Thousand	
Wages	$ 30,000	
Payroll taxes	2,000	
Promotional activities	2,000	
Purchases	22,500	
Gaming and local taxes	27,500	
Illinois corporation tax	1,800	
Federal corporation tax	11,628	
Retained profits	22,572	
Retained Money from Casino Operation/Portion Retained within 35-mile Radius	**$ Thousand**	**% of Total**
Wages	$ 27,000	90
Promotions	2,000	10
Purchases	13,500	60
Gaming and local taxes	6,875	25
Retained profits	2,257.2	10
Total	$51,632.2	

Source: Thompson, William N., and Ricardo Gazel. 1996. *The Economics of Casino Gambling in Illinois.* Chicago: Chicago Better Government Association.

population). This additional $120.43 per adult translates into an extra loss of $12,043,000 (or $24,086,000 with a multiplier of two) for an economic area of 100,000 adults when the first casino comes to town.

Wisconsin Native American Casinos
A similar impact study was made for Wisconsin Native American casinos in 1994 by this editor, Ricardo Gazel, and Dan Rickman. We interviewed 697 players at three casinos. Using casino descriptions as well as player information, we calculated that the state's casinos won $600 million from the players. Interpolating data for one casino with $120 million in revenues, we determined how much of the gambling revenue was attracted to and retained in the area of 35 miles around the casino.

The players' interviews indicated that 37.2 percent were from the 35-mile area surrounding the casino. Of their $44.64 million in gambling revenues, 20 percent

is money that would otherwise be gambled elsewhere. On the other hand, 10 percent of the $75.36 million gambled by "outsiders" would have otherwise come to the area in other expenses by these players. Hence we consider that $43.248 million of the losses are from the local area, and $76.752 million comes from the "outside."

The expenses of the casino are as shown in Table 2. With a multiplier of two, the direct positive impact of such a Native American casino is $88,776,000.

The positive impacts are lessened by the social costs due to crime and compulsive gambling. As most of the casinos are in rural areas, the population rings of 35 miles will not contain in excess of 200,000 or 300,000 adults, making these costs considerably less than the positive benefits shown.

A Comparison of the Empirical Applications The positive local area economic impact of Native American casinos

TABLE 2. Economic Impact of Wisconsin Casinos

Casino Expenses	$ Thousand	
Wages	$ 25,600	
Payroll taxes	1,700	
Promotions	2,000	
Purchases	29,240	
Management fees	8,000	
Tribal share (66,540)	53,460	
Retained Money from Casino Operations/Portion Retained within 35-mile Radius	**$ Thousand**	**%**
Wages	$ 20,480	80
Promotions	2,000	100
Purchases	11,696	40
Tribal share	53,460	100
Total retained	$ 87,636	

Direct economic impact: $87,636,000 − $43,248,000 = $44,388,000

Source: Thompson, William N., Ricardo Gazel, and Dan Rickman. 1995. *The Economic Impact of Native American Gaming in Wisconsin.* Milwaukee, WI: Wisconsin Policy Research Institute.

in Wisconsin contrast to the negative impacts in Illinois for several reasons. The Illinois casinos are purposely put into urban areas as a matter of state policy. As a result, a higher portion of gamers are local residents; therefore, fewer dollars are drawn into the area. The urban settings also exacerbate social problems, as the negative social costs are retained in the areas. The two major factors distinguishing the positive from negative impacts are (1) the Native casinos do not pay taxes to outside governments, and (2) the ownership of the casinos by local tribes keeps all the net profits (less management fees) in the local areas.

OTHER FORMS OF GAMBLING

The economic model can be applied to all forms of gambling. Other findings may arise from studies, however. For instance, for horse race betting, there would have to be a realization that the commercial benefits of racing are spun-off to a horse breeding industry. Today those benefits could be seen merely in terms of dollars. In the past, however, those benefits were seen in terms of a valued national resource. By encouraging breeding, the nation's stock of horses was improved in both quality and quantity, and that stock was a major military resource in times of war. Even though the Islamic religion condemned gambling as a whole, exceptions were made for horse race betting precisely because it would provide incentives for "improving the breed." Another consideration affecting race betting is the source of funds that are put into play by widely dispersed off-track betting facili-

ties, and then how those funds are distributed. The employment benefits of racetracks are also more difficult to put into a geographical context, as many employees work for stables and horse owners whose operations are far from the tracks.

Lotteries also draw sales from a wide geographic area. Funds are all given to government programs; however, the funds are often designated for special programs. The redistribution effects are difficult to trace and are dependent on the type of programs supported. When casino taxes are earmarked, the same problem exists; however, a casino tax will be much less than the government's share of lottery revenues. Lotteries do not provide the same employment benefits for local communities as are provided by casinos, because they are not as labor intensive. Benefits from sales tend to go to established merchants, often large grocery chains, in the lottery jurisdiction.

National lottery games, such as Lotto America, only further complicate the economic formulas. Such is also the case with Internet gambling. For race betting and lotteries, there is very little activity by nonresident players.

WHAT DO NEGATIVE GAMBLING ECONOMIC IMPACTS MEAN FOR A LOCAL COMMUNITY?

Negative direct costs, imposed on an area by the presence of a casino facility, simply mean there can be no economic gains for the local economy. There can be no job gains, only job losses. Purchasing power is lost in the community; local residents play the gambling dollars, and those residents do not have funds for other activities. Our survey of Wisconsin players found that 10 percent would have spent their gambling money on grocery store items if they had not visited the casino. One-fourth indicated they would have spent the money on clothing and household goods. Additionally, there can be no real government revenue gains, except at a very high cost imposed upon local residents in severely reduced purchasing powers and high social costs. Negative impacts simply mean the facilities are economically bad for an area.

References

Cohn and Wolfe. 1999. *The 1999 Industry Report.* Washington, DC: American Gaming Association.

Evans Group. 1996. *A Study of the Economic Impact of the Gaming Industry through 2005.* Evanston, IL: Evans Group.

Grinols, Earl, and J. D. Omorov. 1996. "When Casinos Win, Who Loses?" *Illinois Business Review* 53, no. 1 (Spring): 7–11, 19.

Midwest Hospitality Advisors. 1992. *Impact: Indian Gaming in the State of Minnesota.* Minneapolis, MN: Marquette Partners, 1.

National Gambling Impact Study Commission [NGISC]. 1999. *Final Report.* Washington, DC: NGISC.

Samuelson, Paul A. 1976. *Economics.* 10th ed. New York: McGraw Hill, 425.

Thompson, William N. 1999. "Casinos in Las Vegas: Where Impacts Are Not the Issue." In *Legalized Gambling in the United States,* edited by Cathy H. C. Hsu, 93–112. New York: Haworth Hospitality Press.

Thompson, William N. 1998. "The Economics of Casino Gambling." In *Casino Management: Past, Present, Future* (2nd ed.), edited by Kathryn Hashimoto, Sheryl Fried Kline, and George Fenich, 306–319. Dubuque, IA: Kendall-Hunt.

Thompson, William N., and Ricardo Gazel. 1996. *The Economics of Casino Gambling in Illinois.* Chicago: The Chicago Better Government Association.

Thompson, William N., Ricardo Gazel, and Dan Rickman. 1995. *The Economic Impact of Native American Gaming in Wisconsin.* Milwaukee: Wisconsin Policy Research Institute.

ECONOMICS AND GAMBLING

The essence of gambling is economics—gambling involves money.

Money is put at risk, and money is won or lost. Money goes into the coffers of organizations such as racetracks, casinos, lotteries, or charities, and that money is redistributed through taxes or public funds, profits, wages, and various supplies. The money associated with gambling can help economies of local communities and regions grow, but gambling operations can also cause money to be drawn out of communities. The existence of gambling represents an opportunity to express personal freedoms, and these have value, although it is not easy to measure in a precise manner. On the other hand, gambling can also impose costs upon societies because of problem behaviors of persons who cannot control gambling impulses.

Gambling enterprises, specifically casino resorts and racetrack operations, involve major capital investments. These may come through expenditures of individual entrepreneurs, sale of stock at equity exchange markets (e.g., the New York Stock Exchange), bond issues, or other borrowing mechanisms. Gambling enterprises are subject to a wide range of competitive forces. Participants in each form of gambling compete against one another, but they also compete against other entertainment providers as well as all other services and products that can be purchased with the consumers' expendable dollars.

The vast array of economic attributes tied to gambling has led to many studies that focus upon gambling economics. Most concentrate on positive sides of the gambling equation, and they tend to overlook a very basic fact: gambling revenues must come out of the pockets of players. Las Vegas was the fastest-growing city in the United States during the 1980s and 1990s, and in the early years of the 21st century. The city had the greatest job growth and wage growth. Yet Las Vegas is in a desert—it does not have trees. On the other hand, the wooded areas of the United States (e.g., Michigan and Indiana) suffered economic declines even during a prosperous period for the general economy. The point is, quite simply, that "money does not grow on trees." A large casino may generate great revenues that can be translated into many jobs; however, those revenues do not fall out of the air. The money comes from people's pockets.

This notion is illustrated by the story of a man whose life is falling apart. As he is driving to church, he sees a sign that says "Win the Lotto, and Change Your Life." In church he prays that he will win. He hears the voice of God telling him, "My Son, you have been good; you shall win the lottery." Convinced his problems are over, the man is much relieved. But he does not win the lottery. The next week, instead of praying to God, he is angry and asks God why He lied, why He has forsaken him. God replies, "Yes, my son, I understand your anger, because I did promise. But my son, you have to meet me half way. You have to buy a ticket." All the money that is discussed in studies of the economics of gambling is money that has to come out of people's pockets. Unless individuals "buy the ticket," there is no gambling phenomenon—no lotteries, no racetracks, and no casinos. The formula for understanding gambling economics is not difficult. It can be expressed in a few words. It involves where the money comes from and where the money goes. In the next section, we will return to this basic formula. First we will look at the revenues in gambling.

GAMBLING REVENUES

In 2007, gambling players spent (another way of saying "lost") over $90 billion on legal gambling products in the United States (this is called the gambling "hold"). The $90 billion represents the money that gambling enterprises retained after players wagered more than a trillion dollars (this is called the gambling "handle"). In other words, casinos, lotteries, and tracks kept over 8 percent of the money that was played. The greatest share of the players' losses was in casino facilities of one kind or another, followed by purchases of lottery tickets.

Table 3 draws information from the annual report of revenues published by Eugene Martin Christiansen in 1999 in *International Gaming and Wagering Business.* The information breaks down where the money was gambled. It can be noted that from 1998 to 2007, gambling revenues increased over 66 percent, from $54.4 billion to $90 billion. Casino revenues grew to $32.2 billion for commercial casinos, with an additional $5.2 billion for racinos (racetrack casinos) and about $25 billion for Native American casinos. Lottery revenues increased to more than $17.5 billion. The gaming increases since 1982, when collective statistics were first gathered, represented increases five times as great as the increases in the Gross Domestic Product.

Gambling growth has been seen in all areas, although only minimally in the pari-mutuel sector of gambling. Much of the growth is due to the fact that new jurisdictions have legalized forms of gambling and that new gambling facilities have been established.

Christiansen found that if all gambling were conducted in one enterprise, the business would be among the 10 largest corporations in the country. Gambling revenues in the United States represent the largest share of entertainment expenditures. Indeed, the revenues surpass those of all live concerts, sales of

TABLE 3.   Gambling Revenues (player losses, or "hold"), 1998, United States

	$ Million	%
Casino Gambling		
Land-based commercial casino	$12,614	
Riverboats	7,294	
Cruise ships/"cruises to nowhere"	539	
Native American (all class III)	7,213	
Noncasino machines	1,830	
Total	**29,490**	**54.3**
Lotteries		
Lottery tickets	15,399	
Video lottery	1,282	
Total	**16,681**	**30.7**
Pari-mutuel Wagering		
Horse racing	3,307	
Dog racing	494	
Jai alai	45	
Total	**3,846**	**7.1**
Charity and Bingo		
Charitable bingo	972	
Native American bingo (all class III)	954	
Other charitable games	1,598	
Total	**3,524**	**6.5**
Other Gambling		
Card rooms	739	
Bookmaking	72	
Total	**811**	**1.5**
Grand total (rounded)	**54,352**	**100**

Note that Internet gambling revenues were estimated to be $651 million for the year; however, much of the wagering was outside the United States and hence not included in the table.

Source: Based on information in Cabot, Anthony N. 1999. *Internet Gaming Report III.* Las Vegas: Trace, 3; and Christiansen, Eugene Martin. 1999. "The 1998 Gross Annual Wager." *International Gaming and Wagering Business* (August): 20ff.

recorded music, movie revenues (theater and DVD), and revenues from attendance at all major professional sporting events combined! The revenues surpass the sales of cigarettes by 13 percent. Gambling revenues approach 1 percent of the personal incomes of all Americans.

In 1998, commercial casinos attracted 161.3 million visits from customers representing 29 percent of the households (or 28.8 million households) in the United States. The average visitor made 5.6 trips to casinos. The visitors spent an average of $123 during each of those visits. Visits to Las Vegas, Atlantic City, and other resort gambling areas typically last for several days, accounting for larger expenditures, whereas those visiting casino boats usually confine their gambling to two or three hours of time; many boats impose time limits. A typical boat visitor will lose $50 to $60 per visit. With approximately 200 million adults in the country, each spends an average of $100 per year in commercial casinos, but $147 in all casinos, including those operated by Native Americans and charities.

A higher percentage of households participated in lottery games—54 percent (or 53.5 million households). They play on a regular basis, buying tickets each week; hence they do not lose as much to this form of gambling at a single time. The average American adult spends $84 a year on lottery tickets or video lottery play.

Approximately 11 percent of households participate in bingo games and 8 percent in racetrack betting. Considering all the forms of legal gambling, the average adult spends (loses) $272 on gambling each year. When that amount is spread over the entire population of 270 million, the per capita expenditure was $200 in 1999, but rose to over $400 in 2007.

EMPLOYMENT AND GAMBLING

Employment is considered one of the leading benefits of gambling enterprise. Proponents of gambling initiatives usually make job creation a central issue in their campaigns. Gambling provides jobs. There is no doubt about that. Estimates suggest that well over 600,000 people are employed by all forms of legal gambling enterprises in the United States. Critics of gaming suggest, however, that specific gambling interests may not provide net job gains for communities, as gambling employees may be people who simply moved from other jobs. Moreover, gamblers themselves may lose jobs because of their behavior, and their gambling losses may also result in a loss of purchasing power in a community, leading others to unemployment. Critics also suggest that gambling jobs are not necessarily "good" in that they may offer low salaries, low job security, and poor working conditions. Gambling proponents counter these claims and argue that jobs produced lead to indirect jobs through economic multipliers.

The different gambling sectors produce different job circumstances. Casinos are labor-intense organizations. Horse racing provides fewer jobs at track locations but generates many direct jobs in the agriculture sector on horse breeding farms. Modern lotteries in North America are not job providers in a major sense. Government bureaucracies increase employment; however, a lottery distribution system using existing retailers adds few jobs to society.

The casino and racing sectors provide jobs in North America in the same manner as they do elsewhere. Lotteries, however, are quite different. In Europe as well as in traditional societies, low-income people and handicapped people may find employment selling tickets. For instance, more than 10,000 blind and handicapped persons support themselves by selling lottery tickets in Spain. They are able to earn about $30,000 a year through their activities. Moreover, administration of a special lottery organization is staffed by the handicapped, and all of the proceeds from ticket sales are designated for programs for the handicapped. In many poorer countries, persons who could not otherwise secure employment buy discounted lottery tickets on consignment and resell them in order to support themselves and their families. In Guatemala City, Guatemala, and Tegucigalpa, Honduras, the lottery sales force gathers in squares near cathedrals or government buildings and creates market atmospheres with its activities. The lotteries in these countries produce revenues for charities. In the United States, Canada, and other modern lottery venues, the sale of tickets is directed almost exclusively to provide general revenues for government activities. Therefore, the goal of the lottery organization is to maximize profits through efficient procedures. Sales are coordinated through banks and major retail outlets, which conduct lottery business along with other product sales. Because the tickets are simply added to other purchases made by the gamblers, there is little if any employment gain through the activity.

Big corporations usually control the lottery retailers. In many cases, however, retailers are small businesses that may be aided considerably by volumes of ticket sales. Ticket sales may provide them with margins of profits that enable their businesses to compete with larger merchants. Video lottery machines (gambling machines) also provide revenue that allow bars and taverns to remain competitive with other entertainment venues and, hence, remain as employers in society.

According to the National Gambling Impact Study Commission, pari-mutuel interests that run horse and dog tracks as well as jai alai frontons employ about 150,000 workers in the United States; however, casinos provided the largest number of gambling-related jobs. A report from the American Gaming Association showed that in 1999 U.S. casinos directly employed almost 400,000 workers.

The Nevada gaming industry indicates that in 1998 tourism in Nevada resulted in 307,500 jobs, with 182,621 directly related to gaming. In that same year, the state led the nation in job growth. Unemployment in Las Vegas was a very low 2.8 percent. Analysts observed that when considering indirect employment, in 1998 casinos were responsible for 60 percent of the jobs in the state. R. Keith Schwer found that each of the casino jobs in Nevada leads to the employment of 1.7 persons in all—that is, an extra 0.7 employee (or 7 employees for every 10 casino employees). This multiplier factor (1.7) is considered rather low. It is low because Nevada is not a manufacturing state. In fact, with a 3 percent manufacturing sector, the state manufactures less per person than any other state. Because the state produces few products, almost the entire casino purchasing activity is directed to imported goods and, accordingly, not to goods produced by Nevada workers.

New Jersey casinos employ approximately 50,000 workers. The industry claims that an additional 48,000 jobs are created through the purchasing activities of casinos and casino employees. In 1998, the 50,000 jobs that directly employed casino workers produced a payroll of $1 billion, or $20,000 per job. Many of the jobs are not full-time. Although Atlantic City gambling halls employ a large number of workers (averaging more than 4,000 per casino), casinos have not solved the problems of poverty and unemployment in the community, a city of 38,000. The population of Atlantic City has continually declined since the introduction of casinos in 1978, and its unemployment rate was 12.7 percent in 1998, a time when the national average and state of New Jersey average were approximately 4 percent.

Mississippi casinos employed 32,000 people in 1998. Since the 1990s, when casinos of the state were established, the effects of construction employment have been noticeable. For instance, from 1990 to 1995, an additional 1,300 construction jobs existed in Biloxi, one of the state's casino centers. The jobs lasted through the end of the century; however, construction jobs must be tied to specific projects, and when the projects are finished, the jobs are finished. Although Mississippi experienced a boom with the introduction of casinos in 1992, the new employment witnessed in the state did not alter unemployment rates to a degree that was any different than that for the entire country. The 1990s were prosperous, and casino communities in the state experienced the same prosperity felt by noncasino communities.

A similar phenomenon has taken place in the Native American community. There, scores of casinos have generated about 100,000 jobs. Most of the jobs, however, are found in casinos on very small reservations. Overall Native Americans still experience the worst economy of any subsector of the U.S. population, with unemployment rates approaching 50 percent on some reservations. Lots of people, mostly non-Native Americans, have obtained jobs in casinos, and small tribes have become extremely wealthy, but generally the Native American community has not "cashed-in."

Other sectors of the gambling industry have not caused job creation. The National Gambling Impact Study Commission reported that there was no evidence whatsoever that convenience store gambling (machine gambling) created any jobs. Charity gambling has produced considerable funding for myriad projects, but it has not produced jobs either.

A study by Grinols and Omorov of jobs produced by the onset of riverboat casino gambling in Illinois found that the multiplier of each job was less than one, but still more than zero. That meant that most of the new jobs were only shifted away from other enterprises, and the available jobs were not filled in all cases. Indeed, a multiplier of approximately 0.2 resulted as the casinos added 10,000 jobs, but the numbers employed overall increased by only 2,000. Some jobs may have remained unfilled because the casinos extracted purchasing power away from the residential populations due to the fact that many residents are also gamblers. Casino jobs can also have a negative impact on a community by depriving other businesses of workers. Atlantic City casinos drew many new employees away from jobs in local school districts and local police forces. In free markets, people can make job and career choices on their own, and such job shifts indicate that some people may see casino jobs as better than other available jobs.

The industry jobs have been both praised and criticized. The positions run the gamut from stable hand to chief executive, from minimum wage without benefits to seven-figure positions with golden parachutes. A stable hand working with horses may be residing in substandard housing conditions, perhaps ever sharing quarters with the animals he or she cares for. The largest number of "good" positions is found in commercial casinos. The bulk of these jobs are unionized and carry very good benefit packages, including full health insurance coverage for families of workers. Dealer positions, for the most part, are not unionized, although they do have good fringe benefits. The dealers usually make low salaries, but they share tips. Where tips are not good (or not permitted, as in Quebec), salaries are higher. The best tip situations are found in Atlantic City and on the Las Vegas Strip. A typical dealer at a casino such as Caesars might expect an additional $50,000 per year in tips.

Working conditions in gambling facilities are often not the best. There is high job turnover due to job dissatisfaction and also to policies that sometimes allow firing at will. Traditionally, people were hired in Las Vegas casinos through friendship networks; however, this practice is now less pervasive, as the industry has grown considerably and is now more a buyer's, that is, an employee's, market. Nonetheless, other adverse conditions surround casino employment. For years the casino atmosphere was one that was dominated by "male" values. Women employees were often placed in situations where they were degraded. This behavior came from fellow employees as well as from customers. It is unacceptable behavior today, yet in some ways it is still tolerated in the casino atmosphere. That atmosphere also has downsides from a health standpoint, as most casinos permit open smoking—and many players smoke—as well as drinking. Casinos can be very loud, and of course, employees work shifts over a 24-hour schedule.

Most workers in the United States have indicated in surveys that job security and salaries are no longer the leading motivators when seeking employment, but rather that factors such as "ability to get ahead," "recognition for work accomplished," and "having responsibility" are more important. A survey of casino dealers found, however, that they desired security and financial compensation over the other factors. This is an indication of the insecurity that persists among the workforce.

Coauthored by Ricardo Gazel and Dan Rickman

References

Bowen, John, Zheng Gu, and Vincent H. Eade. 1998. *The Hospitality Industry's Impact on the State of Nevada.* Las Vegas: UNLV International Gaming Institute.

Christiansen, Eugene Martin. 1998. "Gambling and the American Economy." In *Gambling: Socioeconomic Impacts and Public Policy* (special volume of *The Annals of the American Academy of Political and Social Science*), edited by James H. Frey, 36–52. Thousand Oaks, CA: Sage.

Christiansen, Eugene Martin. 1999. "The 1998 Gross Annual Wager." *International Gaming and Wagering Business* (August): 20ff.

Cohn and Wolfe. 1999. *The 1999 Industry Report: A Profile of America's Casino Gaming Industry.* Washington, DC: American Gaming Association.

Grinols, Earl L., and J. D. Omorov. 1996. "When Casinos Win, Who Loses?" *Illinois Business Review* 53, no. 1 (Spring): 7–11, 19.

National Gambling Impact Study Commission [NGISC]. 1999. *Final Report.* Washington, DC: NGISC.

Schwer, Keith. 1989. "Why the Las Vegas Multiplier Is Less Than 3." *Las Vegas Metropolitan Economic Indicators.* Las Vegas: Center for Business and Economic Research, University of Nevada, Las Vegas, 1–4.

Thompson, William N. 1999. "Casinos in Las Vegas: Where Impacts Are Not the Issue." In *Legalized Gambling in the United States,* edited by Cathy H. C. Hsu, 93–112. New York: Haworth Hospitality Press.

Thompson, William N. 1998. "The Economics of Casino Gambling." In *Casino Management: Past, Present, Future,* edited by Kathryn Hashimoto, Sheryl Fried Kline, and George Penich, 306–309. Dubuque, IA: Kendall-Hunt.

EUROPEAN CASINOS AND AMERICAN CASINOS COMPARED

The institution that we call the casino had its origins in central and western European principalities in the 17th and 18th centuries. It was here that governments gave concessions to private entrepreneurs to operate buildings in which games could be legally played in exchange for a part of the revenues secured by the entrepreneurs. Whereas from time immemorial, players had competed against one another in all sorts of private games, here games were structured to pit the player against the casino operators—known as the "house." These gambling halls were designed to offer playing opportunities to an elite class in an atmosphere that allowed them to enjoy relaxation among their peers. Even though casinos in the United States seek to achieve goals that are primarily financial by offering gaming products to as many persons as possible, the notion of having a European-style casino often resonates where proponents meet to urge new jurisdictions to legalize casinos.

In some cases, casino advocates actually believe they can somehow duplicate European experiences, but rarely do they meet such goals, for a variety of reasons. If they indeed knew about the way European casinos operate, they would not want any of the experience repeated in casinos they controlled. Other times, they may actually try to establish some of the attributes of these casinos, only to realize later that the attributes are quite adverse to their primary goals: profits, job creation, economic development, or tax generation.

The European casino is offered in campaigns for legalization as an alternative to having a jurisdiction endorse Las Vegas–type casinos. In reality, however, it is the Las Vegas casino that the advocates of new casino legalizations in North America wish to emulate. Among all the casino venues in North America,

Las Vegas best delivers on the promise of profits, job creation, economic development, and tax generation. However, the imagery of the European casino is so often used in discussion of casino policy outside of Europe that a descriptive commentary is pertinent here.

In June 1986, this editor visited the casino that operates within the Kurhaus in Wiesbaden, Germany. In an interview, Su Franken, director of public relations for the casino, was describing a new casino that had opened in an industrial city a few hours away. With a stiff demeanor, he said, "They allow men to come in without ties, they have rows and rows of noisy slot machines, they serve food and drinks at the tables, and they are always so crowded with loud players; it is so awful." Then with a little smile on his face, he added, "Oh, I wish we could be like that."

The reality is that, even with the growth in numbers of casino jurisdictions and numbers of facilities, Europe cannot offer casinos such as we are used to in North America—those in Las Vegas and Atlantic City, the Mississippi riverboats, those operated by Canadian provincial governments or by Native American reservations—because a long history of events impedes casino development based upon mass marketing. Actually, the rival casino to which the Wiesbaden manager was referring, the casino at Hohensyburg near Dortmund, was really just a bigger casino, where a separate slot machine room was within the main building as opposed to being in another building altogether. Men usually had to wear ties, but the dress code was relaxed on weekends, and the facility had a nightclub, again in a separate area. It was crowded simply because it was the only casino near a large city, and the local state government did not enforce a rule against local residents entering the facility.

Table 4 shows a pattern of differences between the prototypical European casino and the Las Vegas Strip casino.

The casinos of Europe are very small compared to those in Las Vegas. The biggest casinos number their machines in the hundreds, not the thousands. A casino with more than 20 tables is considered large, whereas one in Las Vegas with twice that number would be a small casino. Even the largest casinos, such as those in Madrid, Saint Vincent (Italy), and Monte Carlo, have gaming floors smaller than the ones found on the boats and barges of the Mississippi River. The revenues of the typical European casino are comparable to those of the small slot machine casinos of Deadwood, South Dakota, or Blackhawk, Colorado. The largest casinos would produce gaming wins similar to those of average Midwestern riverboats.

Another distinguishing feature of the European casino is that most are local monopoly operations. Where casinos are permitted, a town or region will usually have only one casino. The government often has a critical role in some facet of the operation, either as casino owner (directly or through a government corporation) or as owner of the building where the casino is located. Where the government does not own the casino, it might as well. Taxes are often so high that the government is the primary party extracting money from the operations. For example, some casinos in Germany pay a 93 percent tax on their gross wins. That means for every 100 euros the players lose to the casino, the government ends up with 93 euros. In France the top marginal tax rate is 80 percent; it

TABLE 4. American and European Casinos: Prototypical Comparisons

	American	*European*
1. Bottom line	Revenue for private enterprise; job creation; tourism as a goal	Community enhancement; tourism as amenity
2. Ownership	Private	Mixed; typically government-owned
3. Location	Concentrated	Diffuse; typically small town; monopolies
4. Taxation	Minimal; consistent with need for private investment; 6–8 percent	High to excessive; 50–90 percent
5. Access	Open, free; no dress codes; no identification; minimal exclusion lists	Restricted; fee charged; dress codes; passport identification; no locals; restricted occupations; voluntary exclusion lists
6. Hours	Continuous	Limited; evenings; closed holidays
7. Clientele	National; international; high volume	Local and regional; low volume
8. Promotions	Many; advertisements; junket tours; complimentaries	Few; no advertisements; no junkets; few complimentaries
9. Credit	Credit operations; open check cashing	No credit; limited check cashing
10. Community involvement	Mixed	Essential
11. Decor	Loud; large; glitzy; bright; red; closed in (no windows)	Quiet; small; elegant; calm; blue; open (windows)
12. Alcohol	Free; open distribution	Limited; restricted distribution
13. Games	Slots and tables mixed; blackjack dominates; craps; poker; some baccarat; limited roulette	Tables dominate; slots nonexistent or separate; roulette dominates; baccarat; some blackjack
14. Labor	High turnover; trained outside; salaried plus large tip volume controlled by dealers individually and in small groups; nonunion	Career employment; all hired at entry level; promotions from within; no salaries; tips controlled by casino, share with all employees; union
15. Compulsive gamblers	Not considered a factor or concern	Discouraged; excluded
16. Crime	Pervasive in atmosphere; ongoing problem in casino control	Not a factor or concern

Source: William N. Thompson.

is 60 percent in Austria and 54 percent in Spain. Nowhere are rates below the top 20–30 percent rates in U.S. jurisdictions (the Nevada rate is less than 7 percent—that is, for each $100 players lose to the casino, the government receives less than $7 in casino taxes).

The European casinos typically restrict patron access in several ways: (1) Several will not allow local residents to gamble. (2) They require identification and register patron attendance. (3) They have dress codes. (4) Many permit players to ban themselves from entering the casinos as a protection from their own compulsive gambling behaviors. They also allow the families of players to ban individuals from the casinos. The casinos themselves also may bar compulsive gamblers. (5) The casinos operate with limited hours, usually evening hours. No casino opens its doors 24 hours a day. (6) The casinos, as a rule, cannot advertise. If they can, they do so only in limited, passive ways. (7) Credit policies are restrictive. Personal and payroll checks will not be cashed. (8) Alcoholic beverages are also restricted. In many casinos (for instance, all casinos in England), such beverages are not allowed on the gaming floors. Only rarely is the casino permitted to give drinks to players free of charge. (Other free favors such as meals or hotel accommodations or even local transportation are also quite rare.)

The clientele of the European casino is generally from the local region. Few of the casinos rely upon international visitors. Moreover, very few have facilities for overnight visitors, although several are located in hotels owned by other parties. The casinos feature table games, and where slot machines are permitted, they are typically found in separate rooms or even separate buildings. The employees at the casinos are usually expected to spend their entire careers at a single location. The employees are almost always local nationals.

There are myriad reasons why the European casino establishment has remained in the past, while modern casino development has occurred in the United States, specifically in Las Vegas. First, Europe is a continent with many national boundaries. The future may see more and more economic and even political integration, but national separateness has been strong and will remain as

a factor retarding casino development. The European Union has, at least at its initial stage of decision making, decided to allow casino policy to remain under the jurisdiction of its individual member states. Although a central congress may decree that all European states must standardize other products, usually following the most widely attainable and profitable standards, there will be no decrees that the entire continent should follow the most liberal casino laws. Each country retains sovereignty in this area.

Language and religious differences separate the various nations of Europe. No European congress can decree away these differences. National rules of casino operation have emphasized that entrepreneurs and employees be local residents. Such rules remain in place in most jurisdictions. In the past, movement of capital has been restricted among the states, making the possibilities of accumulating large investments for large resort facilities and for large promotional budgets difficult. Additionally, it was difficult for players to move their gaming patronage across borders, as they also would have to be able to move capital with that patronage. Advertisement restrictions also tied casino entrepreneurs to local markets. These small local markets never beckoned as attractive opportunities for foreign investors even when they could move funds.

Second, employment practices have not fostered the kind of cross-germination that is present in the North American casino industries. Typically, the employees of European casinos are local residents, and they are expected to stay with one casino property for an entire career. Promotions come from within. The work group is very personal in its interrelationships. The work group is also unionized and derives much of its wage base from tips given by players at traditional table games. The employment force is simply not a source for innovative ideas.

Third, because almost all of the casinos are monopoly businesses, the industry has had little incentive to develop competitive energies that could be translated into innovations. Also, the entrepreneurs have not been situated to take advantage of the forces of synergy, which are quite obvious in the Las Vegas and U.S. gaming industry.

Fourth, the basic political philosophy that dominates government policy making in Europe has its roots in notions of collective responsibility. Americans threw off the yoke of feudalism and its class system of noblesse oblige when the first boats of immigrants reached its Atlantic shores in the 17th century. The colonies fostered a spirit of individualism. Conversely, a spirit of feudalism persists in European politics. Remnants of monarchism remain, as the state has substituted official action for what was previously upper-class obligation. Socialist policies now assure that the working classes will have their basic needs guaranteed. The government is the protector as far as personal welfare is concerned, and those protecting personal welfare (that is, the government officials) also are expected to guide personal behavior, even to the point of protecting people from their own weaknesses.

In the United States, and especially in the American West, the expectation was that people would control their own behaviors; such was not the case in Europe. In Europe, but not in the United States, viable socialist parties developed. Coincidentally, Christian parties also developed. They too fostered notions that the state was a guardian of public morals. Christian parties saw casinos as anathema to the public welfare and permitted their existence only if they were small and restricted. Socialists also saw casinos as enterprises that exploited the bourgeois and that had to be out-of-bounds for working-class people.

Fifth, and perhaps the overriding force against commercial development of casinos, has been an almost perpetual presence of wartime activity in Europe over the past three centuries. The many borders of Europe have caused a constant flow of national jealousies, alliances, and realignments, all of which contributed to one war after another. Often the wars engulfed the entire continent: the Napoleonic wars, the Franco-Prussian wars, and World Wars I and II. A modern casino industry cannot flourish amid wartime activity. Casinos need a free flow of people as customers, and people cannot move freely during wartime. Casinos need markets of prosperous people, but personal prosperity is disrupted for the masses during wartime. Wartime destruction consumes the resources of society. Moreover, a society does not allow its capital resources to be expended on leisure activities when the troops in the field need armaments. And wars change boundaries, governments, and rules. Casinos need stability in the economy and in political policy in order to grow; Europe has lacked stability over the last three centuries.

The United States has benefited from not being a war battlefield for over a century. Following World War II, the new industrial giant of the world accepted an obligation to help European countries rebuild their industrial and commercial bases. The Marshall Fund was created to infuse U.S. capital into European redevelopment. The Marshall Fund could have been a vehicle for infusing the individualistic American spirit of capitalism into European commercial policy as well. The fund stipulated, however, that the new and revitalized businesses of Europe had to be controlled by Europeans. U.S. entrepreneurs were not allowed into fund-supported businesses. The fund actually supported the reopening of a casino at Travemunde, Germany. But the policy of the U.S. government in not allowing Americans to directly participate in the commercial enterprise of rebuilding Europe blocked U.S. casino operators from legitimately entering Europe with the modern spirit they were utilizing in Las Vegas gambling establishments. On the other hand, less than fully legitimate Americans sought to bring slot machines to the continent. They were rooted out, however, and as these "operators" were deported, the image of the slot machine as a "gangster's device" became firmly rooted into casino thinking in Europe.

The impact of these many forces is felt today even though the existence of the forces is not as strong. There is much expansion of casino gambling in Europe. It is generally an expansion in the number of facilities, however, not in the size or scope of the facilities. Each of the former Eastern Bloc countries now has a casino industry, but restrictions on size and the manner of operations are severe, as are tax requirements. France authorized slot machines for its casinos for the first time in 1988. But a decade later, its largest casinos were producing revenues less than those of a typical Midwest riverboat,

revenues measured in the tens of millions of dollars—nowhere near the hundreds of millions won by the largest Las Vegas and Atlantic City casinos. In Spain, casino revenues have been flat as the industry begs the government for tax relief. Austria has developed a megacasino at Baden bei Wien, but it would be almost unnoticeable on the Las Vegas Strip. Casinos Austria and Casinos Holland, two quasi-public organizations, are viewed as two of the leading casino entrepreneurs of the continent. But both derive much of their revenue from operations of casinos either on the sea or in Canada. Twenty Las Vegas and a dozen Native American properties exceed the revenues of the leading casinos in Germany.

The European casinos have a style that would be welcomed by many North American patrons. In achieving that style, however, the casinos must forfeit what most entrepreneurs, governments, and citizens want from casinos—profits, jobs, economic development, and tax generation.

Reference

Thompson, William N. 1998. "Casinos de Juegos del Mundo: A Survey of World Gambling." In *Gambling: Socioeconomic Impacts and Public Policy* (special volume of *The Annals of the American Academy of Political and Social Science*), edited by James H. Frey, 11–21. Thousand Oaks, CA: Sage.

FEDERAL LOTTERY LAWS

In the early days of the republic, gambling policy was considered the prerogative of state governments. The new government was structured to be one of delegated powers. The government of the constitution was created by "We the

People," and officials of the government were empowered to make policy only in the areas designated by the "People." Congress was delegated certain powers in Article I, Section 8, and nowhere on the list were powers to regulate gambling activity. Moreover, the Tenth Amendment of the U.S. Constitution specifically reserves the "powers not delegated to the United States . . . [nor] prohibited" to the "States, respectively, or to the people." Accordingly, the federal government stayed away from gambling for nearly a century—that is, except for the few lotteries actually run by the government or authorized by the government. Congress was empowered to raise money.

Congress was also given the power to "establish post offices" and to "regulate commerce . . . among the several States." Congress turned to these powers when concerns were raised, first about illegal lotteries, and then about the legal but disrespected Louisiana lottery. In 1872, the use of the mails was denied to illegal lotteries. This was followed by a series of laws aimed at curbing the interstate activities of the Louisiana Lottery

On July 19, 1876, President Grant signed an act that provided legal sanctions against persons using the mails to circulate advertising for lotteries through the mails (44th Congress, Chapter 186). On September 2, 1890, an act was signed that proscribed any advertisements in newspapers for lotteries (51st Congress, Chapter 980). The Louisiana Lottery managers saw a loophole in these antilottery laws, and they moved their operations to Honduras. They were only a few years ahead of the law, however. On August 27, 1894 (53d Congress, Chapter 349), legislation was passed prohibiting the importation "into the United States from any foreign country . . . [of] any lottery ticket or any advertisement of any lottery." All such articles would be seized and forfeited. Penalties of fines up to $5,000 and prison time of up to 10 years, or both, would be assessed against violators. The next year (March 2, 1895; 53d Congress, Chapter 191), Congress passed an act for the suppression of all lottery traffic through national and interstate commerce. Very specifically, the mails could not be used by lotteries to promote their interests.

These federal laws had a desired effect. They put severe restrictions upon the operators of the Louisiana Lottery. Also, the citizens of Louisiana came to recognize that the operators were bribing state political leaders and extracting exorbitant profits from the lottery, whereas state beneficiaries were being shortchanged. There were also exposures of dishonest games. Under pressure from citizens, the legislature ended the state sponsorship of the lottery in 1905.

In two U.S. Supreme Court decisions, the acts of Congress were determined to be constitutional. That is, they were passed within the scope of the powers of Congress. In 1891, the Court ruled in the case of *In re Rapier* (143 U.S. 110) that the 1872 prohibition was a valid exercise of congressional power to regulate the use of the mails. In 1903, the justices held in *Champion v. Ames* (188 U.S. 321) that Congress had the power to pass an appropriate act against a "species of interstate commerce" that "has grown into disrepute and has become offensive to the entire population of the nation."

Although there were no other legal state-authorized or state-operated lotteries until New Hampshire began its sweepstakes in 1964, there were lotteries that sought markets in the United States. There were illegal numbers games in all major cities, and there was the Irish Sweepstakes. The Irish Sweepstakes was created by the Irish Parliament in 1930 as a means of benefiting Irish hospitals. The Irish were well aware that they did not have substantial marketing potential if they aimed the lottery only at customers within the Free State, so they looked outward to Europe and to the United States. At first, they used the mails to promote and sell tickets to customers in the United States; however, the U.S. Post Office successfully intervened with legal action to stop this blatant violation of the 1895 law. Then the Irish Sweepstakes operators turned to smuggling tickets onto U.S. shores. Using ship-to-shore operations, as well as Canadian border cities, they were quite successful into the 1960s and 1970s, when U.S. states began to meet them with competition from their own lotteries.

When radio became established as a viable entertainment media, the federal government found that it was necessary to create the Federal Communications Commission (FCC) and to establish uniform regulations for operations of radio stations across the country. The Communications Act of 1934 stipulated rules for advertising "on the air." Within a few decades, the rules applied also to television signals.

The broadcasting law held that persons would be subject to fines of $1,000 or penalties of one year in prison, or both, if they used radio stations to broadcast or knowingly allowed stations to broadcast "any advertisement of, or information concerning, any lottery, gift enterprise, or similar scheme, offering prizes dependent in whole or in part upon lot or chance" (Federal Communications Act of 1934, Public Law 416, June 19, 1934).

But that was 1934, when no government in the United States had its own lottery. That situation changed in 1963, when New Hampshire authorized a lottery that began operations the next year. By 1975, 11 states had lotteries. The limitations on advertising seemed to be adverse to the fiscal interests of state budget makers. Congress responded to a demand for exemptions to the 1934 act.

In 1975, Congress passed legislation that allowed a state-run lottery to advertise on radio and television stations that only sent signals within the state. Courts later held that the substantial portion of the signals had to be within the state. In 1976, the exemption was expanded to allow advertisements on the air that extended into adjacent states as long as the other states also had state-run lotteries.

In 1988, the exemption included signals into any other state that had a lottery. (Nonprofit and Native American gaming was also exempt from the 1934 act; in 1964 the FCC issued rules allowing horse race interests to advertise "on the air" as long as the advertising did not promote illegal gambling.)

By the last years of the century, the application of the law was in reality an anomaly, with only commercial casino gambling subject to the ban on "lottery" advertising. Lotteries were fully exempt. The anomaly was short-lived, as the 1934 provision was deemed unconstitutional as a violation of freedom of speech after a 1996 U.S. Supreme Court case in a related matter (44 *Liquormart v. Rhode Island;* 517 U.S. 484 [1996]).

References

Cabot, Anthony N. 1999. *Federal Gambling Law.* Las Vegas: Trace, 39–80.

Federal Communications Act of 1934, Public Law 416, June 19, 1934.

Thompson, William N. 1997. *Legalized Gambling: A Reference Handbook.* 2nd ed. Santa Barbara, CA: ABC-CLIO, 130–134.

See also Louisiana Lottery Company (in Venues and Places section).

FEDERAL WIRE ACT OF 1961

The Federal Wire Act of 1961, passed with the support of Attorney General Robert F. Kennedy, was aimed at illegal horse race bookies and bettors on sports events. The law prescribed penalties of up to two years in prison and a $10,000 fine for persons who "knowingly" use "a wire communication facility for transmission" of bets, wagers, and information assisting betting and wagering on any sports event or contest. Telephone companies could be ordered to cut off service from betting customers when notified of the activity by law enforcement agencies.

Legitimate reporting on sports events by newspaper media was exempt from the act. Similarly it was permissible to transmit messages for betting from one state to another as long as the betting activity was legal in both the states.

The Federal Wire Act was written at a time when telephones with physical wire lines represented the major avenue for interstate communication. Also, horse race betting was the most prevalent form of illegal gambling. Attorney General Kennedy's testimony to Congress on the bill mentioned only sports and race betting. Since 1961, telephones have used wireless signals, and there are also other forms of satellite communication signals. The Internet is replacing the telephone for many communications. Moreover, the Internet carries many kinds of wagering activity in addition to bets on races and sports events. The imprecise fit of the act to current gaming forms has necessitated discussion regarding new legislation to clarify the application of the law. A bill sponsored by Senator Jon Kyle of Arizona won approval in the U.S. Senate but had not come to a floor vote in the House of Representatives for approval. That bill would make all gambling on the Internet illegal. Amendments were added to make exceptions for legal race betting and lottery organizations. The bill would give the Department of Justice and the Federal Trade Commission power to enforce the law.

References

Federal Wire Act of 1961 (Public Law 87–216, signed 13 September 1961).
Kelly, Joseph M. 2000. "Internet Gambling Law." *William Mitchell Law Review* 26: 118–177.

THE GAMBLER'S BOOK CLUB

The Gambler's Book Club is perhaps the only bookstore devoted exclusively to selling books about gambling and gambling-related topics. The store is located on Tropicana Ave., just two miles east of the famous Las Vegas Strip. With more than a thousand titles in stock, it is also the largest gambling bookstore in the world.

The bookstore's founder John Luckman began his gambling career as a player and then a bookie in California. He moved to Las Vegas in 1955 to work as a blackjack and baccarat pit boss. From that experience, he became convinced that players did not know the games and that business could be increased in the casinos if players were more knowledgeable. He started writing pamphlets describing each casino game. From that start he developed a mail-order book business for his pamphlets, as well as books that others wrote on gambling. With his wife, Edna, he secured his location and bought a printing press. Soon he was publishing 120 titles and stocking them for sale.

John Luckman died in 1987, but his store remains under the operation of his wife and Howard Schwartz, a true scholar of Las Vegas gambling history. Schwartz not only knows the name of every important gambler in Las Vegas history, but he has met and interviewed every one of them who was alive in the last 30 years. Edna Luckman and Howard Schwartz make most of their sales now through a mail-order catalog and the Internet. The store itself, however, is a marvel. It is a place where all gather: players, local historians, the intelligentsia of gambling, casino entrepreneurs as well as dealers, FBI agents, and all sorts of other people just interested in some aspect of gambling. The store has several local competitors who do well but tend to concentrate their sales efforts on other gambling merchandise, from chips to antique machines. The Gambler's Book Club remains the essential bookstore for the industry.

References

Barrier, Michael. 1991. "How Bookmaking and Bookselling Came Together in Las Vegas." *Nation's Business,* November 29, 4–8.

Hopkins, A. D., and K. J. Evans. 1999. "John Luckman." *The First 100: Portraits of the Men and Women Who Shaped Las Vegas.* Las Vegas: Huntington Press, 232–233.

GAMBLERS' MOTIVATIONS: WHY DO THEY GAMBLE?

A clear majority of American adults participate in legalized gambling activities each year. Many reasons can be suggested for the activity. The results of a random national survey of 1,522 respondents taken by a research group at Mississippi State University in 1995 offered insight into the motivation to gamble.

People may gamble because it is a logical thing to do. It simply makes economic sense to do so—sometimes, with some games. Sometimes players have skills that permit them to outperform other players in games played for money. Certainly this is the case with most live poker games—not poker machines. This is also the case with horse race betting and sports betting. The player who has the necessary skills to outperform other players may choose to make wagers because it is a way to make money. Also, some blackjack players may be able to memorize and count cards that have been played and thus discern moments at which the remaining cards in a deck will give advantages to the players and disadvantages to the casino. If these players can use their special memory skills in the games, they may play the games for the very logical reason of making money.

At other times, the odds of a game may also favor players. In slot machine and lottery games where there is a progressive jackpot, a point may be reached where the jackpot offered may exceed the odds of winning the jackpot. For instance, the odds may be a million to one, but because part of the losses of earlier players is put into the jackpot, the jackpot may be $2 million. Although the game is a long-shot chance game, the playing of the game is logical and rational from an economic point of view. Even when, as is normally the case, the odds do not favor the player, the play can still make some economic sense. A lottery player may wager a single dollar. That dollar has very little value (marginal value) to the player. It might represent a cup of coffee in a cafe or four cigarettes. The player may forgo the pleasure of the cigarettes or coffee in order to play, and in such a case, the player does not suffer any loss in his or her quality of life. In practical terms, nothing is risked. On the other hand, no matter how remote the possibility of a large jackpot is, the large jackpot represents a major factor that could drastically improve a person's quality of life. The logical player who calculates this proposition must be wary

not to make excessive wagers that could subtract from his or her quality of life.

Although players can play for logical economic reasons, most of the players must know that even at games of skill, more players lose than win. Also there are not very many big lottery winners, whether or not the odds, relative to the jackpots offered, favor the player. If players are approaching gambling activity from a more logical point of view, they should see the activity in exchange terms. As they are most likely giving up money, they should expect something in return for the money. Gambling offers things of value for the money invested. Gambling offers a source of entertainment. The entertainment industry is very large in the United States. People pay money to be entertained by movies, television, music, and sports events. Entertainment helps people achieve a distraction from the boredom and the difficulties of daily life. People use entertainment outlets as hobbies. Gambling entertainment can be seen in the same way.

The gambling opportunity can be an opportunity for social interaction for people who crave interaction. People socialize around gambling activities. Also, gambling can bring excitement to lives. One professor at a Las Vegas university suggested that gambling opportunities should be brought into homes for senior citizens. The thrust of her argument was that gambling could give meaning to lives of seniors, a hope for the future, and something to look forward to. The excitement can have positive health consequences for otherwise sedentary people. (See also the entry titled The Positive Case for Gambling.)

Some people may participate in gambling activities because they wish to support the cause of a group sponsoring a gambling event. Private schools, amateur athletics, health care facilities, and many other causes sponsor gaming events, and people can be drawn to gambling to support those causes.

Many people, especially first timers, may gamble just for the curiosity of gambling. As new forms of gambling are coming to many areas of the country, people may be drawn to the activity simply to see it and try it out.

Having looked at the reasons for gambling, we can now look at the study previously mentioned. In early 1995, the Social Science Research Center at Mississippi State University formed a gambling study group. The group is directed by Arthur Cosby. (The editor of this volume has also been a member of the group.) The group designed a survey questionnaire that covered many aspects of gambling. People were asked what games they played and also why they played. Information was collected on the backgrounds of the respondents. The questionnaire was administered through telephone calls to a national random sample. Of the 1,522 respondents, 937 (61.6 percent) had made a wager during the previous 12 months (Thompson 1997, 25–32).

These respondents were asked to indicate why they gambled. They were permitted to offer more than one response. Even though only a very few gamblers can use their talents and skills to regularly win money from gambling, as discussed earlier, a clear majority indicated that the reason they gambled was "to win money." The second category—"for entertainment"—was offered by one-third of the gamblers. Fewer than one-fifth said "for excitement"; "curiosity," "socializing," "worthy causes," "distraction," and "hobby" followed. The responses given are reported in Table 5.

The overall responses are somewhat disturbing, as they indicate that the general population is buying into a false concept of the true product of the gambling industry. Of course, winners and winning are featured in advertising about gambling, but the simple truth is that most cannot win. There may be consequences for the gambling industry because of these attitudes. A collective disillusionment may soon encompass the industry if majorities persist in being drawn to the activity as a way of gaining money. Indeed, some of the recent defeats of gambling propositions may spring from such disillusionment. The overall numbers need to be examined more closely, however, before such conclusions are evident.

Respondents were asked which games they had played during the previous 12 months. Again, they were permitted to name one or more form of gambling (as well as more than one reason for gambling). Of the gamblers, 817 (87.2 percent) had played the lottery. Casino players (both in commercial and Native American casinos) numbered 367 (39.2 percent); 127 (13.6 percent) had wagered at horse races or dog races, and 117 (12.5 percent) had played bingo games.

TABLE 5. Why People Gamble (N = 937)

Motivation	*No.*	*%*
To win money	473	50.5
For entertainment	313	33.4
For excitement	172	18.4
For curiosity	99	10.6
To socialize	89	9.5
For worthy causes	38	4.1
As a distraction	38	4.1
As a hobby	34	3.6

Source: Thompson, William N. 1997. *Legalized Gambling: A Reference Handbook.* Santa Barbara, CA: ABC-CLIO, 31.

The survey indicates that players at different kinds of games play for different reasons. Without trying to isolate persons who played at only one kind of game, the survey sought to compare those playing different games. The differences shown are probably smaller than the real differences, because people will be reported in more than one category. Nevertheless, the differences appear to be major ones in many cases. Table 6 reports the leading categories of responses of players of each type of game. Table 7 indicates other responses.

Clearly the lottery players appear to be the most unrealistic of the gamblers. Over half (53.7 percent) gamble to "win money." Yet, the lottery game is the one in which skill plays the smallest role—basically no role at all—in determining the winner. Moreover, except for special times when lotto jackpots exceed the odds of winning, the lotteries give the lowest return of any of the games. Only about half of the money gambled at lotteries is returned to the players in money prizes. Even in the case of large lotto jackpots, the number of players who win is extremely low—one in hundreds of thousands. Playing the lottery "to win" is indeed an unreasonable fantasy, even if on occasion it may be economically logical. Only 31.7 percent see lottery play as "entertainment," and only 17.7 percent find it exciting.

The next most luck-oriented game is bingo. Here, the skills of listening and paying attention help, but the luck of the draw really determines the winner. Payoffs are only marginally better than lottery payoffs. Yet 43.6 percent of bingo players play "to win money." An equal portion indicated "entertainment" as their motivation, and 20.3 percent said they played bingo for "excitement."

Casino players and race bettors indicated that the desire for "entertainment" was the leading reason for gambling. Of the race bettors, 48.8 percent cited "entertainment" as the first reason, 36.2 percent said it was "to win," and 30.7 percent indicated "excitement" as the reason for gambling. Of casino players, 48.8 percent sought "entertainment," 37.3 percent played for the purpose of "winning," and 27.2 percent played "for excitement." The casino card games and the race betting allow players the greatest opportunity to exercise skill. The ambience of the games, however, puts a premium on their entertainment value. The responses suggest that most of the people drawn to the games are not chasing false dreams or false promises of easy wealth. Rather they

TABLE 6. Players' Games and Reasons for Play

Game	To Win	Entertainment	Excitement	Hobby
Lottery (N = 817)	439	259	145	84
	53.7%	31.7%	17.7%	10.3%
Casino (N = 367)	137	177	100	38
	37.3%	48.8%	27.2%	10.4%
Race bets (N = 127)	46	62	39	16
	36.2%	48.8%	30.7%	12.6%
Bingo (N = 117)	51	51	24	9
	43.6%	43.6%	20.3%	7.7%

Source: Social Science Research Center, Mississippi State University. 1995. *National Gambling Survey.* Jackson: Mississippi State University.

TABLE 7. Players' Games and Reasons for Play

	Curiosity	Socialize	Worthy	Distraction
Lottery (N = 817)	66	33	35	31
	8.1%	4.0%	4.3%	3.8%
Casino (N = 367)	52	19	17	17
	14.2%	5.2%	4.6%	4.6%
Race bets (N = 127)	13	5	5	10
	10.3%	3.9%	3.9%	7.9%
Bingo (N = 117)	20	8	8	10
	16.9%	6.8%	6.8%	8.5%

Source: Social Science Research Center, Mississippi State University. 1995. *National Gambling Survey.* Jackson: Mississippi State University.

are exchanging their time and money for entertainment experiences.

Curiosity seekers are marginally more likely to be drawn to racetracks. Bingo is clearly seen as the game most likely to draw those desiring a social experience (16.9 percent). Casinos follow closely (14.2 percent), whereas lottery players are least likely to be drawn to the games for social reasons (8.1 percent). Bingo play-

ers are most likely to play in order to support "worthy causes." They are also most likely to play as a "hobby" and as a "distraction" from the problems of daily life.

Gender differences reveal that males are more likely to gamble "to win" than females (54.4 percent to 46.4 percent) but less likely to play games for entertainment (27.7 percent to 39.0 percent) or for social reasons (7.8 percent to 11.3 percent).

Not all the risks on the Las Vegas Strip are inside the casinos—for years tourists tried their "luck" on this giant waterslide.

Males show a greater inclination to play for "excitement" (20.4 percent to 16.3 percent), whereas females are more likely to play as a distraction from daily problems (5.0 percent to 3.2 percent).

Whites and nonwhites express many of the same reasons for gaming. They can be distinguished on two factors, however. Nonwhites are more likely to gamble "to win money" (58.1 percent to 49.3 percent); they are less likely to gamble for social reasons (4.7 percent to 10.6 percent).

The survey also asked if people had traveled in order to gamble. Of those who had, a much greater portion gambled for entertainment (39.4 percent to 29.5 percent) and for excitement (26.8 percent to 12.8 percent). Persons who indicated that they had gambling opportunities in their communities were less likely to gamble out of curiosity (10.2 percent to 21.4 percent) and more likely to gamble to "win money" (50.8 percent to 41.4 percent). Local gambling was also more socially oriented (9.7 percent to 3.6 percent).

The bottom line? People gamble for many reasons. With the exception of a small portion of skilled players, those who do so for the purpose of winning money are quite simply fooling themselves. It appears that some gamers are more likely than others to fall under the false allure of the notion that they can win. It is regrettable that the lottery players are most prone to these feelings. Lotteries are not only the most luck-oriented games, but they also give the player the worst odds of any of the games. What is even worse is the fact that only the lotteries, of all the games, are offered by government entrepreneurs. At a time when the politicians are seeking to raise their voices against gambling in Washington as well as several state capitals, it is disconcerting that the one gambling game directly operated by politicians is the game most apt to be sold for something it is not—an opportunity to win money. Casino gambling is the target of gambling's political opposition. Yet the casino players appear to have the most realistic rationale for their play. The gambling industry offers many games. Some offers are more responsible than others. Policymakers examining the impacts of gaming on society should be very mindful of the differences among different games and among the way the games are offered to the public.

References

Social Science Research Center. 1995. *National Gambling Survey.* Jackson: Mississippi State University.

Thompson, William N. 1997. *Legalized Gambling: A Reference Handbook.* 2nd ed. Santa Barbara, CA: ABC-CLIO, 25–32.

GAMBLING DEVICES ACTS (THE JOHNSON ACT AND AMENDMENTS)

One of the primary accomplishments of the Kefauver Committee's investigations of organized crime was the passage of the Gambling Devices Act of 1951, also known as the Johnson Act (Public Law 81–906, passed 2 January 1951) (*see* The

Kefauver Committee). The act prohibited the transportation of slot machines across state lines, except when they could legally be used in the state of destination.

No slot machines were permitted on federal enclaves such as domestic military bases, national parks and forests, and Indian reservations. The machines were also prohibited for use in waters under the maritime jurisdiction of the United States, unless they were on vessels authorized for legalized gambling by state governments. As U.S. flag ships were prohibited from having gaming operations on international waters by 1949 legislation, the Johnson Act made the transportation of machines to these ships also an illegal act.

Under provisions of the act, every manufacturer of machines had to register with the U.S. attorney general. All machines had to be specially marked and numbered for identification. Records of all sales and distributions of machines had to be filed with the attorney general each year.

The Johnson Act of 1951 defined "gambling devices" as mechanical devices "an essential part of which is a drum or reel . . . which when operated may deliver, as the result of the application of an element of chance, any money or property." The act also included other machines that are activated by coins for purposes of gambling. The act applied to parts of these machines as well.

In 1962, the Gambling Devices Act was amended to include gambling machines other than traditional slot machines, such as video games, digger or crane machines, quarter drop machines, and pinball machines that allow free replays, and also devices for gambling such as roulette wheels and wheels of fortune. The act did not apply to nonmechanical devices such as paper products for bingo games. Pari-mutuel equipment was also exempt, as were certain games designed especially for carnivals.

Subsequent legislation such as the Indian Gaming Regulatory Act of 1988 and the Cruise Ship Competitiveness Act of 1992 added further exemptions to the act.

References

Gambling Devices Act (Public Law 81–906, signed into law January 2, 1951).

GAMBLING ON THE HIGH SEAS, THE LAWS OF

For more than 80 years, the subject of gambling on the high seas has been a policy concern for U.S. officials. In 1926, operators anchored barges three miles off the coast of California and welcomed gamblers from San Francisco and, later, Los Angeles, who would take smaller speedboats from the shore to the boats. The barges were well lit and could be seen from the shore. State officials did not like the boats, but they were frustrated in attempts to enforce state anticasino laws, as the boats were considered to be in international waters. The boats could accommodate as many as 600 players, and they soon appeared off the Atlantic Coast as well.

In 1948, U.S. Senator William Knowland (R-California) introduced legislation aimed at these barges. In the process he won passage of a bill that stopped all gambling on the high seas by U.S. flag-bearing ships worldwide.

The law supposedly applied to vessels used "principally" for gambling, but in actuality, it applied to all ships whether gambling was the major activity of the ship or merely a side activity—as gambling is on most cruise ships. Gambling was prohibited on the vessels if they were registered under the laws of the United States or if they were "owned by, chartered to, or otherwise controlled" by citizens or residents or corporations of the United States. Persons violating the law could be fined up to $10,000 and jailed for two years and also could lose their vessel.

The law also made it illegal to transport passengers from the shore to a gambling ship in international waters, regardless of whether the ship was under the American flag or a foreign flag.

In 1951 (and as amended in 1962), the Johnson Act made it illegal to transport gaming equipment onto any U.S. ship. There was no change in the law until 1992. Over the intervening decades, U.S. shipping interests seemed to have suffered considerably. Although gambling activity provided only a small part of the revenues of cruise ships, the extra revenues probably helped the ships achieve overall net profits. As of 1991, there were 82 cruise ships that docked at U.S. ports. Only two of these were U.S. ships.

In 1992, as part of the Flower Garden Banks National Marine Sanctuary Act, Congress amended the Johnson Act to remove the prohibition on transporting gambling equipment to U.S. ships and also authorized those ships to permit gambling in international waters or in national waters if permission was granted by states. Under the new law, states could still stop such international waters gambling if the ships simply made "cruises to nowhere." States could prohibit gaming unless the ships docked in ports of other states or countries before they returned to the port in the state of origin.

In 1996, the federal law regarding gambling ships changed again, allowing ships to have gambling on Lake Michigan if they were authorized to do so by the state of Indiana. Voyages to Alaska were also allowed to have gambling if they stopped twice in Alaska and also either in Canada or another state. The ability of states to prohibit gaming was also restricted. The boats could have gambling if they returned to the original state without going to another state or country as long as the cruise was tied to a longer cruise. The new law stimulated new interest in what were referred to as "cruises to nowhere," as these were allowed unless specific state action prohibited them. The state action had to be expressed in new legislation, and cruise boat interests were adept at lobbying against the restrictions.

The growth in the number of gambling ships caused the 1997–1999 National Gambling Impact Study Commission to recommend new legislation to allow states to more easily stop "cruises to nowhere" that did not have explicit permission to operate under the state law. Such legislation has yet to be passed into law.

*Coauthored by Anthony N. Cabot
and Robert Faiss*

References

Cabot, Anthony N., William N. Thompson, Andrew Tottenham, and Carl Braunlich, eds. 1999. *International Casino Law.* 3rd ed. Reno: Institute for the Study of Gambling, University of Nevada, Reno, 605–612.

National Gambling Impact Study Commission [NGISC]. 1999. *Final Report.* Washington, DC: NGISC.

Thompson, William N. 1997. *Legalized Gambling: A Reference Handbook.* 2nd ed. Santa Barbara, CA: ABC-CLIO, 131–132.

See also Cruise Ships; Gambling Devices Act (Johnson Act and Amendments).

GAMBLING SYSTEMS

Gambling is as old as human existence and so too are the attempts to beat the game. Players have used cheating schemes and have also used more or less legitimate systems and strategies for winning from the first moment that cards were dealt or dice were rolled. Although the basic truth is that an honest random game cannot be beaten, systems can indeed be effective. At times they can produce wins that are beyond normal expectations. But more often systems can be used to protect a player from excessive losses or to maximize playing time when the player is seeking game play for entertainment.

The most effective winning systems are tied to games in which skill is a greater factor than luck in determining winners. Applications of systematic play can produce results in live poker games, at blackjack tables, and with sports betting and horse race betting. The most important part of systematic play is having a full knowledge of the odds in the game; for instance, knowing the likelihood that particular cards will be dealt at a particular moment. In a player-banked game such as poker, the systematic player will also be cognizant of his or her bankroll and the bankroll of opponents. Systematic skills at poker also involve being able to "read" the other players: that is, finding "tells," or mannerisms that might reflect the strength of their hands. Another essential skill at poker or at other games involving calculations and interpretations of situations is the ability to have a clear head; for instance, it is important to remain fully sober during play. In blackjack, good playing strategies keep the house edge down to one or two percentage points. Card-counting strategies, however, if properly executed, can give the player a positive return, as discussed in Edward Thorpe's book *Beat the Dealer* (1962).

Sports bettors can gain an edge over the casino by carefully studying records of teams and game situation histories. The sport bettor can use information to assess the likelihood that one team will win a game or the likelihood that it will win by a certain margin. The sports bettor has an advantage over the casino in that the casino oddsmakers are not assessing the results they feel will occur in the game but rather are assessing how the betting public will play the game. For instance, the casino knows that players will favor teams such as Michigan and Notre Dame in their betting. Given this situation, the casino will add greater handicaps to these teams. When the oddsmakers think Notre Dame will beat Northwestern by 11 points, they put the point spread at 15 points, knowing that half of the public will bet on each side of the game at that level. The true student of the game with no emotional attachment to either team will see that Northwestern has a definite advantage in the betting situation. That player is getting an extra 4 points by betting on Northwestern. As long as the betting is balanced on both sides, the casino does not care who wins or loses. The casino is hurt only if the betting is heavily on one side. In such cases, it will move the point line to seek an adjustment. If the casino moves the line too much—more than 2 or 3 points—the smart, skillful bettors will bet when the spread is low on one team and when it is high on the other team and hope they can win on both sides.

In horse race betting, most systems are also based upon having full information about a horse's pedigree and prior experiences in similar situations (dry track, muddy track, long race course, short race course). Again, the odds that will be given on a particular horse are balanced according to how other bettors are making wagers on the race. If one bettor gets better information or can better analyze information, he or she can make money on the wagers. One system assumes that the bettors on first-place horses—the win bets— are knowledgeable. Therefore, the system player analyzes betting on the board

(at the track or at an off-track betting parlor). He or she sees the possible return on the favorite. It might be two for one—a $4 payout for a $2 wager. The next-best horse may pay off $10, $12, or $14. The bettor then looks at the bets to show—that is, that the horse will finish in one of the first three places. This is a different pool. The other bettors might overlook the favorite here, and that horse's return could be $3, compared to $4, $5, and $6 on the other horses. This is proportionally much more favorable to the favorite. Under the system, a bettor placing his or her money on the favorite to finish in one of the top three places can gain a very good edge on the others and even on the track, which takes up to 20 percent from the pool of bets.

In games involving skillful choices, systems can provide an edge, as most of these games—even when house banked (as sports betting is)—pit one player's skill against that of other players. In luck games such as roulette, baccarat, or craps, however, the player is foolish to believe he or she can sustain an edge over the house with any system. Of course, with luck, any system can provide short-term winnings, but luck can do that for a nonsystem player as well. Systems can help with managing the player's money, but every system first directs the player toward finding the best bets on the table. For instance, system players at craps would avoid all but the pass/come bets combined with the odds bets. Blackjack bettors would avoid insurance bets, and roulette bettors would seek out wheels with only one zero and would not bet on a five-number combination at a double-zero wheel. The optimum bet would be one offering *en prison,* on a single-zero wheel, preferably in England, where tipping is prohibited.

Bettors playing total chance games have pursued several systems with some frequency over the centuries wherever the games have been played. One very simple system is called flat betting. Under this system the bettor simply bets the same amount every time. At games such as blackjack, the player would double down and split when it was advantageous to do so. At a roulette game, such players would bet on even-money choices such as red and black. Which way they bet would make no difference. They could bet pass or no-pass on a craps table whether they thought the table was hot or cold, but it would make no difference. Using this system or strategy, the player can be assured that over the long run, he or she will lose at the rate of the house percentage. As the house edge is 5 percent or less, the system can sustain play for a long period of time. A streak of luck can provide the player with a win. And the one big advantage all players have, but reluctantly use, is that they can walk away from the game at any time. The casinos really cannot do that.

The most popular system—one that has broken many players but never a casino—is called the Martingale progressive system. In this system the player raises bets by doubling them after losses. If the first bet is $1 on red and it is a loss, the player next bets $2 on red. A player who wins goes back to betting $1 the next time. If he or she loses again, the next bet is $4. Another loss and he or she bets $8, then $16, then $32 if there are five losses in a row. The player is now putting $32 at risk. A player who wins is $1 ahead. A player who loses is risking in turn $64 and then $128, all in order to get ahead by $1. This system is very much dependent upon the nerve of the gambler. Will he or she really be willing to put out $64 in a bet after losing six in a row, when he or she started out with a $1 bet in hopes of winning $1? But even more

than nerve, there is the question of house limits. The limits usually involve a spread of 100 times or less. In this case, if the player has seven losses, he or she is forced to bet $128 to get the $1 win. A $1 table will probably have an upper limit of $100 for bets, so the system can no longer be used. The laws of probability and streaks indicate that with thousands of rolls of dice or wheels, there will be streaks occurring with some regularity. Wheels show red seven in a row times every night. The same is true for odds and evens and for high and low numbers. The streak can kill the system player, wiping out his or her bankroll very quickly. If, on the other hand, the player is betting with the streak, he or she wins only $1 each time. In a streak of seven, the player loses $131 if he or she is on the wrong side but wins $7 on the right side.

Cognizant of these facts and knowing that wheels and dice do indeed follow streaks, some of the Martingale progressive system players will watch a wheel (or dice table) for several minutes and wait for a streak to develop. Then, depending upon their disposition, after five or six reds in a row, they will start their system by playing black, or if they sense a wheel bias, by continuing to bet on red. All of this is a futile exercise, assuming that the casino does monitor its wheel against biases, because the wheel does not remember what it has rolled the previous five times, ten times, or ten thousand times. Casinos with roulette and baccarat games encourage these Martingale system players by furnishing them with pencils and paper so they can track the numbers on the wheels. They also publish books of numbers for the past month, or past year, to try to get players to practice their systems. Evidently, the casinos are not afraid of the Martingale. Nor are they afraid of Great Martingale systems that find the bettor tripling bets after losses.

A cancellation system is offered as a sure winner. The bettor writes down three numbers: 1, 2, and 3. He or she now bets $4, the total of the first and third digits (1+3). A player who wins cancels out the 1 and 3 and bets $2. A winner cancels out the 2 and starts over. If he or she loses, he or she adds the $2 loss to the 2 and now bets $4. A player who wins crosses off 4 from the total and starts over. A player who loses adds the 4 to the 1, 2, and 3 and bets 5 (4 + 1). Wins bring the player back to the 1, 2, 3. Although under this system one can show a profit with an even number of wins and losses, streaks can be as deadly as with the Martingale system.

Another system, which is simpler, suggests that the player should go with the flow, raising bets one unit whenever there is a win and lowering them one unit (or keeping the original bet amount) when there is a loss. Under this method, over the span of play the player should be able to keep his or her losses within the house percentages.

Casinos as an entertainment experience offer play at house games. The best systems cannot change that fact. Good money management demands the ability to set limits. The player should determine his or her budget before play begins and be willing to walk away from the table when the budget is spent. If the player wishes to sustain play over a period of time for enjoyment of the games, the initial bet should not exceed 1 percent of his or her bankroll. The player should also consider a winning limit. If with a $100 bankroll the player achieves wins of $20, he or she should remove this amount from the bankroll and play it no more during that session. A player who experiences a streak of more than five or six bets might pause and consider going to another table or game.

References

Scarne, John. 1986. *Scarne's New Complete Guide to Gambling.* New York: Simon and Schuster, 409–420.

Sifakis, Carl. 1990. *Encyclopedia of Gambling.* New York: Facts on File, 24–27.

Thorpe, Edward O. 1962. *Beat the Dealer.* New York: Random House.

See also Cheating Schemes.

Gambling Taxes. *See* Taxes, Gambling.

Games, House-banked. *See* House-banked Games (in Games section).

Games, Player-banked. *See* Player-banked Games (in Games section).

Gaming Institutes: Research and Political

The rapid growth of legalized gambling, both domestic and international, has been responsible for the number of organizations being formed in recent years to analyze, teach, manage, and research many areas of the gaming industry and to train personnel to work in the industry. There is a great need for understanding and planning when evidence of social, economic, and political effects is seen as a result of gambling. The associations and institutes presented in this entry vary in purpose and size, but all of them have the common objective of managing information related to the gaming industry.

UNIVERSITY OF NEVADA, LAS VEGAS, INTERNATIONAL GAMING INSTITUTE

The International Gaming Institute (IGI) is part of the College of Hotel Administration located on the campus of the University of Nevada, Las Vegas (UNLV). The institute was started in 1993 to provide executive development programs, seminars, training, classes, and conferences for the gaming industry and for gaming regulators. The IGI utilizes experts in the gaming and hospitality industries to provide a unique learning environment in its casino lab and support facilities as well as in Las Vegas casino/resorts and gaming-related businesses. The institute has five centers: the Gaming Regulation Center, the Publication and Information Center, the Hospitality Research and Development Center, the Gaming Management and Development Center, and the International Gaming Technologies (IGT) Gaming Resource Center.

Gaming Regulation Center

The purpose of the Gaming Regulation Center at IGI is to create a venue where gaming regulators can meet to discuss topics related to public policy and the regulation of gaming. The center conducts seminars on law enforcement for gaming regulators, background and licensing investigation procedures, casino auditing, surveillance, and financial issues relating to casinos.

Publication and Information Center

The IGI has authored or sponsored several publications relating to the casino industry, and these are made available through the institute's Publication and Information Center. One objective of the IGI is to conduct research for the gaming industry, and toward this end, the IGI publishes a biannual academic journal called the *Gaming Research and Review Journal.* This professional journal is dedicated entirely to research and management of gaming operations, and it is designed to benefit gaming operators, industry consultants and researchers, and government policymakers and regulators.

Hospitality Research and Development Center

The Hospitality Research and Development Center (HRDC) is part of the university's College of Hotel Administration, a situation that allows the HRDC to draw upon the experience of faculty members who are experts in the hospitality industry. HRDC provides nongaming educational seminars and workshops, customized executive programs, market research and customer surveys, expert witness testimony, and sessions on time management and team building.

Gaming Management and Development Center

The Gaming Management and Development Center designs, coordinates, and markets seminars as well as contracting conferences, seminars, and symposia for the gaming and casino industry. Seminar topics include table game management, mathematics of table games, slot volatility, game protection, casino marketing, analysis of customer game participation, rebates on losses, gaming financial issues, management of human resources in the gaming industry, general management and leadership issues, and customer service. The center also offers a fast-track, rigorous Gaming Management Certificate Program, which focuses on several key areas of casino management.

International Masters of Gaming Law

The International Masters of Gaming Law (IMGL) was founded in 2002 by the world's leading gaming attorneys. They represent major gambling concerns. The association also includes regulators and educators concerned with gambling law. Membership is restricted with two general members per gambling venue. The organization holds twice annual general meetings as well as a variety of workshops. Its active program of publications includes its major journal, *Casino Lawyer,* as well as *Canadian Casino Lawyer* and *European Casino Lawyer.* Additionally it published a loose-leaf compilation titled *International Casino Law and Regulations.*

Reference
www.gaminglawmasters.com.

The International Gaming Technologies Gaming Resource Center

The International Gaming Technologies (IGT) Gaming Resource Center offers reference and referral services for researchers, businesspeople, and students. Questions beyond the resources of the center are sometimes referred to gaming professors, government agencies, gaming organizations, and gaming resources in other libraries. The core of the IGT Gaming Resource Center is the Gary Royer Gaming Collection, an extensive compilation of documents and information relating to gaming.

Reference
http://www.unlv.edu/Research Centers, UNLV International Gaming Institute.

GAMING STUDIES RESEARCH COLLECTION, SPECIAL COLLECTIONS DEPARTMENT, LIED LIBRARY, UNIVERSITY OF NEVADA, LAS VEGAS

The Special Collections department at UNLV's main campus library serves as a central research repository for information relating to gambling and commercial gaming as it developed in Las Vegas and became an international model for the industry. Special collections house materials that provide important documentation of the history of gaming, casinos, and entertainment in Las Vegas. The collections document the history and statistical basis of games and gambling; the economics and regulation of the gaming industry; psychological, social, and political effects of gambling; and the history of specific Las Vegas hotels and casinos. Significant collections have been developed in the related fields of organized crime and prostitution. Cultural aspects of gaming are represented in collections of literature and periodicals concerning Las Vegas and gambling, as well as in photographs and motion pictures. The Taxe Collection is an important resource for the study of 19th-century gaming.

Reference

University of Nevada, Las Vegas. 1999. *Graduate College Catalog.* Las Vegas: University of Nevada, Las Vegas, 13.

INSTITUTE FOR THE STUDY OF GAMBLING AND COMMERCIAL GAMING

The Institute for the Study of Gambling and Commercial Gaming was established by the University of Nevada, Reno, in 1989. The first academically oriented program of its kind, the institute promotes the understanding of gambling and the commercial gaming industries and encourages research and learning.

The institute is directed by William Eadington, an international authority on the legalization and regulation of commercial gambling. Eadington is a prolific author on the topics of economic and social impacts in the commercial gaming arena and has also edited a variety of gaming publications. Eadington has organized a number of conferences, including the 15

International Conferences on Gambling and Risk Taking that took place between 1974 and 2009.

The institute serves as an important resource for Nevada's major industry. It also responds to information and research requests from the public, maintains contact with domestic and international media, and directs an annual executive development program, as well as gaming management education for the College of Business Administration.

Reference

http://www.unr.edu/unr/colleges/coba/game.

CENTRE FOR THE STUDY OF GAMBLING AND COMMERCIAL GAMING

Located at the University of Salford, Manchester, England, the Centre for the Study of Gambling and Commercial Gaming was established by a consortium of companies to actively research and encourage serious discussion of the gaming industry and to offer university students options for pursuing careers in gaming. The increasing interest in England's national lottery has led to the perception that the country is deficient in academic- and government-sponsored research on gambling. The centre is a response to the need for examining policy alternatives and economic issues with respect to the gaming industry.

The objective of the centre is to encourage scholarly research and teaching in all aspects of gambling and commercial gaming. It provides a reference point for individual scholars and researchers interested in the economic, social, cultural, and mathematical studies of gaming, with emphasis on policy, regulatory, and organizational aspects. The centre provides a sequence of courses at the undergraduate and postgraduate levels that fall under the area of business economics with gambling studies. The series of courses introduces students to some of the practical problems associated with gaming and gambling and provides a firm foundation in the basic principles of economic theory and quantitative economics. The degree course of economics and gambling is designed to establish a good base for a career in management, finance, or marketing.

Reference

http://www.salford.ac.uk/gambling.

NATIONAL INDIAN GAMING ASSOCIATION

The National Indian Gaming Association (NIGA) was established in 1985 as a nonprofit organization. As of 2001, its members include 168 Indian nations and 55 nonvoting associate members representing organizations, tribes, and businesses engaged in tribal gaming enterprises from around the United States. NIGA has an executive committee headed by a chairman and other officers, including delegates from tribal nations throughout the country. The association's headquarters are located in Washington, D.C. NIGA's commitment and purpose is to advance the lives of Native Americans economically, politically, and socially. Its stated mission is to protect and preserve the general welfare of tribes striving for self-sufficiency through gaming enterprises in Indian country. To fulfill its mission, NIGA works with the federal government and the U.S. Congress to develop sound policies and practices and to provide technical assistance and advocacy on gaming-related issues. NIGA also seeks to maintain and protect Indian sovereign governmental authority in Indian country.

NIGA operates a Library and Resource Center that houses and provides educational research materials related to Indian gaming and other issues affecting Native Americans. To facilitate its research objectives, the center is developing a National Indian Gaming Survey to document the historic impact of Indian gaming on tribal communities and governments as well as on their non-Indian neighbors. The National Indian Gaming Library's goal is to become the most comprehensive library of printed material on Indian gaming in the country. The center also has a Web site that includes basic information about Indian gaming, a searchable database, and an impressive set of links to other Native American Web sites. Its virtual library has more than 50 research and impact studies related to Indian gaming available online. NIGA also publishes a monthly newsletter that provides updates on legislative activities, Indian gaming casinos, and related national events.

Reference

http://www.indiangaming.org.

AMERICAN GAMING ASSOCIATION

In 1993, major gaming/casino executives discussed forming a trade association to represent their industry to the nation and to the powers that be in Washington,

D.C. As a result of these talks, the office of the American Gaming Association (AGA) opened in Washington, D.C., in June 1995. Its primary purpose is to use education and advocacy to promote a better understanding of the gaming entertainment industry among the general public, elected officials, the media, and other decision makers.

The AGA represents the commercial casino entertainment industry by examining federal legislative and regulatory issues that affect its members and their employees and customers. Some of these issues include federal taxation, regulation, and travel and tourism.

The AGA has an aggressive public education program designed to convey the industry's message to key audiences. It provides leadership and guidance when new issues emerge and helps develop industry-wide programs that respond to important issues such as problem gambling and underage gambling.

The association has approximately 80 members from different organizations affiliated with the gaming industry, including casinos and equipment manufacturers, suppliers, and vendors; companies that provide professional and financial services; a pari-mutuel/sports book; and a variety of associations, publications, and unions. The AGA's membership also includes some of the most recognized names in the industry, such as Harrah's Entertainment, International Game Technology, Mandalay Resort Group, MGM Mirage, Park Place Entertainment, Gtech, and the Nevada Resort Association. The AGA is supported by dues from its member casinos and organizations.

The AGA's Web site has a section on its publications, which includes selected articles from the AGA's membership newsletter, *Inside the AGA,* and a third-party newsletter, *AGA Ally.* There is a library of AGA documents and studies that can be received through the mail. The Web site also features gaming industry videos available for viewing online; media updates that contain the AGA's latest press releases, speeches, op-eds, letters to the editor, and archival materials from 1995 to 2000; and member services that outline information about member benefits. The American Gaming Association was also instrumental in establishing the National Center for Responsible Gaming (NCRG) in 1996.

Reference
http://www.americangaming.org.

NATIONAL CENTER FOR RESPONSIBLE GAMING

The National Center for Responsible Gaming (NCRG), located in Washington, D.C., is an independent nonprofit organization founded in 1996. It is the first and only funding source dedicated solely to scientific research on gambling disorders, particularly problem gambling and underage gambling. Its mission is to assist individuals and families affected by problem gambling disorder and eliminate underage gambling by:

Supporting the finest peer-reviewed basic and applied research on gambling disorders

Encouraging the application of new research findings to improve prevention, diagnostic, intervention and treatment strategies

Enhancing public awareness of problem and underage gambling

The NCRG is a division of the Gaming Entertainment Research and Education Foundation and is governed by a board of directors. The membership of the board includes representatives of the gaming industry and leaders from the civic, charitable, educational, community, and public service sectors.

The center is supported financially by the commercial casino industry and has received pledges of more than $7 million from gaming and gaming-related organizations. The NCRG administers its research grant program using peer review panels. Panel members, who are recognized as experts in their areas, follow review procedures and criteria guided by rigorous standards established by the National Institutes of Health to evaluate the scientific merit of proposals submitted to the NCRG (a list of members who have served on the panel is available on the NCRG's Web site). The center has granted $2.5 million to renowned research and medical centers, such as Harvard Medical School, in support of research in the fields of neuroscience, behavioral and social science, and epidemiology. Ideally, these research projects will help to expand our knowledge about gaming disorders and lead to effective prevention and treatment programs.

Reference
http://www.ncrg.org

THE NATIONAL COALITION AGAINST LEGALIZED GAMBLING

The National Coalition against Legalized Gambling (NCALG) is the creation of its executive director, Tom Grey. In 1991, Grey, a Vietnam Infantry veteran and a United Methodist minister, became concerned about gambling. Grey was a graduate of Dartmouth College and the Garrett Evangelical Theological Seminary, and he had led four congregations. He was pastoring a Methodist church in his hometown, Galena, Illinois. Illinois had authorized riverboat casinos, and an operator expressed interest in running a boat out of Galena. Grey supported a local referendum to vote against the proposal. Over 80 percent of the local voters said no to the idea of a local casino. Nonetheless the county commissioners supported the casino, and in 1992, the Illinois Gaming Board ignored local opinion and awarded a license for the Galena site. Grey was incensed. He soon discovered that many people around the country were faced with the same problem—having casinos placed near their communities in spite of local opposition. Grey decided to organize these opposition forces.

In May 1994, Grey formed the NCALG to unify the opponents of gambling expansion. He structured a network of people in almost every U.S. state as well as in Canada, and he began holding annual conferences and issuing a newsletter. The NCALG established the National Coalition against Gambling Expansion to serve as its political arm. The NCALG makes education its top priority and provides research, information, and technical support to those battling the expansion of gambling. Staff leaders—especially Grey—travel the country helping local groups organize grassroots efforts to oppose gambling. They help build bridges to other local groups that do not want legalized gambling. The e-mail net of the NCALG serves as a clearinghouse for antigambling information.

Tom Grey and his groups have challenged gambling proponents wherever they have appeared. The campaigns are ongoing, and Grey finds himself traveling about the country, usually driving by himself, popping into communities, dining at church suppers, and being a house guest of local clergy. He energizes the local population by providing facts and speaking with the local media and key community leaders. He offers a zeal that is usually associated with the pulpit. One political consultant labeled the 60-plus-year Grey (born in 1941) as the gambling industry's nemesis: "Our most dangerous man in America" (*U.S. News and World Report,* January 15, 1996). Grey and his coalitions have seen major victories as well as defeats. He was instrumental in getting Congress to establish the National Gambling Impact Study Commission, which began work in 1997. The efforts of the group defeated casino gambling in Ohio, Arkansas, and Florida but fell short in Michigan. They were key in the fight to defeat a lottery in Alabama and to close down slot machine operations in South Carolina.

Reference

http://www.ncalg.org.

ALBERTA GAMING RESEARCH INSTITUTE

Recommendations came from the Alberta Lotteries and Gaming Summit '98 for the government to spend more money on gaming research. The Alberta Gaming Research Institute was established in November 1999 in response to those recommendations. The purpose of the institute, which is a consortium of the universities of Alberta, Calgary, and Lethbridge, is to sponsor research on gaming-related topics such as the social impact of gaming, aboriginal gaming issues, and trends in gaming.

The institute supports the collaborative research efforts of faculty researchers, graduate students, visiting scholars, and postdoctoral fellows. The Alberta Gaming Research Council directs most of the institute's research activities. Its 14 members, who represent both the public and government sectors, have been appointed to serve for three years.

For the first three years, $1.5 million per year was allocated to the institute from the Alberta Lottery Fund. The Alberta government earmarked an additional $3.4 million from the Alberta Lottery Fund for 1999–2000 to go to the Alberta Alcohol and Drug Abuse Commission (AADAC) to provide support for the prevention of problem gambling and to promote education and treatment programs.

The Web site of the Alberta Gaming Research Institute provides basic information, including historical background, the purpose of the institute, its organization, budget, and methods of operation. The site also has links that provide access to information about gaming in Alberta, research and education, and legislation, as well as various reports, news releases and updates, business plans, and forms.

Reference

http://www.gaming.gov.ab.ca/what/agr _institute.html.

THE CANADIAN WEST FOUNDATION

The Canadian West Foundation (CWF)—a nonprofit research institute— was established in 1970 to pursue research and to promote civic education in Canadian public policy. The CWF sponsors conferences on myriad policy issues and has an active publication program. In 1998, the CWF embarked upon a three-year "gambling in Canada" project. They have explored: (1) the impact of gambling on the nonprofit sector, (2) opinions, attitudes, and public policy implications of gambling, (3) the history and scope of gambling in Canada, and (4) the socioeconomic impact of gambling on communities. A series of monographs has been published as a result of the project.

The CWF is headquartered in Calgary, Alberta. The gambling research project has been directed by Jason J. Azmier and has been supported by researchers including Garry Smith, Harold Wynne, and Colin Campbell.

Reference
www.cwf.ca.

AUSTRALIAN INSTITUTE FOR GAMBLING RESEARCH

The Australian Institute for Gambling Research (AIGR) is a research center located at the University of Western Sydney (UWS). It is the only independent national center of gambling studies in Australia. The AIGR has an advisory board with representatives from both the community and academia. It has a worldwide reputation for in-depth gaming research, including the areas of policy and social impact.

The AIGR was established in 1993 with a grant from UWS and was supported through the collaborative efforts of experienced Australian researchers. UWS was instrumental in appointing Australia's first faculty Chair of Gaming, and in January 1997 Prof. Jan McMillen was named executive director of the AIGR, broadening the research focus of the institute.

The AIGR has received various research grants from the Australian Research Council as well as Australian and international governments. This has resulted in the publication of articles in scholarly journals, as well as books and research reports. The AIGR is involved in community service and engages community groups in its research programs. AIGR researchers also provide voluntary service to the community.

The Library and Information Services of UWS supports the needs of the AIGR. Its gambling collection has over 1,000 items, including reports, videos, journals, games, books, and newspaper clippings. The AIGR sponsors various annual conferences related to gaming issues.

Reference
http://fassweb.macarthur.uws.edu.au/AIGR.

EUROPEAN ASSOCIATION FOR THE STUDY OF GAMBLING

The European Association for the Study of Gambling (EASG), located in the Netherlands, strives to improve communication among its members, who represent many different areas of the European gaming industry. It also provides a forum for the study, discussion, and dissemination of knowledge about European gambling issues.

The EASG promotes comparative studies that examine the historical, economic, and social impact of gambling; developmental and regulatory gambling issues; ethical management and marketing of gaming; and pathological gambling issues, including prevention and treatment programs.

EASG membership is open to both individuals and institutions affiliated with the gaming industry, either within or outside Europe, as well as to academic researchers. The association is governed by an executive committee, which includes a chairman and several subordinate officers.

The association's Web site provides pertinent information about gambling and gaming literature. It also highlights several international gaming conferences and provides links to related Web sites.

Reference

http://www.easg.org.

LIONEL, SAWYER, AND COLLINS; AND LEWIS AND ROCA

Two American law firms are important in gaming research endeavors. Lionel, Sawyer, and Collins, a Las Vegas law firm, was founded in 1967 by Samuel Lionel and Grant Sawyer, the retiring governor of the state of Nevada (*see* Sawyer, Grant). One of their first functions was conducted under the leadership of attorney Robert Faiss, who helped pen significant amendments to the Nevada Gaming Control Act. In subsequent years,

the firm assisted in drafting gambling regulatory bills for legislative consideration. The firm has also been the leading sponsor of the International Gaming Law Association, and Anthony Cabot, an attorney with the firm, served as a coeditor of the *Gaming Law Review* (with Joseph Kelly). No other law firm has published as many law materials on gambling. When Cabot moved to the Las Vegas offices of Lewis and Roca, he continued his role as a leader in gaming publications, serving as the senior coeditor on three editions of *International Casino Law.* He has also authored or contributed to a number of publications, including *Nevada Gaming Law, Federal Gaming Law, Legalized Gambling in Nevada, Casino Gaming Policy, Economics and Regulation,* and *Casino Credit and Collection Law.*

Coauthored with Sidney Watson and Maria White

Reference

www.lionelsawyer.com.

Hoca and E-O. *See* Roulette, Wheels of Fortune, and Other Wheel Games.

HORSE RACING

Horse racing is one of mankind's oldest sports, dating back to the earliest days of recorded time. There has been a variety of types of races, and many different breeds of horses used for racing. Thoroughbreds are the most recognized breed of

racehorses, but quarter horses, Arabians, and standardbreds may also race.

There are races over straight courses and oval tracks, from one-fourth mile to several miles. The standard distance of races is measured in furlongs; one furlong is one-eighth of a mile. Tracks may be made of grass, dirt, or synthetic materials. (A synthetic racing surface, called Polytrack, was first introduced in the United States at Turfway Park in Kentucky in 2005. It was designed for easier maintenance and also in the hopes of reducing injuries to horses.) In addition to mounted races (called flats) and harness races, there are obstacle races called steeplechases.

Certain races command much more attention than others. These include the American championship races known as the Triple Crown and the Breeders' Cup for thoroughbreds, the Breeders Crown and the Hambletonian for standardbreds (harness horses), and the American Futurity for quarter horses. There are races for two-year-olds, three-year-olds, and older horses. There are also maiden races for horses that have never won a race before. Other varieties of races include allowance and handicap races, stakes races, and claiming races.

The majority of U.S states have some forms of race betting. Thirty-seven states allow thoroughbred racing, 27 states allow quarter horse racing, and 26 states have harness racing. Additionally, 25 states allow off-track betting, and 39 states have inter-track betting facilities. Every Canadian province has pari-mutuel betting on horse races. The 10 provinces and the Yukon permit harness racing, 7 provinces and the Yukon allow thoroughbred racing, and 9 provinces and the Yukon allow quarter horse race betting. All provinces and the Yukon permit inter-track betting as well as telephone betting and off-track betting. There are also major tracks throughout the world.

In the United States, approximately 6 percent of all gambling losses come from pari-mutuel horse bettors. Although on-track betting has declined a great deal

One of America's leading jockeys—Pat Day—mounts up for a run at the Breeders' Cup at Santa Anita, California.

over the past three decades, the total amount bet on horse races has increased slightly, going up an average of 2.3 percent per year since 1982. (Until 2009, all gambling in the United States increased 10.4 percent each year since 1982.) There are approximately 150 tracks in the United States, with several of these operating only during short fair seasons. Canada has approximately 40 tracks, most of them for harness racing events (National Gambling Impact Study Commission 1999, 2–11; www.HorseRacing .Gambling.com).

Gambling operations have supported racing ever since it became a popular form of entertainment. A variety of betting systems exist, but in modern times, the pari-mutuel system has replaced almost all other systems at North American tracks. Other systems still used in Europe and Asia include pooled and auction betting, as well as betting with bookies who guarantee a horse's odds at the time a bet is placed. In recent years betting revenues have shown only minuscule growth, and tracks have sought other opportunities to gain revenues. They have benefited from inter-track, off-track, and even telephone betting. Many tracks see their future in adding slot machine and video machine gambling (*see* The Racino).

HISTORY OF RACING

Records of horse racing date back to 4000 BCE or earlier. At that time Babylonian soldiers used chariots not only in wartime battles but also in staged races. By 1500 BCE, the Assyrians had developed chariot races as a form of recreation. The early breeds of horses that were available to the peoples of histori-

cal western societies were small in size. It would take two or more horses to pull a chariot, and individual horses could not be mounted by riders. A statue dating to 2000 BCE in a New York museum shows an Egyptian racing a mounted horse, however. In 624 BCE there was a mounted horse race during the 33rd Olympic games in Greece. Records suggest that the Greeks captured stronger horses from Arabs and Persians.

There was very likely betting on the Greek races, as gambling was part of their society. There is little question that the Romans bet on horse races. Races were held in Rome very soon after the city was founded, and racing events became an essential part of the entertainment of the masses of Roman citizens. Racing was also seen as a way of encouraging the development of a better, stronger, faster stock of horses for military use. Romans are credited with bringing their horses to the British Isles, where they raced against and also mixed with Celtic ponies. In about 200 CE, the Romans held their first formal race meeting in England.

During the first millennium, racing captured the attention of civilizations throughout the Mediterranean world and farther east. Arab societies, which fell under the influence of Islam, adhered to prohibitions against gambling, but they made two exceptions. It was permissible to bet on scholarship contests involving children, as doing so encouraged learning the Koran, and it was permissible to bet on horse races, as doing so encouraged improvements in breeding that would result in better horses that could be used in holy battles with the infidel.

In England, horse racing and betting flourished. In the Middle Ages; horse race betting took on its identity as the

Sport of Kings. Henry II established weekly races at fairgrounds in about 1174, and his son John kept a royal stable of racehorses. Serious breeding efforts and formal racetracks date back to the 16th century. Henry VIII passed laws that sought to isolate racing stallions from ordinary horses. He also demanded that each of his dukes and archbishops keep at least seven stallions. The oldest sponsored British race was probably the Chester Cup, which was run in 1512 during Henry's reign. The first stakes race (a race requiring owners to pool money for the winner's prize) was held during King James's reign in the early 17th century. Under James's direction, the racetrack at Newmarket initiated racing. During the Cromwell interlude, a Puritan dominance of England precluded racing, but the activity came back with a vengeance with the Restoration and Charles II. He established new stakes royal races, and in 1674, the king himself mounted a steed and rode to a first-place finish at Newmarket.

Racing developed over the course of the 17th century in England as breeding practices were regularized, lineages were recorded, and tracks were improved. The notion of accurate lineage became even more critical with the arrival of three special horses in England toward the end of the 17th and beginning of the 18th centuries. Every thoroughbred horse running in the world today is descended from one of these three horses: the Byerley Turk, Darley Arabian, and Godolphin Arabian.

In the 17th century, the purest breeds of horses were to be found in Turkey and Arabia. In 1688, British captain Byerley captured a horse from a Turkish officer at Buda. The horse that became known as the Byerley Turk had probably been born in 1680. He was brought to England, where his breeding career began. The second horse was called the Darley Arabian. He was 20 years younger than the Byerley Turk. He was bought by Englishman Thomas Darley at Aleppo in 1704 and sent to a farm in Yorkshire, where he performed stud duties until 1730. One of his sons was sent to North America. The third horse, the Godolphin Arabian, was born in Yemen in 1724. He was first exported to Syria and then to Tunis, where he was given to the king of France. Englishman Edward Coke of Derbyshire purchased the horse in Paris and later sold him to the second Earl of Godolphin for stud at his estate near Newmarket.

The first horses to arrive in the Western Hemisphere came west with the second voyage of Christopher Columbus in 1495. Columbus used horses in his conquest of the indigenous populations in the Caribbean region. Thereafter, every ship from Spain carried horses. Their numbers multiplied in the Caribbean islands, and Spanish conquistador Hernando Cortez took horses from Cuba to Mexico in 1519 and used them as he overwhelmed his Aztec adversaries. Horses soon were being exported to the far reaches of South America. Many were also captured by Native Americans, and some ran off to start a wild horse population on the American plains and into the Southwest. On some occasions horses became part of the food supply for desperate conquistadors and explorers. The Spanish also raced the stock in Cuba and Mexico during the 16th century.

English settlers came to Virginia and New England in the early decades of the 17th century. The first horses arrived at

Jamestown Colony in 1610, but the six mares and one stallion were eaten as other food supplies dwindled during the next winter. Subsequent ships brought more horses, including 20 mares in 1620, and a solid permanent stock of horses was established. The Virginia colonists also purchased horses, descended from Spanish imports, from Native American peoples. As soon as horses were in the American colonies, horse racing began. The Virginia colony passed a law allowing racing in 1630. The previous year, horses arrived in New England. By mid-century, racing was common all along the Eastern seaboard, as the stock of horses was pervasive.

Cleared land was at a premium in these early Colonial years, so most of the racing was on village streets or on narrow paths through woods. The notion of the sprint race developed, a precursor of quarter horse racing, which was popularized in the American West. Originally the betting on races was conducted among the owners of the horses. Disputes over betting and the results of the races were submitted to the law courts for resolution. The first racetrack in the Americas was established by Richard Nicholls, the British governor of New York, immediately after his countrymen had taken hostile possession of New York (New Amsterdam) from Dutch settlers in 1665. Nicholls built a large, oval, wide-open, grass track in present-day Jamaica, Long Island.

Other colonies followed by building their own tracks. The tracks allowed for much longer races. Indeed, the four-mile race became common. Racing was formalized, and large purses were offered to winners. At first, all betting had been among players, but with tracks, entrepreneurs developed systems of pooled betting. A pool seller would offer a wager at set odds, and then he would seek to sell chances on all the horses. If he could not sell all the horses and all the bets in the pool, he would be subject to taking losses on the races. The popularity of the tracks led more and more people to betting, including members of the less wealthy classes. As a result, several colonies passed laws banning racing.

Nevertheless, betting continued through the years leading up to the Revolutionary War. Then the stock of racing horses became critical to the war effort, and racing stopped. Prior to the war, several colonies had developed jockey clubs that established the rules for all the races and to a degree replaced the civil law courts as the arbiters of disputes regarding wagers and race results.

The development of racing stock in Canada has been related to events in other countries, as well as indigenous factors. The French began settlements in Quebec City in 1608. Because the weather was quite severe there and also in other French Canadian settlements, horses were viewed as work animals. They ate and they worked, performing tasks on the farm. They were also used for transportation. The population did not see them as frivolous objects that could be raced for fun. The motherland in Europe—France—did not send horses to Quebec for racing purposes. In France, racing was an activity of royalty. During the French Revolution the rebels who brought down the royalty purposely killed all the racehorses in France, as they were viewed as a symbol of autocracy. There the activity of racing was lost for generations and also lost as an activity that could be exported to North America. By the time of the American Revolution, Quebec was part of a British colonial system. Some French farmers did experiment in developing trotters; however, most of these horses were sold to be raced in the United States. Nonetheless, a horse track opened in Montreal in 1828. Most of the thoroughbreds running in Montreal were initially from the United States. In 1836, however, King William IV of England commissioned a flat race (alternatively called the King's Plate and Queen's Plate) for Canadian-bred horses. Montreal remained the center of Canadian racing for a quarter-century.

Ontario (Upper Canada) developed steeplechases, as an elite aristocratic population familiar with fox hunting had migrated northward during the American Revolution. With an increasing population, Ontario turned its sights to thoroughbreds. In 1860 the Toronto Jockey Club was able to persuade racing officials and horse owners to move the Queen's Plate race to the Woodbine racetrack, where the race is still run. The Civil War years in the United States saw many horses from the South being moved to Ontario. More Canadian tracks developed. Canadian racing also received a boost when the moral authority in the United States caused most racing to be declared illegal in all but a few states in the first decade of the 20th century. This boost, which resulted in many small Canadian tracks being opened, also brought in many corrupting elements. An epidemic of rigged races and other untoward practices resulted in Canada banning racetrack betting in the 1920s. In the 1930s racing was revived with a pari-mutuel system in place.

In the United States, racing had a revival after the Revolutionary War, with most of the action being found in the South. Kentucky established itself as the premier location for horse breeding.

Newly settled western areas attracted racing interests. The era brought an end to long endurance races, as one-mile dashes and quarter-mile runs became popular. Quasi-official "stud books" were initiated to record the identities of all racing horses.

The Civil War devastated racing in the South. Only in the border state of Kentucky did racing continue without interruption. In the meantime, New York reestablished its earlier predominance in the sport. Saratoga Race Course opened in 1863 and became the country's leading facility. Major stakes races were started, the first being the Travers Stakes run at Saratoga in 1864. Three new stakes races were established that later became known as the Triple Crown. These were the Belmont Stakes, first run in New York City in 1867; the Preakness, first run at Baltimore's Pimlico Race Course in 1873; and the Kentucky Derby, which had its initial run at Louisville's Churchill Downs in 1875.

In 1894, the Jockey Club of New York was formed by the leading horse owners. The club set down rules for all thoroughbred racing, and the next year the state legislature decreed that the rules would be enforced on all tracks. Lawmakers in other states also accepted the New York Jockey Club's rules for their own tracks. The Jockey Club also took over the American Stud Book and made it the universal book of registry for all thoroughbreds in the country. The rules and strong organization helped race-track betting survive in New York at the turn of the century, while it was being rendered illegal in most other states. In Kentucky, racing survived with state intervention in the form of the creation of the first state racing commission in the United States in 1906.

A wave of reform at the turn of the 20th century that led to the demise of lotteries and the closing of casinos in the New Mexico Territory, the Arizona Territory, and the state of Nevada also brought most racing to a standstill. Kentucky and Maryland survived as the only states allowing horse race betting through the reform era; policy in New York vacillated between tolerance and prohibition. Racing began its comeback in the 1920s and 1930s as states looked toward gambling activity as a source of tax revenue. The movement for a return to racing was helped with the introduction of the pari-mutuel system, as it centralized all betting, facilitating both control and also taxation. Florida opened the Hialeah racetrack in 1925. A course opened in 1929 at Agua Caliente, Baja California, near Tijuana, serving the desires of California bettors before that state joined nine other states in legalizing pari-mutuel betting in 1933.

Other innovations also strengthened the growth of the sport. Power starting gates ensured that all horses were given an even beginning. Saliva tests were developed that could help ensure that horses were not drugged; they were first used at Saratoga in 1932. In 1936, the first photo-finish camera was used. The popularity of racing was also facilitated by illegal betting, which was encouraged by national bookie organizations that used wire services to instantaneously send information across the country to local street bookies and bookie shops.

During World War II, racing remained a sport demanding public attention. Two horses, Count Fleet and Citation, won the Triple Crown, in 1943 and 1948, respectively. Their presence made racing activity common conversation throughout the land. Horse racing peaked in the 1950s and 1960s with performances of star thoroughbreds such as Nashau, Swaps, and Native Dancer.

In 1966, Walter D. Osborne wrote, "The United States today is in the midst of the greatest boom in horseflesh since the invention of the gasoline engine" (Osborne 1966, 11). What goes up sometimes comes down, however, and since the end of the 1960s, horse racing has been in steady decline. Attendance at races has plunged drastically, and betting at on-track pari-mutuel windows has suffered accordingly. In the last three decades, betting on racing at the tracks has gone from being the most popular form of gambling, with almost a legal monopoly on gambling activities in the United States, to being a very small sector of legal gambling—producing revenues under 7 percent of all legal gambling revenues. Only two factors have saved the betting sport from almost certain oblivion: (1) the introduction of revenues gained from off-track wagering and telephone betting, and (2) the introduction of revenues from other gambling activity taking place on tracks and in card rooms (Hollywood Park, California), gambling machines (nine states and four provinces), and sports betting (Tijuana).

There have been many theories about why racing has declined. Many have suggested that racing lost its edge by clinging to old "proven" methods that worked in an atmosphere of no competition. Racing rejected opportunities to put its entertainment products on television as that media swept American culture in the 1950s and 1960s. Other professional sport events rushed to television. The public gave endorsements to baseball, football, and basketball as never before.

The baby boom generation that began to reach the age of majority in the 1960s did not relate to horses as did their fathers or grandfathers. They were more focused on automobiles as their form of transportation. More important, this emerging and now middle-aged generation was action oriented. Its members wanted their entertainment now, and they wanted entertainment to be constant. They did not see the excitement in watching horses run at a 25-mile-per-hour clip for two minutes and then sit for 30 minutes before the action began again. They might ask why a sports fan would prefer horse racing to an auto race, where cars spin around a track at 200 miles per hour for several hours.

The entertainment consumer of the latter part of the 20th century did not want to have to devote time and energy to understanding what he or she was watching. It was not easy to understand the fine points of horse racing—that is, understanding enough to become a reasonably astute bettor-handicapper. When other forms of gambling—lottery, casino games—became available to these consumers, their desire for racing products naturally declined.

Gaming competition is generally considered to be the major factor in the decline of racing. Additional factors surrounding the decline include the declining and aging condition of racing facilities—stands, betting areas, restrooms. The tax reform legislation in the mid-1980s also took investment incentives away from businesspeople interested in racing.

The decline fed upon itself, because prizes for horse race winners were taken from a betting pool. As bets were reduced in size, so too was money available for prizes. Lower prize money discouraged investors and also kept many from entering their horses in races. The quality of racing was affected as lesser-quality entries were led to the post. In turn, public interest in racing lessened again. The state (and provincial) governments made the situations worse as they often responded to lower betting activity by increasing their tax take from the betting pool. This not only affected prizes but also made the return for bettors less desirable, hence reducing the incentive for betting.

Although tracks realize these factors, they find that reforms are at best stopgap measures allowing them only to barely survive. They must run faster and faster just to stay in place.

TYPES OF RACES

Most horse races involve multiple horses; however, some of the most exciting events in history have been match races between just two horses. One of the most famous was a four-mile run held in 1878 in Louisville, Kentucky, between Ten Broeck, an eastern colt, and Mollie McCarty, a filly from California. The race inspired the song "Molly and Tenbrooks," which as performed by the Stanley Brothers is considered the first song in the bluegrass music genre (see book preface). Other notable match races include a Canadian contest between Man o' War and Sir Barton in 1920, won by Man o' War; a 1938 victory by Seabiscuit over War Admiral at Pimlico; and the race between Nashua and Swaps in 1955. The last famous match race, held in 1975 at Belmont Park, was between the colt Foolish Pleasure and the filly Ruffian. The race ended in tragedy when Ruffian fractured a foreleg during the early stages of the race. Emergency surgery to repair the fracture failed, and the filly was later euthanized. Her remains are buried in the Belmont Park infield.

In addition to races of various distances and races for certain kinds of horses (for example, races for fillies, mares, or colts only, races for horses that have never won before—called maiden races—or races only for two-year-olds or for three-year-olds), there are four basic kinds of races for multiple horses: claiming races, allowance races, handicap races, and stakes races.

Claiming Races

Most races are claiming races. An owner who puts a horse into a claiming race is, in effect, putting the horse up for sale. Registered persons can claim the horse for a price, generally equal to the purse of the race. The claimers must present cash or a certified check to a race official before the race starts. If two or more persons claim the same horse, a roll of the dice decides who purchases the horse. The ownership of the horse changes when the race begins; however, the old owner retains the purse for the race if the horse is a winner. Claiming races are a mechanism for selling horses that have not met the expectations of their owners. The prices received for the horses are generally below those that are exchanged in horse auctions.

Allowance Races

Allowance races are usually a step above claiming races in quality. The track secretary accepts applications for entry and then balances the qualifying horses by adding or subtracting the weight carried by individual horses. A horse that has performed well in the past by winning races and bigger purses carries more weight on the saddle, making the horse have to work harder in the race. A horse that has not won or has won only maiden races or claiming races typically carries less weight. The weights are assigned by a specific formula. There could be a 10-pound difference or more between the horses with the best and worst records.

Handicap Races

As in allowance races, the track secretary assigns extra weight to favored horses in handicap races. The weights, however, are assigned not according to a fixed formula but in accordance with how the secretary feels the horses will perform. The secretary is seeking to truly make the contest "a horse race," that is, a race in which all horses stand relatively the same chances for reaching the finish wire in the lead. In handicap races, the trainers and jockeys know that the racing secretary is seeking to have a balanced race. Therefore, if they gain a very large lead in the race, they tend to adopt a strategy of holding back somewhat so their margin of victory will not be as large as it could be. By winning closely instead of running away with the race, there is a chance that the secretary may not assign as much weight the next time the horse runs in a handicap.

Stakes Races

The most important races are stakes races. In these races the owners pay a fee at the time they apply to enter a horse in the race, then another fee when the track secretary accepts their entry, and a subsequent fee or fees when they appear at the track on the day of the race. All the fees are added into the purse. The leading stakes race in the United States is the Kentucky Derby; other races such as those in the Breeders' Cup series have large fees. An entrant in the Kentucky Derby may incur fees as large as several hundreds of thousands of dollars. The track may also add money into the purse for a stakes race. These races attract the best horses, and they all run carrying the same weights. Most run all out and seek to win by the biggest margins possible. Strong wins in stakes races can be translated into very good prices if the owners wish to sell the horse and also for stud services if the horse is retired.

In all the races fillies and mares are given a five-pound weight allowance— that is, they run with a weight load five pounds lighter than all the other horses in stakes races or claiming races, or five pounds less than they would otherwise carry in allowance or handicap races. There are special races just for fillies and mares; however, there are no races that are exclusively for colts.

RACING PARTICIPANTS

Owners

Owners of horses cover all costs for maintenance and training of the horses, as well as track entry fees for stakes races. Although owners may be serious businesspeople who see racing as a way of accumulating wealth, few owners can actually make money in horse racing. Costs for maintaining a racehorse average $30,000 a year, whereas the typical racehorse achieves winnings that are less than $10,000. In the past, racing attracted many moderately successful businesspeople who calculated the excitement of being in the "racing game" and assumed

there would be losses but that the losses could be subtracted from their business income for tax advantages. The 1986 tax reforms made such write-offs much more difficult; hence many businesspeople moved out of racing. Racing also attracts the rich, who wish to be in the game and have no serious qualms about losses they might incur because their horses cannot win races. Some of these owners willingly pay the very high fees to have their horses entered in major stakes races even if their horses appear to be outclassed, thus giving the best fields of horses several "sure losers," running at odds of 50–1, 60–1, 70–1, or even greater. But then, maybe 1 out of 70 times their horses can score a major upset. The winning owners are given 80 percent of the purse of the race if their horse is the winner. In most cases, to be a winner—of some of the purse—the horse must finish in one of the first four spots. In major races, part of the purse may go to the fifth-place horse. One of the major jobs of the owner is to select a trainer for the horse.

Trainers

The trainer is in charge of the horse 24 hours a day, every day. He or she has been called the "Captain of the Stable" (Scott 1968, 47). The trainer is responsible for doing everything that gets the horse ready to come to the track and race, makes decisions regarding the races in which the horse will run, and advises owners when to sell the horse or when to buy horses. Of course, in these decisions—and the decision to put a horse into a claiming race—he or she must have the approval and confidence of the owner. If there is not a good relationship when these major decisions are made, the trainer may refuse to work for the owner. A trainer receives 10 percent of the purses won by the horses he or she has trained, as well as fees from the horse owner for training services. The trainer picks the facilities for training and keeping the horse and also makes another big decision: he or she chooses the jockey for the races.

Jockeys

Jockeys have to be small, or at least light in weight. The upper weight limit for a jockey is less than 120 pounds. There are no real qualifications for beginning a career as a jockey other than size. Most jockeys just appear at tracks and ask for the work. They are first given menial tasks around the stalls. A person who shows the appropriate amount of dedication, wins the support of stable personnel, and, most important, can get close to a trainer or assistant trainer may move toward being a jockey. The first step in that movement would be to become an "exercise boy." This is a low-status job consisting of walking a horse, either for exercise or for cool downs after an exercise run or a race. After fulfilling a set of general requirements, an aspiring jockey can apply for an apprenticeship license. Once the license is approved by the track stewards, the jockey is able to ride as a professional. He or she must usually start with horses that are not expected to win. The jockey is given a minimal fee for running each race in addition to 10 percent of the purse. On the other hand, jockeys incur expenses. They must invest in all their equipment and outfits including boots, pants, and saddles. They do not have to pay for the specific colors they wear, as these represent the owner. The job of the jockey is very dangerous, and often careers are cut very short by small or major injuries. Many jockeys return to earlier roles such as that of exercise boy or groom—essentially stable hand. Others, of course, become very famous. Those in the latter category use agents, who also take part of their winnings.

RACE OFFICIALS AT THE TRACK

Stewards

Every race meet at a track has three stewards. One is appointed by the track—that is, the racing association; another by the state racing commission; and a third by the local jockey club. The three are essentially the "Supreme Court" of the track. They resolve all disputes arising in races. They also enforce rules, certify the identification of horses, and conduct investigations into any perceived misconduct. For instance, if horses do not run up to their performance, or if a long shot mysteriously finishes in the lead, the stewards will examine the matter closely. They also authorize drug tests for horses, either with reason or on a random basis. All winning horses must be subjected to saliva and urine tests after races. Stewards are empowered to fine or suspend jockeys or trainers for misconduct. Their suspension takes effect on all tracks in the country.

The Racing Secretary

The track secretary creates the races. He or she seeks out the horses to run in the races and in allowance and handicap races is the one who assigns weights to horses. The goal is to produce races that are well matched and even. Sometimes when strong favorites are selected for races, the secretary will use considerable powers of persuasion with trainers and owners to fill a field of horses. The secretary also arranges for the stable accommodations for the racehorses.

The Paddock Judge

The paddock is the area between the stables and the track. The grooms bring the horses out of the stable and walk them around the paddock ring for the entire world—the owners, bettors, and officials—to see. After a walk around the ring, the jockeys mount their horses, and again they walk around the ring. Then they walk off to the track. The paddock judge inspects each horse, examining its appearance, markings, and a tattoo on its lip in order to ensure that there is no "ringer" in the race. In the history of racing, substitute horses have many times been secretly put into the field in order to give selected insiders betting advantages.

The Starter

The starter oversees the entrance of the horses into the starting gate. He encourages the jockeys and grooms to settle the horses down and to ready them for the start. When he is satisfied that all the horses are set, he pushes the button that releases the gate, and "they're off."

Patrol Judges

Each track has at least four patrol judges who closely watch all facets of the race. They seek to see if one horse bumps another or one jockey commits unfair actions, such as grabbing another horse or prodding his mount illegally. They alert other officials to examine a film of the race if they discern irregularities.

They also help the steward resolve complaints registered by race participants.

Placing Judges

Three judges watch the finish line and independently declare which horse finishes first, second, third, and fourth (or fifth if that spot is "in the money.") If they do not have a unanimous agreement, they request a photo of the finish. They also seek photos if the race is close for any of the four positions.

Track Veterinarians

There are veterinarians at each track. The official vet must certify that each horse is physically able to compete in the race. He determines that no illegal drugs have been put into the system of the horses if he suspects they might have been.

The Eclipse Awards

American thoroughbred racing has established the Eclipse Award as its most prestigious award for the leading horses, jockey, owner, and trainer each year. It is named after the great British horse of the 18th century. The awards were first given in 1971, and several of the winners are described in the Selected List of Leading Thoroughbred Horses below.

THE RACING HALL OF FAME AND MUSEUM

The National Museum of Racing and the Thoroughbred Racing Hall of Fame have been established in Saratoga Springs, New York, near the historic Saratoga racetrack. The museum opened its doors in 1950, and the Hall of Fame was created at the site in 1955. As of 2007, the most recent year for which statistics are available, the Hall of Fame included 176 thoroughbreds, 88 jockeys, and 84 trainers. They are selected by a special panel of 125 experts from nominations made by leading media writers and commentators (www.Hall.racingmuseum.org). Among the leading members of the Hall of Fame are the following horses and competitors.

A SELECTED LIST OF LEADING THOROUGHBRED HORSES

Affirmed

Affirmed, the great-grandson of Native Dancer, won the Triple Crown in 1978 under the saddle of Steve Cauthen. In a three-year career, Affirmed won 22 of 29 races and finished out of the money only one time. Affirmed was owned by Louis Wolfson and trained at his Harbor View Farm in Florida. As two-year-olds, Affirmed and his great rival Alydar began a series of 10 races that captured the attention of all horse enthusiasts. They raced six times as two-year-olds, with Affirmed victorious four times. As three-year-olds, Affirmed finished first and Alydar second in all Triple Crown races—the only time two horses have done that. In a subsequent meeting, the Travers Stakes, Affirmed won again but was disqualified. Affirmed finished his Triple Crown year with a loss to previous year's Triple Crown winner, Seattle Slew, and then had an out-of-the-money finish in a race where his saddle slipped. Nonetheless, Affirmed was proclaimed Horse of the Year. As a four-year-old he repeated the honor of being Horse of the Year.

Barbaro

"America's Horse," "An Inspiration," "An American Tragedy." In a name: Barbaro. This remarkable horse became the nation's hope to win the Triple Crown in 2006. Three-year-old Barbaro, born April 29, 2003, entered the Kentucky Derby undefeated, with major victories in the Laurel Futurity, the Tropical Park Derby, and the Florida Derby. His run for the roses satisfied all as he galloped to a six and one-half length win—the largest margin of victory since that of Assault in 1946. The decisive victory gave American racing fans hope that they would finally see another Triple Crown winner.

But it was not to be. Barbaro went to post two weeks later as the heavy favorite to win the Preakness. However, before the race began he bolted out of the starting gate. He had to be settled down before the race could officially start. Then he broke cleanly with the pack, but within a hundred yards he appeared to take a bad step. Veteran jockey Edgar Prado brought him to a gentle stop, but the damage was done. Barbaro had shattered his right hind leg in more than 20 places. Barbaro was taken to the New Bolton Center at the University of Pennsylvania. There he underwent many operations and constant treatment. The nation began an eight-month vigil, many praying for his recovery. However, racehorses are not built to withstand such serious injuries. They are too top heavy and unbalanced, and when they shift weight away from one injured leg, the pressure on other legs takes a toll. Barbaro developed a severe case of laminitis, first in his left hind leg, and then in both front legs. In early 2007, the complications became overwhelming, and on January 29, 2007, Barbaro was peacefully euthanized.

The case of Barbaro has raised several issues for animal lovers. Was he prepared for the rigors of the race? Are racehorses bred to have brittle bones in order to enhance their speed? Is a three-year-old too young to race? Many animal rights advocates suggested that racing itself was brutal for horses. The issues have come front and center for debate, but without resolution, the controversy goes on.

Cigar

Cigar ran to 19 victories in 33 starts over a four-year career. His mark of fame came in 1996 when as a six-year-old he galloped to his 16th consecutive win, tying a record set by Citation. Cigar was raised at Allen Paulsen's Brookside Farm in Kentucky, after being born in Maryland. He was the great-grandson of Northern Dancer. The future champion did not race until he was three years old, and he bypassed the Triple Crown races. He won only two of nine races as a three-year-old, and it was discovered that he had chips in the bones of each knee. Arthroscopic surgery corrected the trouble, but he still won only two of six races as a four-year-old. The wins came in his last two races that year, and they were the beginning of a streak. In 1995, in the Donn Handicap, his leading challenger was Holy Bull, the 1994 Horse of the Year. Holy Bull took a misstep during the race and incurred a career-ending injury, and Cigar went on to win. Critics discounted Cigar's victory even though he was leading when Holy Bull's accident happened. Soon, however, Cigar was defeating other top-class fields, winning the Pimlico Special Handicap, the

Massachusetts Handicap, the Hollywood Gold Cup, the Woodward Stakes, the Jockey Club Gold Cup, and, most impressively, the 1995 Breeders' Cup Classic. The season was a perfect 10 for 10, and Cigar's winning streak was at 12. Cigar won Horse of the Year honors as well as the Eclipse Award as the older male champion. In 1996, Cigar raced to four straight victories, winning the Dubai World Cup, the Donn Handicap, the Massachusetts Handicap, and finally the Arlington Citation Challenge, which tied Citation's record. That sixteenth win came in a race especially created for a national television audience.

Cigar had tied Citation's record, but the chance for 17 victories in a row was lost when his jockey, Jerry Bailey, could not slow his pace, and he succumbed to exhaustion and a second-place finish, three and a half lengths behind Dare and Go in the Pacific Classic at Del Mar. He won one more time before being retired to stud. His career produced winnings of $9,999,815. The prize money was his crowning glory, as he was a failure at stud. He was sterile. Cigar was moved to the Kentucky Horse Park in Lexington so that his many admiring fans could come and look him over—another kind of pleasurable retirement.

Citation

Citation, a bay colt, won the Triple Crown for Calumet Farms in 1948. He competed four years: 1947, 1948, 1950, and 1951. He ran 45 times, with 32 firsts, 10 seconds, 2 thirds, and only 1 out-of-the-money run. Injuries kept Citation off the track in 1949, and the horse never regained his Triple Crown form afterwards, but his owner, Warren Wright, requested that he keep running in order to become the first $1 million purse winner. Citation accomplished that for his owner, retiring in the middle of the 1951 season. In the course of his racing career, Citation put together a string of 16 wins, a record that held for over five decades until it was equaled by Cigar. Citation was a horse with both speed and staying power and a "killer's instinct" that craved victory.

Count Fleet

Count Fleet ran only two years, competing in 21 races, winning 16, placing second in 4, and third in 1. Among Count Fleet's victories were the Triple Crown races in 1943, in which he was ridden by the legendary Johnny Longden. Count Fleet was the offspring of the 1928 Kentucky Derby winner, Reigh Count, and Quickly, a sprint filly. Because Count Fleet had suffered a hoof injury during the Wood Memorial, many horses showed up to challenge him in the Kentucky Derby. He was still the favorite, and he won over Blue Swords by three lengths. That did it for most of the others. Only three challengers showed up for the Preakness, where he galloped to a win over Blue Swords by eight lengths. That made the Belmont only a three-horse race, and Count Fleet flew by the competition, winning by 25 lengths, a margin unsurpassed in any Triple Crown event until Secretariat's Belmont run of 1973. Count Fleet's time was a record for the Belmont, and he actually won with an injured ankle. He was immediately retired to stud. There he continued his greatness, as he became racing's leading sire. He fathered 38 stakes winners, as well as female offspring that produced another 119 stakes winners, including the great Kelso. Count Fleet lived until age 33, dying in 1973.

Curlin

Curlin was born March 25, 2004, in Kentucky. Both as a three-year-old and as a four-year-old, Curlin won the Eclipse Award for Horse of the Year. Curlin amassed in excess of 10 million dollars in winnings, making him the all-time leading earner in North America. As a three-year-old, Curlin entered the Kentucky Derby as the favorite. However, he only finished third. Two weeks later he won the Preakness by a head, and he became the favorite to win the Belmont Stakes. There he lost to Rags to Riches in a fantastic sprint to the finish. The best was yet to come. In October 2007, Curlin won the Breeders' Cup Classic at Monmouth Park, New Jersey. As a four-year-old, Curlin triumphed in the Dubai World Cup.

Eclipse

The "first champion" English thoroughbred, Eclipse, was foaled in 1764. Eclipse was a great-great-grandson of the Darley Arabian. He began training and racing at age five and ran matched heats of four miles each. He won every race he entered, but his true fame is for posterity. Over 80 percent of all racing thoroughbreds today can trace their bloodlines to this champion.

John Henry

John Henry started in 83 races over an eight-year career. He won 39 and was second 15 times, while amassing $6,591,860 in prizes. He was born in 1975 at Kentucky's Golden Chance Farm, and with his humble pedigree and poor conformation, seemingly no one wanted the horse. After being sold several times early in his career, when he was a three-year-old, he was purchased sight unseen for the modest amount of $25,000. His career got off to a slow start, but in 1980, he hit his stride as he won 6 straight stakes races. In 1981, he won 8 of his 10 starts. In the most recognized of his runs that year, he was ridden by Bill Shoemaker as he won the inaugural running of the Arlington Million. John Henry won the Eclipse Award for older horses and also was named Horse of the Year. Over the next two years, injuries kept his starts down, but in 1984 he returned to prominence with 6 victories in 9 races. In 1985, he retired to the Kentucky Horse Park as the leading money winner at that time. John Henry died in 2007 at the age of 32.

Kelso

In 1960, Kelso was voted the champion male three-year-old and also the Horse of the Year. He won 8 of 9 races. The honors came even though he did not run that year until after the Triple Crown series had ended. But once running, he kept running, for six more years, amassing a total of 39 victories (31 in stakes races), as well as 12 seconds in his 63 starts. He won $1,977,896 in prizes. Kelso was durable, winning a record five designations as Horse of the Year. He also set track records at eight different courses. Often he ran with the disadvantage of extra weights as race organizers tried to give the competition a chance. Kelso was born in 1957 at Claiborne Farm in Paris, Kentucky. He retired after running only one start in 1966 at the age of nine. He lived to be 26, dying at owner Allaire du Pont's Woodstock Farm in Maryland in 1983.

Man o' War

Man o' War was designated the greatest horse of the 20th century by the *Blood-Horse* magazine. All agree that he was the "super horse" of 1919 and 1920, winning all of his eleven races the latter year. As he was not entered in the Kentucky Derby, he did not achieve the Triple Crown. Nonetheless Man o' War, called "Big Red," is still considered by some to be the greatest racehorse in history. In his two-year career, out of 21 starts he had 20 first-place finishes and only one second place. His second-place finish came in the 1919 Sanford Stakes when he lost to a decided underdog by the name of Upset. As a result of that race a new word, *upset,* was introduced into the vocabulary of sports enthusiasts and applied to victories by underdogs. In his final race, the Kenilworth Gold Cup, he defeated Sir Barton, the previous year's Triple Crown winner, by seven lengths. Man o' War also was accomplished at stud, as he fathered War Admiral, the Triple Crown winner of 1937. Man o' War lived to be 30. He died in 1947, and his funeral was broadcast by radio to the nation. The site of his grave, now at the Kentucky Horse Park, is marked by a 3,000-pound sculptured likeness.

Native Dancer

Native Dancer was born on the Scott Farm near Lexington, Kentucky, in March 1950, and he was raised on owner Alfred Vanderbilt's Sagamore Farm in Maryland. In 1952, as a two-year-old, Native Dancer ran to nine straight victories, sharing Horse of the Year honors with One Count. He won his first race at Jamaica in April 1952, and his second race only four days later. The frequency of his races was probably a training error, as he had to be rested for three months with bruised shins. He again picked up his frantic pace, however, winning the Flash Stakes at Saratoga and then three more races within the next three weeks. He added four more victories before the end of the season. In 1953 he earned victories in the Gotham Stakes and the Wood Memorial and became the heavy favorite to win the Kentucky Derby going away. That victory proved to be elusive, however. In the first turn of the race he was bumped by a long shot, and he ended up in heavy traffic. Finally he burst loose from the crowd and charged at the leader, Dark Star, gaining on him all the way. Alas, "all the way" was not long enough; the finish line came too soon. Native Dancer finished second by a head. Two weeks later, Native Dancer defeated Dark Star and the field in the Preakness. He kept on winning—the Belmont Stakes, the Dwyer Stakes at Aqueduct, the Arlington Classic, and the Travers Stakes. At age four, he added three more victories, and once again earned Horse of the Year honors, after which he was retired, with a record of 21 wins in 22 races. At stud at Sagamore Farm, he sired 44 stakes winners, including Kentucky Derby winner Kauai King. Native Dancer was the grand sire of Mr. Prospector—one of the greatest sires of all time—and he also sired the mother of Canada's greatest horse, Northern Dancer. Native Dancer died in 1967.

Phar Lap

Phar Lap was born in New Zealand in 1926. He was given his name by a stable hand. The name means "lightening" in Thai. Phar Lap became known by many as "Australia's Wonder Horse." In 1928, he was purchased by Australians and moved to the place of his many triumphs. He got off to a slow start, as he lost his first four races before winning a maiden race in 1929. Soon his winning ways were established. In 1930, he won the famous Melbourne Cup race, and in 1931 he won 14 consecutive races. In a four-year career, he posted 37 wins out of 51 starts, often carrying much greater weight than his competition.

Phar Lap's final race was run at Agua Caliente in Tijuana, Mexico. The race offered the largest purse ever given in a North American race. Almost without noticeable effort, he won by a large margin. After the race, his owners arranged for him to tour America. First they took him to a ranch in Menlo Park, California, for a rest. There, on April 5, 1932, only a month after his race, he was taken ill with a stomach affliction. Within hours, he hemorrhaged to death.

There has been speculation to this day about the cause of his death. Did he eat the wrong food, or perhaps grass that had been sprayed with chemicals? Or, was he deliberately poisoned? Some feel organized crime elements wanted him dead because bookies lost considerable amounts of money each time he ran.

Rags to Riches

"Queen for a Day." Rags to Riches was born on February 27, 2004, in Kentucky. She was a granddaughter of Triple Crown winner Seattle Slew, and a great-granddaughter of Secretariat. As a two-year-old she only had a single race, a sprint in which she could not even show. As a three-year-old, her trainer, Todd Pletcher, made sure to place her in longer races. In these, she developed a powerful finishing kick. She won the Santa Anita Oaks, but Pletcher decided to keep her out of the

Kentucky Derby as he had two other horses in that race. After she won the Kentucky Oaks, Pletcher set his eyes on the longest of the Triple Crown races—the Belmont, at one and a half miles long. It was her first race against male horses. After a stumble at the start, Rags to Riches recovered and moved around the track with the leading pack. At the top of the stretch she pulled even with Curlin, and it was a two horse sprint to the wire, with Rags to Riches winning by a head under jockey John Velazquez. She had become the first filly to win the Belmont in more than one hundred years and the first to win a Triple Crown race since 1988.

In the fall of 2007, Rags to Riches suffered a hairline fracture during her run in the Gazelle Stakes at Belmont. She trained again as a four-year-old, but was retired after a re-injury to her leg.

Secretariat

Secretariat was a very strong chestnut colt born on March 30, 1970. He was known as "Big Red," the same nickname as Man o' War had. Secretariat's father was Bold Ruler, Horse of the Year in 1957, and his mother Somethingroyal, a horse who never ran a race. The greatest horse of the last half-century was owned by Penny Chenery and carried the blue and white colors of Meadow Stable. Secretariat was trained by Lucien Laurin and ridden by jockey Ron Turcotte. As a two-year-old he lost his first race but then showed dominance in the next eight runs, winning all but the last, which he lost as a result of a disqualification. He was named Horse of the Year in 1972. In 1973, he was ready for the Triple Crown. His warm-up races went fine until he had a weak performance in the Wood Memorial owing to a painful abscess. Although many doubted

that he had the stamina, he was ready for the Kentucky Derby. He won going away in record time of 1:59:40, becoming the first horse to win the Derby in under two minutes. In the Preakness, he won by two and a half lengths, in what would have been a record time if the track clock had not malfunctioned. His competition was intimidated, and there were only five horses entered in the Belmont. Secretariat left them in the dust, winning by a phenomenal 31 lengths, in a record time of 2:24, more than two seconds faster than the track record. His final race was at the Canadian International at Woodbine Racetrack in Toronto, after which he again was named Horse of the Year. He retired to stud at Claiborne Farm in Lexington, where in addition to the mares, he attracted over 10,000 visitors a year until he died in 1989. The source of Secretariat's extraordinary stamina was discovered after his death, when an autopsy revealed that his heart was 50 percent larger than normal size.

LEADING THOROUGHBRED JOCKEYS

Eddie Arcaro

Eddie Arcaro was born in Cincinnati in 1916. He rode in his first race at the age of 15 in Cleveland, but he had to wait almost a year for his first victory, which came at the Agua Caliente track in Tijuana. He soon won a contract to ride exclusively for Calumet Farms and then with the Greentree Stable of the Whitney family. In 1946, he became an independent. Arcaro was the first and only jockey to have ridden two Triple Crown winners—Whirlaway in 1941 and Citation in 1948. Over a career spanning 30 years he rode in 24,092 races, winning 4,779 of them and finishing in the money almost 12,000 times. He won the Kentucky Derby five times and the Preakness and the Belmont six times each. His success was earned with a riding style that seemed to have horse and rider always as one. It also came from the quality of his many mounts: five-time Horse of the Year Kelso, Bold Ruler, Native Dancer, Nashua, and, of course, the two Triple Crown winners. Eddie Arcaro died in 1997 at the age of 81.

Jerry Bailey

Jerry Bailey was born in Dallas in 1957. He was drawn into racing when his father purchased several horses at claiming races. Bailey started racing quarter horses when he was only 12. When he was 17, he turned to thoroughbreds and took his first mount in a professional race. He has been racing ever since. Seven times he has been selected as the winner of the Eclipse Award for jockey of the year. He won two Kentucky Derbies, with Sea Hero in 1993 and Grindstone in 1996, and rode 15 winners in Breeders' Cup races. In 1995, he was inducted into the racing Hall of Fame. One of his most notable claims to fame came as the jockey who rode Cigar in 1994 and 1995, as the horse was Horse of the Year both years. Bailey has been the president of the Jockeys' Guild. He retired from racing in 2006 having amassed 5,892 wins.

Steve Cauthen

Steve Cauthen became a sports phenom as a teenager. He was named *Sports Illustrated* Sportsman of the Year in 1977 at the age of 17. Steve began riding when he was only five. He began racing in 1976, immediately setting track records. At River Downs he won 94 races in his first 50 days of racing. From there he moved on to Arlington Park, Aqueduct, and Belmont. In his second year, records continued to fall as he won a record $6.1 million in purses. But the best came in 1978 as he guided Affirmed to victory in the Triple Crown. He was the youngest jockey ever to win any Triple Crown race. In 1979, however, he experienced a losing streak and then accepted an offer to move to England, where he rode for the rest of his career. While fighting weight problems and also alcohol dependency, he was still able to win, becoming the number-one English rider in 1984, 1985, and 1987. A severe fall in 1988 kept him out of action for most of a season; nevertheless he returned to race for another year, after which he retired at age 33. He moved back to his home state of Kentucky, where he raises horses.

Angel Cordero

Angel Cordero Jr. was born on May 8, 1942 in Santurce, Puerto Rico. In a career spanning 31 years, he registered 7,057 wins in 38,646 starts and won purses totaling $164 million. His wins included three in the Kentucky Derby, two in the Preakness, and one in the Belmont Stakes. He also had four winners in Breeders' Cup races, with more than $6 million in Breeders' Cup earnings. Cordero won the Eclipse Award for outstanding jockey two times, in 1982 and 1983. An inspirational figure, he once remarked, "If a horse has four legs, and I'm riding it, I think I can win."

But he could not win them all. In 1992, he retired after almost dying in a spill at Aqueduct racetrack in New York. He then became an agent and trainer. However, in 1995, he did saddle up for one more run in the Breeders' Cup. Tragedy struck the Corderos again in January 2001, when Angel's wife, Marjorie, was killed in a hit-and-run accident while jogging at night. Marjorie herself had been a very popular jockey, winning 71 races between 1982 and 1985.

Pat Day

Pat Day was born on October 13, 1953, in Brush, Colorado. He was drawn into racing after competing in high school and amateur rodeos. He thought he should turn to racing because of his slight build. At age 19 he moved to California and started riding thorough-breds. He won his first race in 1973. Notable wins include a victory in the Kentucky Derby aboard Lil E.Tee in 1992, five wins in the Preakness, and three wins in the Belmont. He became one of the leading winners among Breeders' Cup jockeys, with 12 wins. He led the country in number of wins six different times. He won the Eclipse Award for outstanding jockey in 1984, 1986, 1987, and 1991. He was inducted into the racing Hall of Fame in 1991. He is ranked first in all-time earnings among jockeys. In 2005, he retired having ridden 8,803 mounts to victory.

Garrett K. Gomez

Garrett K. Gomez was born in Tucson, Arizona, in 1972. He learned racing from a father who was also a jockey. Gomez began competitive racing in New Mexico in 1988 and continued his early career at the Ak-Sar-Ben track in Omaha. After achieving notable victo-ries in the Arkansas Derby, he moved his activities to California where he rode for prominent trainer Robert Frankel. In 2006, Gomez won two Breeders' Cup races, which launched two very success-ful years to follow. In both 2007 and 2008 he won the Eclipse Award for being the top jockey in America. In 2007 he won 76 stakes races—a record—in addition to two more Breeders' Cup races. In 2008, he won the Pacific Clas-sic and the Travers Stakes.

Bill Hartack

Bill Hartack was born in Blacklick Valley, Pennsylvania, in 1932. He took up riding in his late teenage years, and in a profes-sional career lasting from 1952 to 1974 he won 4,272 races, capturing purses of $26 million. His many winners included five mounts at the Kentucky Derby, a feat equaled only by Eddie Arcaro. Hartack was the leading jockey in number of wins in four different years and the leading money winner twice. He was known as a stickler for many details and an antagonist to the press and the general public. He was always at his best while steering his horse around the track and at his worst in the winner's circle, refusing to give interviews and making caustic remarks to those around him. It was reported that he hated the media because they insisted on calling him "Willie." After retirement in 1974, he worked as a steward at racetracks in California. Hartack died in 2007 at age 74.

Julie Krone

Julie Krone was born in Benton Harbor, Michigan, in 1963. She is a Hall of Fame member with the all-time most wins of any female jockey—3,704. She accomplished this record over a career that spanned nearly 20 years. Her most notable win was in the 1993 Belmont Stakes, when she became the first woman to win a Triple Crown race. She also matched Angel Cordero's and Ron Turcotte's record of having five winners on the same day at Saratoga. Besides winning the Belmont, Krone rode winners in the Arlington Classic, Meadowlands Cup, Jersey Derby, Carter Handicap, and Delaware Handicap. Her career was marred by several accidents that eventually led to her first retirement in 1999. She subsequently returned to racing in 2002, but retired again in 2004, although she has run in an "old timers" race. In 2000, she became the first female rider elected to racing's Hall of Fame.

Johnny Longden

Johnny Longden was born in England in 1907. He was raised in Canada. He became the leading jockey of his era. He was the first jockey to win 6,000 races; by the end of his riding career at the age of 59 in 1966 he had won 6,032 races. This stood as a record until Willie Shoemaker surpassed the number in 1970. Longden's purses totaled $24.6 million. His most notable achievement was riding Count Fleet to victory in the Triple Crown in 1943. His career demonstrated his great spirit and his love of horses. He broke both arms, both legs, both ankles, his feet, and his collarbone in racing accidents, along with six ribs and several vertebrae. His arthritis slowed him down enough to cause his retirement as a jockey. But his maladies could not keep him away from the track. Three years after retiring as a rider, he became a trainer, leading Majestic Prince to a

Kentucky Derby win. He is the only person to have Kentucky Derby wins as both a jockey and a trainer. But there was more—he was also Majestic Prince's exercise boy, groom, and stable-cleaner.

Laffit Pincay

Laffit Pincay was born in Panama City, Panama, on December 29, 1946. He started racing professionally at the Presidente Ramon racetrack in Panama at age 17, and two years later he moved to the United States. Success followed as he became the all-time leading jockey at Hollywood Park, Santa Anita, and Del Mar. One day he won a record seven races at Santa Anita. He was the nation's leading jockey in earnings seven times, and he won the Eclipse Award as the top jockey five time. He biggest win came at the 1984 Kentucky Derby. He also won the Belmont Stakes three times in a row and had seven wins in Breeders' Cup races. He took several spills with his victories, showing great fortitude. He broke his collarbone 11 times and his ribs 10 times; he had two spinal fractures, two broken thumbs, and a sprained ankle. At the time of his retirement in 2003, Pincay's 9,530 wins placed him as the all-time leader in career victories. (In 2006, jockey Russell Baze surpassed his number of wins.) Pincay passed Willie Shoemaker's accomplishments in a 35-year period. He retired in 2003.

Willie Shoemaker

Willie Shoemaker was born in 1931 in Fabens, Texas, moving to California as a child, where he started riding. At age 17 he rode in his first professional race, and after a month he rode his first winner. By age 22 he had ridden a record 485 wins in a single year. He just kept winning and winning. On six occasions he won six races in a single day. In 1970, he passed Johnny Longden as the leading winner as he rode across the finish line in first place for the 6,033rd time. By the end of his 41-year riding career in 1990 he had ridden 8,833 winners. In 10 different years he was the leading money winner among jockeys. Overall he produced purse wins of more than $123 million, being the first jockey to have wins of over $100 million. He won 1,009 stakes races. On four occasions he won the Kentucky Derby, the last time in 1986 at age 54. He was the oldest jockey ever to win the race. He also had two wins in the Preakness and five wins in the Belmont stakes. After retiring, he became a trainer. His career success came at serious costs. He suffered broken legs and hips from falls during races. His most devastating injury came in a car accident in 1991, however, the year after he retired from racing. The accident left him paralyzed below the neck. He continued in an advisory role as a trainer at Santa Anita, the scene of so many victories over his career, until his retirement in 1997. He died October 12, 2003.

Ron Turcotte

Ron Turcotte will always be known as the jockey who rode the great Secretariat to the Triple Crown in 1973. But he did more than just that outstanding feat. He also won the Kentucky Derby and Belmont aboard Riva Ridge in 1972, giving him victories in five of six Triple Crown race in two years. He also rode Tom Rolfe to victory in the Preakness in 1965, and he rode Northern Dancer as a two-year-old. Turcotte was a French Canadian, born in Drummond, New Brunswick, on June 22, 1941. He was one of 12 children. He dropped out of school at the age of 13 in order to work as a logger. In that work, he began to ride horses. As a result, he was drawn to racetracks and set his sights on becoming a jockey, but he had to work up to it. He moved to Toronto and its Woodbine track in 1959 and started cleaning stables, then walking horses, and then giving them workout rides. In 1961, he became an apprentice jockey. Success followed each step of the way. In 1962, he had 180 wins, and in 1963 he was the leading jockey in Canada. In that year he also began racing in the United States at Laurel and Saratoga. His U.S. career received a big boost with his Preakness win on Tom Rolfe in 1965. He was hired to ride for Meadow Stable, where he was given the reins of Secretariat when the horse was a two-year-old and won Horse of the Year honors. He retired in 1978 and was elected to the Hall of Fame the next year.

John R. Velazquez

John R. Velazquez won the Eclipse Award winner for outstanding jockey in both 2004 and 2005. He was born in Puerto Rico in 1971 and learned to ride under the tutelage of Angel Cordero Jr. When he came to the United States, he first raced in New York, where his titles at Belmont, Saratoga, and Aqueduct launched a career that now includes more than 4,000 victories. His most notable wins include six Breeders' Cup races, the Kentucky Oaks, the Dubai World Cup, and the Woodbine Mile. In 2007, he won his first Triple Crown race aboard Rags to Riches in the Belmont Stakes.

TRAINERS

Steve Asmussen

Steve Asmussen won the Eclipse Award for trainers in 2008. He was born in South Dakota in 1965, and raised in Laredo, Texas. At the age of 16, he was a jockey. However, he had to give up that career as he added body weight, and at 21 he began training thoroughbred and quarter horses. In 2002, he produced 407 winners, and in 2004, a record 555 wins. His most notable triumphs were with Curlin, the 2007 winner of the Preakness and the Breeders' Cup Classic. In 2008, Asmussen had another record year, with 622 victories.

Bob Baffert

Bob Baffert was born in Nogales, Arizona, on January 13, 1953. He was a professional jockey before turning to training quarter horses. He trained Gold Coast Express, the champion quarter horse of 1986, before turning his attention to thoroughbreds. Within his first decade as a thoroughbred trainer, he guided the careers of five national champions. He won the Eclipse Award as the leading trainer in 1997. In both 1997 and 1998, he won the first two legs of the Triple Crown with Kentucky Derby and Preakness victories with Silver Charm and Real Quiet. In 2001 he won both the Preakness and Belmont stakes with Point Given, and in 2003 the Kentucky Derby and Preakness with War Emblem. He has also won two Breeders' Cup races. In 2009, Baffert was inducted into racing's Hall of Fame.

Jim Fitzsimmons

James E. "Sunny Jim" Fitzsimmons was born in 1874. He began exercising horses when he was 10, and he paid his dues by cleaning stables, grooming horses, and then becoming a jockey. He went on to become one of the most famous trainers of all time, not retiring until he was 89 years old in 1963. In a training career spanning three-quarters of a century, his horses won 2,275 races and purses exceeding $13 million. His most notable claims to fame were his two Triple Crown winners, Gallant Fox in 1930 and Omaha in 1935. He also won the Kentucky Derby with Johnstown in 1939. In addition, he trained Eclipse Award winners Bold Ruler, Granville, High Voltage, Misty Morn, Vagrancy, and Nashua. Fitzsimmons was inducted into racing's Hall of Fame in 1958. He died at the age of 92 in 1966.

Robert J. Frankel

Trainer Robert J. Frankel was born in Brooklyn, New York, in 1941. He started training on his own in 1966 in New York, afterwards moving to California. There he won 60 races at Hollywood Park in 1972. Since that time he has won Breeders' Cup races several times. In 1995, he was inducted into racing's Hall of Fame. He won the Eclipse Award for best trainer in 1993, 2000, 2001, and 2003.

Ben Jones

Ben Jones was born in 1882. He spent 47 years as a trainer. He was the key figure in building Calumet Farms into the leading owner of winning horses eleven times in the 1940s and 1950s. He trained Triple Crown winner Whirlaway for Calumet, and he took over the general managership of the farm in 1947, just as

Citation's racing career began. He gave the reins of Citation to his son Jim, who trained the colt for his successful run at the Triple Crown in 1948. Ben Jones produced 1,519 winners as a trainer, earning purses of nearly $5 million. Counting Citation, his six wins at the Kentucky Derby are the most ever for a trainer.

Lucien Laurin

Lucien Laurin was born in 1912. He began his career with horses as a jockey, riding 161 winners before he turned to training in 1942. Laurin trained 1973 Triple Crown winner Secretariat and also 1972 Kentucky Derby and Belmont winner Riva Ridge for Meadow Stable. His four consecutive victories in Triple Crown races stood as a trainer's record until D. Wayne Lucas won five in a row. Laurin trained 36 stakes winners over the course of a career that spanned four decades. Lucien Laurin died in May 2000 at the age of 88.

D. Wayne Lucas

D. Wayne Lucas was born in Antiga, Wisconsin, in 1935. By the mid-1980s he emerged as the leading contemporary trainer. He has also been important as the purchasing agent selecting several champion horses. Lucas graduated from the University of Wisconsin, where he was also an assistant basketball coach. He began training horses in the late 1960s. Lucas was inducted into the racing Hall of Fame in 1999 after having been the top money-earning thoroughbred trainer in 14 different years. His wins have included the Kentucky Derby on four occasions, the Preakness five times, the Belmont four times, and eighteen Breeders' Cup races. He won the Eclipse Award as the leading trainer in 1985, 1986, 1987, and 1994. In 1994, 1995, and 1996 he set a trainer's record when he won six consecutive Triple Crown races.

William I. Mott

William I. Mott was born in Mobridge, South Dakota, in 1953. He started training horses while he was still in high school, winning many races in the unrecognized meets of South Dakota. In 1978, he joined the stable of trainer Jack Van Berg, where he worked until 1986. Then he became the trainer for owners Bert and Diana Firestone before becoming independent. At age 45, Mott was the youngest trainer ever to be inducted into the racing Hall of Fame. His major claim to fame was supported by the record of Cigar, who twice earned Horse of the Year honors. Mott has also won five Breeders' Cup races.

Todd Pletcher

Todd Pletcher was born in Dallas, Texas, in 1967. While a student at the Race Track Industry Program of the University of Arizona in the late 1980s, he began working with D. Wayne Lucas and Charles Whittingham as a groom. In 1991, he became assistant trainer for Lucas. In 1995, he ventured out on his own. In 2004, Pletcher had two winners in the Breeders' Cup, and another in the Kentucky Oaks. In 2005, his horses won the Travers Stakes and the Blue Grass Stakes, and in 2006 he led all trainers in the numbers of stakes winners. In 2007, his Rags to Riches won the Belmont Stakes. Pletcher won four consecutive Eclipse Awards as the top trainer of 2004, 2005, 2006, and 2007.

Woody Stephens

Woodford Cefis "Woody" Stephens was born a sharecropper's son on September 1, 1913, in Midway, Florida. He died in 1998 just before his 85th birthday. Woody Stephens started his career with horses as a jockey in 1930. Ten years later he became a trainer, a trade he continued for 57 years. Stephens's most notable achievement was winning the Belmont Stakes five consecutive times in the 1980s. He also had two Kentucky Derby winners and one Preakness winner. He also trained eleven national champions—only D. Wayne Lucas trained more. He was elected to the Hall of Fame in 1976 and was given the Eclipse Award as the leading trainer in 1983. Stephens retired in 1997.

Charlie Whittingham

Charlie Whittingham was born on April 13, 1913. He lived to the age of 86 and came to be known to some as the greatest trainer ever. It was certain that he was the oldest trainer ever to have a Kentucky Derby winner. He was 73 when Ferdinand claimed the roses, and he was 76 when Sunday Silence was first across the finish line in Louisville. Whittingham's leading rider during his career was Willie Shoemaker.

Whittingham followed horses from the age of eight, as his older brother was a jockey. He began training horses in 1934. His 60-year career brought him three Eclipse Awards as the leading trainer and Hall of Fame induction in 1974. He trained 11 national champions and three horses named as Horse of the Year—Ack Ack, Ferdinand, and Sunday Silence. He was the all-time winningest trainer at both Santa Anita and Hollywood Park. His amazing career also included a tour of duty with the marines in the South Pacific during World War II. He died in California on April 20, 1999.

Nicholas Zito

Nicholas Zito was born in New York City in 1948. When he was nine years old he started attending the horse races with his father, who had done service as an exercise attendant. At the age of 15, Zito got a job as a handyman in the race-track stables. He moved up the career ladder as an exercise boy, then a groom, and slowly worked toward being a trainer. He learned every step of the way. In the early 1970s, he won his opportunity, training his first horse in 1972. But even then success came slowly. In the 1980s, he teamed up with owner B. Giles Brophy and the keys to success were in his hands. In 1996, he won his first Triple Crown race with a victory in the Preakness. In 1991 he won the Kentucky Derby with Strike the Gold and again in 1994 with Go for Gin. He was only the fifteenth trainer ever to have two Kentucky Derby winners. He won Belmont Stakes races in 2004 and 2008. In 2005, Zito was elected to the Hall of Fame.

TRACKS AND TRACK ORGANIZATIONS

Churchill Downs, Inc.

Churchill Downs is the premier thoroughbred racing track in North America. The track is part of a larger organization (Churchill Downs, Inc.) that has included Hollywood Park, Arlington International, Ellis Park, Hoosier Park, and Calder Race Course as well as the New Orleans Fair Grounds and the Churchill Downs Sports Spectrum (an off-track facility) and other interests.

Churchill Downs is located within the city of Louisville, Kentucky, close to the bluegrass horse farms that breed a majority of racing stock in the United States. Racing started at Churchill in 1875, and that was also the inaugural year of the Kentucky Derby, the most famous race in the United States and the lead event in the Triple Crown. The Kentucky Derby is run over a one and one-quarter-mile distance. Colonel M. Lewis, who was the president of the track for 20 years, established the race. As racing fell into disrepute around the turn of the century (as did all gambling-related activities), the Derby declined in prominence. Its rejuvenation became the life work of Matt Winn. Winn had been with the track in 1875 and saw all of the first 75 Kentucky Derby races before his death in 1949. The Derby now draws in excess of 150,000 fans each year. The track's icon is its twin spires that were built atop its stands in 1895. In addition to hosting America's leading race each May, the track has been the site of the Breeders' Cup six times.

Hollywood Park was organized by the Golden State Jockey Club in 1936 and began offering races on June 10, 1936. Although the 350-acre park and track facility is located in Inglewood, California, it was called Hollywood because its founders included film industry celebrities Jack Warner, Walt Disney, Sam Goldwyn, Al Jolson, and Bing Crosby. The track has been open continuously during this time except

for the World War II years, when the land was used for military purposes. The track was also closed for the 1949 season owing to a fire that destroyed the grandstand. Hollywood Park had the honor of holding the first Breeders' Cup races in 1984. They also hosted the event in 1987 and 1997. In 1994 the facility became a racino, as it opened a cardroom casino (*see* The Racino). The facility was purchased by Churchill Downs in 1999 and sold in 2005.

In 2000 the Arlington Park International Racetrack was merged into the Churchill Downs Corporation. The Chicagoland Arlington Park has enjoyed a history of glamour and a reputation for elegance. Yet the track that opened in 1927 has had its problems. In 1985 the original grandstand was devastated by fire. Four years later, however, the course made its comeback, reopening with the word "International" in its title and having even more elegant facilities. Arlington track has been a pioneer in several track developments. In 1933, the track installed the first all-electric totalizator that projected ongoing betting activities onto a board that could be followed by patrons. In 1936, the track used the first photo-finish cameras, and in 1940, the first electric starting gates were installed. The track banked its turns in 1942—another first. Arlington also initiated the trifecta bet (a bet on which horses will finish first, second, and third in a race) in 1971. In the same year Arlington began a commercially sponsored race that offered a prize of $100,000. Ten years later, Arlington hosted the first race with a $1 million purse. The inaugural Arlington Million race was won by John Henry. In 1996,

Arlington was the site of the Citation Challenge, the race in which Cigar matched Citation's record of 16 consecutive wins.

Churchill Downs purchased Ellis Park in 1998. The racecourse had been built in 1922 by the Green River Jockey Club. It is located in Henderson County, Kentucky, just across the Ohio River from Evansville, Indiana. The track suffered a decline after the opening of the Aztar Riverboat Casino in Evansville. Ellis Park was sold in 2006.

Churchill Downs, Inc., won a license to open Indiana's first racetrack, Hoosier Park, which is located north of Indianapolis in Anderson. The track began racing standardbreds in 1993. The first thoroughbred races were held one year later. The leading race is the Indiana Derby, held in October. The track was sold in 2006.

Churchill Downs purchased one of Florida's leading venues, Calder Race Course, in January 1999 for $86 million. The course had begun operations near Miami in 1970, featuring a special formula track surface designed by the 3M Company. Churchill is dedicated to returning Florida to the glory days of racing that were enjoyed in the mid-20th century. The racetrack at the New Orleans Fairgrounds was purchased in 2004.

Del Mar

Del Mar Racetrack is located near the ocean, just north of San Diego. The track's short race meet traditionally opens just as Hollywood Park's summer season closes down. The two tracks do have a short overlap of seasons during the Hollywood fall meeting. Del Mar opened on July 3, 1937. The track was founded by Hollywood celebrities Bing Crosby and Pat O'Brien. Many outstanding events have taken place at Del Mar, including Bill Shoemaker's 1970 ride for win 6,033—surpassing Johnny Longden's record. New grandstands were built in an $80 million renovation during the early 1990s to make the facility one of the most modern and comfortable in the world. Bing Crosby immortalized the track with his song, "Where the Surf Meets the Turf." In 2007, Del Mar, Santa Anita, and all California tracks were required to install synthetic racing surfaces.

El Comandante

El Comandante is Puerto Rico's only horse racing track. It is located 12 miles east of the San Juan tourist and casino district, on the edge of the Yunque Rain Forest National Park. It is a rare track in that racing is ongoing throughout the year five days a week. In the early 20th century, there were several tracks in the commonwealth. In 1954, however, the government gave the San Juan Racing Association a monopoly over track operations, and they developed El Comandante in 1959 as a modern facility. A newer facility was built in 1976, offering a one-mile oval, 257 acres of landscaped property, a 65-foot-wide exercise track, and a 12,000-seat six-level grandstand. Eight thousand cars can park in the lot. Puerto Rico offers 675 off-track outlets for online television betting. In 2002, the Puerto Rico government helped keep the track open by investing $3.5 million in development funds in the facility. In 2004, the track corporation was permitted to gain revenues from VLT gaming machines.

Keeneland Race Course and Sales Operations

Keeneland Race Course is located in the heart of the Kentucky bluegrass country, just six miles away from Lexington. Keeneland offers a beautiful track with a short season that features the Bluegrass Stakes, an event for three-year-olds that is a warm-up for the Kentucky Derby. Fourteen Derby winners have won the race. Keeneland is also a year-round training facility and a research center, with a library collection of 2,000 volumes on pedigrees, breeding, and racing information. The key activity at Keeneland is horse sales. The track holds five sales annually. The January sale is for all horses and the April sale is for two-year-olds; a yearlings sale is held in July and September, and a sale of breeding stock in November. Sales began in the 1930s, but they gained their premier standing during World War II. Prior to the war, horses would be transported by trains from Kentucky farms to Saratoga Springs, New York, for auctions. The military precluded such heavy use of trains during the war, however, and sales activity remained close to the source—at Keeneland. Many stories revolve around the sales. Foals of Northern Dancer sold for over $2.8 million; John Henry was sold for $1,100 in the sale for all ages in 1976 and for $2,200 in 1977. A late bloomer, he commanded only $25,000 as a three-year-old. The gallant steed went on to win $6,591,860 in his amazing career. The Keeneland organization is unique, as it is a non-dividend-paying corporation. All profits are reinvested in capital improvements, used for purses in races, or distributed to charitable or educational operations.

The New York Racing Commission Tracks

The New York Racing Commission owns and operates three major tracks—Saratoga, Belmont, and Aqueduct.

Saratoga Race Course in Saratoga Springs, New York, opened its race card in 1864 to a jam-packed crowd of 10,000. The president of the track was William Travers. The first major race at the track was named in his honor—the Travers Stakes. A detailed history of the track and also the other gambling (casino) activity of Saratoga Springs is found in Ed Hotaling's book *They're Off,* which is described in the Annotated Bibliography. Saratoga has been known for many of the great surprises of racing. In 1919 Upset defeated Man o' War in the Sanford Stakes at Saratoga. In 1973, Secretariat lost to Orion in the Whitney Stakes. The 1930 Travers Stakes provided that year's only defeat for Triple Crown winner Gallant Fox. That race was won by a 100–1 long shot named Jim Dandy. Until World War II, Saratoga was the leading venue for horse sales; however, transportation restrictions caused that honor to pass to Keeneland.

Belmont Park is the home of the Belmont Stakes, the Triple Crown's last and longest event. Like that race, the track is a one and-a-half-mile oval. The course was named after banker and horseman August Belmont. It opened in 1905 but had to suffer through an era of prohibition on race betting that closed down its 1911 and 1912 seasons. The Belmont Stakes was begun in 1867 and run at Jerome Park and Morris Park before coming to Belmont in 1905. Belmont has undergone several renovations, the major one being a $30 million grand stand construction project in 1968.

During the period of construction activity, the Belmont Stakes was run at Aqueduct. Belmont has another mark of historical significance. In 1910, the Wright Brothers held an international air flight tournament at the track and drew 150,000 people. Belmont was the site of the Breeders' Cup in 1990 and 1995.

Aqueduct Racetrack began operations in Queens, New York, in 1894. The track facilities were completely rebuilt in 1959. In 1975 an inner track was designed, and a winter meet is held with that track. The facility runs a summer meeting each season featuring two major handicaps—the Brooklyn Handicap and the Suburban Handicap. The Breeders' Cup was held at Aqueduct in 1985.

Pimlico

The Pimlico track in Baltimore is the home of the middle race of the Triple Crown—the Preakness. The track opened in 1870. The major race of the 1870 season was the two-mile Dinner Party Stakes, which was won by an impressive colt named Preakness. When a stakes race for three-year-olds was established in 1873, former governor Oden Bowie, the track president, chose to name the race after the popular horse. The Preakness was run at Pimlico between 1873 and 1889. Then for 15 years the race was moved to the Gravesend track in Brooklyn, New York. From 1889 until 1909, Pimlico racing was confined to standardbred and steeplechase events as scandals touched thoroughbred race gambling. The Maryland Jockey Club brought respectability back to the Baltimore track, and in 1909, they once again held the Preakness. Since 1925 the race has been one and three-sixteenths miles in length. The winner receives the Woodlawn Vase, which was created by the Tiffany Jewelers in 1860. The Pimlico track features sharp turns that have proved to be very demanding for horses that have won other Triple Crown events.

Santa Anita

Santa Anita first began its racing program on Christmas Day 1934. Now it opens each season the day after Christmas. The track offers a very beautiful setting, as it is situated in the San Gabriel Mountains in the city of Arcadia, 20 miles northeast of Los Angeles. The track was founded by the Los Angeles Turf Club led by Dr. Charles Strub. Strub ran the operations until his death in 1958. Santa Anita runs the top stakes races in the country during the winter months. The leading events are the $1 million Santa Anita Derby and the Santa Anita Handicap. The handicap gained instant fame when it offered a $100,000 purse at its first running in the midst of the Depression years. The race has a list of winners that includes Spectacular Bid, Affirmed, Seabiscuit, Ack Ack, and two-time winner John Henry. The Santa Anita Derby has been won by eight Kentucky Derby winners including Sunday Silence, Affirmed, Majestic Hill, and Swaps, the first California-bred horse to win the Churchill classic. Both Johnny Longden and Bill Shoemaker rode their last mounts at Santa Anita, and Laffit Pincay had a record seven wins in one day in 1987. Santa Anita hosted the 1986, 1993, 2003, 2008, and 2009 Breeders' Cup and also the equestrian events for the 1984 Olympic Games. In 2006 the track became the first major racecourse to install an artificial racing surface. The track facility has been in continuous operation since its 1934 beginnings except for the years of World War II, when it served as the staging area for the removal of Japanese Americans from their homes and into internment camps in the desert. Not all the millions of visitors to Santa Anita over its eight decades have been able to fully appreciate its luxury and elegance during racing seasons—certainly not these unwilling visitors.

Woodbine and the Ontario Jockey Club

Canada's leading race venue, Woodbine, is located northwest of Toronto. It began racing with trotters in 1874. The track was developed on Joseph Duggan's horse farm. As elsewhere, the era found bad elements congregating around the racers. In a reaction against the negative reputation that was gathering, Duggan and others formed the nonprofit Ontario Jockey Club in 1881. The club took over the track. The Ontario Jockey Club has also been active in the operation of other tracks, including Fort Erie and Mohawk.

The Woodbine facility was originally in the city of Toronto. A new facility was built in 1956, however, on the outskirts of the metropolitan area. In 1959, the old track was renovated and became Greenwood Race Course. The Fort Erie track across from Buffalo, New York, was developed by the Ontario Jockey Club, but it was sold to private interests in 1997. Today it is the second thoroughbred track in Ontario. The Mohawk track, 25 miles west of the Lester Pearson International Airport at Toronto, offers only standardbred racing. Mohawk is the home of the $1 million North American Cup and the Breeder's Crown, the standardbred version of the Breeders' Cup. Woodbine itself offers seasons of both thoroughbred

and standardbred racing. The track was the home for the Breeders' Cup in 1996, but its most famous race was the 1973 Canadian International that was won by Secretariat—the famous steed's last contest. Racing's popularity in Canada has waned somewhat, as it has elsewhere. The Ontario tracks, including Woodbine, have gained economic strength, however, by becoming racinos. The Woodbine facility now operates approximately 2,000 slot machines.

OWNERS: FARMS AND INDIVIDUALS

Brookside Farms / Allen E. Paulson

Iowa native Allen Paulson made his fortune by creating the Gulfstream Aerospace Corporation. Horses became his passion, and he developed his Brookside Farms in Kentucky, California, Florida, and Georgia. Paulson won the Eclipse Award for top owner in 1995 and 1996 and for top breeder in 1993. His most notable success has been Cigar, Horse of the Year in 1995.

Calumet Farm

In 1924, William Monroe Wright, a man who made his fortune with Calumet Baking Powder, purchased a horse farm outside of Lexington. He named it after his company. Until his death in 1931, the farm was devoted to the preparation of standardbred horses for racing. Wright was able to produce the winner of the Hambletonian in 1931. His son took over the farm that year and converted it into a thoroughbred racing farm. Warren Wright Sr. had his first major winner with Nellie Flag in 1934. Over the

68 years that the farm was in the Wright family, it became synonymous with winning. In 12 separate years Calumet horses had more wins than those of any other owner. They had 11 years in a row as the leading breeding farm. The farm produced 38 divisional winners of horse of the year designations. Of course, their most notable feats were with Triple Crown winners Whirlaway and Citation. The property was held by Warren Monroe Wright's widow until her death in 1950 and then by their son-in-law until 1992. Substantial economic setbacks caused the farm to be sold at a public auction. It was purchased by Henryk de Kwaitkowski.

Coolmore Stud

The most sought-after studs in the horse industry are found at Coolmore Stud. With its main farm located in Ireland, the Coolmore organization also runs facilities on four other continents, including a 350-acre spread near Lexington, Kentucky. The Coolmore operations were established in 1975 as a partnership among owner-breeder Robert Sangster, trainer Vincent O'Brien, and stallion master John Magnier. The organization uses a dual-continent notion of sending stallions from the Northern Hemisphere to Australia for the Southern Hemisphere breeding season. Fifty stallions are under Coolmore management on the five continents.

Golden Eagle Farm

John and Betty Mabee, founders of the Big Bear Grocery chain, used profits from the sale of that business and earnings from the sale of the Golden Eagle Insurance Company to purchase and stock a 560-acre farm near San Diego in 1997. Their operation grew to include more than 500 horses at the farm as well as a stable of broodmares based in Kentucky. The farms have bred more than 140 winners of major races. They also have produced leading California-bred horses. In 1992, Golden Eagle Farm was the leading North American owner of racehorses, winning purses exceeded $5 million. The farm also led the nation in breeding fees, earning over $7 million. The Mabees earned the Eclipse Award for the leading breeders of 1991, 1997, and 1998. Mabee was an original member of the Breeders' Cup board of directors. John Mabee died in 2002.

Robert and Beverly Lewis

Best-known for campaigning Silver Charm, who won the Kentucky Derby and the Preakness in 1997, Beverly and Robert Lewis began their involvement in the racing industry in 1990. In addition to Silver Charm, they raced a number of other champions, including Charismatic, winner of the Kentucky Derby and Preakness in 1999. Based in California, their horses have been trained by such notables as D. Wayne Lucas, Bob Baffert, and Gary Jones. Lewis served as the chairman of the Thoroughbred Owners of California and also as director of the National Thoroughbred Racing Association. Robert Lewis died in 2006.

Overbrook Farm / William T. Young

Lexington, Kentucky, native William T. Young made a fortune developing Jiffy peanut butter and selling the brand to Procter and Gamble. These and other business ventures enabled him to pursue Overbrook Farm in Lexington as an avocation. The 1,500-acre breeding facility produced a number of leading horses in North America. The farm is perhaps best-know for Storm Cat, a modest runner who went on to become one of the most influential sires in the modern thoroughbred racing era. Other notable Overbrook horses include Kentucky Derby winner Grindstone and Belmont Stakes winner Editor's Note. Young's Cat Thief won the Breeders' Cup Classic in 1999. Young also won the Eclipse Award as the outstanding breeder in 1994.

Young died in 2004 and his family kept operations at Overbrook active until 2009, when they sold all their thoroughbred holdings.

The Sheikhs of Dubai

The ruling family of oil-rich Dubai has been involved in horse racing for several generations. Among their members are Sheikh Hamdan bin Rashid al Maktoum, who has more than 300 thoroughbreds stabled in England, Ireland, Australia, Dubai, and the United States. He also owns 155 broodmares. In the United States, the sheikh owns the 1,350-acre Shadwell Farm in Lexington. He was the leading owner of winning mounts in England in 1995. In 1981, Sheikh Maktoum al Maktoum, a member of the ruling family of Dubai, came to prominence in horse racing circles when he and his brothers spent $6.5 million at the Keeneland July yearling sale. He went on to develop a stable of top-class racehorses that went on to great success worldwide. Upon Sheikh Maktoum's death in 2006, the majority of his racing and breeding stock were absorbed into the Godolphin racing empire run by his brother, Sheikh Mohammed bin Rashid Al Maktoum.

Stronach Stable / Frank Stronach

Frank Stronach was born in Austria, but he generated his fortune as a Canadian industrialist with Magna International, Inc. In 1998, Stronach purchased Santa Anita Park and 300 nearby acres for $126 million. He stables about 100 racing horses. Notable runners include Awesome Again, who won the $5 million Breeders Cup Classic in 1998, and Touch Gold (which he owned in a partnership), who won the Belmont Stakes in 1997, denying Silver Charm the Triple Crown. Stronach was given the Eclipse Award for outstanding owner in 1998.

The Thoroughbred Corporation / Prince Ahmed Bin Salman al-Saud

Prince Ahmed Bin Salman al-Saud, a member of the royal family of Saudi Arabia, and four other partners lead the Thoroughbred Corporation. Salman and his Saudi partners have 45 horses in training in the United States and an equal number of broodmares that are kept at the Mill Ridge Farm in Kentucky. Other horses are kept in England and Saudi Arabia, as well as at a sixteen-acre facility near Santa Anita in California. The corporation's horses include the leading stallion, Skip Away; Breeders' Cup winner Distaff; and Sharp Cat. The corporation's purchase of a yearling for $1.2 million at Keeneland's September sale in 2000 was an all-time record price at the time.

The prince died unexpectedly of heart failure in 2002 at the age of 43. The corporation was controlled by his brother, who sold most of its holdings in 2004.

COLORS: THE JOCKEY AND THE MOUNT

Colors are an important part of the tradition and mystique of horse racing. Each major stable is identified by the registered colors worn on the silks of their jockeys. For example, jockeys for the Calumet Farm stable wear red and blue; those riding for Meadow Stable wear blue and white colors. This practice of using colors dates to England's Newmarket track in 1762. Bettors who favor certain owners may clearly see which numbers are carried by their champions.

Bettors may also look at the colors of the horses themselves for clues about performance; however, their luck is bound to fail them if they bet that way for long. Although seasoned bettors may exclaim that one or two white hooves are good but more are worse, such coloring is unrelated to performance. So, too, is the general coloring of the horse. Bay and chestnut horses are the most common colors, and accordingly they register the most wins. In the Kentucky Derby, bays have won the most times, followed by chestnuts, dark bays or browns, gray or roans, and black horses.

Colors are important in that they are used in the registration of thoroughbreds for identification purposes. The following color definitions are used by the Jockey Club:

- Bay: A horse with a coat of yellow-tan to bright autumn, with black mane, tail, and lower legs. Some white markings may be present.

- Black: A horse with an entirely black coat, but some white markings may be present.

- Chestnut: The coat is red-yellow to golden-yellow, with some white markings.

- Dark bay/brown: The coat varies from brown to dark brown, with areas of tan. Mane, tail, and legs are black, with some white markings present.

- Gray/roan: A horse with combined colors of the gray and roan.

- Gray: The majority of the horse's coat has a mix of white and black colors.

- Roan: The majority of the coat has a mix of red and white colors.

Written with the research assistance of Bradley Wimmer

References

"Angel Cordero." 1975. *Current Biography Yearbook.* New York: H. W. Wilson, 90–92.

Bolus, Jim. 1990. *The Insider's Pocket Guide to Horse Racing.* Dallas: Taylor Publishing.

Christiansen, Eugene Martin. 1999. "The 1998 Gross Annual Wager." *International Gaming and Wagering Business* (August): 20ff.

Churchill, Peter. 1981. *Horse Racing.* Dorset, England: Blandford Press.

Everson, R. C., and C. C. Jones. 1964. *The Way They Run.* Los Angeles: Techno-Graphic Publications.

Hollingsworth, Kent. 1976. *The Kentucky Thoroughbred.* Lexington: University of Kentucky Press.

Hotaling, Edward. 1995. *They're Off! Horse Racing at Saratoga.* Syracuse, New York: Syracuse University Press.

"Julie Krone." 1989. *Current Biography Yearbook.* New York: H. W. Wilson, 314–317.

Litsky, Frank. 1975. *Superstars*. Secaucus, NJ: Derbibooks.

National Gambling Impact Study Commission [NGISC]. 1999. *Final Report*. Washington, DC: NGISC.

"Ron Turcotte." 1974. *Current Biography Yearbook*. New York: H. W. Wilson, 418–420.

Scott, Marvin B. 1968. *The Racing Game*. Chicago: Aldine.

Smith, Sharon B. 1998. *The Complete Idiot's Guide to Betting on Horses*. New York: Alpha Books.

"Willie Shoemaker." 1966. *Current Biography*. New York: H. W. Wilson, 373–375.

INSURANCE AND GAMBLING

Insurance has sometimes been compared with gambling. After all, an insurance company acts like a casino as it asks its clientele to wager on whether they will live or die, whether they will be healthy or sick, whether their house will burn down or not, whether they will be victimized by thieves, or whether other sad circumstances will occur. It would seem that insurance has many of the elements found in the definition of gambling: Customers put up money (consideration), and they win a settlement (prize) depending upon a factor of chance (whether or not they become a victim). And of course, like a casino, the insurance company charges a fee for the service of offering its product, and the insurance company also sets the prize structure so that the company will make a profit—the odds are in the favor of the insurance company.

These things being said, or to a degree admitted to be true, there are still major distinctions between gambling and insurance. Paul Samuelson's seminal volume on economics points out the differences (Samuelson 1976). In his section on economic impacts of gambling, Samuelson writes that gambling serves to introduce inequalities between persons and create instabilities of wealth (425; *see* The Economic Impacts of Gambling). Insurance has the direct opposite consequences. Insurance gives people the opportunity to achieve stability in the face of risks that are often inherent in the nature of things—risk of disease, of fire, of lost property. For a small sum of money, people can purchase policies that will guarantee that the costs of a disaster will not ruin their lives or their families. Gambling purposely introduces risk into a society that is stable; insurance purposely exists to avoid risk. Actually the insurance company takes the risk of disaster faced by a single person and spreads that risk among a very large number of persons who buy insurance policies.

Insurance companies may sell policies that cover only a certain set of circumstances. The person purchasing insurance is limited to buying coverage only for "insurable interests." The insurable interest cannot be as frivolous as the turning of a card or a ball falling on a spinning wheel. The interest must be a real concern to the policyholder. One can insure his or her own life but not the life of a total stranger. Insurance companies must limit the amount of insurance sold to values relative to the risk the insurance seeks to avoid. A house can be insured against fire, but only up to the full value of the house. Similarly, health can be insured up to the cost of treatment and collateral losses, such as wage losses. The limits on insurance coverage preclude the gambler's behavior of chasing losses. If the "bad" event does not occur, and a premium payment is thus lost, the insured person cannot simply double the bet for the next period of time. The insurance company and the insured both have disincentives for purchasing excessive policies. Insurance companies make people wishing to purchase large life insurance policies subject to many medical examinations, including full health screenings. Newly covered persons with health insurance may not be able to receive benefits for a number of months.

By gambling, a person is seeking risk that might severely upset his or her financial stability. By buying insurance, a person is avoiding risk. On the other hand, if a person with a house or other property, or a family dependent upon him or her, does not insure the house or property against destruction or himself or herself against illness or death, that person is gambling with fates that strike people, often randomly, albeit with some rarity (in short periods of time), but almost certainly over long periods of time.

Gambling activity can be and often is very destructive to personal savings. Insurance, on the other hand, can be seen as an alternative means of saving— saving for a rainy day in some cases. In the case of whole life insurance, saving and investment are encompassed into the policies. Although in some respects the notion of insuring against the occurrence of certain natural events and betting on the occurrence of contrived events may appear quite similar, in actuality they are not very much alike.

Reference

Samuelson, Paul A. 1976. *Economics*. 10th ed. New York: McGraw Hill, 425.

INTERNET GAMBLING (INCLUDING UNLAWFUL INTERNET GAMBLING ENFORCEMENT ACT OF 2006)

Gambling through the Internet became an established activity in the mid-1990s, causing great concern to many interests— governments as well as private parties that saw danger in easily accessible gambling.

The Internet was developed three decades ago by the U.S. Department of

Defense in order to connect the computer networks of major universities and research centers with government agencies. The growth of the system into what has now become potentially the most active and most encompassing form of communication had to await the advent of the personal computer before it found widespread acceptance. By the end of 1998 there were over 76 million Internet stations providing access to 147 million persons in the United States—mostly in their homes. An equal number of computers with Internet access are found in other countries.

There are an estimated 800 host computer sites that either provide gambling directly or provide information services for gamblers. Approximately 60 Internet sites, located mostly in foreign lands, accept bets on a variety of events. Most wagering is on sports events, but several sites also conduct lotteries or casino game–type betting. In order to make a wager, a player with Internet access must first establish a financial account with an Internet gambling enterprise. Although the enterprise is typically located in another country, the bettor can send money to the enterprise by using a credit card, debit card, a bank transfer of funds, or personal checks. Wagers can then be made, and the account is adjusted according to wins and losses.

Internet gambling activity has not yet become a major part of the worldwide gaming industry, but it appears to be growing, and it possesses possibilities for becoming much larger than at present. The National Gambling Impact Study Commission reported that in 1998 there were nearly 15 million people wagering on the Internet from the United States, providing the Internet gaming entrepreneurs with annual revenues of from $300 million to $651 million. This represents an amount equaling about 1 percent of the legal betting in the United States. Gaming analyst Sebastian Sinclair estimated that revenues could reach $7 billion in the early 21st century. A November 20, 2005, report on the CBS television show *60 Minutes* suggested that Internet gambling revenues were as much as $10 billion per year. If the expansion comes, it will essentially be because the Internet offers bettors a very convenient way to gamble, and it also offers a privacy they may especially want because of the illegal (or at best quasi-legal) nature of the activity. It is easier to sit at home and wager on a computer than it is to drive to a casino sportsbook—especially when we consider that the only legal sportsbooks are in Nevada. The computer is also quicker than bookie telephone betting services. It is also less likely to be intercepted by law enforcement officials.

There are downsides to Internet betting that may hinder wagering activity. The first issue is integrity. Although a player betting on a sports event has an assurance that he has legitimately won or lost a bet (assuming there are independent news reports on the sports event bet upon), players wagering on lotteries or, especially, casino-type games have no firm guarantees that the results of the wagering are totally honest. To be sure, some Internet sites are licensed by governments, giving an appearance of legitimacy. The very staid government of Liechtenstein authorizes operation of an Internet lottery, and several Caribbean entities, such as Antigua, St. Kitts, and Dominica, oversee many Internet sites offering a variety of games, as well as sports betting. The government oversight activities, however, consist almost entirely of collecting fees from the operators.

The Federal Wire Act of 1961 was confined to betting on races and sports events. It did not address casino-type games and lotteries. Hence, some betting on some computer-type games may possibly have been legal, at least in the eyes of the federal government—up to 2006.

To address these questions with clarity, and to fill the possible gap in the 1961 law, U.S. Senator Jon Kyl of Arizona promoted legislation to amend the Federal Wire Act. His proposed amendment was maneuvered through Congress at the end of the session in 2006. The Unlawful Internet Gambling Enforcement Act of 2006 made illegal essentially all Internet gambling that was not precisely skill based, and it gave the Department of Justice and the Federal Trade Commission the power to enforce the law by placing penalties on institutions that facilitated the betting by conducting financial transactions for operators and players. The bill did allow exceptions for some legal race betting and lottery organizations under limited operations within state borders.

References

Cabot, Anthony N. 1999. *Internet Gambling Report III*. Las Vegas: Trace, 115–124.

Kelly, Joseph M. 2000. "Internet Gambling Law." *William Mitchell Law Review* 26: 118–177.

National Gambling Impact Study Commission (NGISC). 1999. Final Report. Washington, DC: NGISC, 2–15, 2–16.

SAFE Port Act, http://en.wikipedia.org/wiki/SAFE_Port_Act, accessed March 25, 2009.

Inter-Provincial Lottery Corporation. *See* Western Canadian Lottery Corporation.

THE INTERSTATE HORSE RACING ACT OF 1978

During the last quarter-century of the 20th century, participation in horse race betting stagnated. Indeed, on-track betting declined considerably, although the decline was offset by a comparable increase in inter-track and off-track betting. New York's state authorization of off-track betting facilities run by a public corporation beginning in 1970 both threatened the viability of on-track wagering and at the same time offered something of a solution to the impending revenue decline. By the mid-1970s there were 100 off-track betting parlors in New York City alone. New York saw the parlors as a source of public revenue as well as a means to discourage patronage of illegal bookies.

Prior to 1970, only Nevada had off-track betting activity. Now many other states examined the New York experience with thoughts of duplicating it. Initially there were no formal provisions requiring that off-track facilities share revenues with tracks, nor were there mechanisms for requiring that wagers be pooled.

Rather, all such arrangements were ad hoc. Racetracks across the country perceived major problems, and they turned to Congress for development of uniform policies to address their concerns. Even though off-track betting operations agreed that they were adding to the race-betting activity and were sharing some revenues, the tracks felt that their share was not sufficient to offset losses resulting from fewer bettors coming to tracks. A compromise measure was hammered out in Congress, resulting in the passage of the Interstate Horse Racing Act of 1978.

The Interstate Horse Racing Act recognizes that there are several interests involved in off-track betting. There are horse owners who realize economic gains through purses when their horses win races. There is the track, which is basically a private entrepreneurial venture; there is also the host racing state and its racing commission. There is the operation (public in New York but private in other places) that runs the off-track betting parlor. And there is the state regulatory commission that oversees the off-track betting activity. Of course, there are always the players—the bettors.

The act stipulated that the tracks and associations of horse owners would meet and agree on how they would split income from fees charged to the off-track betting operations. The state racing commission would have to ratify the agreement. As with on-track betting revenues, it would be expected that portions of the off-track betting wagers would go to the track owners, to the state as a tax, and to horse owners through purses. The three parties would then negotiate with the off-track betting operators for a fee that essentially would be a portion of the money wagered on races (the "take-out").

The take-out portion going to the track, the owners, and the host state would be less than the amount taken from the track bettors, as it also had to be shared with the off-track betting facility and the off-track betting state. The Interstate Horse Racing Act requires that the overall take-out percentage from the off-track betting activity be the same take-out rates as charged to on-track bettors. This protects the tracks from price competition.

The act also stipulated that the off-track betting facility cannot conduct operations without the permission of any track within 60 miles of the facility, or if there are no such tracks, then the nearest track in an adjacent state. The act did not address the subject of simulcasting of race pictures between the tracks and the off-track betting facilities.

Reference

The Interstate Horseracing Act (Public Law 95–515, signed into law October 25, 1978).

Johnson Act. *See* Gambling Devices Acts (Johnson Act and Amendments).

THE KEFAUVER COMMITTEE

The Kefauver Committee is the popular name for the U.S. Senate Special Committee to Investigate Organized Crime in Interstate Commerce. The committee, which met in 1950 and 1951, was the first federal entity to make a comprehensive study of organized criminal activity in the United States. The investigations concentrated much attention upon gambling. The idea of a Senate investigating committee came from Estes Kefauver, a first-term senator from Tennessee. Kefauver's initiative came as a reaction to reports from several state and local crime commissions that had met in the post-war years. These local investigatory efforts had found that criminal organizations experienced great growth during the World War II years. They had moved from Prohibition-era bootlegging activities to gambling, narcotics, and prostitution activities. They did so at a time when the nation's collective attention was focused upon world events.

The crime commissions' reports were accompanied by a widely reported series of sensational newspaper investigations and stories. It seemed to Kefauver that the national public was making a call for action. The ambitious senator had served as a member of the U.S. House of Representatives for five terms before winning election to the Senate in 1948. His election resulted from a bitter fight against a corrupt political machine that had dominated Tennessee politics for decades.

During 1949, Kefauver developed the idea that the federal government should follow the lead of the local commissions and have its own study of crime. On January 5, 1950, he introduced Senate Resolution 202 in order to create a new subcommittee of the Judiciary Committee on which he served. After jurisdictional objections from the leader of the Commerce Committee, the resolution was amended, and an independent special investigating committee was approved on May 3, 1950. Vice President Alben Barkley (president of the Senate) selected five members to serve on the committee. The members included Democrats Kefauver, Herbert O'Conor (Maryland), and Lester Hunt (Wyoming) and Republicans Alexander Wiley (Wisconsin) and Charles Tobey (New Hampshire).

The committee gained widespread national attention for its televised hearings. Kefauver achieved celebrity status and soon afterwards launched a presidential campaign. He failed in attempts to get the presidential nomination of the Democratic party in 1952, but in 1956 he was nominated for the vice presidency on an unsuccessful ticket with presidential candidate Adlai Stevenson.

The committee held its hearings in a Senate office building in Washington, D.C., and in 13 other cities, including Las Vegas, Miami, New York City, New Orleans, Kansas City, Detroit, and Los Angeles. Over 600 witnesses testified. These included federal, state, and local officials as well as many persons who participated in gambling enterprises both legal and illegal. Among these were members of the Desert Inn Group of Las Vegas, including Moe Dalitz and Wilbur Clark. Several thousands of pages of testimony were recorded.

The committee issued its report on April 17, 1951. The committee concluded that "organized criminal gangs operating in interstate commerce are firmly entrenched in our large cities in the operation of many different gambling enterprises . . . as well as other rackets" (Kefauver 1951, 1). The committee found that there was a "sinister criminal organization known as the Mafia" that was operating throughout the country.

Gambling profits were considered the "principal support" for the criminal gangs. The committee strongly opposed legalization of gambling, as they found that the "caliber of men who dominate the business of gambling in the state of Nevada is on par "with those operating illegal establishments" (91). The committee members concluded that "as a case history of legalized gambling, Nevada speaks eloquently in the negative" (94). The committee wrote, "It seems clear to the committee that too many of the men running gambling operations in Nevada are either members of existing out-of-state gambling syndicates or have had histories of close association with the underworld characters who operate those syndicates." They criticized Nevada's licensing system for not resulting in the exclusion of undesirables but rather seeming only to give the individuals a "cloak of respectability" (94).

The committee's report included 22 recommendations for federal government action and 7 for state and local governments. The federal recommendations included (1) the creation of a racket squad in the Justice Department; (2) the establishment of a Federal Crime Commission in the executive branch; (3) a continuing study by the committee of interstate criminal organizations and support of social studies related to crime; and (4) new legislative initiatives, to be suggested by the committee. The committee also applauded the establishment of a special fraud squad in the Bureau of Internal Revenue (now the Internal Revenue Service) to deal with taxation of illegal gamblers and other gangsters. It was recommended that casinos be required to keep daily records of wins and losses of gamblers and provide the records to the bureau. Officials of the bureau should have access to casino records at all times. The transmission of wagers and of betting information interstate by means of telephone, telegraph, or radio and television should be prohibited.

While the committee was meeting, the Johnson Act was passed, which prohibited the transportation of slot machines across state lines for illegal uses. The committee recommended that the prohibition be extended to other gambling devices such as roulette wheels and punchboards. Congress also increased the federal slot machine licensing tax to $250 for each machine. The tax had been established in 1941 and levied at an annual rate of $150.

State and local governments were urged to appoint committees to study the problem of organized crime in their jurisdictions, with special grand juries having extensive powers appointed in communities with wide-open illegal gambling. Greater cooperation among police agencies was suggested. Each jurisdiction was also asked to consider depriving businesses of licenses if illegal gambling was taking place on their premises. Several additional recommendations were urged upon both federal and state authorities in areas of criminal activity that did not involve gambling.

The committee had impact beyond the presidential campaigns of Estes Kefauver. As a result of the hearings, many persons were charged with being guilty of committing contempt of the Senate for their misinformation. The report of the committee listed 33 notorious individuals who were cited for contempt and other charges as a result of the hearings. Additionally, many states followed recommendations and set up their own committees and commissions where they had not done so before. Through the

1950s many local gambling establishments across the country were closed down—in some places one by one, in other places en masse.

The effects on Nevada gaming were mixed. The efforts of other states to crack down on gambling pushed many illegal operators from other jurisdictions to Nevada. The state also experienced growth, as it became known as the singular place where many casinos could operate openly. Also, the attention of the committee influenced Nevada to improve its gaming regulatory structures with the creation of a specialized Gaming Control Board in 1955 and the Nevada Gaming Commission in 1959. Also influential in pushing regulatory improvements in the state were the work of the McClellan Committee and the administration of Governor Grant Sawyer.

References

Kefauver, Estes. 1951. *Crime in America.* Garden City, NY: Doubleday.

Moore, William Howard. 1974. *The Kefauver Committee and the Politics of Crime, 1950–1952.* Columbia: University of Missouri Press.

See also Crime and Gambling; Gambling Devices Acts (Johnson Act and Amendments); McClellan Committees.

THE KNAPP COMMISSION (1970–1972)

The Knapp Commission (officially known as the Commission to Investigate Allegations of Police Corruption and the City's Anti-Corruption Procedures) consisted of five leading citizens of New York City. The commission was instituted by an executive order of Mayor John V. Lindsay on May 21, 1970. Lindsay appointed Whitman Knapp as chairman. Joseph Monserrat, Arnold Bauman (later replaced by John E. Sprizzo), Franklin A. Thomas, and Cyrus Vance (later secretary of state in the Carter administration) were commission members. The commission met for two years and issued its final report on December 26, 1972.

The creation of the commission was not driven by policy considerations of Mayor Lindsay. Quite to the contrary— city officials, as well as top police administrators, were said to be quite content to allow on-street corruption of policy activity through bribery in exchange for having a police force that could basically ensure publicly acceptable levels of social control and criminal activity. Their priorities were often directed toward overlooking certain illegal activities by police if strict enforcement would negatively impact police morale.

Allegations of police corruption have dogged the police force of New York City since its creation in 1844. Investigations have been conducted on a periodic basis. A New York state senate committee (known as the Lexow Committee) looked at police extortion of houses of prostitution and gambling operations in

1894. In 1911, the city council appointed a committee led by Henry Curran to look into police involvement in the murder of a gambler in Times Square. The gambler had revealed to city newspapers a pattern of bribes that he had paid to the police. In 1932, the state legislature again sponsored an investigation under the leadership of Samuel Seabury. It examined cases of bribes paid to police by bootleggers and gamblers. In 1950 and 1951, the district attorney again held grand jury hearings into bribery tied to gambling. Harry Gross, the head of one of the largest gambling syndicates in the city, agreed to testify. Twenty-one policemen were indicted, but charges were withdrawn when Gross ceased to cooperate in the hearings.

In the mid-1960s, it could be expected that the issue would somehow resurface. This time the catalyst for investigations was a policeman whose quest was to be an "honest cop." His name was Frank Serpico. Serpico's story was the subject of a popular book by Peter Maas and a widely acclaimed movie, *Serpico,* released in 1973, starring Al Pacino in the role of Frank Serpico. Shortly after joining the police force, Serpico became aware that officers were taking bribes from persons involved in numbers betting and illegal sports betting. Soon he discovered the depth of a network of bribes tied to protection given to various games. Operators of different kinds of games would pay different levels of bribes depending upon the volume of their activity and the public exposure needed for their activities. Open gambling games would require higher bribes. All the police of a precinct would participate in the police bribes, with varying shares given to uniformed officers, plainclothes officers, detectives, and higher administrators.

At first Serpico simply refused to accept his share of the bribe money. But as he could not escape personal involvement with the situation on a daily basis, he confided his displeasure to higher police officials. Although he was very reluctant to name any fellow officers in his discussions, he was eager that an investigation follow so that the practices would cease. He found little satisfaction within the police hierarchy and instead was severely ostracized. Even contacts with the mayor's office were futile. The highest politicians in the city were more concerned that police morale be high, as race riots were anticipated and general social "peace" in the streets was their priority. Serpico's persistent actions led to internal proceedings that resulted in individual convictions of lower-level policemen. He saw little action at the top levels where general reform had to start, although a higher-level investigation was initiated. In frustration and fear for his personal safety, Serpico and two supportive fellow officers decided to go on record and make their story public.

On April 25, 1972, the *New York Times* reported Frank Serpico's story on the front page "above the fold." The cat was out of the bag, and Mayor Lindsay could no longer hide behind bureaucratic values. He immediately appointed an interdepartmental committee to recommend action. The committee asked for public complaints that would back up the *New York Times* story. They received 375 complaints within a couple of weeks. The committee told the mayor that as regular city employees they did not have time to follow-up with an investigation. They urged the mayor to create what became the Knapp Commission (Knapp Commission 1972, 35).

The city council approved a budget for the commission and also gave it subpoena power. Additional funds were received for the work through the U.S. Law Enforcement Assistance Administration. An investigating staff was formed, and several inquiries into illegal activity were made in the field. The commission also held two sets of hearings. Five days were spent with Frank Serpico and his fellow confidants. The commission also invited public complaints, and they received 1,325 in addition to those sent to the mayor's earlier committee. In addition to the Knapp Commission's report, their work led to the indictments of over 50 police officers. Over 100 were immediately transferred after the hearing began.

The commission spent considerable time discussing what is known as "the rotten apple theory," specifically that corruption is not pervasive but rather the result of a few "rotten apples" that somehow get into every barrel. They rejected that supposition, as their report began with the words, "We found corruption to be widespread" (Knapp Commission 1972, 12). In one precinct they found that 24 of 25 plainclothes policemen were involved in receiving bribes from illegal gamblers. Although group norms motivated police to participate in networks of bribery, so did their realization that the enforcement of gambling laws was not taken seriously by the judicial system. The commission reported that between 1967 and 1970 there were 9,456 felony arrests for gambling offenses. These resulted in only 921 indictments and 61 convictions. Of these, only a very few received jail sentences, and the sentences were generally light.

Although the commission's report dealt with a wide range of corrupting activities, a special focus was upon gambling and the bribes gamblers paid to the police in their part of the city. The activity was found in all parts of the city. Ghetto neighborhoods were especially susceptible to this police activity. One witness indicated, "You can't work numbers in Harlem unless you pay. If you don't pay, you go to jail. You go to jail on a frame if you don't pay" (Knapp Commission 1972, 71).

The commission found that the "most obvious" result of the gambling corruption was that gambling was able to operate openly throughout the city. Although those with no moral opposition to gambling were not upset, they realized that the pattern of bribery in this area opened the police up to other corruption— looking the other way during drug activity, during certain Mob larcenies, and during other Mob activity. The commission saw a definite link between Mob organizations and gambling activity. The bribery pattern also taught the public that the police were not to be respected. This was especially harmful for children.

An additional danger to police corruption was that the police neglected their specific law enforcement duties as they concentrated on collecting bribes and protecting gamblers. One remark from Serpico was telling. In effect, he said that all the crime in New York City could be ended if the police were not so busy seeking payoffs" (Knapp Commission 1972, 76–77). The police responded to the commission by indicating that they were no longer concentrating on small gambling operatives but rather would focus on leaders in gambling operations. The commission felt that this might be admirable, but that it was not sufficient. They believed that "gambling is traditional and entrenched in many neighborhoods, and it has broad public support" (90). Such being their belief, they recommended that numbers, bookmaking, and other gambling should be legalized. Moreover, the regulation of such legalized gambling should be by civil agents and not by the police (Knapp Commission 1972, 18).

The commission rejected the "rotten apple" theory and so too did the Commission on the Review of the National Policy toward Gambling. They reported that a Pennsylvania Crime Commission that began its study in 1972 also found bribes from gamblers to be pervasive in Philadelphia, and the same was also found in other large cities.

References

Commission on the Review of the National Policy toward Gambling. 1976. *Gambling in America: Final Report.* Washington, DC: Government Printing Office.

Knapp Commission. 1972. *The Knapp Commission Report on Police Corruption.* New York: George Braziller.

Maas, Peter. 1973. *Serpico.* New York: Viking Press.

McClellan Committee

In January 1955, Democratic Senator John McClellan of Arkansas became chairman of the Senate's Permanent Subcommittee on Investigations. Previously Senator Joseph McCarthy (R-Wisconsin) had used the chair position to conduct his discredited investigations into communist influences in the national government. Under McClellan's direction, the committee turned toward other topics. Initially McClellan looked at corruption in government contracts and trade with communist China. He selected a young attorney named Robert Francis Kennedy to be the chief counsel and chief investigator for the committee. Kennedy sensed the presence of the International Brotherhood of Teamsters (the Teamsters' union) in certain contract abuses, and he began to probe the Teamsters' activity. During 1956, he stumbled upon evidence of corruption by Teamster president David Beck. Kennedy was influential in having McClellan's committee transformed into a Select Committee on Labor Corruption. The eight-member bipartisan committee met for two years, during which Robert Kennedy's efforts were directed first at Beck, who was forced to resign his union position after a conviction for stealing from the union, and then at Beck's successor, James Riddle Hoffa. The investigation of Hoffa revealed a widespread involvement of Teamsters' union funding of casinos in Nevada, as well as other connections between union officials and organized crime figures; in turn, union activity was linked to illegal gambling. The committee reiterated the conclusions of the Kefauver Committee that there was indeed an organized crime association known as the Mafia and that its major illegal activity concerned gambling.

Following the 1960 elections, McClellan was appointed to be the chair of a newly organized crime committee, while Kennedy became the attorney general in the presidential administration of his brother, John F. Kennedy. The crime committee met for three years.

Kennedy created a crime task force within his office and pursued gamblers and their activity, whether it was legal or illegal. He also pursued Jimmy Hoffa, seeking to expose him as a thief and gangster within the union. Kennedy and McClellan often worked in tandem, especially in the legislative field. Their joint efforts led to the passage of two major pieces of legislation in 1961 that grew out of the Kefauver Committee report. One law banned the use of interstate commerce for any illegal gambling equipment—hence expanding the thrust of the Johnson Act. The other prohibited the use of any interstate communication devices (wire services) in order to transmit information used for wagering activities.

Reference

U.S. Senate Committee on Government Operations. 1962. *Gambling and Organized Crime—Report.* Washington, DC: U.S. Government Printing Office.

See also Federal Wire Act of 1961; Gambling Devices Acts (Johnson Act and Amendments); Hoffa, Jimmy; Kefauver Committee; Kennedy, Robert F.

National Center for Responsible Gaming. *See* Gaming Institutes: Research and Political.

National Coalition against Legalized Gambling. *See* Gaming Institutes: Research and Political.

THE NATIONAL GAMBLING IMPACT STUDY COMMISSION (1997–1999)

The National Gambling Impact Study Commission met from June 1997 through June 1999, producing a report recommending 66 changes in public policy toward gambling activity. The commission was the creation of a new set of political forces in U.S. politics.

As casino-style gambling rapidly spread across the United States in the early 1990s, forces in the debate on gambling turned their attention to the national policymaking arena. Under the leadership of Tom Grey, a United Methodist minister and Vietnam War veteran from Galena, Illinois, the National Coalition against Legalized Gambling emerged to fight gambling wherever the issue arose as an issue of public policy. The coalition also urged politicians in Washington, D.C., to examine gambling and to consider regulation and taxation of gambling activity. In 1994, President Clinton sought to increase the federal budget by $1 billion dollars after Congress had established spending caps for the year. To do this, he would have had to either reduce other spending by a billion dollars or find a new source for the money. He suggested a new source: a 4 percent tax on all gambling profits in the United States. As his real target was the commercial casino industry, casinos reacted. Major Las Vegas and Atlantic City properties quickly came together and formed the American Gaming Association (AGA). The association selected Frank Fahrenkopf, formerly the chairman of the Republican National Committee, to be its spokesman and executive director. The tax measure was silently killed, but national politics were changed forever as the gaming industry moved onto the stage as a major contributor to political campaigns for both parties.

The forces were joined in battle in 1995 when Congressman Frank Wolf (R-Virginia) introduced H.R. 497, a bipartisan bill to create a national study commission to examine gambling in the United States. Senators Paul Simon (D-Illinois) and Dick Lugar (R-Indiana) cosponsored companion legislation in the Senate. The AGA immediately feared that Grey and Wolf had their sights set on destroying big casino gaming with a "witch hunt" that would lead to recommendations for national taxation and regulation of gambling, as well as restrictions on the spread of legalized gambling. The AGA was outmaneuvered in committee hearings on the bill, as Grey and others emphasized the many negative consequences of gambling and indicated that political leaders did not have full knowledge of the impact of gambling. The AGA had to back off of its effort to simply kill the bill. Instead it used its power base—its campaign funding potential as well as congressional voices from gaming states—to make the bill less offensive to its interests.

The bill to create the national commission was substantially changed from the bill Wolf wanted. The commission was charged with investigating the impact of all gaming, whereas Wolf had wished to target casino gaming only. The AGA knew it could deflect much of the criticism of casino gaming by having investigators look at lotteries, charities, and Indian gaming. The commission was denied wide-ranging subpoena powers, whereas Wolf had desired that the commission be able to subpoena casino files and data on players.

The casino interests also negotiated a selection process that allowed them to have a strong voice on the panel. It appeared that Congress wished to satisfy conservatives by establishing the commission, but members of Congress were also quite aware that casinos were a major source of campaign funds. Unfortunately for the state lotteries, they were not able to make campaign contributions. They were not given an "inside voice" in the membership on the commission. The amended bill was quickly passed by each house, and on August 3, 1996, it became Public Law 104–169 as it was signed by President Clinton.

Three of the nine members of the National Gambling Impact Study Commission were appointed by the president, three by the Speaker of the House, and three by the majority leader of the Senate. The two congressional leaders each allowed minority party leaders in their chambers to select one of the three respective appointments. The commission ended up as a bipartisan group including both vocal antigambling advocates and commissioners who were close to the casino industry.

Two strong voices against gambling won appointment: James Dobson, the president of a religious-right organization;

and Kay James, a former dean at religious-based Regent University in Virginia. On the other side, one major casino executive—Terrence Lanni of the MGM Grand—was selected, as was John Wilhelm, the head of the largest labor union in Nevada's casino industry, and Bill Bible, the head of the Nevada Gaming Control Board. A Native American from a nongaming Alaska tribe was selected—Robert Loescher. He turned out to be very much an advocate not only for Native American gaming but also for the industry as a whole.

Three "neutrals" seemed to hold the balance of power. One was radiologist Paul Moore, a close friend of Senate majority leader Trent Lott. (Lott became the target of a public interest group as it was revealed in the commission's last days that he had received an exorbitant amount of campaign funding through the casino interests.) Also considered in the center were Leo McCarthy, former lieutenant governor of California, and Richard Leone, a former New Jersey state official.

The commission selected Kay James to be its chair. She set an antigambling tone to the proceedings from the very start, and it appeared that it would be very difficult for the commission ever to come together for a final report. Nonetheless, many hearings were held across the country, and although there was much verbal acrimony, the commission did unite to make a final report. Operating on a budget of $5 million, the commission engaged in a wide variety of activities. Public hearings were held in Washington, D.C.; Atlantic City; Boston; Chicago; San Diego; Tempe, Arizona; Biloxi, Mississippi; New Orleans; and Las Vegas. Several hundred citizens, public officials, industry officials, and academic experts offered testimony. Information was also gathered from more than a

thousand documents examined by the commission staff. The National Opinion Research Center of the University of Chicago was contracted to conduct a survey of compulsive gambling. It surveyed 2,417 adults and 534 adolescents by telephone and 530 adults in gambling facilities. The center's study also involved making case studies of one hundred communities that were located near gambling facilities. As a result of the work, the center concluded that approximately 1.8 million adults were currently "pathological gamblers" and another 4 million were currently "problem gamblers." Thirteen percent of patrons at gambling facilities indicated attributes of either pathological or problem gambling at some time in their lives (National Gambling Impact Study Commission 1999, 4–5). All the information resources were utilized in making recommendations, which appeared in the final report.

The report had many antigambling messages in it, but on most substantive matters, the casino industry of Nevada came out on the winning side. The gaming industry was bothered by an initial recommendation that states and tribal governments accept a moratorium on new legalizations of gambling activities. That recommendation was passed over in the final report that was issued on June 18, 1999. Instead, the commission urged that the jurisdictions make comprehensive socioeconomic impact statements before they endorsed new legalizations. Other recommendations gave great comfort to the casino industry. Their fears were completely defused with the initial recommendation of the panel. The initial findings of the National Gambling Impact Study Commission included a definitive statement that gambling policy should remain a matter for state governments to control. With two exceptions—Native American gaming and Internet gaming—the commission felt that the federal government should stay out of gaming. There should be no special federal taxes on gaming, and there should be no direct regulation of the gaming industry by the federal government. The policy arena for making laws and rules about the casinos and the other gaming venues of Nevada should be in the hands of state leaders and in the counties and cities of the states.

The commission followed its first recommendation with a full set of suggestions for changes to be made at state and local levels. Many of these were quite critical of current gaming operations around the country. Nevada casino operators had been criticized before—this was not new. But the criticisms were much easier to take from sources that recognized that they should have no power over the choices that the state makes regarding gaming.

The commission recommended that the minimum age for gambling be 21 in all jurisdictions. They also recommended that children not be permitted to linger or loiter in gambling facilities. Gambling "cruises to nowhere"—that is, ships that dock in a nongaming state then go beyond the international waters boundary, allow gambling, and then return to docks—should not be allowed unless the nongaming state specifically approved their activity. The commission also suggested that gaming interests not be allowed to make campaign contributions. Convenience gambling, such as slot machines or other gaming machines in grocery stores, was condemned.

In addition, the national commission opposed money machines in gaming areas. They claimed that "the easy availability of ATMs and credit machines encourages some gamblers to wager more than they intended" (National Gambling Impact Study Commission 1999, 7–30). Therefore, they recommend that "states, Tribal governments, and pari-mutuel facilities ban credit card cash advance machines and other devices activated by debit or credit cards from the immediate area where gambling takes place" (7–30).

The commission took a slap at sports betting by recommending that no betting be allowed on college or amateur contests. There was also a recommendation against the sale of instant tickets by lotteries and the use of machine gaming by lotteries. Lotteries were also chastised for excessive and false advertising. Pari-mutuel racing facilities were urged not to have slot machine–type gambling.

All gambling areas were requested to have warning signs telling players about the dangers of compulsive gambling. States were encouraged to devote funds from gaming taxes to programs for research, prevention, education, and treatment programs for problem gamblers.

The commission urged that Congress pass legislation making all Internet gambling illegal. Moreover, it indicated a desire for legislation to make credit card debts incurred for Internet gambling unrecoverable in courts. The commission also recommended that Indian gaming be subjected to more stringent reporting requirements and that the federal government fully enforce the provisions of the Indian Gaming Regulatory Act.

The commission lamented that even with its extensive study, too many gaps remained in our knowledge of gambling. They recommended an extensive program of continued research.

Generally, the gambling industry was happy with the *Final Report*; it had feared a more severe condemnation of casino gambling. Nonetheless, opponents of gambling received encouragement from the *Final Report* as well. They used the study effectively in a campaign in the fall of 1999 to defeat a proposed lottery in Alabama and to win a court decision ending machine gambling in South Carolina.

Reference

National Gambling Impact Study Commission [NGISC]. 1999. *Final Report.* Washington, DC: NGISC.

National Indian Gaming Association. *See* Gaming Institutes: Research and Political.

NATIVE AMERICAN GAMING: CONTEMPORARY

The U.S. government recognizes over 562 Native American tribes. In 1990 there were almost 2 million Native Americans. In 2000 the number grew to nearly 2.5 million, with another 4.1 million claiming to have mixed ethnicity with some Native American heritage. Of the tribes in the United States, 225 had some kind of gambling operation in 2007. The operations included bingo games, which are considered Class II games, and various kinds of casino-type games, or Class III games (classifications found in the Indian Gaming Regulatory Act of 1988). The Class III operations are found in 28 states. As described below, the Class III games are conducted in accordance with agreements—called compacts—made between the tribes and the state governments.

Since 1990 Native American gambling has been the fastest-growing sector of casino gambling in the United States. Several hundred billion dollars are wagered at the Native American bingo halls and casinos each year. As a result of player losses, tribes take in approximately 30 percent of all the gambling revenues in the United States. In 2007, the Native American gambling facilities in 28 states had wins exceeding $26 billion. The revenues support several hundreds of thousand employees as well as critically needed social programs for many Native Americans who have collectively been the most economically deprived subpopulation in the United States. Gambling monies have also been vitally important for economic development projects, making many tribes self-sufficient. Gambling has not been a panacea for all, however, as a majority of the revenues go to the largest casinos. The 25 biggest casinos in terms of floor space (in 1997) each earned more than $250 million a year, collectively winning

High-stakes bingo at an Indian casino in New York.

42 percent of total revenues from tribal gaming. Over one half of the Native American gaming operations earned less than $25 million a year each. Some of the largest tribes in terms of population have no gambling operations at all.

One of the tribes, the small Mashantucket Pequot tribe of Connecticut, has the largest casino in the world. The 300 members of this community control a casino complex that wins well over $1 billion a year. Their main casino, Foxwoods, is located in Ledyard, Connecticut, near the interstate highway that links New York City with Boston. For most of the 1990s, the casino was the only casino in all of New England. The gaming complex facility has more than 340,000 square feet of gambling space, with casinos that feature more than 7,200 machines and 300 table games, plus a 3,200-seat bingo hall. The gaming resort complex also has three hotels, several theaters, amusement game rooms, and a sports arena. The facility is larger than any casino in Las Vegas, and it earns three times the revenue of the largest Las Vegas casinos. Except for the state government itself, the casino is the largest employer in Connecticut.

Other leading Native American casinos include the Mohegan Sun, also in Connecticut, and casinos on Oneida reservations in both Oneida, New York, and Green Bay, Wisconsin; on Chippewa reservations at Sault St. Marie and Mount Pleasant, Michigan, and Mille Lacs, Minnesota; on a Dakota Sioux reservation at Shakopee, Minnesota; and on the Choctaw reservation near Philadelphia, Mississippi. Any of these gaming facilities could be transplanted to the Las Vegas Strip, and customers would be hard-pressed to notice the difference in gambling operations, although their markets all tend to be located within a one-day car drive and few have large hotels.

HISTORICAL DEVELOPMENT

In the 1970s, many Native American tribes began to participate in charity gambling in accordance with state rules regarding how the games would be played and the types of prizes that could be offered. In 1979, the Seminole Nation decided to do something different for the bingo hall on its reservation in Hollywood, Florida. Faced with considerable competition from other charities, the tribe threw aside the state's prize limits and began a high-stakes game with prizes in the thousands of dollars. The Broward County sheriff filed criminal charges and sought to close down the Seminole bingo game. His actions led to a series of law cases, culminating in the 1981 approval of the games without state limits by a federal court of appeals (*Seminole Tribe v. Butterworth,* 658 F. 2d. 310). In 1982 the U.S. Supreme Court refused to review the ruling (455 U.S.1020). In a very similar case in 1982, another federal court of appeals permitted a California tribe to conduct bingo games and other card games in manners that violated state rules (*Barona v. Duffy,* 694 F. 2d 1185). Key to the cases was the fact that in both Florida and California the games themselves were legal and could be played. The tribes were only violating the manner in which the games were played. The courts of appeals ruled that states did not have regulatory authority over Native American nations' activities unless the activities were totally prohibited by the states as a matter of public policy.

Tribes across the United States took notice of the very successful gambling activities of the tribes and especially of the legal cases, which seemed to affirm the special status the tribes enjoyed in this realm of economic enterprise. During the early years of the 1980s, gambling began to appear on most of the reservations of the United States. Except for internal tribal regulations, there was almost no oversight for the gambling activities. As the activities involved larger and larger sums of money, there were both perceived and real problems. There were cases of non-Native managers setting up games and then taking the bulk of the revenues. Evidence of cheating emerged. Members of organized crime families made their presence felt on some reservations. There were also some unscrupulous tribal members who used gaming for personal advantages in ways adverse to their tribes' interests. Organized commercial casino interests, especially those in Nevada and New Jersey, expressed fears that corruption and organized crime activity on the reservations could result in a popular backlash against all casinos, along with calls for federal regulation of commercial casinos. Of course, they also had concerns about the competitive positions held by unregulated casinos in monopoly-like markets. Congress began to explore the manner in which Native gambling could be regulated.

Congressional action was held back, however, as the U.S. Supreme Court had not ruled on the legality of Native gambling, and many state governments sought to have the highest court overrule the previous decisions of lower federal courts. This did not happen. In 1987, the U.S. Supreme Court upheld the earlier rulings by a 6 to 3 vote in *California v. Cabazon Band of Mission Indians* (480 U.S. 202). Moreover, the Court endorsed Native gambling as being consistent with federal policies designed to promote self-sufficiency for tribes. The Court pointed out that the Bureau of Indian Affairs had actually given grants for construction of some of the gambling facilities, that gambling revenues were accomplishing goals for federal policy, and that gambling revenues "provide the sole source of revenues for the operation of tribal governments, and the provision of tribal services. They are also major sources of employment on the reservations." The Court added, "Self-determination and economic development are not within reach if the Tribes cannot raise revenues and provide employment for their members. The Tribes' interests obviously parallel the federal interests."

The Court added that state regulation or any other regulation by a nontribal entity could take place only if there were a specific act of Congress authorizing the regulation. Now the states besieged members of Congress to act. Conversely, the tribal interests were less inclined to endorse congressional action, as the status quo was quite acceptable to their desires. A compromise was reached with the passage of the Indian Gaming Regulatory Act of 1988, signed into law by President Reagan on October 25, 1988.

THE INDIAN GAMING
REGULATORY ACT
OF 1988

The 1988 Indian Gaming Regulatory Act (IGRA) established a three-member National Indian Gaming Commission. Two of the three members must be enrolled members of Native tribes. The chairman is appointed by the president and the two other members by the

secretary of the interior. The commission is given some direct regulatory authority over bingo-type gaming. It is also empowered to make general rules for gambling operations. The chairman has subpoena powers, and the commission may assess fines against tribal gambling operations and even close them if it feels they are not sufficiently abiding by the rules. The commission approves all agreements outside operators make with Native gambling establishments and conducts background checks on gambling personnel.

Casino-type gambling was to be regulated in accordance with rules established in negotiations between the tribes and the state governments. These negotiated compacts would be given the force of law by the secretary of the interior. If the states refused to negotiate compacts in good faith, tribes could sue the states, and the states could be mandated by federal courts to negotiate. On March 27, 1996, in a 5 to 4 vote (*Seminole Tribe v. Florida,* 517 U.S. 1133), the U.S. Supreme Court ruled that the provision of the act that allowed tribes to sue states in federal courts over the lack of good faith negotiations was unconstitutional because of the Eleventh Amendment. The amendment implies that states are sovereign units and generally cannot be sued in federal courts.

The Court did not rule the entire act unconstitutional, nor did the Court address how impasses would be resolved in the future—whether states could simply say "no" to tribes, or whether tribes could seek relief from the secretary of the interior. In 1999, the secretary of the interior issued guidelines for tribes to take appeals to the secretary's office when states refused to negotiate compacts. However, in the 10 years since the issuance, the guidelines have not once been put into effect.

The act defined three classes of gambling. Class I gambling consists of small prize games between tribal members. It also consists of games traditionally played by tribes in ceremonies or celebrations. These activities are regulated entirely by the tribes. No issues have arisen over Class I games since the passage of the act.

Class II gaming encompasses bingo in its various forms as well as pull-tab cards, punch boards, and tip jars (jars filled with a fixed number of pull tabs, hence guaranteeing a predetermined number of winners). Certain card games such as poker are also included as long as the games are nonbanking, that is, do not involve bets between the casino and the player instead of bets among players. Tribes can conduct Class II gaming as long as the game involved is permitted in the state to be played "for any purpose, by any person, organization or entity." The tribe must pass an ordinance in order to offer Class II games. The ordinance is then approved by the National Indian Gaming Commission chairman. The commission conducts background investigations on the gambling facility and its employees.

The commission then regulates the gambling for a period of three years, after which the tribe can apply for permission to self-regulate the Class II games. Most tribes have successfully won permission for self-regulation. The permission can be revoked if the commission feels that the self-regulation efforts are inadequate. Although the commission regulates the gambling, the commission may assess the tribes a fee for the cost of regulation.

The gaming tribes have been aggressive and innovative in applying the law to their benefit. Where states have not agreed to allowed them to have Class III slot machines, they have used the provisions for "electronic aids" for bingo games found in Class II game descriptions in order to justify installing "bingo" gambling machines that to the player appear very much like traditional slot machines. However, as opposed to the slot machines which operate independently of one another in a casino, these bingo machines are linked together so that all money wagered by the player goes into a central computerized pool of money. Winning prizes are then awarded as money is electronically drawn out of this pool. In this way the machines operate—conceptually—much like live bingo games. The National Indian Gaming Commission has allowed such machines to operate under the rules for Class II games.

Class III gaming consists of all forms of gambling not covered by Class I and Class II definitions. Basically, the Class III category covers all casino-banked games including blackjack, baccarat, roulette, craps, and all (non-bingo) slot machines. Class III also includes lottery games as conducted by state governments and pari-mutuel racing wagers. As with Class II games, the Class III games may be played only if the tribe has an ordinance permitting them and if the games are permitted "for any purpose, by any person, organization or entity" in the state where the tribal facility is located. Additionally, for Class III gambling to be permitted, the tribe must enter into a compact with the state. The compact will provide a detailed provision on games allowed in the facility, the manner of offering the games, and the regulatory structures for oversight of the games.

The Class III negotiated compacts may provide very specific authority for tribal and non-tribal (be they county, city, or state) law enforcement agencies to supervise and enforce provisions of the gaming agreements. Without such specific authority being granted to non-tribal authorities, all enforcement activities regarding gaming on Indian lands remain in the hands of the tribal government and the federal government. In other words, if there is no compact, and tribes are permitting games the state believes to be Class III games, the state cannot enforce the law. The state must wait for federal district attorneys and marshals to make all enforcement actions. As these officials operate under direction of the U.S. attorney general, the basic enforcement activity is on the shoulders of one federal officer.

State governments may not impose taxes on the Native American gaming facilities as requirements in negotiations for Class III compacts. However, the state may charge the tribes sums of money to cover the actual costs of state regulation of the facilities. In fact, many tribes have acquiesced in state requests for special fees in order to finalize negotiations. The secretary of the interior willingly closes his eyes to the legal violation and accepts that the fees are somehow quid pro quos for some mysterious services the state or local governments might give the gambling facilities. One of these services has been a grant by the state of a limited monopoly to offer specific games such as machine games.

The gaming tribes may use money from Class II and Class III games for specific purposes indicated in the IGRA. These include: (1) funding of tribal

government operations or programs; (2) providing for the general welfare of tribal members; (3) promoting economic development for the tribe; (4) making charitable donations; (5) funding of operations of local governments; and (6) making per capita payments to tribal members, when specifically approved by the U.S. secretary of the interior. In regards to the final provision, if the tribe shows that it is meeting its obligations to provide for the social welfare of its members, the tribe may authorize up to 40 percent of net revenue to go to individual members in a per capita distribution. Some tribes have done so; others have not. Some have given the full 40 percent in per capita distributions; others have given smaller proportions. In the case of one Minnesota tribe with a small membership, the per capita distribution of funds was in excess of $800,000 per individual member for one year. Several other tribes have allocations exceeding $100,000 per member per year; however, most of the per capita payments are not so large.

The National Indian Gaming Commission also regulates non-Native persons who wish to work with the gambling facilities on reservations. Moreover, arrangements for outside management of games are regulated, with the outside managers being limited to agreements for no more than 30 percent of the net revenue of the facility going to them in exchange for their services. Agreements cannot last for more than five years. Under special cases outside managers may receive as much as 40 percent of net revenues for seven years if they also provide financing for the Native casino facilities.

The IGRA anticipated that tribal leaders and other entrepreneurs would see opportunities in creating new tribes in order to place gambling facilities in certain locations with outstanding market possibilities. The law provided that new lands designated as Indian lands by Congress or the Department of the Interior could have gambling only if such was approved by the secretary after some (unspecified) consultations with local residents of the area as well as rival gambling tribes in the vicinity. Moreover, the governor of the state would have to specifically approve the gambling, and of course there would have to be a compact. Plans for new tribes and new tribal lands proliferated, and many applications were made to Congress, the Interior Department, and governors. Only about a dozen tribes have been given new recognition by federal authorities, and several now have a casino operating. Only three existing tribes have been given authorization for gambling on new lands not adjacent to their existing reservations.

SELECTED DEVELOPMENTS— CONNECTICUT AND CALIFORNIA

Every state with organized and recognized Native populations has had a special history with its tribes over gambling, with one exception—Utah. As that state has no legal gambling, the federal law is clear that the tribes in the state may not have any Class II or Class III gambling operations. Hawaii, the only other state without any non-Native gambling has no Native lands. Certain state situations deserve extra attention.

Negotiations in Connecticut took many unusual turns on the way to creating the largest casino in the world, Foxwoods. Originally, the Mashantucket Pequot tribe sought a compact so that they could have table games only, as the state did permit charities to use table games in their fundraising events. Governor Lowell Weickert refused to negotiate, however, claiming that the games were commercially illegal in the state. The tribe won a court mandate ordering the governor to negotiate. He refused. A mediator was appointed, to whom the tribe and the governor both submitted proposed compacts. The governor's proposal actually included provisions for allowing the games. The mediator selected the governor's proposal. The state then appealed the selection, asking the secretary of the interior to reject its own proposal. The secretary instead signed the proposal, which became the compact. The state lost its further court appeals.

It was clear that the state did not permit anyone—charities or commercial operators—to have slot machines. Also, the IGRA clearly says states cannot tax tribal gaming. Nonetheless, in 1993 the state and its governor reached a "side agreement" with the tribe to allow them to have as many slot machines as they wanted, providing they paid the state 25 percent of the revenue from the machines. The agreement was never approved by the secretary of the interior (it could not be; it was patently illegal), but the casino offers 7,200 slot machines for its customers. The 25 percent tax was called a monopoly fee that would go to the state only as long as the Mashantucket Pequots had a monopoly on the machines (which could not be legally possible, as the law could allow machines only if they were permitted for others). The monopoly ended in 1996 when a second tribe opened a casino, and the 25 percent share was renegotiated with the governor's office, without the approval of federal authorities. The state of Connecticut receives over $400 million a year as its share of the tribes' slot revenues. The state certainly has not sought to appeal the legality of the slot agreement. While of dubious legitimacy, the gambling situation in Connecticut has widespread support.

The most protracted battles over Native American gambling have occurred in California, one of the states to pioneer Native American gambling. After the federal court rulings in the Seminole and Barona cases in the early 1980s, gambling expanded on California Native lands. The tribes went beyond bingo and player-banked games and started offering games that appeared to have the qualities of Class III games. After 1988, however, California governors George Deukmejian and Pete Wilson declined to negotiate compact agreements to allow tribes to have Las Vegas–style slot machines and house-banked casino games, claiming that casino-type gambling was unconstitutional in California. As all enforcement of gambling laws on tribal lands was placed into the hands of the federal government, the governors could not demand closure of tribal casinos. An impasse ensued for several years during which the tribes expanded machine operations, operating as many as 15,000 of them outside the boundaries of the federal law.

Eventually the tribes turned to the ballot to win their compacts. In 1998, they sponsored Proposition 5, and in 2000 they sponsored Proposition 1A. Governor Wilson opposed Proposition 5; Governor Grey Davis helped design Proposition 1A, and he supported it. Both passed, but a court ruling held that a 1984 constitutional ban on casinos precluded enforcement of Proposition 5. Hence, Proposition 1A was initiated as a constitutional amendment. The measure allows individual tribes to have casinos with up to 2,000 slot machines in each, with an overall state limit of approximately 43,000 machines. This represents a doubling of the number of existing machines in the state.

The 1998 Proposition 5 in California presented the greatest threat to Nevada casinos since the Kefauver hearings of the 1950s. The Native Americans in California wanted a compact and felt they were being stonewalled by Governor Wilson. But in their proposition they did not stop at merely asking for a compact. They asked for wide-open unlimited casino gambling on all 100-plus reservations in the state. The Native interests put almost $70 million into the campaign—one tribe in San Bernardino contributed $26 million of the amount. Nevada casinos responded with $25 million in opposition. Money won the contest, as the voters gave the proposition over 60 percent approval. Unfortunately the proposition was in the form of a legislative initiative, and the courts found it to be constitutionally defective. Nevada paid for the court challenge. The tribes quickly gathered and lobbied the California governor for support of a constitutional initiative to grant them compacts. The new compact (Proposition 1A) limited the number of slot machines that the tribes could have and provided for more definitive regulations—including the possibility of having labor unions for employees. The proposition also provided that the tribes would share a small portion of gaming revenues with other California tribes that did not have gaming, as well as sharing some funds with the state. Nevada interests had been stung by the amount of money that the Native Americans were willing to spend on the campaign in 1998. They were happy with the Proposition 1A compromises, and they were happy that they did not have to advance money against casinos again—a position that makes them feel somewhat hypocritical—but a position they had to take. It is possible that 1A will now allow the casinos of Nevada and the Nevada political establishment to build important bridges to California tribes. Some Nevada companies were quick to seize the opportunity to enter the California gaming scene as managers of new casinos in the Golden State.

A CANADIAN NOTE

The situation in Canada has some parallels to that in the United States. Native peoples (or First Nations) in Canada are the poorest residents of the country. They want to have gambling operations to help them deal with problems arising from their impoverished situations. There is no national Canadian law on Native gambling, unlike the situation in the United States.

It had been well established that all relationships between Native bands (tribes) and non-Native peoples must be conducted with the federal government in Ottawa. In 1985, however, the federal government delegated all authority over gambling to the provinces. Since then the Native bands have felt like political footballs, as provinces say "go talk to Ottawa," and Ottawa says "go talk to the provinces." In the mid-1990s, however, several provinces entered into agreements somewhat similar to compacts in the U.S. states. Tribal casinos are operating in Alberta, Saskatchewan, Manitoba, and Ontario. Disagreements persist between bands and provincial authorities in several of the other provinces.

A unique arrangement was negotiated in Ontario, as one band (Rama) was permitted to have a casino at Orilla, as long as it shared revenues with other bands in the province. Another casino in Ontario, the Blue Heron Casino in Port Perry, also has been authorized to operate under the control of a Native band. The Canadian and U.S. tribes in the United States have generously shared their revenues with many charities in many communities. No Canadian tribe, however, has willingly allowed any other tribe to have a precise share of its gaming revenues.

In 2000, the Alberta government provided guidelines for Native casino operations. At the same time, the Manitoba government held hearings and took advice from people throughout the province before designating five communities as sites for Native casinos. In one case there was no band in the community, and arrangements had to be made to create First Nation land for the casino. Saskatchewan created four native casinos when it established its own provincial casino in Regina. All participate in revenue-sharing provisions.

References

Light, Steven Andrew, and Kathryn R. L. Rand. 2008. "The Hand That's Been Dealt: The Indian Gaming Regulatory Act at 20." Paper presented to Gambling Law Symposium, Drake University Law School, September 12.

Ponting, J. Rick. 1994. "The Paradox of On Reserve Casino Gambling: Musings of a Nervous Sociologist." In *Gambling in Canada: The Bottomline,* edited by Colin Campbell, 57–68. Burnaby, BC: Simon Fraser University.

Thompson, William N., and Diana R. Dever. 1994. "The Sovereign Games of North America: An Exploratory Study of First Nations' Gambling." In *Gambling in Canada: The Bottomline,* edited by Colin Campbell, 27–55. Burnaby, BC: Simon Fraser University.

Thompson, William N. 2005. *Native American Issues: A Reference Handbook.* 2nd ed. Santa Barbara, CA: ABC-CLIO.

NATIVE AMERICAN GAMING: DATA

As mentioned in Native American Gaming: Contemporary, the 25 largest tribal casinos produce 42 percent of the revenue in Native American gambling. The question of how many Native Americans win by having gambling facilities can be examined more closely by looking at these 25 largest Native American casinos and the 25 largest tribes in terms of population. Although it is obvious that some tribes have been helped immeasurably in many good ways because of gambling, have all Native Americans been helped? The 1990 Census reported that there were 1,959,234 Native Americans and that 437,079 of these lived on reservation lands. Of those living on reservations, 50.7 percent were living below the poverty line. Their median family incomes were $13,489, with a mean income of $17,459. The median national family income for all Americans was $32,225, and less than 10 percent were below the poverty line. The Native American population in 2000 numbered 2,475,956, with 512,032 living on reservation lands. Of those on reservations, 39.4 percent were living under the poverty line, with family incomes averaging $23,966. Unemployment rates were still over 20 percent on reservations. Native Americans remained the poorest of all groups in American society. More than gaming was needed to change the circumstances of Native Americans.

Table 8 lists the 20 largest tribes and gambling. Table 9 lists the tribes with the 20 largest casinos. Only one of the largest casinos is located on one of the largest reservations. The Mississippi Choctaw, the 20th-largest tribe, has the 15th-largest casino.

Using data from the July 1997 issue of *Casino Executive Magazine,* the editor discovered that there were 6,037,223 square feet in gambling space in all Native American casinos. The casinos employed 96,584 persons, and collectively they had 5,044 tables and 88,892 gambling machines.

The 25 largest reservations in terms of population do not have the largest casinos. Indeed only 14 have casinos. For these tribes, averaging the casino attributes among the 25 indicates that gambling floors average less than 19,000 square feet and employee numbers average 288 persons. The tribes have an average of 10 tables each and 318 machines at the casinos. Although the 25 largest tribes had over half of the Native American population living on reservations, they had less than 8 percent

TABLE 8. The 20 Largest Tribes and Gambling

Tribe	Gaming Square Footage	Employees	Tables	Machines	Native Population*	Household Income Median	% Below Poverty
Navajo AZ, NM	0	0	0	0	143,000	9,769	54.20
Pine Ridge, SD	30,000	129	8	113	11,181	10,633	75.00
Ft. Apache, AZ	5,300	700	5	299	9,823	12,403	49.90
Gila River, AZ (2)	68,000	1,200	40	771	9,113	12,744	62.80
Tohono O'odham	48,000	750	28	500	8,476	8,552	62.80
Rosebud, SD	0	0	0	0	8,041	10,887	54.40
San Carlos, AZ	65,000	350	10	500	7,106	8,360	59.80
Zuni, NM	0	0	0	0	7,073	15,536	47.40
Hopi, AZ	0	0	0	0	7,059	13,418	47.70
Blackfeet, MT	0	0	0	0	7,025	13,315	45.70
Turtle Mt., ND	22,800	323	10	0	6,770	11,033	51.90
Yakima, WA	0	0	0	0	6,165	14,807	42.50
Ft. Peck, MT	0	0	0	0	5,782	13,822	41.80
Wind River, WY	0	0	0	0	3,674	13,463	47.80
Cherokee, NC	25,000	180	0	874	5,387	16,330	30.00
Flathead	0	0	0	0	5,110	14,898	31.80
Cheyenne River	0	0	0	0	5,100	9,885	57.20
Standing Rock, ND	42,000	400	12	470	4,866	9,493	54.90
Crow, MT	20,000	70	0	100	4,724	14,031	45.50
Mississippi, Choctaw	90,000	2,000	96	2,800	3,932	16,702	37.60
Total of Larger Reservations	415,300	6,489	204	6,432	271,400		
Percentage of All	6.90%	6.70%	4%	7.20%	62.10%		
All Native America	6,037,223	96,584	5,044	88,892	437,079	13,570	
Average	20,765	324	10	322	6,758	—	—
Median	0	0	0	0	6,898	13,030	49

*On reservation only. This collectively represents approximately 35% of enrolled memberships.

Source: Based on information in June 1997 *Casino Executive* magazine, 1990 Census, and other research.

TABLE 9. Tribes with the 20 Largest Casinos

Tribe	Gaming Square Footage	Employees	Tables	Machines	Native Population*	Household Income Median	% Below Poverty
Mashantucket Pequot, CT	284,236	10,687	312	4,585	55	41,667	
Saginaw Chippewa, MI	205,000	2,500	80	3,600	735	15,083	39.80
Mohegan, CT	150,000	5,600	180	3,000	**219	23,611	46.20
Ft. McDowell, AZ	150,000	1,400	0	475	560	15,982	23.70
Mille Lacs (2), MN	270,000	2,334	87	2,875	428	6,796	84.00
Viejas, CA	120,000	1,600	73	1,132	227	18,170	26.00
Barona, CA	115,000	1,100	32	1,000	373	25,625	25.00
St. Ste Marie (5), MI	97,507	2,183	96	2,284	315	21,875	46.80
St. Croix (2), WI	95,000	1,112	44	1,270	459	9,287	44.60
Oneida, WI	95,908	1,520	80	2,500	2,447	19,133	27.50
Cabazon, CA	94,000	550	10	800	20	27,500	50.00
San Manual, CA	92,000	1,400	50	1,000	56	11,250	81.80
Shakopee Mdewakanton, MN	90,000	4,000	120	2,500	153	62,661	5.80
White Earth, MN	90,000	1,000	32	850	2,759	11,867	46.40
Choctaw, MS	90,000	2,000	96	2,800	3,932	16,702	37.60
Prairie Island Mdewakanton, MN	80,000	1,400	60	1,500	56	5,714	71.40
Morongo, CA	80,000	800	49	1,627	527	18,929	30.10
Coushatta, LA	71,000	2,100	60	2,010	33	7,111	61.50
Sycuan, CA	70,000	1,100	72	444	0	—	
Oneida, NY	68,000	2,000	148	1,000	37	16,250	
Total of Larger Casinos	2,407,660	46,380	1,680	37,260	13,120		
Percentage of All	39.90%	48.00%	33.30%	41.90%	3.00%		
All Native Americans	6,037,223	96,584	5,044	88,892	437,079		
Average	120,383	2,319	84%	1,863	656	—	
Median	94,954	1,560	72.50%	1,564	315	16,702	40%

*On reservation only. This collectively represents approximately 35% of enrolled memberships.

**Tribal District Statistical Area.

Source: Based on information in June 1997 *Casino Executive* magazine, 1990 Census, and other research.

of the gambling space, less than 8 percent of the casino employees, 4 percent of the gambling tables, and 9 percent of the gambling machines.

On the other hand, the tribes with the 25 largest casinos employed an average of 2,024 in gambling, whereas their reservation populations averaged one-third of that number. The large casinos had average floor spaces of 115,566 square feet, with 73 tables and 1,761 machines each. The tribes owning the casinos had 4 percent of the 1990 reservation populations, but they had 47.8 percent of the gambling space, 52 percent of the casino employees, 36 percent of the gambling tables, and 51 percent of the casino machines. It can be suggested that these big facilities produced about half of all the gambling revenues generated in Native American facilities.

Although there is little doubt that gambling has been the best economic development tool available to Native Americans since the occupation of their lands by European settlers, the tool has not reached its potential for helping large numbers of the economically poorest people in the United States. Some attention should be given to mechanisms such as those utilized in Canada for spreading this wealth and the opportunities it can engender to more Native American peoples.

References

Light, Steven Andrew, and Kathryn R. L. Rand. 2008. "The Hand That's Been Dealt: The Indian Gaming Regulatory Act at 20." Paper presented to Gambling Law Symposium, Drake University Law School, September 12.

Thompson, William N. 1996. *Native American Issues: A Reference Handbook.* Santa Barbara, CA: ABC-CLIO.

Thompson, William N. 2005. *Native American Issues: A Reference Handbook.* 2nd ed. Santa Barbara, CA: ABC-CLIO.

Thompson, William N. 1998. Testimony presented to the National Gambling Impact Study Commission, Tempe, Arizona, July 30.

NATIVE AMERICAN GAMING: TRADITIONAL

Long before the ships of Columbus brought playing cards to North America, the indigenous peoples engaged in gambling activities. The Native populations of the Western Hemisphere have been no different than other populations since the beginning of time. They have had games and have wagered valuable possessions on the outcomes of the games.

Stewart Culin's *Games of the North American Indians* (Culin 1907) classifies hundreds of Native games into two categories: (1) games of chance, including dice games and guessing games; and (2) games of dexterity, encompassing archery, javelin and darts, shooting, ball games, and racing games. Both categories were found among all North

American tribes when European intruders arrived on the continent.

Guessing games usually involved sticks that one person would hold in his or her hands behind the back. Another person would seek to determine which hand held the most sticks or held a stick with a particular marking. Other guessing games involved having to find a hidden object such as a stone or a ball that might be placed into one of several moccasins or in some place in a room.

The most prevalent game of chance involved objects that had characteristics of today's dice. Tribes of every linguistic group had dice games. Most often the dice were stones with two distinguishable sides. They were tossed by hand into baskets or bowls, and counting systems were used to keep score for two individuals or two groups competing with one another.

All tribes in North America had some game involving throwing or shooting an arrow, spear, or dart through a hoop placed at a distance. A variety of other targets would be used as well. Also, some contests involved keeping arrows in the air for a long time or achieving great distances with shooting. Ring and pin games were also quite popular. A ring (the target) was tied to a stick by a string. The string was then used to swing the stick into the air, with the object of having the stick go through the ring.

Although most arrow-type games and running games were based upon individual skills, Native Americans also had a wide range of team games involving kicking balls or moving balls toward goals by means of rackets or clubs. Europeans learned the game of lacrosse from the indigenous populations of the North American continent. In addition, all tribes had varieties of running games involving individual runners as well as teams of relay runners.

Wherever there was a game or a contest, schemes existed to place wagers on the results. In most of the skill games, the participants in the games were men; however, those making wagers would often include both men and women, and the betting activity could become rather excessive.

Culin relates some harmful effects of tribal gaming, citing an account of a bowl and stick-dice game among the Assiniboin of the northern plains: "Most of the leisure time, either by night or by day, among all these nations is devoted to gambling in various ways, and such is their infatuation that it is the cause of much distress and poverty in families" (Culin 1907, 173–174). He suggests that if a young man gained a reputation for being a heavy gambler that this would be an obstacle in the way of gaining a wife. Many arguments ensued among the people because of gambling. Culin writes, "We are well acquainted with an Indian who a few years since killed another because after winning all he had he refused to put up his wife to be played for" (174).

According to Culin, among the Assiniboin women could become as addicted to gaming as men; however, as they usually did not control property sources as much as men, their losses were not as "distressing" (174).

Other accounts of Native American games have been more positive. Burt and Ethel Aginsky found that among the Pomo of California, gamblers were a highly honored group and a family would happily welcome an apprentice gambler as a son-in-law. Gaming was also sanctioned by tribal religion, and the whole society participated in games that involved wagers. Tribal members, however, were cautioned against winning too many possessions from one another as this would cause "hard feelings" (Aginsky and Aginsky 1950, 109–110).

Henry Lesieur and Robert Custer reviewed several studies of Native American gaming and found patterns of activity that mitigated the possibilities of the development of pathological gambling behaviors: (1) Games were formalized rituals with many spectators; (2) players could not go into debt as a result of the games—they could wager only those possessions they brought with them to the games; and (3) individuals had to have permission from their family in order to make wagers (Lesieur and Custer 1984, 149).

Although the modern era has seen a massive expansion of Native gaming facilities in North America, today's Native games are patterned almost exclusively upon games developed by Asian and European newcomers to the continent. Similarly, while the new Americans very early established contact with Native peoples and also incorporated gambling practices into their new communities, there is very little evidence that they borrowed games from Native peoples, lacrosse being one exception.

The lack of a general cross-fertilization of game development among tribes and settlers of European origin is evidenced in the almost complete lack of mitigating controls over pathological gaming, such as those identified by Lesieur and Custer, in modern Native American casinos. Today's Native American gaming is simply an outgrowth of emerging patterns of non-Native gaming.

References

Aginsky, Burt W., and Ethel G. Aginsky. 1950. "The Pomo: A Profile of Gambling among Indians." In *Gambling* (special volume of *The Annals of the Academy of Political and Social Science*), edited by Morris Ploscowe and Edwin J. Lukas, 108–113. Philadelphia: The American Academy of Political and Social Science.

Culin, Stewart. 1907. *Games of the North American Indians.* Washington, DC: Government Printing Office.

Desmond, Gerald D. 1952. "Gambling among the Yakima." Ph.D. diss., Catholic University of America.

Devereux, George. 1950. "Psychodynamics of Mohave Gambling." *American Imago* 7: 55–65.

Flannery, Regina, and John M. Cooper. 1946. "Social Mechanisms in Gros Ventre Gambling." *Southwestern Journal of Anthropology* 2: 391–419.

Lesieur, Henry, and Robert L. Custer. 1984. "Pathological Gambling: Roots, Phases, and Treatment." In *Gambling: Views from the Social Sciences* (special volume of *The Annals of the American Academy of Political and Social Science*), edited by James H. Frey and William R. Eadington, 146–156. Beverly Hills, CA: Sage.

ORGANIZED CRIME CONTROL ACT OF 1970

President Richard Nixon signed the Organized Crime Control Act into law on October 15, 1970. The act was in reality a long list of ideas rather than a comprehensive, coherent package of tools with which to deal with organized crime. Some called it "a smorgasbord of legal odds and ends" and a series of "nuts and bolts" for dealing with crime.

Among the matters of concern in the act was gambling. The act provided federal tools for enforcing state provisions on gambling under certain conditions. Penalties were provided for persons who financed, owned, managed, supervised, or directed an illegal gambling enterprise. The illegal enterprises had to involve five or more persons who acted contrary to state and local law to participate in gambling over a period of 30 days or more with revenues involved exceeding $2,000 for a single day. If two people conspired to break a state law on gambling and one was a public official, the federal government was also empowered to take action against the offenders. The act also authorized the appointment of the Commission on the Review of National Policy toward Gambling, which was appointed in 1974 and made a report of its findings in 1976.

References

Graham, Fred. 1970. "Nixon Finally Gets Crime Bill He Wanted." *New York Times*, October 18, IV-9.

Organized Crime Control Act of 1970 (Public Law 91–452, 84 Stat. 922, signed into law 15 October 1970).

See also Commission on the Review of National Policy toward Gambling (1974–1976).

Pachinko. *See* Japan and Pachinko Parlors.

Pachi-slo. *See* Japan and Pachinko Parlors.

Pai Gow Poker. *See* Poker (in Games section).

POLITICAL CULTURE AND NEVADA: REASSESSING THE THEORY

How can the culture of a people be related to policies regarding gambling? A political culture is a collective set of beliefs and values that can define how a people orient themselves toward government in general and what their feelings are about their own political jurisdiction, political participation and rules of participation, their obligations as citizens, their attitudes toward their fellow citizens, and their attitudes toward their leaders. The late Daniel Elazar, a renowned political scientist, postulated that although there was a dominant type of political culture for the United States reflecting our national heritage and our national system, there were major subtypes of political cultures in different parts of the United States. He identified three such sub-types: the (I)ndividualistic, (M)oralistic, and (T)raditionalistic.

The I culture envisions a democratic order expressed through a marketplace of issues. Government does not exist to create "a good society" but rather to respond to demands of citizens on economic and other issues. Mass political participation is not encouraged, as politics is an activity reserved for "professionals," not amateurs. Policymaking is transactional, a bargaining process between self-interest groups and individuals. People who seek political office do so as a means of controlling the distribution of rewards of government, not for pursuing programs or ideology. Politics is like horse trading.

The M culture was brought to the New World by the Pilgrims and then the Puritans who set up a series of religious colonies in New England. The M culture emphasizes the commonwealth as the basis for democratic government. Politics is considered a lofty pursuit in humankind's search for the "good society." Although politics is a struggle for power, it is also an attempt to exercise that power for the betterment of the commonwealth. Government is a positive instrument to promote the general welfare, which is more than a balance of or the sum of individual interests. Citizen participation is an essential ingredient in the M culture. Politics is the concern of every citizen. Thus it is the citizens' duty to participate. Those who serve in government and politics assume high moral obligations.

The T political culture had its roots in British royalty. It persisted past the revolutionary years within the United States in the plantation South, where citizens were seeking economic opportunity through their agricultural system. That system relied to some degree upon the institution of slavery. According to Elazar, the T culture is based upon an ambivalent attitude toward the marketplace coupled with an elitist conception of society. The T political culture reflects an older, precommercial attitude that accepts a largely hierarchical society and expects those at the top of the social order to take a special and dominant role in government. That role is defined as keeping the existing social order. Government functions for the purpose of confining real political power to a comparatively small and self-perpetuating elite, who often inherit their "right" to govern through family or social ties. Those who do not have a definitive role to play in the political system are not expected to become active in politics.

Elazar seeks to categorize each state as well as regions within states with one of the three subtypes, or with a combination of the subtypes of political cultures. Elazar placed Nevada clearly under the I culture category, although he did not specifically discuss Nevada politics. Nevada historian James Hulse offers a commentary. He correctly reads Elazar's description of I culture, saying that it "assumes that the function of the marketplace is given top priority" by the government. He goes on to indicate, "Nevada as a society has been relaxed, permissive and at times even reckless in its receptivity to the individualistic prospector and promoter. The contemporary gamblers on both sides of the betting tables belong in that category" (6).

Furthermore, the position that Nevada is an I culture is espoused by Nevada Congresswoman Dina Titus, also a professor of political science at the University of Nevada, Las Vegas. She offers that Nevadans are notoriously antigovernment, indicating that their greatest antipathy is directed toward Washington and that they resent any mandates imposed from "inside the Beltway." Indeed, in support of the argument, both the Sagebrush Rebellion (an effort to have the federal government return lands to state control) and a County Supremacy Movement originated in Nevada. Closer to home, Nevadans' suspicion of government is reflected in the maintenance of a "citizen legislature" that meets for only 120 days every other year and is hamstrung by such constitutional restrictions as a requirement for a two-thirds majority vote on any new tax levy and also a term limit of 12 years for service. There are also provisions for extensive direct democracy via recall and initiative procedures. Although Nevadans do cherish their ability to keep government at a minimum, Titus relates that they seldom exercise the power they have, which is also consistent with the I culture identified in Elazar's model.

Congresswoman Titus also points out the fact that the state has very low voter registration and turnout. In addition, partisanship is extremely weak, as many if not most voters split their tickets frequently. Pragmatic politics prevails over ideology, and libertarian values are espoused by both major parties. Finally, Titus, as did Hulse, emphasizes that Nevada's independent attitude is reflected in a myriad of "anything goes" policies adopted over the years. Protecting personal freedoms is a priority, as she points out in policies such as the prohibition against one-party wire taps, the legalization of medical marijuana, and the existence of lawful prostitution in parts of the state. Nevada also prides itself on being the "Delaware of the West" when it comes to corporation statutes; moreover, the state has promulgated fewer environmental regulations on business than most states.

"Individualism?" Titus asks. "Where else, for example, can you build a roller coaster atop a 115-story tower next door to a wedding chapel with a drive-through window and a mechanical arm that throws rice on your windshield? Where else can you breast-feed your baby in public while carrying not one but as many concealed weapons as you desire?"

The arguments that Nevada has essentially an I culture may be many, but are they necessarily conclusive?

A REASSESSMENT OF THE CATEGORIZATION OF NEVADA AS AN I CULTURE

The editor's research leads him to offer a dissent to the distinguished trio, claiming instead that Nevada represents a prototypical example of the T culture. Indeed, the editor suggested that Nevada may be the only pure example of a state T culture in the United States today. The states identified by Elazar as T states included most of those in the Old South (former Confederate states). They, of course, were isolated in their defense of slavery, and then after emancipation, in their defense of states' rights policies designed to support an apartheid posture to life. Isolation of the South grew during the Civil Rights era of the 1950s and 1960s, and as the racist separation policies fell under the force of national edicts for change, a wave of change ensued throughout the South. Nevada had also been isolated, with its adherence to gambling policies, and a national political establishment also demanded change—an elimination of Mob-controlled casino gambling—in the same decades as the civil rights era. While Nevada was resisting that change, gambling enterprise entered into the economic and political fabric of many other states. Gambling spread first with horse racing, then with government-operated lotteries, and finally with casino gambling that in the form of games was quite similar to that found in Nevada. On the one hand, the T culture of the Old South was overwhelmed with national opposition; the T culture of Nevada, on the other hand, survived to a point where the rest of the nation came to accept the critical element of the Nevada political establishment—the defense of a casino industry.

To a large degree, communities in both California and Nevada began in a similar way. People were attracted to the possibilities of "getting rich quick." John A. Sutter, a pioneer settler in California, discovered gold on his land near Sacramento in 1848. Word quickly spread. Between 1848 and 1860 the population of California went from less than 30,000 to nearly 400,000. Statehood came in 1850, and California entered the union as a wild and sinful place. Nevada's society developed around the discovery of the Comstock Lode of silver in 1859. Populations rushed in from both the East and the West (California prospectors), creating a society that mirrored that of its wild neighbor to the west. Nevada statehood came not as a natural response to the growth of an American population but as a response to political needs in Washington, D.C. Abraham Lincoln had political struggles. Congress had proposed the Thirteenth Amendment abolishing slavery, but states (even some northern states) had been reluctant to ratify the amendment. Lincoln needed another vote, and Nevada's ratification vote was the one necessary for the Thirteenth Amendment to take effect. The state's birth thus can be associated with freedom. Lincoln also wanted congressional support for the proposed Fourteenth and Fifteenth amendments, and Nevada gave that support—especially in the Senate, where it had two votes, just as did the biggest states. And, of course, Lincoln also wanted to be reelected, and Lin-

coln thought his 1864 opponent John McClelland would have a strong campaign. Nevada gave Lincoln its three electoral votes—just in time. Statehood was granted on October 31, 1864, just one week before the presidential election. (The timing was perfect, as today Nevada is the only state that makes Halloween an official state holiday!)

After the initial wave of miners, Nevada's population development slowed. The second wave of family population that hit California completely missed Nevada in the 19th century. When mining resources dwindled, Nevada communities became ghost towns. The state's population fell from a peak of almost 63,000 to less than 50,000 in 1890. There were actually discussions in the 19th century and even later that pondered the notion of revoking statehood status because of depopulation. It also can be noted that in 1922 the Methodist church removed "district status" from the state and designated Nevada as a "mission." Early on, sin represented a style of life as well as an economic opportunity for part of the population; and when mining collapsed, there were no serious efforts to interfere with the jobs provided by alcohol, gambling, and prostitution, albeit a prohibition and antigambling crusade was played out to formal success, then totally ignored.

Early in the state's history a defense against the outside world was necessitated by the declining mining industry. Control of politics was in hands of railroad giants. The Big Four (Leland Stanford, Mark Hopkins, Colis Huntington, and Charles Crocker) who controlled California also controlled Nevada. Nevada was in a sense their colony. Gilman Ostrander has chronicled the era in his book *Nevada: The Great Rotten Borough 1859–1964*. One force kept Nevada's neighbor California supporting Nevada's existence as a state—its two votes in the U.S. Senate. The California railroad interests wanted the votes to support their interests, but also the seats represented desirable commodities for social reasons. During the latter decades of the 19th century, on at least five occasions California-based Senate candidates made overt purchases of elections from the Nevada legislature. In Washington they did not distinguish themselves in any way, and the representation they gave to Nevada interests was minimal—beyond resisting attempts to place the issue of rescinding statehood on the national agenda.

The system of boss selection of senators changed little as the state embraced popular election of senators along with the rest of the nation. By the time the Seventeenth Amendment took force, Nevada had a political boss—George Wingfield—who effectively controlled both parties. Personality battles over offices manifested themselves, but the contestants made little noise on policy matters that counted.

At the turn of the century, Francis Newlands, one of the senators who purchased his seat, emerged as a national leader of Progressives. He was the son-in-law of another Nevada senator who had purchased his U.S. Senate seat—William Sharon. Newlands distinguished himself in the field of conservation. In that role he served Nevada well, as he advocated a national involvement in projects that could reclaim lands for farming and provide water for western communities. The progressive Newlands Reclamation Act of 1902 bears his name. Although Newlands believed that the national government should be a positive force in people's lives, and such notions may have been against fears Nevadans

had of federal control of their activities, a pattern was being established. Nevadans then and even now show a tremendous tolerance for its national leaders' pursuing a variety of causes—liberal, conservative, moderate—as long as they adhere to the central cause of protecting the state's economic base and its right to pursue its economic future as it pleases.

Nevadans survived threats to statehood, but they still had to make their own way economically. In the 19th century, many individual Nevadans felt that "making their own way" meant they had to leave the state, and many did. Those who stayed tried many things. They always fought to make mining work, but could not do so in a reliable way over generations. The state occupied space and took advantage of that simple fact. The state sought to become a center for business incorporation in the way that Delaware was in the East. This effort was short-lived, as California refused to recognize Nevada corporations unless they met California standards. The state allowed boxing matches when California refused to; the Jeffries versus Jackson "Great White Hope" match of 1910 in Reno was the most famous one until the modern era. The state permitted prostitution to remain legal in registered brothels; even today this activity continues in several of the state's counties. Nevada sought to become the divorce capital of the country, as it had very lax rules on exactly who was a resident of the state—it being necessary that one party of a divorce be a resident. The state also sought tax revenues from commerce moving across its borders to and from California. Additionally, the state became a warehousing center by eliminating inventory taxes. In all these things, Nevada was somewhat different or even exceedingly different from other states. The first duty of the political establishment was to protect the economic life of the state, and often this meant protecting the ability of the state to be different. Populism was acceptable when it accomplished the essential goals, progressivism was acceptable when it accomplished the essential goals, and so too were activities that seemed to be of an I, M, or T culture.

THE 20TH CENTURY— PRELUDE TO THE NEW GAMBLING ERA

While California was establishing itself as the Golden State, Nevada was sinking constantly into disrepute. In that disrepute, however, Nevada found the final solution to its economic conundrum—Nevada found wide-open mass-marketed casino gambling. Before that discovery in the 1940s and 1950s, the state had built in its style of political power. During the Progressive era and through the 1920s, 1930s, and 1940s, the state had essentially abolished a notion of competitive two-party politics. As alluded to earlier, George Wingfield was the "boss" of both parties early in the century. Wingfield's office was in room 201 of the Reno National Bank Building, and that room was considered the "real capitol of Nevada." Wingfield was the head of the state Republican Party. Anyone who wished to speak to the head of the Democratic Party did not have to seek out a different address, however. The party chairman was in the same office—he was Wingfield's junior law partner. They shared the same telephone number, 4111. The bipartisan Wingfield machine purposely sought to send one Democrat and one Republican senator to Washington.

This pattern allowed the state to have two members on the same committee in the Senate—the committee of choice was the one with power over mining issues. The pattern also allowed the state to have a Senate delegation with considerable seniority. Two "key" Democrats gained control of important committees, where they could trade favors and votes in manners that could benefit the state in different ways. The incurable alcoholic Key Pittman became the chair of the Senate's Foreign Relations Committee during President Franklin D. Roosevelt's difficult years prior to World War II. Pittman's considerable embarrassments were overlooked; he died in 1940 before he could ruin U.S. international relations during the war years. Toward the middle decades, Wingfield's role was absorbed by the jingoist Senator Patrick McCarran (for whom, ironically, the Las Vegas McCarran International Airport was named). Senator McCarran used his seniority to join hands with U.S. Senator Joseph McCarthy (R-Wisconsin) in his witch hunts against real and imagined communists. He sponsored very restrictive immigration legislation as well. McCarran was a force in putting boundaries around the anticasino work of Senator Estes Kefauver of Tennessee. And both McCarran and Pittman managed to get considerable "pork" for the state in the form of military facilities as well as that plum of all plums—the Nevada Test Site, the facility for atmospheric atomic bomb testing. Fortunately (for Nevadans), most "downwinders" lived in Utah.

State leaders measured their performance in political office in very mundane terms, and most were judged on their personalities. Although individual leaders were permitted to pursue progressive or populist causes on a wide range of issues, they pursued one general protection on all essential issues: they did what was necessary to guarantee that the state's primary industry was protected. There were no noticeable differences in defending gambling policies whether the governor was civil libertarian Grant Sawyer, arch conservative Paul Laxalt, education reformer and labor advocate Mike O'Callahan, Republicans Bob List or Kenny Guinn, or Democrats Richard Bryan or Bob Miller. The public showed a great willingness to elect to the Senate extreme conservatives such as Laxalt and Chic Hecht (who called Jesse Helms "my liberal friend"), or liberal activists such as Harry Reid and Howard Cannon. All were free to pursue any national policies they wished to pursue. They had to be united, however, on defending gambling and on funding state military projects, including nuclear testing. More recently, they have had to staunchly oppose the storage of nuclear waste in the state.

NEVADA GAMBLING

Gambling activities persisted in early Nevada, although casinos were made illegal for a brief time after statehood was granted. By the turn of the century, however, the Progressive movement was gaining strength across the United States and in the Silver State. In concert with temperance organizations, civil leaders attacked the local sin industries. They approached the state legislature and gained passage of a bill that closed the casinos on September 30, 1910.

By 1911, the legislature had second (and third) thoughts. Certain card games were legalized, only to be made illegal again in 1913. In 1915, limited gaming was permitted again. Enforcement of the gaming limits was sporadic at best and nonexistent as a rule. In lieu of fees when gaming was legal, operators now paid bribes to local officials, who pretended that gaming did not take place.

A move to legalize gambling was revived in 1931 when Nevada assemblyman Phil Tobin of Humboldt County introduced the legislative measure. Although opposition was voiced by religious groups, Tobin's bill passed the assembly on a 24–11 vote and the state senate by 13 to 3. On March 19, 1931, Governor Fred Balzar signed the measure to legalize casino gambling. A second law passed later in 1931 permitted local governments to regulate gambling and fixed fees for gaming statewide. The fees were shared, with 75 percent going to local governments and 25 percent to the state. Licenses were granted by county commissions, and all regulations were enforced by the sheriff.

State regulation began in the 1940s as larger gambling operations were established, and casino gambling began to emerge as the state's dominant industry. In 1950 the state weathered the first concerted national attack on its casino industry. The U.S. Senate Special Committee to Investigate Organized Crime in Interstate Commerce (the Kefauver Committee) targeted Nevada. The state resisted the attack through the efforts of its congressional delegation and also by the adoption of new rules for licensing and controlling casinos. In 1955, a full-time Gambling Control Board was established. In 1959, the state responded to continuing attacks that now came from the McClelland Committee, which included Senator John F. Kennedy (D-Massachusetts) and had his brother, Robert, as its special counsel, by adding the Nevada Gaming Commission to strengthen its regulatory framework. During the 1960s, more federal attacks ensued, and Governors Grant Sawyer and Paul Laxalt coordinated the state's response by inviting Howard Hughes to the state in 1966 to become a major player by buying out casinos tied to Mob interests.

In 1969 the state authorized publicly traded companies to own casinos, hence welcoming a type of federal control over big operators—through the Securities and Exchange Commission. The state also strengthened its control over casino operators by banning licensees from having gambling operations in other jurisdictions. This ruling was later modified in 1977 to allow licensees to go into New Jersey. This change was effectuated after Nevada reviewed New Jersey regulatory structures to assure that they would adequately oversee casino operations in such a way that no federal authorities would challenge their industry.

The Las Vegas casino interests had not taken a role in the New Jersey casino campaigns of 1974 and 1976 (when the vote was successful). The competition from the East blindsided Nevada. Coupled with a general national economic slump, in the early 1980s, Nevada casinos had their only three-year period (since statistics were gathered) when gambling revenues fell in terms of constant-value dollars. Nonetheless, the casinos stood by silently during the 1984 California lottery campaign. Nevada was very much aware of the possibilities of harm that could be done to its industry by Indian gambling, however, seeing the harm in terms of unregulated gambling that would draw organized crime and consequently discredit all casinos. Native Americans saw it differently. They saw Nevada as only fearing the competition they would give. In any event, the Nevada congressional delegation came forth with the proposals for a national law to regulate Native American gambling after the U.S. Supreme Court in the *Cabazon* case of 1987 said states could not regulate gambling without an act of Congress. After the Indian Gaming Regulatory Act was passed, Nevada interests provided research help for state attorneys general throughout the nation who stood in opposition to Native American gambling. In most cases the Nevada interests and state attorneys general lost their battles.

During the 1990s, Nevada interests, with the support of Nevada political leaders, continued to fight for the gambling industry. Nevada participated in a congressional initiative to limit sports betting to Nevada and three other states where it already existed—although not in the open way it exists in Nevada. In 1993, the Nevada legislature abolished its rule precluding Nevada licensees from participating in gambling elsewhere. Other states had succumbed to the inevitability of Native American casinos, and eventually nine additional states permitted commercialized casino gambling. The Nevada casino industry was quite eager to be able to cash in on opportunities to manage Native American casinos or to have their own gambling halls in other states.

A new threat to the gambling industry came in 1994 when President Bill Clinton proposed a 4 percent surtax on all gambling winnings in the United States. As lotteries and Native American casinos were exempted, it was clear that the impact of the tax would fall upon the casinos of Nevada. The state (which cast majorities for Clinton in both 1992 and 1996) rallied together in opposition. While the congressional delegation did its job in Washington, the casinos formed a new national lobbying bloc—the American Gaming Association (AGA). The AGA read Clinton's message well, and campaign funds started to flow. Ironically, the Clinton election team was probably the biggest beneficiary of this money spigot. In 1996, the AGA and Nevada forces sought to prohibit the creation of the National Gambling Impact Study Commission. Failing in this endeavor, they succeeded in limiting the powers of the commission, and they gained control over several of its appointments. The venom of the commission—which was led by a decidedly antigambling chairwoman—was deflected away from commercial casinos and onto targets such as Native American casinos, lotteries, and Internet gambling. Betting on college games also attracted commission opposition, leading to proposed legislation to effectuate a ban. Again the Nevada political forces closed ranks in defense of the status quo monopoly the state's gaming industry has over this form of gambling.

The 1998 approval of Proposition 5 in California presented the greatest threat to Nevada casinos since the Kefauver hearings of the 1950s. After it was set aside by California courts, Nevada interests were content to accept the compromises of the new Proposition 1A. It is possible that Proposition 1A will now allow the casinos of Nevada and the Nevada political establishment to build important bridges to California and its power structure (*see* Native American Gaming: Contemporary).

WHICH CULTURE IS NEVADA'S?

These events suggest a misread of the I culture that may also have been implicit in Elazar's placement of Nevada in the I complex. The culture is not the activity of private individuals. That Nevada has many free spirits and gamblers does not mean that the government is also a "free spirit" for sale to the highest bidder. Rather, Hulse seems to offer more poignant words in support of the notion that Nevada has been a Traditionalistic (T) state, quite like the states of the South that seemed the only major bastions of T culture in Elazar's study.

James Hulse writes, "Nevada as a political and social entity has from the beginning been especially vulnerable to [an] ambitious and wealthy oligarchy . . . largely because of its inherently weak and impoverished economic situation." He goes on to suggest that the pattern has survived to this day, with the state being "exceptionally receptive to those with large amounts of money" (6). He then singles out persons of the gambling industry: William Harrah, Howard Hughes, Kirk Kerkorian, and Steve Wynn. Hulse even indicates that the state was exceedingly warm to mobsters who were essential in the expansion of the casino industry. Then he adds that "gambling control agencies were designed not only to regulate [gambling] but also to protect it from those elements that might . . . endanger its prosperity. Likewise, Nevada's Senators and Representatives in Washington and the elected state officials have assumed the position of feudal knights protecting their domain from challengers" (7). The leaders were not merely brokers giving government favors to the winners in some marketplace of policymaking.

A new population influx has made Nevada what California was just a few decades ago—the fastest-growing state in the union. Great population influxes changed California's collective political orientations, as illustrated by Peter Schrag's *Paradise Lost* (1998). The state moved away from an M culture as a lower-income population both grew and demanded more services at the expense of older Californians. So too did population changes make the Old South different in the latter decades of the past century. The population growth of Nevada, however, has not made noticeable changes in the orientation of politics in the Silver State.

Of course such growth could have an influence if it continues. Many of the newcomers, however, are drawn to the state because of its low-cost and high-employment environment. In both cases, these attractive attributes are tied to the state's reliance upon domination by a single industry. Quite frankly, although the state's business climate regularly ranks at the top or in the top two or three places in *Inc. Magazine* rankings, the state does not attract nongambling enterprises in numbers sufficient to absorb employment demands of new residents. Newcomers also appreciate the very low state taxes, which are among the lowest in the nation. This is especially the case with senior citizens attracted to the several new Sun Cities of the Las Vegas area.

Nevertheless, there is a crisis of public services much like that witnessed in California. The school population is growing, and the Clark County school district does not have the tax resources to hire sufficient teachers or to build new school buildings fast enough. The state is also facing crises in transportation and the environment.

The casino industry is quite willing to let the politicians have a "free vote" on school issues or almost any other issue that does not directly affect their interests. They closely keep their eyes on tax policies, however. Here they are like residents— they appreciate low taxes. There have been calls for incremental tax increases from some and for monumental increases in gambling taxes by others. In the latter case, one state senator has called for a doubling of the gambling tax rate. In the 1998 gubernatorial primary, he also advocated higher gambling taxes. This was a unique stand, as all legislators in the state have taken campaign funds from the gambling industry. But the word *unique* is not a word to crave when

seeking votes. The good senator won 15 percent of the vote. That 15 percent probably represents a reasonable number for a subculture of Nevada that wants the casinos to pay much higher taxes.

In 1994, a feature story in *Time* magazine called Las Vegas "America's City" and indicated that the city was not becoming like the rest of the nation but that rather the rest of the nation was becoming like Las Vegas. Perhaps the rest of the nation finds the "free spirit" life of Las Vegas inviting. The other states have embraced the gambling industry, and by doing so, they have allowed Nevada to have allies in its fight against federal interference with casinos. No other state has fallen into a posture of allowing gambling interests to completely dominate its politics, however. In the other states, such as California, the gambling interests have to fight out their battles against other interests that are already organized. The welcoming of gambling is an indicator that these states in many cases may have abandoned Elazar's M culture. It is not an indicator that I cultures have fallen.

Nevada has played its politics game within the tenets of the T culture. In the past, Nevada felt it had to fight competition from other states that might have desired to have casinos. But now gambling has spread to all corners of the nation, and the game on gambling issues need not be played in a way that precludes compromises with competing states. The fear that a national political establishment will now ban all gambling, once a major fear for Nevadans, no longer grips the state. Unlike the Old South, which embraced a T culture when it was opposed by all the other regions of the nation, Nevada has seen much of the nation become as it is—gambling territory. Nevada now has allies in every region, something the South never had on race issues.

CONTEMPORARY CULTURES AND INTERSTATE COOPERATION ON GAMBLING ISSUES

California voices are occasionally heard calling for wide-open casino gambling in order to check the outflow of money that its citizens take to Nevada casinos. Internal fights among various components of California's gambling interests—tracks, card clubs, Native Americans, the lottery—will probably preclude this real threat to Nevada gambling from occurring within the foreseeable future. The compromise of Proposition 1A has also made California Native American gaming acceptable to Nevada—not only acceptable but also an opportunity for Nevada industry investment. Moreover, Nevada's failure to attract manufacturers that can provide a large portion of supplies to the casinos means that the Silver State's main industry will continue to support California's industries with purchasing activities that will largely offset the Golden State's

citizens' losses in the green-felt jungles of Glitter Gulch.

*Coauthored by Carl Lutrin
and Dina Titus*

References

Andersen, Kurt. 1994. "Las Vegas: The New All American City." *Time* 143 (January 10): 42–51.

Cabot, Anthony N., William N. Thompson, Andrew Tottenham, and Carl Braunlich, eds. 1999. *International Casino Law.* 3rd ed. Reno: Institute for the Study of Gambling, University of Nevada, Reno, 101–120.

Elazar, Daniel. 1972. *American Federalism: A View from the States.* 2nd ed., New York: Crowell, 79–94.

Hulse, James W. 1991. *The Silver State.* Reno: University of Nevada Press.

Hulse, James W. 1997. "Nevada and the Twenty-First Century." In *Towards 2000: Public Policy in Nevada,* edited by Dennis L. Soden and Erick Herzik, 1–14. Dubuque, IA: Kendall-Hunt.

Ostrander, Gilman. 1966. *Nevada: The Great Rotten Borough 1859–1964.* New York: Alfred A. Knopf.

Schrag, Peter. 1998. *Paradise Lost: California's Experience, America's Future.* New York: New Press.

Skolnick, Jerome H. 1978. *House of Cards: Legalization and Control of Casino Gambling.* Boston: Little, Brown.

THE POSITIVE CASE FOR GAMBLING: ONE PERSON'S VIEW

Editor's Note: At my invitation, in this entry Felicia Campbell presents her interesting analysis concerning the positive aspects of gambling.

My doctoral dissertation, "The Gambling Mystique: Mythologies and Typologies," is the first major study of the positive effects of gambling for the nonproblem gambler (Campbell 1973). Until 1973, the literature dealing with gambling behavior had been overwhelmingly negative and focused almost entirely on compulsive gamblers. Wire service coverage and an article, "The Future of Gambling" in the *Futurist* magazine (Campbell 1976), gave me more than my 15 minutes of fame, and I must admit that it was rewarding to pick up the newspaper and find Dr. Joyce Brothers quoting me saying that "casinos don't cause compulsive gambling any more than soap causes compulsive handwashing." It was even rather entertaining to walk into a session at a gaming conference in Montreal and hear my words in slightly altered form supposedly coming from the mouths of other gamblers.

It is my view that gambling represents a preservative rather than a destructive impulse. When I began writing about gambling, the prevailing view was that all gamblers were masochistic and had a profound desire to lose. Leading the attack was Edmund Bergler, who saw gambling as an attack on bourgeois values, reducing them to absurdity, and the gambler as a "private rebel" who attacks societal norms with dice, stocks, and chips rather than guns or ballots. One wonders what he would think of today's trading revolution (Bergler 1957).

Although I have continued to take an essentially phenomenological approach to gambling, viewing the gambler as part of the entire context in which he or she exists, today's context is wildly different from that of 25 years ago. The 21st century has arrived with a vengeance in all of its cyber and virtual glory. In a world of cybersex, daytrading, extreme sports, and robot technology rivaling anything in science fiction, the casino gambler no longer stands out as one of Bergler's social rebels, although I believe the rebel still

gambles for the same reasons—an altered state of consciousness that offers hope, opportunities for decision making, possible peak experience, and a respite from the day's cares—a minivacation, if you will. Note that I am speaking here of normal gamblers, not desperation gamblers.

For its adherents, gambling is a form of adventure and sometimes of therapy. As far back as the 16th century, universal genius and gambler Girolamo Cardano prescribed gambling to alleviate melancholy, noting that "play may be beneficial in times of grief and the law permits it to the sick and those in prison and those condemned to death" (Cardano 1961). Although the altered state of gambling provides part of the therapy in the action, it is the wins, few as they may be, that count. As a young friend of mine who prefers casinos to tranquilizers after a hard day teaching high school says, "It's ecstasy, it's Paris, France, that is. I've been to Paris on a handful of quarters. On my income by the time I saved enough I would be too old to go. Oh, the casino is a wonderful place."

Today's adventurer gamblers can enhance their experience by prowling the alternate reality of their choice, the Las Vegas Strip obligingly having turned into a form of virtual reality. Almost as quickly as you can change channels on your television set, you can move from Mandalay Bay to Egypt or Rome or a horde of other destinations. You pay your money and walk into the fantasy of your choice, which may be one of the reasons that the Wizard of Oz theme failed at the MGM. Although the casino is definitely not Kansas, it seems to me unlikely that many people revving up for an evening at the tables or machines want to identify with Dorothy or the Tin Woodman. The casino gambler may have isolated himself or herself from nature, but not from a need for sensate experience, an experience that for good or ill moves ever closer to virtual reality, a concrete fantasy that provides escape from the mundane.

Casinos even present a kind of in-house camaraderie. A fellow feeling exists among card players that may not always be present in the real world. At the black-jack table, players all face the same odds whether they are betting $5 or $500 and have a common adversary in the dealer. Here cultural and racial differences and biases disappear during the action, often, sadly, to be replaced after the players leave the tables and reality returns.

Even machines take on personalities in these palaces of escape. I have always been fascinated by relationship between machine gamblers and their adversaries. In my early research I cited an elderly woman who said that she played because she was lonely, and the machines seemed friendly and acknowledged her existence. To her the ringing bells and flashing lights of even a small payoff said, "I like you."

To see that this feeling is not isolated, one need only observe the give-and-take that goes on between player and machine. I have created a brief typology that illustrates some of the major behaviors. Except where noted, these behaviors are common to both genders. There is the Lover, whose hands move softly over the machine or gently slide up and down the handle, when such exists, as though it were a beloved other, caressing it, trying to lure it into spewing its riches into his hands. Not for nothing is gambling parlance studded with sexual terms such as betting "the come" or the "don't come." The Patter, a variation on the Lover, softly pats the sides of the machine, all the while talking to it. More violent, Thumpers beat a rhythmic tattoo on the side of the machine, while Ragers, almost always male, literally pound the machines with their fists and both cajole and threaten them in language fine for television but probably not appropriate for this entry, seeming to believe that they can bully the machines into submission. In contrast, the Pleader maintains a constant dialogue with the machine, usually referring to it as "baby" as he begs for its favors. Prayers sit silently in front of their idols, lips constantly moving.

Perhaps the most annoying to other players are Singers, usually out of tune, and Whistlers, totally oblivious to those around them (at least I hope they are) and seemingly less in communication with the machine than the others I have mentioned. All, however, regardless of their annoyance factor, are totally absorbed in "the action" within the world of the machine, largely unaware of anything going on around them and often of their own behaviors. They have for the moment escaped. You have probably noticed as have I an uncanny resemblance to the relationships between hackers and their machines, which also carry their users to alternate realities.

Clearly everything about casinos is designed to assist gamblers in slipping the perceptual boundaries of their worlds. Linear time and space are smashed. Themed casinos representing diverse historical eras and geographical settings help to destroy the concept of an orderly, linear time line and traditional geography. I think we need note that theming is not confined to businesses but has become a part of home decor and planned communities everywhere.

In the 21st century, we no longer collectively believe in a linear universe of simple cause and effect. We now know that we dance on a web of intersecting realities, where the effect of the flapping of a butterfly's wing in Hong Kong can escalate to create a dust storm in Las Vegas. In essence, as chaos theory explains, everything influences everything else.

Greed is not the primary motive for these new beliefs. The motive is the slipping of ordinary perceptual bounds and moving into the intensity of another reality.

By Felicia Campbell

References

Bergler, Edmund. 1957. *The Psychology of Gambling.* New York: Hill and Wang. Reprint 1985. New York: International Universities Press.

Campbell, Felicia. 1973. "The Gambling Mystique: Mythologies and Typologies." Ph.D. diss., Department of English, United States International University.

Campbell, Felicia. 1976. "The Future of Gambling." *The Futurist,* 1 April, 84–90.

Campbell, Felicia. 1976. "The Positive View of Gambling." In *Gambling and Society: Interdisciplinary Studies on the Subject of Gambling,* 219–228. Springfield, IL: Thomas.

Cardano, Girolamo. 1961. *The Book on Games of Chance.* Translated by Sydney Henry Gould. New York: Holt, Rinehart, Winston.

PRESIDENT'S COMMISSION ON LAW ENFORCEMENT AND ADMINISTRATION OF JUSTICE

On July 23, 1965, President Lyndon Baines Johnson issued Executive Order 11236, establishing the Commission on Law Enforcement and Administration of Justice. Attorney General Nicholas Katzenbach was asked to chair a 19-member commission whose numbers included former attorney general William P. Rogers; American Bar Association and later Supreme Court justice Lewis F. Powell; Julia Stuart, president of the League of Women Voters; New York City Mayor Robert Wagner; Yale University president Kingman Brewster; *Los Angeles Times* publisher Otis Chandler; San Francisco police chief Thomas Cahill; California Attorney General Thomas Lynch; director of the Urban League, Whitney M. Young; federal judges Luther Youngdahl, James Parsons, Charles Breitel, and future Watergate prosecutor Leon Jaworski; and several leading law professors and attorneys. This blue ribbon panel worked for two years with 63 staff members and 175 consultants to produce its report, titled *The Challenge of Crime in a Free Society* (1967). The report, issued in February 1967, made more than 200 recommendations. This effort placed a new focus on victimization, as the commission conducted a survey of 10,000 households regarding their experiences with crime. A secondary focus was given to organized crime activity. Although gambling did not receive much attention, the report offered some strong words about the activity:

> Law enforcement officials agree almost unanimously that gambling is the greatest source of revenue for organized crime. . . . In large cities where organized crime groups

exist, very few of the gambling operators are independent of a large organization. Anyone whose independent operation becomes successful is likely to receive a visit from an organization representative who convinces the independent, through fear or promise of greater profit, to share his revenue with the organization. (188)

The report suggested that each year gross revenues from gambling in the United States resulted in profits of $6 to $7 billion for individuals associated with organized crime.

The recommendations did not include any that focused specifically upon gambling crimes; however, new weapons for dealing with organized crime were advanced, including a clarified statute on the use of wiretapping, witness immunity and protection programs, special grand juries, and extended prison terms for criminals involved in illegal businesses (that is, gambling enterprise). Every law enforcement organization from the federal government down to the municipal level was urged to have an organized crime section, and citizens and business groups were urged to create permanent community crime commissions.

Reference

President's Commission on Law Enforcement and Administration of Justice. 1967. *The Challenge of Crime in a Free Society.* Washington, DC: U.S. Government Printing Office.

PRESIDENT'S COMMISSION ON ORGANIZED CRIME

On 28 July 1983, President Ronald Reagan issued Executive Order 12435, creating the President's Commission on Organized Crime under the auspices of the Federal Advisory Committee Act. The commission was given the charge to make a "full and complete national and region by region analysis of organized crime; define the nature of traditional organized crime, as well as emerging organized crime groups, the sources and amounts of organized crime's income; develop in-depth information on the participants in organized crime networks; and evaluate Federal laws pertinent to the effort to combat organized crime." The commission was to have up to twenty members.

The president appointed U.S. Court of Appeals Judge Irving Kaufman to chair the three-year work of the panel. Kaufman was certainly one of the most prominent federal jurists on any bench. As a federal district judge, he had presided over the trial of Julius and Ethel Rosenberg. The two were executed in 1950 for being spies for the Soviet Union and stealing atomic secrets. Kaufman had also been the judge during the trials arising from the raid on the organized crime meeting at Apalachin, New York, in 1957. The commission membership also included U.S. Supreme Court Associate Justice Potter Stewart, U.S. Senator Strom Thurmond (R-South Carolina), U.S. Representative Peter W. Rodino (D-New Jersey), Louisiana State Attorney General William J. Guste, Associate Watergate Prosecutor Thomas McBride, and Law professor Charles Rogovin of Temple University. The other members included the sheriff and district attorney for San Diego County, a former U.S. attorney, members of congressional investigating staffs, police officials, private attorneys, and the editor of *Reader's Digest* magazine.

The commission had an overall budget of $5 million. Its staff of thirty-six included sixteen investigators and seven lawyers. The commission met in a series of hearings on selected topics over a three-year period. Hundreds of subpoenas were issued by the commission. Major topics examined included money laundering by organized crime, Asian gang activity in the Unites States, labor union violence, involvement of legitimate business with organized crime, illicit drugs, and gambling. The commission issued reports on the separate topics during the course of its work; however, it limited the scope of its recommendations to only a few topics.

Special importance was given to money laundering. Forty-one banks were investigated. One in Boston was shown to have "knowingly and willfully" allowed $1.22 billion in cash transfers with Swiss banks on behalf of clients who were not asked why they were bringing in large sums of money in paper grocery bags. In a court action the bank was fined $500,000 for failing to abide by provisions of the Bank Secrecy Act of 1970. That was not enough. In October 1984, the commission recommended that a new law be passed making money-laundering activities more clearly illegal under federal law. A first offense could be punished by fines of up to $250,000 or twice the value of the laundered money and imprisonment up to five years. Illegal gambling was seen as a problem area in money laundering, and legal casinos were viewed as agents of potential money laundering. In 1985, regulations of the Treasury Department were amended so that casinos with revenues in excess of $1 million a year were to be considered banks for purposes of the Bank Secrecy Act of 1970. In 1986 Congress passed the Money Laundering Act of 1986, which made money laundering illegal for the first time. The new law indicated in excess of 100 specific activities that would constitute illegal sources of moneys restricted from exchanges by banks and casinos. Illegal drug sales and illegal gambling proceeds were included.

Hearings on Asian gangs found a high level of involvement in gambling operations that were both legal and illegal. Gang members were involved in running Chinese games such as mah-jongg in legal poker rooms in California, and they also attempted to use a front business to buy a casino in Las Vegas. It was feared that Asian organized criminals such as the Japanese-based Yakuza and the Bamboo gang of Taiwan could grow into an influence that would exceed that of the Mafia.

The commission focused its investigatory energies on the misuse of labor unions in order to achieve the goals of organized crime interests. The commission recommended more rigorous implementation of provisions of the antiracketeering statutes already on the books. They sought to have such involvement by labor considered as "unfair labor practices" under provisions of the National Labor Relations Act.

Hearings on gambling activity looked closely at Cuban-American racketeers who were discovered to be operating a $45-million-a-year gambling syndicate in New York City. This activity was a major component of organized crime's control over $1.5 billion in the New York metropolitan area. There were also hearings on gambling and its effect on professional and amateur sports activity.

A study made by Wharton Econometric Forecasting of Philadelphia for the commission concluded that organized crime activity exceeded $100 million a year in drug trade alone. Overall organized crime activity cost Americans 414,000 jobs each year and $6.5 billion in lost tax revenues.

The commission ended its work somewhat in disarray. A final report recommended that bar associations take steps to self-police lawyers who worked for Mob groups. The commission also endorsed wiretapping to discover illicit practices by lawyers. Moreover it sought expanded drug testing in the workplace. Nine of eighteen commission members refused to endorse the final recommendations. The commission was criticized for having too many hearings and not enough meetings to discuss the substance of its investigations.

The topic of gambling pervaded all the investigations. The commission did not issue a separate report on gambling, however. Although commission chairman Irving Kaufman hinted that illegal gambling was a major source of income for organized crime, the commission chose to allow the transcripts of its hearings to suffice to cover the area. The federal administration did not consider organized crime to be a major factor in legal casinos in the United States. The silence was a statement (*New York Times* 1986, I-1).

The commission did not conduct any original research into gambling activi-

ties, but it did contract for a consultants' report on policy options. The report was written by professors John Dombrink of the University of California–Irvine and William N. Thompson of the University of Nevada–Las Vegas. The report lamented that a wave of legalizations of gambling across North America had not been accompanied by serious research and thoughtful consequences of legal gambling for society. A program of federally supported research was recommended. It was especially important that the extent and impacts of compulsive gambling be known before more gambling was legalized, making it advisable to have a moratorium on new legalizations for a time during which research could take place. Also during the time of a moratorium (three years was suggested), state officials, industry personnel, and other interested parties should be brought together by the U.S. Department of Justice to create a set of minimum standards for gambling activity to assure a uniform integrity and to assure that organized criminals would be excluded from operations. The minimum standards could then be enforced by state governments or, alternatively, by the Department of Justice if the states chose to ignore the standards. States could be given incentives to follow the standards through law enforcement grants. The consultant's report rejected the notion that the federal government should be involved in either direct regulation or taxation of gambling operations. There is no evidence that the commission used the consultant's report. Later in 1996, however, a bill to regulate Native American gambling was introduced in Congress. The bill included a moratorium provision such as the one in the report.

Coauthored by John D. Dombrink

References

Dombrink, John, and William N. Thompson. 1986. "The Report of the 1986 Commission on Organized Crime and Its Implications for Commercial Gaming in America." *Nevada Public Affairs Review* 1986 (2): 70–75. *New York Times*, 2 April 1986, I-1.

See also Cash Transaction Reports and Money Laundering

PROBLEM GAMBLING

From the earliest moments of humankind when gambling became the second-oldest "diversion," the activity has been laden with potential problems. Considering the consequences, Eve's wager that picking the forbidden apple represented a good bet may have been labeled an act of excessive, impulsive, and reckless gambling. Humankind did survive, only to face painful and finite years of life. But even with the results, no lesson was learned. Betting activity has continued recklessly, impulsively, and excessively for many players.

Problems seem to be present wherever and whenever gambling occurs. Some players lose control over how they participate, and their activity may be labeled as compulsive, pathological, addictive, troubled, disordered, or simply problem gambling. These players are usually a minority of the players in a game, and a minority of the population in a society. Nevertheless their activity can have very severe and negative effects not only in their own lives, but also in the lives of larger numbers of people, including their families, their friends, others in their communities, and society in general.

This entry explores several questions about problem gambling—a term that will be used to encompass all the labels indicated above. First, what is "problem" gambling, what are its symptoms, and how can it be recognized? Second, what are the causes of problem gambling? Third, how many people (what proportion of the population) are problem gamblers, or may be susceptible to becoming problem gamblers? Next, what are the consequences of problem gambling for individuals, their family and friends, their community, and society in general? What price tag may be placed upon these consequences? And last, how might problem gambling be avoided, and, if not, treated and cured?

DESCRIPTIONS OF PROBLEM GAMBLING

The nature of problem gambling has been captured in descriptions found in literature dating back to ancient times. The Hymn of the Gambler appears in the Hindu book of Rig Veda (circa 4000–1500 BCE):

> As alluring as a draught of Soma on the mountain, the lively dice have captured my heart. . . . I've driven her (my wife) away for the sake of the ill-fated throw of a dice . . . I make a resolve that I will not go gaming. . . . But as soon as the brown nuts are rattled and thrown, to meet them I run, like an amorous girl.

In *The Vedic Reader for Students,*
A. A. Macdonell. 1994. Delhi:
Motil Banarsidass, x.34

Millennia later, the author Dostoyevsky
wrote an autobiographical account of his
problem gambling:

> I can't miss! . . . If I start very care-
> fully. . . . Why am I really such an
> irresponsible infant? Can't I see that
> I am a doomed man? But why can't
> I come back to life? All I have to do
> is to be calculating and patient once,
> and I'll make it! I have to hold out
> for just one hour, and then my whole
> life will be different. Just remember
> what happened to me seven months
> ago in Roulettenburg, before I lost
> everything. Oh, it was a beautiful
> instance of determination. . . . I lost
> everything I had then . . . I walked
> out of the Casino, and suddenly dis-
> covered that I still had one gulden in
> my waistcoat pocket. Well, that'll
> pay for my dinner at least, I said to
> myself. But after I had taken a hun-
> dred steps or so, I changed my mind
> and went back to the roulette table. . . .
> I won, and twenty minutes later I left
> the Casino with one hundred and
> seventy gulden in my pocket. It's the
> absolute truth! That's what your very
> last gulden can do for you! But sup-
> pose I had lost heart then? What if I
> hadn't dared to risk? Tomorrow,
> tomorrow, it will all be over!

Final lines from Dostoyevsky's
(The Gambler)

Of Dostoyevsky, Sigmund Freud
wrote (1928) that he "knew that the chief
thing was gambling for its own sake—*le
jeu pour le jeu.*"

This is consistent with the notion that
for the problem gambler "winning is the
best thing, losing is the next best thing,
and nothing is in third place."

Modern students of problem
gambling reached a consensus that
problem gambling involves four categories of symptoms. These have been
identified by Richard Rosenthal (1989).
First, the compulsive gambler is
involved in a progression of behavior.
The phenomenon is dynamic—ongoing.
The compulsive gambler bets more and
more and more—more often and with
more money—as time moves on. Second, the compulsive gambler cannot
accept losing. When he or she loses, the
gambler takes it as a personal defeat,
which must be quickly rectified by winning bets that can make up for the loses.
Losses generate feelings of guilt, which
are concealed from other people. Third,
the compulsive gambler is preoccupied
with gambling at all times. When not
gambling, the gambler is reliving old
gambling experiences and is craving
future gambling opportunities. Fourth,
the compulsive gambler exhibits a disre-
gard for the consequences of gambling.
He or she borrows money while consciously knowing that repayment is
unlikely, lies to those nearby, and gets
drawn into criminal behavior, such as
check forgery, embezzlement. The gambler neglects family obligations. Rosenthal also lists what he calls ancillary
factors and predisposing factors that
enable the compulsive gambler. However, the major enabling factor is not
mentioned in his work, and that is the
factor around which this study is oriented: the presence of a gambling activity—the availability (more or less
immediately or conveniently present) of
an opportunity to gamble.

In 1980, after years of study, the American Psychiatric Association declared that problem gambling is a disease. They labeled it as an "impulse control disorder," and they described its traits in the *Diagnostic and Statistical Manual*. Revisions in the first list resulted in the current listing of attributes:

1. Progression and preoccupation: reliving past gambling experiences, studying a system, planning the next gambling venture, or thinking of ways to get money.

2. Tolerance: need to gamble with more and more money to achieve the desired excitement.

3. Withdrawal: became restless or irritable when attempting to cut down or stop gambling.

4. Escape: gamble in order to escape from personal problems.

5. Chasing: after losing money gambling, often returned another day in order to get even.

6. Denial: denied losing money through gambling.

7. Illegal activity: committed an illegal act to obtain money for gambling.

8. Jeopardizing family or career: jeopardizing or loss of a significant relationship, marriage, education, job or career.

9. Bail out: needed another individual to provide money to relieve a desperate financial situation produced by gambling. (DSM IV)

This list, as well as other lists of factors, have been used to screen potential problem gamblers and also to research rates of prevalence of problem gambling in society.

CAUSES OF PROBLEM GAMBLING

For centuries problem gambling behaviors were seen as resulting from a depravity of moral character. The troubled gambler was simply a bad and evil person. Because uncontrolled gambling has negative consequences that are often imposed upon persons who are not even involved in gambling, the notion that the gambler is depraved remains a prevalent view in society. However, the modern era has found that other theories may explain why people become problem gamblers. Four categories have received the most attention: (1) physiological theories, (2) psychological theories, (3) sociological theories, and (4) behavioral theories.

Many believe that there is a chemical basis underpinning gambling addictions. While there may be no evidence that gambling actually introduces chemicals into the body, as do other addictive activities (drug use, alcoholism), several scholars have found that the pathological gambler has certain chemicals in his or her neurological system that are not found in other peoples. For instance Robert Perkins of the Keystone Treatment Center asserts that, "pathological gamblers do not have the choice to gamble . . . (when gambling) they are in a chemical psychoactive high. The moment the gambling is over, they slip into a chemical psychoactive low, an irritable depression they cannot tolerate . . . pleasure hormones become used up, and (they) must gamble (again) to feel normal. . . . They are gambling to feel normal" (www.robertparkinson.com/gambling-treatment.htm).

Durand Jacobs discovered that gamblers enter into dissociative states that include trances and memory blackouts. These may result from different excitement levels in different peoples, and may be related to preconditions that could be genetically based, although the literature does not establish this supposition.

Most psychological theories derive from Sigmund Freud's explanation for excessive gambling. His major study in this field focused upon the life of Fyodor Dostoyevsky. Freud suggested that the gambler's early childhood conflicts led him to a behavior that resulted in self-punishment. More recent scholars identify the oedipal complex, conflicts arising from breast-feeding experiences, and other childhood traumas as the sources of adult gambling problems.

Sociologists such as John Rosecrance see gambling as part of the process of role identification, role behavior, and social class orientation. Men gamble more often than women because gambling can be associated with the traditional male role of acquiring financial resources for the family, while the female remains at home and converts these resources into items to satisfy family needs. Gamblers also form communities, which provide a range of socially supportive opportunities for the player. Gambling communities can become alternative locations for playing out life roles for people who find it difficult to cope in other social groups or the larger society.

People may also be drawn to gambling because games are played in places where "normal" business contacts can be made. Certainly Las Vegas is not one of the nation's leading business convention centers because businesses *want* their employees to gamble. However, conventions put the employees in an atmosphere where gambling is available. Sociological scholars may also find wide variations in gambling behaviors among age groups, religious groups, and national identity groups.

Several students of gambling have found explanations for compulsive activity in the theories of behavioral conditioning made popular by B. F. Skinner. People gravitate toward activities that bring pleasure, and they avoid activities that bring pain. The schedule of rewards that are associated with an activity may determine how much a person participates in the activity. Frequent gamblers have defined the anticipation of a gambling win as a very pleasurable experience. However, to get the pleasure, the person must actually be in a place where a bet can be made, and he or she must be able to make the bet. To be sure, there is pain, very serious pain, that accompanies gambling losses. However, compulsive gamblers are able to project that pain off into a distant future, neglecting it, as they seek an opportunity for pleasure that is immediately available.

Theorists and scholars argue about which theory has the most merit, but most students of the subject see both merits and limits within each line of reasoning. Some have developed approaches which incorporate aspects of all these theories.

HOW MANY PROBLEM GAMBLERS

The question of the prevalence of problem gambling has been a major concern of gambling researchers for more than three decades. The first attempt to quantify prevalence came with a University of Michigan study made in 1976 for the Commission on a National Policy on Gambling. The study found that 0.77

percent of a national sample consisted of people considered to be pathological gamblers. The researchers also found the rate in Nevada to be 2.5 percent. Other studies of general populations of states or provinces found rates ranging from 1.4 percent pathological gamblers (present time) to more than 8.0 percent lifetime pathological gamblers (having had attributes of pathology some time during lifetime). A study of Native Americans in North Dakota revealed a lifetime rate in excess of 14 percent. The Michigan study used but one question to determine the results. Subsequent studies have used a list of questions, such as those in the *Diagnostic and Statistical Manual.*

In 1997 a group of scholars at Harvard Medical School combined all the results from 125 surveys taken in U.S. and Canadian venues up to that time. Their meta-analysis study found that 1.60 percent of the adult general population in the United States were lifetime Level 3 (severe or pathological) gamblers and 1.14 percent fell into the past-year Level 3 category. Among individuals in the same populations, 3.85 percent qualified as lifetime Level 2 (problem) gamblers and 2.80 percent as past-year Level 2 gamblers.

In 1998, the National Gambling Impact Study Commission hired the National Opinion Research Center (NORC) to conduct a nationwide poll to track gambling behaviors in the adult population of the United States. They telephoned 2,417 households and conducted 500 face-to-face interviews at gambling locations. Respondents were classified as being "not at-risk," "at-risk," "problem," or "pathological"

TABLE 10. Prevalence of Gambling Problems among Selected Populations

Demographic	Problem Gambling		Pathological	
	Lifetime	Past Year	Lifetime	Past Year
Gender				
Male	2.0	0.9	1.7	0.8
Female	1.1	0.6	0.8	0.3
Race				
White	1.4	0.6	1.0	0.5
Black	2.7	1.7	3.2	1.5
Hispanic	0.9	0.7	0.5	0.1
Other	1.2	0.5	0.9	0.4
Age				
18–29	2.1	1.0	1.3	0.3
30–39	1.5	0.8	1.0	0.6
40–49	1.9	0.7	1.4	0.8
50–64	1.2	0.3	2.2	0.9
65+	0.7	0.6	0.4	0.2
Education				
Less than high school	1.7	1.2	2.1	1.0
High school graduate	2.2	1.1	1.9	1.1
Some college	1.5	0.8	1.1	0.3
College graduate	0.8	0.2	0.5	0.1

Source: National Opinion Research Center, 1999. "Gambling Impact and Behaviour Study." *Report to the National Gambling Impact Study Commission, 26–27.*

gamblers. In addition, NORC examined these behaviors over the course of a lifetime and over the previous year.

The survey found that 7.7 percent qualified as "at-risk" gamblers at some point during their lifetime, and another 2.9 percent were categorized as "at-risk" gamblers based on their past-year activity. Meanwhile, 1.5 percent were "problem" gamblers at some point in their lives, and 0.7 percent were labeled as past-year problem gamblers. Finally, 1.2 percent of Americans qualified as "pathological" gamblers at some point during their lifetime, and 0.6 percent of the sample qualified as pathological gamblers for the past year.

The survey also identified the prevalence of gambling problems among different demographic groups. For instance males were more likely to be current-year pathological gamblers than females (0.8% to 0.3%) and whites less likely than blacks (0.5% to 1.5%).

The study also found that the problem and pathological gambling rates for adults living within 50 miles of a casino are roughly double the rates found elsewhere.

Assessing and Addressing Social Costs

Many social costs are associated with problem gambling as the troubled gambler imposes a wide range of burdens not only onto himself or herself but also onto family members, friends, coworkers, those with whom he or she has business relationships, and the general public as well. Lesieur and Custer estimated that between 10 and 15 persons are directly and adversely affected by a pathological gambler. These gamblers often will bor-row from close associates and even resort to stealing or "creatively rearranging funds" when the money runs out. Unfortunately, the popular notion that pathological gamblers somehow have a financial "cap" on the damage they inflict is flawed. In fact, these individuals often are able to locate funds far beyond their own means. And finally, when the individual or his or her family can no longer pick up the pieces, the entire society may have to pay for welfare, for treatment costs, for police service, and for jails and prisons.

Unfortunately, it is not easy to come up with definitive money figures that can discern the exact social costs caused by each compulsive gambler. There are definitional issues in deciding exactly what a "social cost" is, and there are methodological problems in calculating costs, even where one knows the specific cost item. Several experts have offered opinions about the social costs associated with pathological gambling. Lesieur and Puig examined several illegal behaviors associated with fraud in general and with insurance fraud in particular. They indicate a monumental cost for society from this fraudulent activity. In their analysis, they conclude that one-third of insurance fraud can be attributed to pathological gamblers. On September 1, 1994, John Kindt testified to the Committee on Small Business of the U.S. House of Representatives that the social costs of an individual compulsive gambler was between $13,000 and $52,000 a year. In 1981, Robert Politzer, James Morrow, and Sandra Leavey made an analysis of the annual costs to society of untreated pathological gamblers. These costs included lost productivity, criminal system costs, and "abused dollars," an illusive term that included not only bad debts but also all money lost at gambling. Their information was gathered from 92 persons receiving treatment at the Johns Hopkins Compulsive Gambling Counseling Center. They found that the average "bottomed-out" gambler imposed a cost of $61,000 upon society over the last year of gambling. A "more average" problem gambler imposed an annual cost of $26,000 upon society.

In 2002, this editor teamed with R. Keith Schwer of the University of Nevada–Las Vegas and conducted a survey with the help of local Gamblers Anonymous chapters. A questionnaire was completed by 99 members. The questionnaire had been used in five previous studies, including partial use by the National Gambling Impact Study Commission in its surveys. From the survey information, a social cost profile was developed. Several factors were considered:

a. Player Losses Respondents estimated the amount of money that they had lost in their lifetimes The median loss was between $50,000 and $100,000, while the mean loss was $112,400.

b. Sources of Gambling Funds The troubled gambler will typically seek funds from others only when his or her personal funds have been exhausted. After other legitimate sources are tapped, the problem gambler may consider seeking money from illegal sources. Over two-thirds indicated that they had to go to other people for gambling money. The largest group (57.7 percent of the 99) went to a spouse, while 30 percent of the 99 went to children. Of the one-third that didn't seek help from others, 63.3 percent passed bad checks, 55.5 percent cashed in securities, and 60 percent sold personal property, while 34.4 percent used casino credit, and 16.7 percent used bookies or "loan sharks." In addition, 18.5 percent gambled with social security funds.

c. Debts Gambling activity did cause major financial problems for the respondents. The median debt was $24,500, while the mean debt was $78,305.

d. Bankruptcies For 45.4 percent of respondents, gambling activity led to bankruptcy court for protection from creditors. This group had median debts of $38,750, while their average debt was $121,646.

e. Creditors in Court In addition to bankruptcy court, the gamblers' debts also resulted in other legal actions. A total of 15 percent were sued in courts by others seeking repayment of debts.

f. Thefts When pathological gamblers run out of legitimate sources of money, they consider illegal sources. Starting close at hand, they pass bad checks, as did 63.3 percent of the respondents. They also look for money in the workplace; 30.1 percent admitted to stealing from the workplace in order to gamble or pay gambling debts.

A total of 43 percent of respondents indicated that they had stolen money or things and used it to gamble or to pay gambling related debts. The average theft amount per gambler was $13,517.

g. Criminal Justice System Activity The thefts reported by a majority of respondents certainly led to many police investigations. However, the respondents were quite adept at avoiding the criminal law consequences of much of their illicit activity.

Only nine were ever arrested for any gambling-related activity, resulting in nine trials. Seven were convicted and five were then incarcerated, with average sentences of just over three months. Spread over the 99 respondents, the average sentences were 0.16 months each. Ten were also placed upon probation for gambling related offenses. Of all, each endured an incidence of probation of 0.10 months.

h. Employment Problem gamblers are not as productive as others in the workplace. One study suggested that a pathological gambler was only 20 percent effective in the workplace. While this study did not attempt to assess financial costs for reduced productivity for those who were on the job each day, such costs do exist and must not be considered nonexistent because they are not calculated here. Answers to the survey questions provide some information that can be used for cost calculations.

It was found that 56.2 percent did indicate that they had lost time by absenting themselves from the workplace in order to gamble or to participate in activities related to their gambling (i.e., seeking funds with which to gamble or to pay gambling-related debts). These gamblers reported missing an average of 17.22 hours of work each month due to gambling. Averaged over all 99 respondents, this represents a loss of 8.69 hours a month, or 104.4 hours a year.

Of the respondents, 22 quit work because of gambling activity or gambling problems. These 22 had periods of unemployment averaging 18.77 months. Spreading the idle months over 99, lost employment averaged 4.2 months due to

gambling. An additional 24.0 percent indicated that they had been fired due to their gambling activity. This group averaged 11.57 months of unemployment as a result; spread across the 99, this represents an average loss of 2.45 months of work because of discharges from the workplace.

i. Welfare Only 3 of 89 had to turn to general welfare because of gambling problems, while 5 of 87 indicated that they received food stamps as a result of gambling.

j. Treatment A small portion of respondents sought professional treatment help. Thirteen were hospitalized, while 20 had outpatient care. Twenty-nine indicated treatment costs which averaged $7,022 each. Spread over all 99, the average cost is $7,094.

k. Suicide The survey found that 60 of 91 (65.9 percent) respondents had planned suicide as a result of gambling. Twenty-six (of 94, or 27.7 percent) indicated that they had made actual attempts to take their own lives.

The factors above were utilized to develop a social cost profile of problem gambling. In formulating the profile, researchers were mindful that some costs of the gambler's activity are absorbed by the gambler and his or her family, others are imposed on others (against their will), while some are imposed upon governments. Yet these and other costs may result in general losses for the economy and for society in general. The term *social cost* typically is used to indicate costs that are imposed upon people other than the gambler and his or her family, that is people who do not participate in the gambling process.

There are many very real costs that are not included in the cost profile presented. There is a very real cost to employers and society when the work productivity of problem gamblers decreases. Only because it would be very difficult (and costly) to develop methodologies to capture the cost are they excluded from the analysis. Students of pathological gambling find that the spouses of problem gamblers suffer major life costs as well. These costs include workplace costs such as missed work and lost productivity, as well as health and other treatment costs. Spouses who are enablers may also participate in illicit fund-raising to deal with situations brought about by the gamblers. There are also major costs to children, and these costs can be relayed onto society as a whole thought their dysfunctional behaviors. When a gambler "steals" from a child's college fund, and education is stifled, society is also a big loser. Also the survey made no attempt to calculate a cost for suicide, given that the respondents had not let their addiction take them to that extreme.

For these reasons, it was suggested that the numbers are conservative and very much below what the real social costs are.

a. Annualizing Costs The social costs were added together with the knowledge that they occurred over a time period. While subjects had indicated they had gambling problems over many years, it was believed that the problems were manifest to a much greater extent in the years immediately prior to joining Gamblers Anonymous. A factor of four was used in determining the annualized social costs.

The following costs were calculated, as outlined in Table 11.

TABLE 11. Social Costs Totals (Annualized)

Cost of Missed Work	$2,364
Cost of Quitting Jobs	1,092
Cost of Fired Jobs	1,581
Cost Unemployment Compensation	87
Debt/Bankruptcy	9,493
Costs of Thefts	3,379
Cost Civil Suits	777
Costs of Arrests	95
Costs of Trials	85
Costs of Jail Time	80
Costs of Probation	170
Costs of Food Stamps	50
Costs of Welfare	84
Costs of Treatment	372
Total Cost	$19,711

Source: Thompson, William N., and R. Keith Schwer. 2005. "Beyond the Limits of Recreation: Social Costs of Gambling in Southern Nevada," *Public Budgeting, Accounting, and Financial Management,* 17, no. 1 (Spring): 62–92.

a. Employment Costs The income of each respondent was revealed in their answers to inquiries about household income. Nonrespondents to the income question were figured to have the lowest wage of all respondents, which was $5.60 per hour. On this basis, the annualized cost of lost work was $2,364.

Productivity losses result when individuals are fired from or quit their jobs. Valued at the hourly wage of the respondent, the losses from "quitters" represented work valued at $1,092 when annualized and spread over all 99 respondents. The annualized cost of lost productivity due to firings because of gambling when spread over the 99 gamblers was $1,581.

Eight of the fired workers also secured unemployment compensation. Over the average of 2.28 months for the eight at $732 a month, this is a social cost (to all society) that is translated to an individualized annual cost of $87 per fired gambler.

b. Debts, Bankruptcies, and Civil Suits. Bad debts represent costs imposed upon other people. If the other people are businesses (e.g., credit card companies), the costs are spread out across society, directly or indirectly. Hence when you do business with a merchant that has filed to collect an obligation owed by a gambler, you pay part of the cost—even though you did not enjoy the excitement of the poker machine, nor did you receive a chance to win the casino's big prize.

While almost all of these gamblers probably failed to pay debts to some degree, researchers calculated debts by looking only at those gamblers who went through bankruptcy proceedings. Researchers reduced one outlying debt to the next highest debt level. Then the average (spread to all 99) was $37,968, or a debt annualized to $9,493.

Social costs are also imposed upon governments as a result of court actions. Additionally, the gambler incurs legal costs that represent lost resources for society, that is, they are resources not available for positive needs. Among the survey respondents, there were 44 bankruptcy actions. There were also 19 civil suits relating to debts. A court action costs $7,500 at the federal level. Researchers assumed half that cost here for 63 cases. This represents an average cost spread over all respondents of $2,540, which is annualized to $635.

The 63 court actions at legal fees of $2,500 each take an average of $1,676 from the gamblers (annualized to $418), money that could be better spent on positive things in the economy.

The 19 gambling-related divorce actions impose court costs on society of another $774 per gambler, or an annualized cost of $194. They impose legal costs on the gambler of $516, costs annualized to $129.

Considering the court costs only and spreading them among 99 respondents, the annualized court costs equal $777 for each gambler.

c. Thefts and Criminal System Actions Thefts are social costs. The average (over all 99) costs of thefts as reported (and reducing the one outlying response) was $3,379 on an annualized basis.

The 13 arrests for the nine reporting being arrested cost society $2,900 for each, representing a career cost of $380, or an annualized cost of $95 for each respondent.

Nine criminal trials at a cost of $3,750 each represents another average gambler cost of $340, a cost to society annualized to $85 for the individual gambler.

Sixteen months incarceration cost $32,000, or an average of $324 per gambler, or an annualized cost of $80.

Ten probation cases among 99 respondents cost society an annualized amount of $170.

d. Social Costs of Treatment The 27 gamblers who undertook to have professional treatment for their problems, either in a hospital or as an outpatient, spent an average of $7,022 each on the treatment. Spread over 99 respondents, the average career treatment cost is $1915, an annual cost $478. The approximately 28 percent paid by the gambler was not considered a social cost, but the remaining $372 was.

e. Welfare Services Researchers assume that those taking welfare and food stamp provisions did so for two years each. Three took welfare. At an average payment of $460 a month, the total costs for three people for two years comes to $33,120. Spread over the 99 respondents, this represents an average annual social cost of $84.

Food stamp costs were set at $2,000 a year. Five gamblers impose a two year cost of $20,000 as a result. This represents a career average cost of $204, or an annualized cost of $50, spread over all 99 gamblers.

Projecting the Costs to the Entire Society

a. Costs for a Pathological Gambler "On the Street" The pathological gambler who is not in treatment is not the same as the one who has sought treatment such as that offered by Gamblers Anonymous. The survey above questioned only members of Gamblers Anonymous. On the one hand, researchers might suggest that the "on the street" gambler (that is, one who is not in Gamblers Anonymous) is still in denial and may actually be more severe in his or her habit, but probably he or she is less severe. Nevertheless James Westphal (1999) and his colleagues in Louisiana applied a gambling screen to the gamblers that were in the treatment groups that they studied in order to assess social costs. They then applied the screen to gamblers identified as pathological to those in a telephone survey. The ones in the telephone survey had social costs equaling 51 percent of the costs of those in treatment, which suggest that the social costs of pathological gamblers could be based upon costs not of $19,711 each, but rather the lower costs of $10,053 each (Westphal).

In using this value, researchers might project the social cost that severe problem gambling has on the entire society. If the United States has 200 million adults, and 1.14 percent are severe or pathological gamblers, that means that these 2.28 million people are imposing costs ($\times$ 10,053) of nearly $23 billion on their fellow citizens. Added to this number would be costs imposed by less severe problem gamblers.

Treatment and Policy Remedies for Problem Gambling

Current-day gaming companies are realizing that if the gambling industry is to survive as a beneficial provider of economic development, with good jobs and with revenues for worthy public (and private) causes, it must confront its "unfriendly" side and deal with it in a responsible manner. The gambling industry is in a position analogous to that of the tobacco and alcohol industries. Although both of these industries have been condemned for the social ills they generate, tobacco's posture of denial has led to major lawsuits and judgments that could potentially threaten its profitability. Alcohol industry leaders, on the other hand, have taken another approach and addressed social costs associated with their product. They have supported measures to mitigate problems (e.g., the concept of the designated driver and stiffer drunk driving laws). The gaming industry would be wise to follow the latter example. Efforts such as the establishment of the Responsible Gambling program under the auspices of the American Gaming Association and support for education and treatment programs are steps in the correct direction.

Treatment of problem gambling can be bifurcated into activities focusing upon the individual and activities focusing on the industry and policy makers at large. Regarding the former approaches, although severe problem gambling (called pathological, or compulsive, gambling) has been designated as a disease by the American Psychiatric Association, there is no accepted pharmaceutical treatment for it. To be sure many problem gamblers show symptoms of depression (one study of pathological gamblers found that 76 percent had "major depressive" disorders) and they are given medications during the course of their other treatments. These other treatments invariably involve counseling therapy both on an individual and a group basis. The most prevalent form of group therapy is through meetings of chapters of Gamblers Anonymous.

Counseling emphasizes personal awareness and responsibility for one's problems, as well as recognition of the irrational nature of problem gambling behaviors. Group therapy often involves a step program. The Gamblers Anonymous 12-step program—which is similar to the 12-step program of Alcoholics Anonymous—is a primary example.

1. An admission that one is powerless over the gambling problem.
2. That he or she needs a higher power to restore normality to life.
3. That he or she will turn to the power for guidance.
4. They will make an inventory of their problems.
5. They will admit to themselves the nature of their wrongs.
6. They will be ready to change these defects.
7. They will ask the higher power to change their lives.
8. They will make a list of all people they have harmed.
9. They will seek to make amends to these people where possible.
10. They will admit their wrongs to others.
11. They will meditate and pray for change.
12. They will take their message to others with gambling problems.

A major issue in treatment is whether or not the problem gambler must abstain from all gambling activity forever. Gamblers Anonymous tenets hold that the "disease" is one that cannot be cured if the gambler keeps on playing. On the other hand, some behavioral therapists as well as researchers see symptoms of the disease as being excesses that can be modified, allowing the person to gamble again without bad consequences. They believe that the problem gambler can be trained to avoid excessive behaviors and thereby return to rational and modest gambling activity. Advocates of this approach such as John Rosecrance also suggest that there is a range of severity in gambling problems, ranging from most problem gambling to the most severe types, which can be labeled pathological or compulsive. Only the most severe problem gamblers would have to undergo complete abstention as a cure.

Arnold Wexler is a compulsive gambling counselor who has experienced the most severe level of the disease. He accepts the notion that any cure demands complete abstention from gambling. He illustrated his position in a commentary to a gambling policy class at the University of Nevada–Las Vegas. He told the class about his problem. He indicated that 30 years had passed since he had made any bet at all. But he told a story about going to New York a few months before to speak to a group in a major hotel. When he entered the hotel lobby, there were big signs indicating that a lottery prize was now in the hundreds of millions of dollars. He passed a stand selling tickets as he went into a conference room. He was in the room for two hours, during which time he made his remarks and listened to others. All that time his mind was obsessed with the lottery prize. He had become very nervous and anxious. As the session came to an end, he noticed that he was in a sweat, and he grew very fearful that he could not pass the stand on the way out of the hotel without stopping. When the session did end, he quickly grabbed his brief case and walked fast and then actually ran to get to the street. He could not breathe normally for another hour. And it had been three decades since he had made a bet. He knew he had to abstain forever.

Public policies can be designed to help control the incidence and the consequences of problem gambling. Policies can be focused upon early education (in schools) and public education (through advertising and the media) about the nature of problem gambling and the need to engage in rational play if one ever gambles. Public education also involves the use of help lines (800 telephone numbers) which can direct people to counseling programs and Gamblers Anonymous meetings. Governments can also support counseling programs. Many venues ask the gambling industry to give funds for such support. Public entities can also ensure that access to gambling is limited and restricted. They can require that facilities screen people so that problem gamblers can be warned or excluded. Many venues have voluntary or even mandatory programs that place bans on problem gamblers under certain conditions. The Social Concept program in Switzerland is a very good example (*see* Switzerland and the Swiss Social Concept entry).

Public policy can also be directed toward reducing access to credit via ATM and credit card machines. Alcohol has a relationship to gambling problems, and access to drinking while gambling can be restricted as well.

A NOTE ON COMORBIDITY

Problem gamblers often have other addictive maladies. In the survey of Gamblers Anonymous members in Las Vegas, it was found that many admitted to these troubles. A question in that study was posed: how does comorbidity affect the severity of gambling problems as measured by the social cost profile? The study found that 22 percent of the severe problem gamblers were addicted to alcohol, 16 percent to tobacco, 9 percent to drugs, 28 percent to food, and 9 percent to shopping.

Did those with other addictions exhibited higher costs? Because some respondents did not report on other addictions, they were eliminated from the analysis and researchers used a base figure of $19,585 in annual costs per pathological gambler.

Only alcohol and drug addiction showed statistically significant relationships regarding costs. The findings suggest a pattern of complementary and substitute comorbidity as it relates to problem gambling. For the alcoholics in the survey, the extra addiction added $14,460 to their cost profiles, holding all other factors constant. However, researchers found a contrary result from respondents who indicated that they were addicted to drugs. Their gambling cost profile was reduced an average of $19,156, other factors being held constant. The results from the analysis of shopping, food, and tobacco addiction were not significant. Nonetheless, they are worthy of note. The shopaholics had cost profiles $4,234 below average. Food addictions added $10,887 to the profiles, while tobacco addictions added $456.

It was surmised that alcohol use complements gambling, as the two activities can be done at the same time and in the same place. Casinos tacitly acquiesce to alcohol addiction; some would likely say that many casinos promote the comorbidity, as drinks are often served to gamblers at the gambling site. In Las Vegas, drinks are considered a free amenity for gamblers. Certainly, a person who is in a drunken state would be denied free drinks at a casino, because a person who outwardly appears to be intoxicated might create a liability situation. (Note: Nevada does not have a "dram" law assigning tort liability to those distributing alcoholic beverages when the person drinking does harm to another.) Thus, other than for individuals who have passed the insobriety threshold, gambling and drinking are accepted, if not encouraged.

Drug use, on the other hand, produced a reduced cost profile in the survey. One is not likely to see a casino acquiescing to drug activity. Indeed, drug activity is neither permitted nor tolerated on casino floors by customers or employees; a person high on drugs would probably be considered disruptive to casinos. Drug use also is more expensive than alcohol use.

The decrease in costs of gambling among compulsive shoppers has two possible explanations. First, a shopper cannot gamble while shopping. Second, shopping, like drug use, demands financial resources that may divert one from gambling activity. Shopping and drug use are substitutes for gambling, not complementary activities.

Food addiction caused a large increase in the cost profile, though it is not statistically significant. While the dynamic is quite different, casinos are certainly associated with food. Casinos use food, mostly in the form of low-cost specials or buffets, as specific, advertised attractions to bring players into the gambling atmosphere. Free drinks are often given to players in Las Vegas, and meals are likely the second or third most prevalent free gift.

Tobacco has traditionally been associated with casinos as well. Like drinking, smoking is something one can do while engaged in gambling. While the cost increase for tobacco addicts was not large, it was expected. The increase was not large, perhaps because tobacco use may lead players to take breaks in their play in order to "light up" or procure cigarettes.

These findings suggest that policy makers should control activities other than gambling that are made available for their patrons.

Coauthored with Bo Bernhard

TWO GIANTS IN TREATMENT AND RESEARCH

Robert L. Custer (1927–1990)

Dr. Robert L. Custer must be recognized as the true pioneer of modern treatment and modern perspectives on pathological and problem gambling. He was born in Midland, Pennsylvania, in 1927, attended Ohio State University, and received his medical education at Western Reserve University with psychiatric training following at the University of Missouri. In 1955 Custer and his wife, Lillian, began careers treating persons with addictions. Soon they were seeing gamblers who had problems. Custer joined the Veterans Administration (VA) in 1974 and began a tour at the VA hospital in Brecksville, Ohio. There, in 1972, he developed the first inpatient treatment program for pathological gamblers combining individual therapy with group counseling. His work with his patients convinced him that Freudian approaches in treatment would not be effective. Instead, he saw the gambling affliction as a disorder that could best be treated as if it were a disease. He pushed his notions within the medical community and as a result of his efforts, the American Psychiatric Association accepted his perspective toward pathological gambling and included the malady along with a list of symptoms in the third edition of the Diagnostic and Statistical Manual of Mental and Nervous Disorders in 1980. The fourth edition refined the definition of what was designated as an "impulse control" disorder. After leaving the VA, Custer organized the Taylor Manor psychiatric center in Ellicott, Maryland, to treat pathological gamblers. Dr. Custer's advocacy for problem gamblers was evidenced by his many appearances as an expert witness in criminal trials and also by his book *When Luck Runs Out*, coauthored with Harry Milt (see Annotated Bibliography).

Henry Lesieur

Henry Lesieur learned about problem gambling as a teenager while working in a gas station near a horse-racing track. He heard story after story from the gamblers, and he started to engage the bettors in conversations. As a graduate student at the University of Massachusetts in Amherst, he formulated discussions with gamblers in Gamblers Anonymous groups and gamblers in the student body into the body of a master's thesis. This in turn led him to expand his studies, resulting in the 1977 publication of *The Chase*. His book (republished in a second edition in 1984) has been recognized as the first sociological study into the lives of serious problem gamblers. Lesieur soon joined the criminology faculty of St. John's University in Jamaica, New York. There he became the founding editor of the *Journal of Gambling Behavior* (now the *Journal of Gambling Studies*). Dr. Lesieur teamed with Sheila Blume to develop the South Oaks Gambling Screen, the most utilized instrument for assessing the prevalence of gambling problems in society. He also developed tools for assessing social costs of gambling. Lesieur's research and his perspectives on gambling have been presented to scores of academic conferences as well as to government policy-making groups. His influence on the modern study of problem gambling has been monumental.

References

American Psychiatric Association. 1987. *Diagnostic and Statistical Manual of Mental Disorders.* 3rd ed. Washington, DC: APA.

Freud, Sigmund. 1928. "Dostoyevsky and Parricide." In *The Complete Works of Sigmund Freud,* edited and translated by J. Strachey, v. 19: 157–170. London: Hogarth Press, reprinted in 1961.

Gamblers Anonymous. 1984. *Sharing Recovery Through Gamblers Anonymous.* Los Angeles: GA.

Jacobs, Durand. 1989. "A General Theory of Addictions: Rationale for and Evidence Supporting a New Approach for Understanding and Treating Addictive Behaviors." In *Compulsive Gambling: Theory, Research, and Practice,* edited by Howard Shaffer, Sharon Stein, Blase Gambino, and Thomas N. Cummings, 35–64. Lexington, MA: D.C. Heath (Lexington Books).

Kallick, M., D. Suits, T. Dielman, and J. Hybels. 1979. *A Survey of American Gambling Behavior.* Ann Arbor: Institute of Social Research, University of Michigan.

Lesieur, Henry. 1984. *The Chase: Career of the Compulsive Gambler.* Cambridge, MA: Schenkman.

Lesieur, Henry R., and Robert L. Custer. 1984. "Pathological Gambling: Roots, Phases, and Treatment." In *Gambling: Views from the Social Sciences* (special volume of *The Annals of the American Academy of Political and Social Science),* edited by James H. Frey and William R. Eadington, 146–156. Beverly Hills, CA: Sage.

National Gambling Impact Study Commission [NGISC]. 1999. *Final Report.* Washington, DC: NGISC.

National Opinion Research Center. 1999. "Gambling Impact and Behavior Study." Report prepared for the National Gambling Impact Study Commission.

Politzer, Robert M., James S. Morrow, and Sandra B. Leavey. 1981. "Report on the Societal Cost of Pathological Gambling and the Cost-Benefit/Effectiveness of Treatment." Paper presented to the Fifth National Conference on Gambling and Risk Taking, October 22.

Rosecrance, John. 1988. *Gambling Without Guilt.* Pacific Grove, CA: Brooks/Cole.

Rosenthal, Richard J. 1989. "Pathological Gambling and Problem Gambling: Problems of Definition and Diagnosis." In *Compulsive Gambling: Theory, Research, and Practice,* edited by Howard Shaffer, Sharon Stein, Blase Gambino, and Thomas N. Cummings, 101–126. Lexington, MA: D.C. Heath (Lexington Books).

Shaffer, Howard J., Matthew N. Hall, and Joni Vander Bilt. 1997. *Estimating the Prevalence of Disordered Gambling Behavior in the United States and Canada: A Meta-analysis.* Boston: Harvard Medical School.

Thompson, William N., and R. Keith Schwer. 2005. "Beyond the Limits of Recreation: Social Costs of Gambling in Southern Nevada," *Public Budgeting, Accounting, and Financial Management* 17, no. 1 (Spring): 62–92.

Thompson, William N., and R. Keith Schwer. 2007. "Nevada and the Win Win Game: Compulsive Gamblers and Alcohol," *Casino Lawyer* 3, no. 3 (Summer): 16–18.

Westphal, James, L. J. Johnson, and L. Stevens. 1999. "Estimating the Social Cost of Gambling for Louisiana." Baton Rouge: Louisiana State University Medical Center.

See also Switzerland (in Venues and Places section); Switzerland and Swiss Social Concept.

PROFESSIONAL AND AMATEUR SPORTS PROTECTION ACT OF 1992

Betting on professional sports and college sports games is very popular in the United States. There can be little doubt that tens of billions of dollars are wagered on these games each year. Most of the betting action is illegal. Only Nevada permits wagers on individual games, and the Oregon lottery allows players to wager on sports cards that require them to bet on at least four games on a single card—meaning they have to pick all four winners in order to have a winning bet. Delaware had authorized a similar system for betting on national football for several years starting in 1976. That system ended operation after a few years as it was not profitable to the state. In 2009, Delaware began plans for a new sports betting program. Montana permits private sports pools to be operated in taverns. The tavern organizes the pool, but all betting is among the players, who retain all of the prizes.

Several public officials expressed concern over a rising level of sports betting in the United States during the 1980s and early 1990s. The concern was attached to the fact that more than a dozen states were entertaining prospects of legalizing betting on games. One concerned official was U.S. Senator Bill Bradley (D-New Jersey), who had been a star player in the National Basketball Association on the world championship New York Knickerbockers team. He deplored

sports gambling, fearing that it would draw children into gambling activity since younger people were more attracted to games. He also saw the wagering as harmful to the honesty of the games, as sports betting could lead to attempts to bribe players in an attempt to alter the results of games in ways favorable to certain bettors. The public confidence in the integrity of the games was in jeopardy.

In February 1991, legislation was introduced in the U.S. Senate to block the expansion of publicly authorized sports betting. On October 28, 1992, the bill was signed into law by President George Bush as the Professional and Amateur Sports Protection Act (Public Law 102–559).

The law provides that no government entity may sponsor or authorize or otherwise promote any lottery or gambling scheme based in any way upon the results of one or more competitive games in which amateur or professional athletes participate. The four states with existing authorizations for sports betting—Nevada, Delaware, Oregon, and Montana—were exempt from the act's provision. Also, New Jersey's standing as the second state with large casinos was recognized, and the state was given until the end of 1993 to legalize sports betting in Atlantic City casinos if it desired to do so. When January 1, 1994 came, New Jersey had not legalized sports betting for the casinos, so the law prohibited sports betting in 46 states. The act does not apply to horse race or dog race betting or to pari-mutuel betting on games of jai alai.

Reference

Professional and Amateur Sports Protection Act (Public Law 102–559, signed into law October 28, 1992).

THE RACINO

A racino is a facility that mixes dog or horse track activity with casino-type activities.

For myriad reasons, racetracks have experienced a steady decline over the past several decades. There have been many efforts to stop the ongoing decline. During the 1990s, a new solution received support from track interests as well as political leaders in many jurisdictions. They recommended that tracks have gaming machines—video poker and slot machines. The recommendations took effect in several states and provinces, as well as in Mexico. Nine states (Iowa, Louisiana, Maryland, New York, Pennsylvania, West Virginia, Rhode Island, Delaware, and New Mexico) and four provinces (Alberta, Saskatchewan, Manitoba, and Ontario) have permitted gaming machines to be installed at racetrack facilities. In addition California's Hollywood Park has a very large card room casino.

The tracks offer advantages as casino-type venues: large parking areas, separation from the core urban populations, and space that is underutilized. On the other hand, critics suggest that the facilities may prey too much on local habitual gamblers, as very few racinos are geared to attracting tourists. Additionally there is debate over whether the casino-type gambling can add to the profitability of racing activity or whether it merely offers more competition to racing betting, hence hastening the doom of the racing events.

One 1998 study of a track in West Virginia found that machine gambling results in decreased pari-mutuel wagering, but that overall revenues at the tracks increased as the machines more than made up for the deficit in pari-mutuel activity. An issue of importance that should be addressed is just what share of the machine profits are assigned to the track and to horsemen, either in purses or through other means.

Pari-mutuel gambling is not fully compatible with machine gambling. Seasoned horse players are renowned as cerebral, educated calculators of the odds and probabilities that indicate a particular horse may win a race. For them, information is critical. Their activity requires a considerable amount of knowledge, which takes a long time to learn. Tom Learmont reports one gaming executive comments that "betting on horse races is a game of skill, unlike the mindless tapping of a slot machine button, and our philosophy is that the customer must be gently educated on how to study form before he places his bets" (S-13).

Where machine gaming is introduced, it dominates other gambling products. Inside Las Vegas's plushest casinos, machine revenues now exceed revenues from tables that cater to high rollers. After the Oregon Lottery introduced video lottery terminals (VLTs), revenues from the machines quickly dwarfed figures from traditional lottery products. Machines bring in 90 percent of the lottery revenues in South Dakota.

RACINO JURISDICTIONS

West Virginia

The West Virginia legislature authorized an experimental installation of video gaming machines—keno machines, poker machines, and machines with symbols—at Mountaineer horse racing track beginning on June 9, 1990. At first only 70 machines were installed. During the experimental time the number grew, reaching 400 in 1994. Most were keno machines. The first machines had payouts of 88.6 percent. During a three-year experimental period, the state agreed not to put machines in other locations. Since then, machine gaming has expanded to all the state's tracks, and tracks have been permitted to have table games as well. The tracks are able to keep 70 percent of the revenues, and 30 percent goes to the state.

Rhode Island

The second state to have machines was Rhode Island. The video machines were authorized for Lincoln Greyhound Park and a jai alai fronton. Operations started in September 1992. The greyhound facility soon dropped the word *greyhound* from its name and directed most of its advertising toward machine-playing customers. By mid-1994 there were 1,281 machines at the track. At first, 33 percent of the revenues went to the track and 10 percent went to purses for the dog races. Later the state took 33 percent, the track took 60 percent, and 7 percent went to purses.

In late 1993 Rhode Island added "reel" machines to the mix, as it was felt that the players should have the same variety of machines that was offered by a casino in nearby Connecticut.

"The introduction of VLTs stopped the bleeding," according to Dan Bucci, vice president and general manager of the track. In July 1994, he commented in *International Gaming and Wagering Business*, "We're living proof it can help. But I'm not sure gaming machines are a panacea. If there's a magic bullet out there for all of racing's problems, I don't know what it is." He commented, "It's a lot harder to create new pari-mutuel patrons than it is to create new machine patrons."

Louisiana

Although Louisiana has a long history of gaming, legal gaming machines appeared only in the 1990s. Pari-mutuel racing was well established when a state lottery was authorized in 1989. Tracks were affected by the new competition, and they immediately began to lobby for machines. VLTs were authorized for truck stops, restaurants and bars, and racetracks in 1992. Tracks were allowed to have an unlimited number of machines. The advantage of having machines was short-lived, as tracks had to compete with 15 newly licensed casino boats.

Ray Tromba, general manager of Louisiana Downs near Shreveport, commented, "It [the installation of 700 machines] was hopefully a way to help the racetrack be more of an entertainment facility; for the first two years it worked extremely well." Attendance at the track went up. Purses were raised and used to attract better horses for races. The patrons enjoyed the better races. Eighteen percent of the machine revenue was authorized for purses. Tromba maintained that "pari-mutuel can stand on its own if it's a good enough product that people will want to wager on it, it's as simple as that. This is not rocket science" (McQueen 1998).

Delaware

Delaware authorized all types of slot machines and other gaming machines for its tracks in 1995 (McQueen 1996). Delaware Park offered the machines first, but that track was soon followed by Harrington Raceway and Midway. Delaware Park pursued a strategy somewhat different from those elsewhere (Rhode Island, Iowa), as it sought to make a strong separation between the machine gaming and the track wagering. According to marketing director Steven Kallens, track efforts to bring slot players to the track windows were simply unsuccessful. "People got too confused. It was clear we had a pretty dedicated group of slot players with no interest in racing." But perhaps the situation was made to be that way. An unused 60,000-square-foot section of the grandstand was converted to slots. No racing monitors were placed in the room, and players had to go to another room to make racing wagers (McQueen 1996).

Iowa

In 1995, the Prairie Meadows horse track in Altoona near Des Moines was the first to have slot machines. Machines are also at two dog tracks, the biggest one in Council Bluffs. Without a doubt, they have turned the finances of the facilities around.

The Prairie Meadows racetrack opened in 1989, but the opening preceded the state's approval of riverboat casinos by only a few months. In 1991, as the boats opened, the last races were held at Prairie Meadows, and the track entered bankruptcy protection. There were no races in 1992. In 1993 a short meet with a mixture of thoroughbred and quarter horse racing was held, but it was not successful. By then a large Native American casino had opened its doors only 60 miles away in Tama. Machines made all the difference. With their installation, racing began anew in 1995, but it was machines that led the way. The 1995 revenues consisted of $118 million from the machines, $4.9 million from on-track race betting, and $25.8 million from simulcasting (McQueen 1996).

Iowa's Prairie Meadows has tried very hard to involve the machine players in track wagering, although the track racing has not become self-supporting. Machines have horse racing themes. One block of quarter machines is called Quarter Horses. The slot players can see track events from the slot area. Staff members circulate among slot players promoting racing and answering questions about race wagering. The players can also make bets to the staff directly while sitting at their machine locations. According to media director Steve Berry, slot players are also able to win free pari-mutuel tickets (McQueen 1996).

Of the retained revenues, $14 million is put into purses for horse races. Purses were only $1 million in 1994 prior to the introduction of slots. As a result of the increased purses, the quality of racing is improving, and simulcast revenues are up 4–5 percent. Attendance is approximately 10,000 a day, and handle has increased 16 percent. No other horse track in the Midwest has done as well as Prairie Meadows.

Maryland

In the 2008 elections the voters of Maryland authorized machine gaming. Some of the sites for this new gaming will include racetracks.

New Mexico

In 1998, the state of New Mexico agreed to let tracks have machines as long as they could all be tied together in a slot information network. The track gives 25 percent of the revenue directly to the state and gives 20 percent to horsemen through race purses. The track keeps 55 percent. Machines are permitted to run 12 hours a day, every day—as long as the track offers some racing products.

There are four tracks in the state with machines. On May 4, 1999, Ruidoso Downs, less than half an hour away from the large Native American casino of the Mescalero Apache tribe, was permitted to start operating 300 machines. Of the machines, 70 percent are traditional reel-type slot machines and 30 percent are video gaming devices. The track has simulcast racing every day, so the slot machines are available to players 365 days a year. Live racing—thoroughbred and quarter horse—occurs four days a week from Memorial Day to Labor Day.

The nation's leading quarter horse race—the All American Futurity—is run on Labor Day.

New York

New York Native American nations were authorized to negotiate compacts for casinos and slot machine gaming in 2001. To aid the state's horse racetracks in the face of this new competition, they were also permitted to offer machine gaming.

Pennsylvania

In 2004, the legislature of Pennsylvania authorized slot machine gaming at 14 locations, including seven horse tracks.

Canada

In 1998, a decision was made to allow 18 race tracks in Ontario to have slot machines under the direction of the provincial lottery corporation (McQueen 1998). Windsor Raceway, a track just a few miles away from the very successful Windsor Casino, was the first to start operations. In December 1998, 712 machines were set into action. The lottery corporation receives 15 percent of the revenues; 10 percent goes to the track and 10 percent to horsemen through purses and other awards. The remaining revenues go to the provincial treasury in Toronto (McQueen 1999).

According to John Millson, president of the raceway, "When the first coin went in, I knew there would be no turning back. It was music to my ears." He was also very supportive of the fact that the lottery corporation ran the machines. "It's a government agency, and quality and proper perception is extremely important, so they do it right." He also commented, "It means a tremendous opportunity for us to market our facility as a gaming and entertainment facility" (McQueen 1999).

The track-machine situation was mixed in other parts of the province. The major track in Toronto—Woodbine—was stymied in its early efforts to get machines, as the city council refused to grant a zoning variance for the activity.

The earliest province to embrace gaming on tracks was Saskatchewan. There a full casino was placed into operation underneath the stands of the Regina Exhibition Park's racing facility. Revenues from the casino were earmarked for Exhibition activities. The casino at the track discontinued operations a year after the provincial government began a major casino in downtown Regina. When the new casino opened, track handle decreased 23 percent.

Racinos are also found at the tracks in Alberta and Manitoba.

Mexico

The Agua Caliente track in Tijuana developed a sports betting complex to supplement dog racing and horse racing activities, but the horses have stopped running at the track. An operation in Juarez also offers dog racing and sports betting.

References

Learmont, Tom. 1998. "Racing's Rebirth." *International Gaming and Wagering Business* (June): S-13.

McQueen, Patricia. 1996. "Not Just for Racing Anymore." *International Gaming and Wagering Business* (August): 98.

McQueen, Patricia. 1998. "Reeling Them In." *International Gaming and Wagering Business* (May): 59.

McQueen, Patricia. 1999. "Slots Debut at Windsor Raceway." *International Gaming and Wagering Business* (February): 45.

Thalheimer, Richard. 1998. "Pari-mutuel Wagering and Video Gaming: A Racetrack Portfolio." *Applied Economics* 30: 531–544.

Thompson, William N. 1999. "Racinos and the Public Interest." *Gaming Law Review* 3 (December): 283–286.

RELIGION AND GAMBLING

Las Vegas and religion have a strange but enduring relationship. For many years, local boosters would proudly proclaim that Las Vegas had more churches per person than any other city in the country. Perhaps that was because the population used to be small, and the boosters probably counted all the wedding chapels as churches.

Actually Las Vegas is pretty well "churched," but not more than any other large city today. What is true even today is this: Las Vegas has more prayers per person than any other city in the country. It is said that there are no atheists in a foxhole, and the same can be said about the people standing around a high-stakes craps table. There just possibly may be a difference between the prayers heard near a casino craps table and the ones mumbled in a church on a Sunday morning—the prayers in the casino may be more serious.

As the casino entertainment industry became entrenched in Las Vegas, various ministries made their appearances on the Las Vegas Strip. In the 1970s, the Southern Baptist Convention assigned a young minister to the Strip to establish a ministry among the employees, entertainers, and players in the casinos. More recently, the Riviera Casino put a clergyman on its own staff. He is available to counsel other staff as well as tourist guests who experience immediate personal and family needs while they are in Las Vegas. He also conducts services in the casino facility.

Religious and gambling institutions need not be incompatible, although leaders in each are often at loggerheads with one another. The primary leader of the opposition to gambling in the United States at the beginning of the 21st century is Tom Grey, a Methodist clergyman. Churches have been prominent in campaigns against gambling, as documented in John Dombrink's and William Thompson's *The Last Resort: Success and Failure in Campaigns for Casinos* (1990). On the other hand, casinos, wary of political opposition from religious groups, have often extended financial support to church groups. The casino at Baden-Baden, Germany, actually constructed both the Catholic and Protestant church buildings of its town. The Berkeley Casino Company of Glasgow, Scotland, aided a local Presbyterian church body by purchasing its old building in order to utilize it as a casino. The pews were removed, but the religious aura seems to hang over the roulette wheels and blackjack tables. On the other hand, the Guardian Angel Church on the Las Vegas Strip features a large stained glass window that depicts scenes of several nearby casinos. Of course, many churches have also used bingo games and raffles for fund-raising.

The relationship between gambling and religion goes back to the dawn of human time. Was the snake tempting Adam and Eve with a gamble when he suggested that they disobey God and eat of the fruit from the tree of knowledge? Could they have known where that quest for knowledge would lead them? Could they have contemplated the nature of life had they not searched for something different?

Moral and religious views on gambling are probably as old as gambling activities themselves. Prehistoric and primitive societies have engaged in exercises to try to make sense of their universe and to control their environment by appealing to the supernatural, forces often expressed as gods or God—that is, powers beyond their world. David Levinson's *Religion: A Cross-Cultural Encyclopedia* describes religion as a "relationship between human beings and the supernatural world" (Levinson 1996, vii). The exercises involving appeals to chance would be part and parcel of a people's religion.

For instance, in all societies from prehistoric times to modern times, the notion of divination has been present. Divination involves beliefs and practices of human beings that enable them to communicate with gods (or God) in order to tell the future. In divining the future, leaders might throw sticks or stones into the air and watch where they fall in order to gain the answers. It was as if they were throwing dice or rolling a

The Strip is featured on the stained glass windows of the Guardian Angel church in Las Vegas.

gambling wheel. Religious leaders might also hold long sticks that would somehow point them in a direction that their people should follow on a journey, perhaps in quest of water or food. A large part of early religions may have involved the use of gambling instruments (Levinson 1996, 53–54, 182–183). The origins of many games played among traditional Native American tribes may have had religious connotations. The following discussion, however, concentrates on early experiences in the Judeo-Christian heritage as well as established Eastern world religions.

The Hebrews were probably carrying on prehistoric traditions as their leaders sought ways to find the "truth" about the future or about the proper decisions they should make. They would throw stones that were in essence two-sided dice, called Urim and Thummim, in order to choose between two alternatives. They would also draw lots in situations calling for choices. There are many references in the Old Testament regarding the use of these gambling devices for decision making. Urim and Thummim are mentioned in the following eight cases.

Aaron was made to carry Urim and Thummim upon himself as he came before the Lord, as the objects would tell him the judgment of the people of Israel. (Exodus 28:30). The Lord commanded that Moses place the Urim and Thummim on Aaron (Leviticus 8:08). In Numbers 27:21, Moses chooses Joshua to lead the people, and he is given Urim and Thummim to help him find the right answers in his leadership. Similarly, Levi is given the objects in order to make choices (Deuteronomy 33:08). As Saul was preparing for war with the Philistines, he was bothered when the Lord did not urge him forward. He thought it perhaps was because of his sins, his son's sins, or those of his peoples. Urim and Thummim told him the sins were not his people's. Then he threw the stones again, and he was told they were sins of his son Jonathan. His son confessed that he had broken the laws. When Saul determined that his son would have to die, the people intervened, and Saul was forced to walk away from battle (I Samuel 14:41). Later Saul threw the stones again in order to get directions he should take in another battle with the

Philistines (I Samuel 28:6). Solomon (Ezra 2:63) and Nehemiah (Nehemiah 7:65) both used Urim and Thummim to determine which of the people who came to the temple were clean—in the sense of having the proper family heritage—and could enter the priesthood and partake of holy food.

The Old Testament also records more than a dozen references to the use of lots, or lotteries. The first was when Aaron used lots to decide which of two goats were to be sacrificed to the Lord as a sin offering (Leviticus 16:08). Joshua divided the land of Israel into seven portions and awarded them to families through a casting of lots (Joshua 17:6). Moses used lotteries to divide the lands of Israel among families (Numbers 33:54). Soldiers were selected for battle by lottery (Judges 20:9). Saul was chosen to be king by the process of a drawing (1 Samuel 10:20–21). David was told which way to go in order to assume command of his troops (2 Samuel 2:1).

Leaders of the Israel church community were chosen by lots (1 Chronicles 24:31ff.), and the music was organized for the temple by using lots to assign duties to individuals (1 Chronicles 25:8–31). Specific duties such as controlling gates and roads, as well as storehouses, were also given by lots (1 Chronicles 26:13–14). In Nehemiah (10:34) it is reported that lots were cast to decide which families would bring wood offerings into the house of God. One-tenth of the people were allowed to live in Jerusalem; the others lived in smaller villages. Those who were allowed into the city were chosen by lotteries (Nehemiah 11:1). Job (6:27) has a reference to one remonstrating with God, saying "you would even cast lots over the fatherless and bargain over your

friend." In a passage that must have been in anticipation of the crucifixion, the Cry of Anguish in the Psalms (22:18) talks of one dying and of dogs who "divide my garments among them, and for my raiment they cast lots."

Joel spoke the word of the Lord condemning the nations that had scattered the Jews, claiming that they "cast lots for my people and traded boys for prostitutes" (Joel 3:03). In Obadiah (1:11) the Lord condemned the people of Edom for allowing foreigners to cast lots for Jerusalem, looking down on your brother "in the day of his misfortune." Jonah (1:07) offers the story of a ship that has been disabled by a storm. The crew believes it is because a sinner is on board, and they cast lots to find that it is Jonah. Nahum records the Lord's anger at Nineveh as he spoke of people casting lots for her nobles and putting her great men in chains (Nahum 3:10).

In Isaiah (36:08) it is reported that Judah is asked to make a wager with the king of Assyria in which he can win 2,000 horses for Israel if he is able to put riders upon them. The story is repeated in 2 Kings (18:23).

These references to lots, throwing of dice-like objects, and wagering are not at all judgmental (collectively) regarding the desirability of gambling or the acceptability of gambling. The same may be said for New Testament references that include the use of lots (some think dice) by Roman soldiers to decide which centurion would receive the clothing of the crucified Christ (Matthew 27:35; Mark 15:24; Luke 23:24; Acts 1:26). Certainly this is a negative light in which gambling is classed. But contemporary with that event was the use of lots to select a replacement for Judas in the group of 12 disciples (Act 1:21–26).

Because the Bible contains no direct condemnation of gambling (not even in the Ten Commandments), different religious groups among Christians and Jews interpret its writings in various ways. Some point to the many uses of gambling devices in decision situations, essentially as objects for divination, as a justification of gambling. Others say that the use of lots to determine God's will is substantially different from using gambling for personal gain. Other biblical passages suggest that there might be evil in gambling. The writers of Isaiah (65:11–12) state, "But you who forsake the lord who set a table for fortune and fill the cups of mixed wine for destiny, I will destine you to the sword, and all of you shall bow down to slaughter." Proverbs (13:11) suggests that winnings from gambling are only temporary: "Wealth hastily gotten will dwindle, but he who gathers little by little will increase it." Other Old Testament references suggest that gambling represents covetousness or stealing, which is condemned (Exodus 20:15–17). The New Testament admonition to give up possessions and follow the Lord suggests that the quest for wealth through gambling is not appropriate. Tom Watson, in *Don't Bet On It,* feels that a further commandment against gambling beyond the Ten Commandments would have been somewhat redundant. "If God didn't get our attention with his laws about stealing and coveting, He probably felt any reference to gambling would be ignored as well" (Watson 1987, 63).

JUDAISM

Religious groups from Judaism through the most modern Christian sects have addressed the issue of gambling, but not at all times and certainly not always in the same way. In Judaism, rabbis and other scholars meticulously analyze historical evidence regarding activities. Jewish law changes and grows with interpretations. The interpretations have differed considerably at times; however, there is a general position of tolerance couched in considerations of the circumstances of the gambling activity.

Occasional gambling in social situations has been moderately acceptable. Indeed, because an enemy king once rolled the dice to determine when to attack Israeli troops, leading him to attack at the wrong time and lose the battle, the Jewish people have come to celebrate a day called Purim. Games involving gambling are played on Purim, a time also known as the Feast of Lots. The winner of money at such a game, however, is supposed to make an offering to the synagogue (Wigoder 1989, 576).

Hanukkah celebrates the miracle of the lamps. As a "lucky day" for the Jewish people, it has also been known as the "New Year's Day for Gamblers."

A person who gambled either professionally, as a means of personal support, or habitually was shunned, despite these other examples. The professional gambler was considered a thief, not earning his money through honest labor, and the habitual gambler was seen as one who harmed society. A gambler was a "parasite engaged in useless endeavor and contributing nothing to the world" (Werblowsky and Wigoder 1966, 152). Time spent in gambling games has been viewed as time away from study and productivity. Jewish courts traditionally will not honor gambling debts. And gamblers could not have weddings or funerals in synagogues, nor could they be witnesses in court, as their word was not considered truthful (Bell 1976, 217).

There have been divided interpretations regarding the use of gambling for charitable and fund-raising purposes. Some synagogues have allowed bingo games on their premises, but an association of synagogues condemned the process. Some scholars have interpreted tragic events suffered by the Jewish people at different times in history as being punishments for sins such as gambling. Leaders in the faith have actively opposed legalization of gambling at certain times, although not taking positions or allowing passive support at other times (Jacobs 1973, 151–153).

CHRISTIANITY

Theologian H. Richard Niebuhr postulates that Christians look at the involvement of Christ in the culture of worldly activity in five basic ways:

1. They see Christ *against* the culture of the world. Here one must choose the sin of this world or a heavenly world that is totally separate.

2. A second approach is that Christ is *of and in* the world. God is the force that directs culture toward its greatest (human) achievements.

3. Christ is *above* the culture. People may live lives directed toward a good, but to achieve the highest human aspirations they must make a supernatural leap to the higher power.

4. Christ *and* culture are forces with dual power over people. As subjects we render unto both God and Caesar, seeking to keep religious and civil authority separate yet together.

5. Christ is seen *as the transforming agent* to remold the culture. People undergo a conversion while they are in the culture (Niebuhr 1951).

Christian views on gambling can be guided by these approaches. Absolutist views—always negative views—toward gambling are found among groups adhering to the first view. For instance, Jehovah's Witnesses seek not to let the materialism of this world become dominant forces in their lives, and accordingly, they disdain all gambling. The Jehovah's Witnesses do not lobby governments or campaign for or against any gambling questions. Members do not vote. Although they show respect for authority, they see governments as worldly, secular institutions, which should not be encouraged, albeit the edicts of government will be obeyed. Their spokespersons make it clear that their members do not participate in or support gambling. The *Watchtower*, the official journal of the faith, regularly reports on gambling, calling it an activity of "greed" and "covetness" stimulating "selfishness and lack of concern for others." Gambling "degrades" people and "entraps them in false worship" (October 1, 1974, 9).

The Salvation Army also rejects gambling in its entirety. However, it subscribes more to the second approach of Christ and culture, that Christ is of the world, that he came and walked among the sinners and gave them the light by which to transform their lives and lift up the culture. With this approach the church does not actively campaign against proposals for gambling, but rather like Gamblers Anonymous groups, it concentrates its efforts on reforming the individual suffering from the influences of gambling.

The third and fourth approaches that churches take toward the role of Christ in culture seem to accept the status quo with regard to public policy. Many of the churches do not oppose gambling outright but look at it in its full context. Churches such as the Methodists (United), Southern Baptist, and Latter-day Saints (Mormons) condemn all gambling by members in all circumstances, adhering to the fifth notion that Christ is the transforming agent sent to earth to remold the culture by converting individuals within the culture.

The Book of Discipline of the United Methodist Church, for instance, proclaims:

> Gambling is a menace to society, deadly to the best interests of moral, social, economic, and spiritual life, and destructive of good government. As an act of faith and love, Christians should abstain from gambling and should strive to minister to those victimized by the practice. Community standards and personal lifestyles should be such as would make unnecessary and undesirable the resort to commercial gambling, including public lotteries, as a recreation, as an escape, or as a means of producing public revenue or funds for support of charities or government. (General Conference of the United Methodist Church 1984, 98–99)

The Southern Baptist Convention is the largest non-Catholic denomination in the United States. Their director of family and moral concerns, Harry Hollis, told the Commission on the Review of the National Policy on Gambling much the same story:

> In all its resolutions, the Southern Baptist Convention has rejected gambling. Obviously, some forms of gambling are more serious than others, but all forms have been consistently rejected in Southern Baptist statements and resolutions. The use of gambling profits for worthy activities has not led Southern Baptists to endorse gambling. . . . The availability of gambling tempts both the reformed gambler and the potential gambler to destruction. For the entire community, gambling is disruptive and harmful. Thus, concerned citizens should work for laws to control and eliminate gambling. (Bell 1976, 172–173)

The Church of Jesus Christ of Latter-day Saints has been equally vehement in maintaining that gambling is always wrong. In 1982, Spencer Kimball, the 12th president of the church, wrote:

> From the beginning we have been advised against gambling of every sort. The deterioration and damage come to the person, whether he wins or loses, to get something for nothing, something without effort, something without paying the full price. Profiting from others' weaknesses displeases God. Clean money is that compensation received for a full day's honest work. It is that reasonable pay for faithful service. It is that fair profit from the sale of goods, commodities, or service. It is that

income received from transactions where all parties profit. (Kimball 1982, 355–356; *See also* Ludlow 1992, 533)

An interesting side issue arose recently over temple privileges. A member of the Church of Latter-day Saints must be in good standing in order to enter a temple. In the past if a Mormon worked in a gambling establishment or in a gambling-related job, especially if the job was on the "frontline" of providing gambling service, such as being a dealer, he or she might be denied good-standing status. When the church decided to build a temple in Las Vegas (about 10 percent of the local population are Mormons), many members who held jobs in casinos wished to have temple privileges. Casinos provide the largest number of jobs in the Las Vegas community, so many members of the Mormon faith do work in casinos. The church stand against casino employment was reviewed, and it was decided that casino workers who did not personally gamble and did not overtly encourage others to gamble could have good standing if they met other church and community obligations.

Churches that accept gambling in some circumstances generally view Christ's role in culture in the third or fourth way as advanced by H. Richard Niebuhr. In *Money, Mania, and Morals,* L. M. Starkey writes, "[A]ll Catholic moralists are agreed that gambling and betting may lead to grave abuse and sin, especially when they are prompted by mere gain. The gambler usually frequents bad company, wastes much valuable time, becomes adverse to work, is strongly tempted to be dishonest when luck is against him, and often brings financial ruin upon himself and those dependent upon him" (Starkey 1964, 90–91). Nonetheless the Catholic Church reconciles gambling with the fact that Christ must have been of the world as God had given people personal freedom that led them into certain activity. *The New Catholic Encyclopedia* relates, "A person is entitled to dispose of his own property as he wills . . . so long as in doing so he does not render himself incapable of fulfilling duties incumbent upon him by reason of justice or charity. Gambling, therefore, though a luxury, is not considered sinful except when the indulgence in it is inconsistent with duty" (*The New Catholic Encyclopedia* 1967, 276).

The Catholic Church believes that it is sinful for a person to gamble if the money gambled does not belong to him or if the money is necessary for the support of others. The Church also condemns gambling behavior when it becomes compulsive and disruptive to family and social relationships. Moreover, the freedom to gamble implies that the participant is entering into a fair and honest contract for play. Cheating at gambling is considered wrong, as are all dishonest games.

The Church also looks at the end result of the activity. If through gambling good consequences may follow, the gambling activity may even be considered good and may be promoted by the Church. Hence, a limited-stakes bingo game conducted honestly by church members within a church building in order to raise funds for a school or hospital is not bad.

On questions concerning the legalization of gambling, Catholic Church leaders ask if the particular form of gambling puts poor people at a disadvantage, if it causes people to become pathological gamblers, and if the gambling will be adequately monitored to assure that it is honest and fair. Church leaders have opposed some public referenda, while they have supported others.

The Church of England and its U.S. offspring, the American Episcopal Church, both essentially reformed Catholic organizations, accept the same approach toward gambling as is taken by the Catholic Church. The National Convention of the church has no stated position on gambling. Individual church organizations have used gambling events to raise funds; others have prohibited the use of gambling within church facilities. Basically the issue of gambling is a low-priority ethical issue. Individuals are left to develop their own attitudes on the subject.

EASTERN RELIGIONS

Middle Eastern and Asian countries usually ban gambling. For the most part Arab states, India, China, Japan, and other Asian countries have no casinos. Regional religions such as Islam, Hinduism, Buddhism, and Shintoism—which are also practiced by many Americans—generally account for the legal prohibitions.

It is written in the Koran—the holy scriptures of the Islamic faith—"Only would Satan sow hatred and strife among you, by wine and games of chance, and turn you aside from the remembrance of God, and from prayer; will ye not, therefore, abstain from them?" Islamic law therefore condemns gambling as being contrary to the word. The activity is viewed as "unjustified enrichment" and "receiving a monetary advantage without giving a counter-value" (Survah V, verses 90–91). The evidence of a gambler is not admissible in an Islamic court. Anyone receiving gambling winnings is obligated to give the money to the poor. There are, however, two exceptions to the general prohibition on gambling: Wagers are permitted for horse racing, as such betting was an incentive for training necessary for the holy wars. Also, prizes may be given for winners of competitions involving knowledge about Islamic law.

Under Hindu law, gamblers are also disqualified as witnesses. Because of their "depravity," they are considered, as are "thieves and assassins," to be people in whom "no truth can be found." The Hindu law books indicate that gambling—among the most serious of vices—makes a person impure and that "the wealth obtained by gambling is tainted" (Eliade 1987, 5:472). The devout Buddhist considers gambling wrong. In the Parabhava Sutta, the Buddha includes addiction to women, strong drink, and dice as one of 11 combinations of means whereby men are brought to loss. The one path to victory is loving the "dhamma"—the Buddha's teaching. Monks are warned that games and spectacles—including fights between elephants, horses, buffalo, bulls, goats, rams, and cocks, and also various board games, chariot races, and dice games—are detrimental to their virtue.

Buddha saw that the world was suffering because of desire. Desires could not be satisfied, and therefore we had frustration. When we achieved our wants we only wanted more, and then we became obsessed with fears that others would take away what we had. In rejecting desires, we had to seek the ten "perfections" in generosity, self-sacrifice, morality, renunciation, energy, forbearance, truthfulness, loving, kindness, and equanimity. These perfections come with a rejection of worldly passions, including those aroused by gambling activity (Eliade 1987, 5:472).

The Shinto faith of Japan emerged after centuries of contact with Buddhism. It became a national religion in the 19th century, incorporating many Buddhist beliefs. It extols the virtue of industriousness and strong will power. Hence, gambling is accorded the status of an evil activity, as it diverts one from the path to virtue and righteousness.

Marxism has replaced religion to a major extent in China and North Korea, although remnants of religious practices can be witnessed. The notions of Marxism are consistent with the prohibitions on gambling found within the major regional religions. Marxist and socialist thought views gambling as an activity that takes people away from productive pursuits, and in an organized sense, gambling is another capitalist activity that exploits the working classes.

The force of Marxism and religious doctrines of Islam, Hinduism, Buddhism, and Shintoism upon the laws of most Middle Eastern and Asian countries has been pronounced. Nonetheless, the affluent among the populations of the region have always found gambling outlets available for their play. Middle Eastern and Asian gambling enclaves thrive in places such as Macao, Beirut, Cairo, Manila, and Kathmandu. And Las Vegas casinos include nationals from the Eastern and Middle Eastern countries, which forbid gambling, high on the lists of their most exclusive high-rolling players. Religions in the East as well as the West do influence the attitudes people have toward the legalization of gambling, but the force of beliefs as a determinant over whether people will personally gamble or not may be less pervasive.

Coauthored by James Dallas

Casino Budapest began in an old church tower.

References

Bell, Raymond. 1976. "Moral Views on Gambling Promulgated by Major American Religious Bodies." In *Gambling in America,* Appendix I. Washington, DC: National Commission on the Policy of Gambling.

Dombrink, John D., and William N. Thompson. 1990. *The Last Resort: Success and Failure in Campaigns for Casinos.* Reno: University of Nevada Press.

Eliade, Mircea, ed. 1987. *The Encyclopedia of Religion.* 16 vols. New York: Macmillan.

General Conference of the United Methodist Church. 1984. *The Book of Discipline.* Nashville, TN: United Methodist Publishing House.

Jacobs, Louis. 1973. *What Does Judaism Say About . . . ?* Jerusalem: Keter Publishing.

Kimball, Spencer, ed. 1982. *The Teachings of Spencer W. Kimball.* Salt Lake City: Deseret Book Company.

Levinson, David. 1996. *Religion: A Cross-Cultural Encyclopedia.* Santa Barbara, CA: ABC-CLIO.

Ludlow, Daniel H. 1992. *Encyclopedia of Mormonism.* New York: Macmillan.

The New Catholic Encyclopedia. 1967. 17 vols. New York: McGraw-Hill.

Niebuhr, H. Richard. 1951. *Christ and Culture.* New York: Harper and Row.

Schacht, Joseph. 1964. *An Introduction to Islamic Law.* Oxford: Clarendon Press.

Starkey, L. M. 1964. *Money, Mania, and Morals.* New York: Abington Press.

Thompson, William N. 1997. *Legalized Gambling: A Reference Book.* 2nd ed. Santa Barbara, CA: ABC-CLIO.

Wagner, Walter. 1972. *To Gamble, or Not to Gamble.* New York: World Publishing.

Watson, Tom. 1987. *Don't Bet on It.* Ventura, CA: Regal Books.

Werblowsky, R. J. Z., and Geoffrey Wigoder, eds. 1966. *The Encyclopedia of the Jewish Religion.* New York: Holt, Rinehart, Winston.

Wigoder, Geoffrey. 1989. *The Encyclopedia of Judaism.* New York: Macmillan.

See also "The Best Gamblers in the World" (in Selected Essays on Gambling section).

Senate Special Committee to Investigate Organized Crime in Interstate Commerce. *See* The Kefauver Committee.

SEX AND GAMBLING IN NEVADA

Public opinion changes on a daily basis in the United States. Perception can slowly shift until practices that were once illegal, or at least taboo, become acceptable and even commonplace. This trend can be illustrated by the recent nationwide explosion of gaming and sexually oriented businesses. Like gambling, a formerly marginal activity now epitomized by glamorous and family-oriented resort casinos, segments of the sex industry have transformed themselves from seedy operations operating without license to socially acceptable and upscale operations that cater to members of both sexes. Nowhere is this transition more evident than in Las Vegas, where the nexus between the casino gamer and the "new" sex industry has replaced the nexus between the miner or military recruit and prostitution of the late 1800s.

Brothels operated openly throughout Nevada from its earliest existence. In 1881, county commissioners were given the authority to regulate and tax or prohibit brothels, and in 1907 city councils were given the same authority. In 1971, the state legislature banned prostitution in any county with a population of 200,000 or more. At the time, this law applied only to Clark County, where Las Vegas is located. Actually most of the brothels had been effectively closed because of military orders first issued in 1942 from nearby Nellis Air Force Base declaring the brothels off-limits.

Historical records suggest that the law banning prostitution in Clark County was the result of two major influences. First was the potential involvement in the Las Vegas area of Joe Conforte, the notorious owner of Nevada's largest brothel, who was opposed by the Las Vegas area gaming community. Second was the belief that maintaining a "good image" was essential for gambling and the exploding convention and tourism industries. In effect, prostitution had to give way because it was a perceived threat to dominant business interests.

Several, but not all, small counties throughout the state continued to allow prostitution. The economic realities of sparse tax revenues and the notion that prostitution depressurizes things—that is, takes the pressure off of wives and daughters in rural communities—helped maintain a status quo that accepted brothels in rural Nevada. In larger communities, Nevada's brothels were simply not as powerful as the industry's gaming community. Any conflict of interest between another Nevada industry and gaming would invariably be resolved in favor of gaming.

Legal prostitution has not grown much in the last 30 years. For example, there were 33 brothels open in Nevada in 1971. Today there are 36 brothel licenses, although three are only open part-time. Most of the brothels are relatively small, and there are only a few hundred licensed prostitutes within the whole state.

When most people think about the sex industry, they usually think about prostitutes and perhaps individuals involved in the adult entertainment or pornography businesses. The scope of the sex industry is much broader, however, than a stereotypical prostitute.

The adult entertainment segment of the sex industry is nationally an $8 billion institution that is becoming a significant part of popular U.S. culture. Like gambling, the adult entertainment industry has changed dramatically over the last three decades. Technological advances such as cable television, videocassettes, and DVDs have allowed individuals access to a wide variety of adult entertainment in the privacy of their homes. Expenditures on adult entertainment are larger than those on Hollywood movies and larger than the revenues for recorded popular music. "Strip clubs" in the United States have seen even greater growth. The number of female exotic dancers grew from fewer than 15,000 in 1980 to more than 300,000 in 2000. It is apparent that the industry's growth is linked to a changing popular culture that tolerates, if not embraces, traditional vices such as gambling and divergent sexual activities. There is no doubt that sex is being used throughout the United States to sell many consumer items and to promote television ratings.

Sex also sells in Las Vegas. Topless reviews are still common at major strip casinos, but more economically significant are "gentleman's clubs" and high-priced outcall and escort services. Las Vegas has maintained its reputation as Sin City. This reputation is based, in part, on a belief that the community has a diverse and extensive sex industry. There is no doubt that the Las Vegas sex industry substantially contributes to the local economy. There are approximately 1,500 to 2,000 illegal prostitutes and between 2,000 and 2,200 active exotic dancers who work and live in the metropolitan area. These numbers often swell on key convention and prize-fight weekends to nearly 3,000 illegal prostitutes and nearly 3,500 exotic dancers.

Prostitution did not disappear from Las Vegas when it was legislatively banned in the 1940s. Illegal prostitution still flourishes despite efforts by local police departments to keep it under control, particularly in the Las Vegas Strip area. The county has implemented an "order out" ordinance that strongly discourages prostitutes from working in or near the Strip casinos. This ordinance has forced low- to medium-level prostitutes who had traditionally worked the Strip's bars and streets into walking high crime areas elsewhere.

It is estimated that street prostitutes in Las Vegas each make between $25,000 and $60,000 per year. Outcall entertainers average between $65,000 and $100,000 per year, depending upon skill and work schedule. (The local Sprint *July 2000 Yellow Pages* carries 104 pages of "entertainers." Only lawyers have more pages in the book—138). Most outcall entertainers work up to four evenings per week. Most do not stay in the business for more than three years. High-priced prostitutes average between $100 and $500 per client interaction.

Private referral escorts cost between $500 and $10,000 per day depending upon the individual entertainer and client. The casinos often arrange the services of these women. There is evidence of one woman who was paid in excess of $250,000 for one weekend's work by a high roller at a major casino.

The largest segment of the sex industry in Las Vegas is the gentlemen's clubs that employ exotic dancers, commonly known as strippers. The number of gentlemen's clubs in the United States roughly doubled between 1987 and 1992. There are now nearly 3,000 clubs in the United States employing between 250,000 and 300,000 women. The Las Vegas area has more than 30 gentlemen's clubs. Their annual revenues range from $500,000 to more than $10,000,000. These clubs span the gamut from old run-down operations to up-scale full-service operations that include food and gambling.

The growth of the local clubs has been fueled by four major developments. First is the rapid growth of convention business. This growth has created a substantive increase in the visitation of professional males aged 25 to 54. Second has been the substantial investments made by local operators to upgrade their establishments in line with other major cities throughout the nation. Only in the last decade did the major operators make facility investments and physical changes to reflect the national trends in upscale clubs. Third, there has been a growing acceptance of upscale gentlemen's clubs by a larger segment of the nation's business community. Last, the relationship between the casinos and the clubs has improved, and a codependence has developed to form a variation of the network prostitution system of the pre-1980s. This relationship recognizes that these clubs provide an entertainment venue that is sought after by many of the casinos' key customers. The clubs provide a safe outlet for many of these important casino customers. For legal prostitution, casino customers can easily take the one-hour cab ride to visit a Pahrump brothel (outside of Clark County). Nevertheless, many casino customers believe they can procure sex at local gentlemen's clubs. As such, casino hosts have developed relationships with individual gentlemen's club managers to enable them to provide their customers with the services desired.

The upper tier of Las Vegas–area gentlemen's clubs independently contract with women for their services. Many of the dancers pay to dance at the local establishments. The fees vary significantly depending on the club's policies and the time of day and the day of the week. Weekend nights (8:00 p.m. to 4:00 a.m.) are generally the most expensive times for dancers to work. Additionally, high-traffic conventions such as COMDEX (a computer dealers' exposition) increase the rates that clubs charge dancers. The typical dancer makes (that is, nets) between $35 and $75 per night plus tips and fees, but at top clubs a good dancer will make between $300 and $1,200. The number of dancers increases by over 40 percent on most weekends in Las Vegas. The majority of this weekend increase in dancers is a result of out-of-state dancers who work only the weekends. The traditional economic concept of supply and demand is clearly at work in the Las Vegas community. These services exist to satisfy the demand.

The major difference between the prostitution network today and that of 1981 is that the managers of the gentlemen's clubs have replaced the prostitutes in the network. Additionally, these establishments have substantially more power than in the past. This is not to suggest that all exotic dancers are prostitutes. Yet, like gambling, the gentlemen's club is about an illusion of winning. Sure, sometimes gamblers win, but mostly they lose. The dancers understand this illusion concept as well. Some dancers will perform a sex act for money, but others will not.

The casinos recognize that it is in their interest to have high-class prostitutes and escorts available—inconspicuously—for their customers. Publicly, casinos denounce the evils of prostitution; privately, they recognize its importance to their customer base and support its continued existence. The casinos come closer and closer to participation, albeit they stay a legal arm's length away. In recent years casinos have opened a new style of night club. These clubs include Christian Audigier, Rain, the Ghost Bar, Risque, LAX, Tao, Pure, and The Bank. Standard fare includes a $60 door charge, and a required bottle purchase of $475 per table—and this is just the start. The guests are certainly not rushed to return to the casino tables. The clubs are "for men," but women "customers" are admitted free of charge, and then given seats at tables with men. Their "job" is to keep the men interested in buying more bottles, and perhaps (without the knowledge of the casino) making arrangements for future "dates."

Nevada's economy was built upon the legalization of activities that were considered vices by the rest of the United States. As the nation becomes more like Las Vegas, Las Vegas becomes more like the nation, and what once were vices are now only minor variances on the norm.

Coauthored with Robert Schmidt

References

Frey, James, Loren Reichert, and Kenneth Russell. 1981. "Prostitution, Business, and Police: The Maintenance of an Illegal Economy." Paper presented to the Pacific Sociological Association, July 1981, 239–249.

Schlosser, Eric. 1997. "The Business of Pornography: Who's Making the Money?" *U.S. News and World Report* 22 (10 February): 42–50.

Schmidt, Robert. 2000. *Illusions of Sex: Lap Dancing in Las Vegas.* Unpublished manuscript.

Thompson, William N. 2008. "Branding Las Vegas," *Casino Lawyer* 5, no. 1 (Winter): 13–15.

Sic Bo. *See* Craps and Other Dice Games (in Games section).

Sports Betting

Sports betting occurs when gamblers make wagers on the results of games and contests played by other persons. The gamblers have no control over the outcome of the games—that is, as long as the wagering is honest. Whether it is legal or not is another matter.

There are sports betting opportunities involving a wide variety of games and contests. Although in a generic sense, sports betting includes wagers made on the results of horse races and dog races, these games (contests) are usually considered to be different than other forms of sports wagering. In this encyclopedia, they are discussed separately, as are jai alai contests and cockfighting.

It may be suggested that making wagers on the results of games is the most popular form of gambling in North America. It is certainly the most popular form of illegal betting in the United States. Estimates from the 1999 National Gambling Impact Study Commission place illegal sports gambling activity between $80 and $380 billion annually.

This illegal sector commands considerably more activity than the few legal outlets for sports gambling in the United States. In Nevada, there are 187 locations, almost all within casinos, that accept legal bets on professional and amateur sports contests. More than $2.4 billion was wagered in these sportsbooks in 2006. The gross revenue from these wagers was $192 million; that is, casinos "held" 7.9 percent of the wagers, owing to the fact that the gamblers bet on the wrong team and casinos structure odds in their own favor. These sports wagers constituted just over 1 percent of all the betting in Nevada casinos. About two-thirds of the wagers were on professional games and the rest on college sports. According to the American Gaming Association, in 2007, 45 percent of these wagers were bet on football, 26 percent on basketball, 20 percent on baseball, and 8 percent on other sports.

Although the profits casinos realize directly from sports bets seem to be low, sports betting is very important in Las Vegas and Reno. Major gamblers like to follow sports, and the wagering possibilities draw them to the casinos. Casinos sponsor championship boxing matches and give the best seats to their favorite gamblers. Super Bowl weekend and the first four days of the NCAA men's basketball tournament, commonly known as "March Madness," are the biggest gambling times in Las Vegas each year. Approximately $93 million was wagered in Nevada on the 2007 Super Bowl and more than $85 million on the 2007 NCAA tournament.

The only other active legal sports wagering in the United States was in Oregon. It had begun in 1989, with the Oregon Lottery offering Sport Action, a parlay card allowing bets on professional football games. This game was structured to produce a return of 50 percent to the players on a pari-mutuel basis. In 1990, NBA games were added, but eliminated the following year due to lack of interest. The sales of Sport Action and its offshoot, Monday Night Scoreboard (introduced in 2003) totaled $12.7 million in 2006. The Oregon legislature ended this form of sports betting at the end of the 2006–2007 football season.

HISTORICAL PERSPECTIVE

Sports betting has developed rapidly in recent decades. The added interest in sports betting has been affected by increased interest in sports in the United States. Although individual sports have different experiences with their growth, one factor that has affected all sports has been television access to games and news media on odds and point spreads. Games in all sports can now be viewed through basic cable television, which is a major upgrade in programming from coverage provided by the three major U.S. networks of the 1980s. In addition to basic cable,

The lottery is advertised at a Louisiana State University football game.

premium sports-specific packages and home satellite systems are also available to allow the sports gambler to view wagered upon games. Lastly, with the continued advent of new forms of technology, games can be watched via "gamecasts" on the Internet and viewed on home computers and personal digital assistants (PDAs), such as the BlackBerry, Palm, and iPhone.

While the ability of fans to watch games they cannot attend is an important factor in the growth of sports, a more critical aspect for the sports bettor is the access to gambling information provided by the popular media. Point spreads are published in the overwhelming majority of daily newspapers, posted on sports Web sites, and constantly discussed on sports-specific television and radio shows. Other factors considered by the sports gambler (weather conditions, injury reports, competitive trends, home field advantage, etc.) are also available via the Internet, television, radio, and newspapers. In some regards, this information was always accessible to the diligent gambler, but the immediate nature of the information, due to scrolling tickers on the television and instant updates on cell phones and pagers, has made entrée into the sports gambling world even easier.

Most Nevada sports betting was confined to small parlors outside of the major casinos until the late 1970s. This gambling activity was discouraged by the fact that the federal government imposed a 10 percent tax on each sports wager; however, this was lowered to 2 percent by 1975. In that year, the amount wagered in Nevada quadrupled. The state of Nevada also changed laws in 1976, making it easier for casinos to have sportsbooks. Then, a final breakthrough came in 1982 when Congress lowered the federal betting tax on sports contests to 0.25 percent, which is where it is today. Major sports betting areas were constructed in many casinos, the largest books (in physical size) being found today in the Las Vegas Hilton, The Mirage, and Caesars Palace, where each are equipped with digital point spreads displays, seating for hundreds of bettors, numerous giant screen televisions, and personal viewing monitors.

Ironically, given the widespread nature of sports betting, this form of gambling is also very controversial. Popular opinion regarding wagering on sports is very mixed and most debate falls strongly against legalizing this particular form of gambling. A survey taken for the Commission on the Review of the National Policy toward Gambling in 1974 found majority acceptance of several forms of gambling, including bingo, horse racing, and lotteries. Fewer than half of the respondents supported the legalization of casinos (40%) and off-track betting (38%), and the fewest (32%) supported legalized sports betting (Commission on the Review of the National Policy toward Gambling 1976, App. II). A 1982 Gallup poll found majority support for all other forms of gambling but only 48 percent approval for betting on professional sports events. However, more recently, in 2006, an ESPN Sports Nation online poll indicated that 71 percent of respondents believed that sports gambling should be legalized. Opponents of sports betting suggest that the activity may have a tendency to corrupt the integrity of games, as those making wagers could try to influence the activity of the players in the contests. This corruption, commonly referred to as "point shaving" or "fixing" will be covered in detail below.

Sports betting is legal in the United Kingdom, Canada, Mexico, and other parts of Central America and the Caribbean region; however, sports betting is very limited in the United States. In reality, only in Nevada can a gambler legally make a wager on an individual contest or game. Nonetheless, sports betting is pervasive in the United States, as bets on almost all sports events take place among friends, coworkers, or social acquaintances in private settings. Almost all of these wagers, as already discussed, are illegal, as are wagers made through betting agents known as bookmakers. These bookmakers (or bookies) run their operations wherever the demand for wagers exists: in small towns, large cities, on college campuses, and in neighborhood sports bars and social clubs.

The widespread availability of the Internet in the 1990s made sports wagering available to most residents, creating a substantial increase in the amount of sports betting by Americans, most of which is also clearly illegal. Christiansen Capital Advisors, a firm that monitors online gambling, states that sports wagering produced over $4.2 billion in revenues in 2005, up from $1.7 billion in 2001. There is some debate, however, as to whether Internet gambling, done through sites that are controlled by an operator in a jurisdiction where sports gambling is licensed and legal, is always illegal if the player is in another jurisdiction.

This discussion initially revolved around the Wire Act of 1961, which dealt with interstate or foreign business of sports wagering or the information that assists in making bets, and the Professional and Amateur Sports Protection Act of 1992, which banned sports betting in all states within the United States, excepting four states with previous gambling operations. The most recent legislation, the Unlawful Internet Gambling Enforcement Act, enacted in 2006, makes it illegal for financial institutions (banks, credit unions, etc.) to collect debts acquired on Internet gambling sites. While ways to most effectively enforce this new legislation are being determined by law enforcement personnel, many major online gambling sites have stopped providing services to U.S. customers, while others have experienced a major drop off in U.S. customers.

The greatest amount of sports betting—both legal and illegal—in the United States consists of wagers made on American football games. Professional (National Football League) games attract the most action, with the championship game (the Super Bowl) being the attraction that garners the most wagering action. The Super Bowl attracts legal wagers over $90 million in the casinos of Nevada and estimates in the vicinity of $8 billion illegally. Most of the illegal gambling on the Super Bowl consists of private bets among close friends or participation in office pools in which the participants pick squares representing the last digit of scores for each of the two teams. Following the Super Bowl in importance for the gambling public are college basketball's March Madness (the NCAA men's basketball tournament), the college football bowl game season, the World Series for professional baseball (MLB), and the National Basketball Association (NBA) finals.

SPORTS BETTING BY SPORT

In the following sections, the structure of betting is discussed for football, basketball, baseball, hockey, and boxing. Each of these games has different structures for gambling. Basically, wagers on sports are made one of three ways: (1) on an odds basis, (2) on the basis of handicapped points for or against one of the contestants (teams), or (3) a combination of odds and handicapped points.

Football

Football did not generate much interest among bettors until the National Football League (NFL) gained television contracts and had the opportunity to display its special kind of action for the public. Two critical events affecting sports wagering were the climax of the championship playoffs of 1957 and the creation and introduction of Monday Night Football.

In the championship game of 1957, the Baltimore Colts defeated the New York Giants in a sudden-death overtime game viewed, nationwide on NBC, by the largest television audience for a sporting event at that time. The game marked a critical point at which national interest in football exceeded interest in baseball, a game that did not translate well to the public over television, as it had too many breaks in the action. Monday Night Football, designed in the mid-1960s, initially brought to television in the 1966 season and launched on ABC for a 39-year run in 1970, created a unique opportunity for the sports bettor. This "end of weekend" game provided sports bettors a chance to capitalize on a successful week or, most likely, one last chance at recouping losses from a week's worth of wagers.

Football betting received a boost in 1966 as a new, upstart professional league, the American Football League, which began operations in 1959, merged with the NFL, bringing teams and games to each major city in the United States. Although wagering on professional football dwarfs other sports, the NFL is not the only football bet by sports gamblers. College football, specifically the NCAA's Football Bowl Subdivision (FBS) formally known as Division I-A, also garners a large amount of interest and wagers. From geographic and conference-driven rivalries to the expanded 12-game season to traditional bowl games and the Bowl Championship Series (BCS), betting on college football is an extremely popular option for sports gamblers.

The Point Spread The growing interest in football was directly tied to betting on the games. Betting increased considerably when a handicap system of point spreads was developed. Prior to the use of point spreads for football wagering, bookies only offered odds on winners and losers of games. Because many games were predictable, odds became very long, therefore, problematic for both bookmakers and gamblers. Players realized that they had little chance to win with the underdog, but at the same time, the bookies did not want to accept bets on "sure-thing" favorite teams, and they were reluctant to accept the possibilities of an underdog winning with odds of 20 to 1 or greater. Therefore, many games simply were not available for the betting public as bookies did not give odds on those games by "taking games off the board." The point spread also effectively created a way to even the playing field for mismatched games and generated an excitement that was not tied to the actual results of the games, but the results of the point spread bet. Consider the following game attended by editor William Thompson in Iowa City in September 2008:

Iowa State University and the University of Iowa were playing their annual in-state rivalry game with Iowa favored by 13½ points. With three minutes to go in the fourth quarter, Iowa ran back a punt for a touchdown and a 17-3 lead. Iowa State received the kickoff, moved steadily down the field to the Iowa five yard line before being held on downs. With two minutes left and Iowa State with no timeouts, Iowa took over on offense with the outcome of the game no longer in doubt. On first, second, and third down, Iowa ran the ball into the line in an attempt to run out the remainder of the time on the clock. With fourth and eight at their own seven yard line, Iowa lined up to punt. The punter took the snap in the end zone and held the ball before running out of bounds for an intentional safety. With only 20 seconds left the Iowa safety gave Iowa State two points and all Iowa State bettors a winning wager as Iowa no longer covered the 13½ point spread. Half of the crowd was cheering an Iowa victory on the playing field, while the other half was cheering the financial windfall of a successful wager commonly referred to as a "back-door cover."

There is a dispute over who invented the point spread. A University of Chicago-trained mathematician, prep school math teacher of John F. Kennedy, and securities analyst, Charles K. McNeil, is credited by most for inventing the spread in the early 1940s. Two other bookies, Ed Curd of Lexington, Kentucky, and Bill Hecht of Minneapolis, are also cited for creating the spread decades later. Bobby Martin, in the late 1960s at Churchill Downs in Kentucky, and Michael "Roxy" Roxborough, through the use of technology, took oddsmaking to the next level, but it was Jimmy "the Greek" Snyder who brought the point spread to the public via his role as a betting analyst on CBS's NFL Today show in the 1970s and 1980s.

Bookies and the few legal sportsbooks in operation in the 1950s and 1960s loved the spread for football and certain other games, as it greatly reduced their risks. Bookies do not want risks. They are businesspeople who want stability in their investments. The essential feature of the point spread was a guaranteed profit for the bookies—if the books could be balanced. Points are set for games with the goal of having an equal (or nearly equal) amount of money bet on either side of the point spread.

The point spread is called "the line" or "the number." The point spread refers to the betting handicap, or extra points, given to those persons making wagers on the underdog in a contest. Those betting on the favorite to win must subtract points from their team before the contest begins. In football, as with all other sports, the home team is indicated in all capital letters. The point spread is used most often for bets on basketball or football games. As an example, the New York Giants are a seven-point underdog against the Green Bay Packers. Thus, the line is Green Bay minus seven (indicated by a – sign). Those betting on Green Bay will lose their bets unless Green Bay wins by more than seven points. Those betting on the New York Giants will win unless the Giants lose by more than seven points. The bet is a tie (called a push) if Green Bay wins by exactly seven points; neither the bettor nor casino/bookie wins or loses.

In 1969, the New York Jets were double-digit underdogs against the Baltimore Colts in the Super Bowl. The point spread was as high as 18 points. Yet New York, under the leadership of quarterback Joe Namath, defeated the Colts 16-7. Although some considered that the point setters failed miserably on that game, the exact opposite was true. Money books were balanced and the bookies won their transaction fees, commonly referred to as "vigorish" or "juice." Although players bet on one side of the line, they must put up $11 in order to win $10. This means that if the books are perfectly balanced, with $10,000 bet on both sides, the bookie pays out $20,000 (the $10,000 wagered plus the $10,000 won) to the winning bettors, and collects $21,000 (the $10,000 bet plus the $11,000 lost) which allows him to make a tidy $1,000 profit. This is a 4.55 percent advantage over the bettors.

In actuality, this theoretical advantage is seldom realized. Bettors do not line up evenly on either side of the point spread, and some bettors have knowledge about the games superior to that of the point setters, taking advantage of the spread numbers. At the 2008 Super Bowl between the heavily favored New England Patriots and New York Giants, Las Vegas casinos lost $2.6 million due to money line wagers on the Giants, who were 17-14 victors. The bookies often find that they have to adjust lines in order to get more even betting on each side. In certain cases, a line may move two or three points, resulting in a situation called "middling" or "tweening," whereby bettors on both sides—early bettors on one side, later bettors on the other side—can be winners. This happened with betting on the Super Bowl in 1989. The three-point line, with San Francisco favored over Cincinnati, was moved to five or more points, as the bettors clearly favored the San Francisco 49ers (they were not only a California team—that is, near Las Vegas—but had also won the Super Bowl twice in the previous seven years). The game finished with a four-point San Francisco victory. Early San Francisco bettors won; later Cincinnati bettors won. Many of the bettors won both ways. The bettor gets the point spread that is listed at the time the bet is made, unlike pari-mutuel wagers on horse racing where odds are based upon the cumulative bets of the players.

Then there are the cases in which the point setters do their job what some might consider "perfectly." In the 1997 Super Bowl game between Green Bay and New England, the Packers were favored by 14 points. The point setters were on target as the Packers won with a 14-point margin. The bookies and legal sportsbooks made no profit on the game. They had to give all the money bet back to the bettors. The bets were a tie, also called a "wash" or "push." Because ties on point spreads are bad for the sportsbooks, there is a tendency to use half points in spreads, although these are moved when betting behavior demands that the points be changed. Specifically with football, these half point spreads are based on scoring numbers: 7 points for touchdowns and 3 points for field goals. Therefore, you frequently see 6½, 7½, 2½, and 3½ point spreads or combinations and multiples of those numbers.

Also, bookies realize that certain spreads will lead to ties more often than others will. More games end with a 3-point victory than any other specific point margin. Moving points up or down around the 3-point margin is also dangerous because of the middling or tweening factor.

The Structure of Football Bets The standard bet on football has a gambler wagering that a favored team will either win by the set number of points or, conversely, that an underdog team will either win the game outright or will not lose by more than the determined number of points. If a game is considered to be an even contest, no points are given either way. Such a bet, with no points either way, is called a "pick-em" or "chalk" by bettors. If the point spread is expressed as a full number, and the favorite team wins by that many points (or an even match ends in a tie), the bet is considered a tie (or push), and the money wagered is returned to the player. In reality, there is no bet.

There are many betting opportunities other than a straight, point spread bet. A very popular bet on professional and college football games is the over-under wager, also called "totals." With the over-under bet, the point setters indicate a score that is simply the total number of points scored by both teams in the game. Bettors wager $11 to win $10 that the total score of the game will be more or less than the set number. Over-under wagers exist for all NFL games and for a large number of college games, specifically games involving conferences with national television coverage.

Parlay bets are combination bets whereby the bettor wagers that several games (with point spreads) will be won or lost. The key to a parlay wager is that the bettor must win all games within the parlay to be considered a winner. For instance, on a two-team parlay, a bettor wagering $10 will win $26 (for a payback of $36) if both picks are correct. At even odds, the player should receive 3 to 1 odds for such a bet, or a return of $40. This means that the house edge on the bet is theoretically 10 percent—again assuming that bets on all sides of the parlay action are even amounts of money. A three-team parlay pays 6 to 1, while the "correct" odds of such a parlay would be 7 to 1. The theoretical edge in favor of the sportsbook would be 12.5 percent. There are two kinds of parlay bets: (1) ones made based upon the point spreads of the moment (available in Nevada casinos, with bookmakers, and via online sites), and (2) ones made on a pre-printed card where only certain games are available and the point spread is fixed until the game is played. The latter type of cards may have a theoretical edge as high as 25 percent or more and are illegally distributed in office settings, factories, bars, and on college campuses. Based on the individual "operator," some cards allow tie bets to be winners; others are figured as "no-bets"; and some treat ties as losers.

There are also parlay wagers called "teaser" bets where the bettor is given extra points (to lessen the points a favorite has to give or to get more points for the underdog) for a game in exchange for having the odds on the bet changed against him. For example, whereas a regular four-team football parlay card pays 12 to 1 odds on a winning card, a four-team teaser having the ability to move each game by seven points (in either direction) pays 2 to 1 odds.

Another category of football bets available to the sports bettor are the wide array of proposition bets that are usually reserved for special occasions. Bettors may wager on hundreds of situations for the Super Bowl or NCAA National Championship game each year. For instance, the bettor is allowed to wager on which team will win the coin toss; which quarterback will complete the most passes; who will score first; how the first score will happen (touchdown, field goal, etc.); how many fumbles there will be in the game; which team will lead at halftime; and many other situations. In the 1986 Super Bowl, a Las Vegas casino offered a wager on whether Chicago Bear William "The Refrigerator" Perry (a 300-plus-pound offensive lineman) would score a touchdown in the game against New England because he had been used as a back on gimmick plays during the season. The betting started with odds at 13 to 1 but quickly came down as the betting public wagered that Perry would score a touchdown. Late in the game, which had become a rout (Chicago won 46-10), coach Mike Ditka called Perry's number. He lined up in the backfield, was given the ball, and scored a Super Bowl touchdown. More recently, in the 2008 Super Bowl pitting the New England Patriots against the New York Giants, over 300 proposition opportunities existed, even including cross-sport proposition wagering. A bettor could wager on which would be higher: the number of Randy Moss receptions or the number of birdies in Tiger Woods' fourth round at the Dubai Desert Classic. They could also bet on number of points scored by the Los Angeles Lakers' Kobe Bryant against the Washington Wizards being more or less than the points scored by the Patriots.

There are possibilities for odds betting (also called betting the "money line") for football games, although the sportsbooks put the gambler at a considerable disadvantage for any games where the point spread betting exceeds seven points. Basically, one can wager on the "sure thing" but only at considerable risk. For instance, on an even, no-points, pick-em game, players betting either side "lay" or bet $11 in order to win $10. With a three-point spread game, those wagering on the favorite bet $15 to win $10, and those wagering on the underdog wager $10 to win $13. For a 7½-point game, those betting on the favorite would be asked to wager approximately $40 to win $10, while those betting on the underdog would wager $10 to win $30. The theoretical house edge thereby moves from 4.55 percent for the even game, to 8 percent for the three-point spread game, to 20 percent for the 7½ point game.

The biggest bet on a football game was made by maverick casino owner Bob Stupak, the former owner of Vegas World and the creator of and an initial investor in the Stratosphere Tower. In January 1988, he bet more than $1 million on Super Bowl XXIII. He wagered $1,100,000 to win $1,000,000 on the Cincinnati Bengals (getting seven points) against the San Francisco 49ers. And he won. It was great publicity all the way around. The Little Caesar's Casino and Sportsbook basked in the glow of publicity as it happily paid the $2,100,000 check (for winnings and original bet) to Stupak. He basked in the light of publicity, as he was seen as the ultimate "macho-man." He put it all on the line for his team, and he had won.

One newspaperman was rather suspicious about the deal, as it seemed too good to be true for both the casino and the bettor. Reportedly, he made an official inquiry of the Nevada Gaming Commission as to the veracity of the bet. The commission confirmed that Stupak had bet $1,100,000 on the game and that his win was legitimate. The commission reported no fact other than it was a legitimate bet. Sometime later, news media personnel uncovered the rest of the story—Stupak had bet on both teams! He was actually a $100,000 loser for the day, but it was worth it to him to gain the desired publicity. The Nevada Gaming Commission has absolutely no obligation to report information on losing bets; in fact, that information is rightfully considered to be very private. Publicly, that information certainly would harm the industry, as Las Vegas seeks to portray itself as a place where "winners" play.

Basketball

Betting on professional and college basketball games follows the same general structure of football betting, with straight bets utilizing a point spread and wagers on total scores (over-under bets) being popular. Parlay bets and teaser wagers, with and without cards, are also used quite often by sports bettors. As margins of victory vary considerably and do not come together on specific numbers (such as with football), the threat of middling or tweening is less for the sportsbook or bookmaker.

The general condition of basketball betting would seem to suggest that theoretical hold percentages would be more likely achieved than with football games; however two factors make this achievement more difficult. First, there are many more basketball games than football games. While the NFL has a 16-game season and college football teams play 12 games annually, the National

Basketball Association (NBA) employs an 82-game season, and college teams routinely play 30 or more games per year. One major area of growth regarding basketball wagers has been with college basketball, as the result of the popularity of the NCAA men's basketball tournament. Not only are many people wagering on the 65-team tournament (1 of every 10 Americans according to the NCAA) via a tournament bracket, but others take advantage of the additional 64 games to place extra point spread and over-under wagers. Second, the results of basketball games are much more dependent upon individual players. One or two players can dominate a team's performance much more than in football (with the general exception of the quarterback). Therefore, there is a greater need to have information about players in order to more accurately predict the outcomes of games.

Yet with the number of games all over the country, bettors may have more information than legal sportsbooks and illegal bookmakers. Key information can include "the inside scoop" about player injuries, emotional disposition of particular players, disputes within teams, and off-field distractions (personal relationships and finance issues for professional athletes and examination schedules and class performance for college players). As a result, basketball is more vulnerable to influences that attempt to affect the outcome of games, called "point shaving" or "fixing."

Most sports betting scandals have hit the college basketball ranks as a result of the sophistication of the college basketball betting public. Some professional gamblers sense that in college basketball they can compromise players who can affect the points of victory, or "shave points," because the college athlete does not have a large amount of disposable income. Because the average NBA player salary is almost $4 million annually, with some players earning more than $20 million per year, these athletes are not vulnerable to offers of money or other favors to shave points. It must be noted, however, that the sportsbooks (and illegal bookies as well) frequently cooperate with authorities in exposing players or teams that are compromising point spreads. If the line is compromised, sportsbooks not only lose customers who feel that games are not honest but also find it more difficult to get equal bets on both sides of the point spread, which means that they struggle to realize theoretical profit margins. While dishonest games negatively affect all aspects of sports, they damage the bookies and sportsbooks where it may hurt the most—in the wallet.

Baseball

Baseball is bet on an odds basis (also called the "money line"). For instance, a bet on a game between the Detroit Tigers and the Chicago White Sox may be listed as Tigers plus 110 (indicated by a + sign) and White Sox minus 120 (indicated by a – sign). This means that the person betting on Detroit puts up $10 to win $11 (collecting $21) if Detroit is victorious. The bettor wagering on Chicago bets $12 for the chance to win $10 (and collect $22). This "dime" line (so called in recognition that there would be a dime difference if bets were expressed as single dollar amounts rather than in terms of 100) produces the theoretical win of $10 per $220 wagered, or 4.55 percent. As the bet odds increase, more money is bet, but the house edge remains at $10, hence the percentage edge falls. If the favored team

demands a $200 wager to win $100, and the underdog a $100 bet to win $190, the house theoretically wins $10 on action of $590 (both player and house money), for a win of only 1.7 percent. For this reason casinos and bookmakers will abandon the dime line and move to 15-cent or 20-cent lines on games with longer odds. Hence, a bet between the Tigers and White Sox may read Detroit +150; Chicago –170.

The odds created for baseball bets are primarily based on the starting pitcher. The better the pitcher, the higher price the bettor will have to pay. Most baseball bets are made with pitchers for both teams listed on the betting proposition. The pitchers are usually listed a few days before a game. If by some circumstances a listed pitcher is withdrawn, there is no action and all money is returned on the bet. For the bet to count, the listed pitchers must each make at least one pitch in the game as a starter.

It is rare for a baseball game to have odds expressed as a run differential or a point spread. If the casino or bookie feels such a line is necessary, it awards 1½ runs or more to one side, and then keeps the odds line (dime, 20 cent, etc.) the same. Baseball bettors are also able to bet on total runs (an over-under bet), usually with a plus 110 and minus 120 edge. If the total runs are expressed in whole numbers, and the number is the actual game result, the bets are returned. Extra innings do not affect bet results. Parlay bets are figured on the basis of the lines offered, with payoffs of each game multiplied.

Hockey

In hockey contests, both goals and odds are used in betting lines. In some cases there is a split line, with one team receiving 1½ goals and the other team giving up 2 goals. Such a bet will be started at even odds. The house would be guaranteed a win of half the money bet if the game ended on the whole goal total. The +2 goal bettor would have their money returned because of the tie (or push bet) and the –1½ goal bettor would lose their wager.

Most hockey betting does not use the split line approach. Usually, an advantage of 1½, 2½, or 3½ goals (or more in very rare cases) is assigned to one team. In addition to the goal-related point spread, there is a money line, usually set as a 40-cent line. With a 40-cent line, a wager between the Boston Bruins and Tampa Bay Lightning may read Boston +140 and Tampa Bay –180. Hockey parlays are figured the same way as baseball parlays. Hockey also offers over-under bets on total goals scored.

Boxing

Boxing matches are bet in many different ways. The simple win-loss bet carries a money line (or odds) that features a large spread. For instance, one favored fighter may be bet at –400 ($400 must be bet to win $100), and the underdog is bet at +300 ($100 wagered to win $300). Fight bets are usually returned if the fight is canceled or postponed for more than a few days, which happens more frequently than one might think. Casinos and bookies also offer odds on whether there will be a victory by knockout or decision and on the round in which a knockout will occur.

FUTURES

In futures contests, the sportsbook or bookie offers odds on results of future competitions—such as who will win next year's Super Bowl, World Series, Stanley Cup, NBA Championship, NCAA tournament, or Masters golf tournament. All bets are placed prior to the start of the particular sports season or individual event. Most of these odds are offered as inducements for bettors to put a wager on their favorite team or player or "home" team. In reality, futures betting produces little serious wagering action.

NONCONTESTS

Boxing is one of the few sports bet in which judges of performance determine the results of the contest. The Nevada Gaming Commission does not otherwise permit bets on "noncontests" in which the outcome is not determined in some arena or field of action. Although sportsbooks in England often allow wagering on political election contests (even election contests in the United States), this is not permitted in Nevada casinos and sportsbooks. Las Vegas bettors are not allowed to wager on the outcome of the Academy Awards, the winner of the Miss America pageant, or on reality television shows like *American Idol* and *Survivor*. Following the lead of legal sportsbooks located in the United Kingdom, online gambling Web sites, based outside the United States, do offer odds on the winners of numerous nonathletic contests. In the 1980s the famous television series *Dallas* ended one season with a revelation about who shot the star of the series ("Who Shot J.R.?"). One casino put odds up on the list of characters that might have done the terrible deed, but the odds were listed only in jest—or as a publicity stunt. No actual bets were allowed.

In the 1990s, the Palace Station casino did post odds and took bets at the beginning of a baseball season on who would be named the Most Valuable Player in the American and National Leagues. One bettor, Howard Schwartz, who just happened to run the Gambler's Book Club in downtown Las Vegas—the largest gambling specialty bookstore in the world—decided he liked the 25 to 1 odds on Andre Dawson, a player with the Chicago Cubs. Schwartz wagered a modest $10. At the end of the season when Dawson was named as the most valuable player, Schwartz retrieved his winning ticket and marched to the Palace Station. The casino cheerfully greeted him and handed back $10. He was told that the Nevada Gaming Commission had heard about the contest through advertisements in the local newspapers. The commission had determined that the contest violated gaming rules and ordered the casino to stop the contest. It was, of course, a stupid move on the part of the commission. They could have warned the casino never to do it again and fined them a sufficient amount of money to assure they and others similarly inclined to have such contests would not attempt such a challenge in the future. Had they known the names of all persons who entered the contests, they could have returned all the entry money. But such names were not known, as bets (unless more than $10,000 in cash) are made anonymously. Instead, they voided bets already taken. Schwartz was, to say the least, irate. Schwartz had a bona fide bet. He had put his money at risk and had won. When told he could have his money back, he inquired if the casino had a plan to return money to all players including losers—including losers who quite naturally would not come

to the casino expecting to cash in their tickets. They had no plan outside of some minimal signage. All the casinos were put on notice not to be put into such a position in the future, as Schwartz used his central location and clout among serious bettors—his bookstore, as well as all the talk radio shows of Las Vegas—to inform the public that one casino would not pay off its winners. Of course, the Palace Station would have liked to pay off the winning ticket, but the gaming commission told it that it could not do so. Considerable public relations damage was done to the casino and to all sportsbooks in Las Vegas over the incident, but the point was made very clear—the only wagers that would be accepted would be bets placed on legitimate sporting events determined on the field of play.

THE "INTEGRITY OF THE GAME" DEBATE

Sports gambling strikes an uneasy chord with many involved in organized sports. Because sports are so ingrained in the social fabric of American culture, everyone from coaches to administrators to governing bodies to fans watch games with a wary eye to any perceived irregularities. Consider the following game:

Baylor, the home team, had fought hard, sometimes uphill, but now it had the game in the proverbial bag. Five points ahead with the ball on the opponent's eight-yard line. Second and goal, ten seconds remaining in the game. Just kneel down and the game's over. Baylor's opponent, the University of Nevada, Las Vegas (UNLV), had no time outs. But instead of kneeling, the Baylor quarterback takes the snap, hands it off, and as the running back swings to the outside he bobbles the ball. A UNLV linebacker somehow grabs the ball in the air, and ninety-five yards later, with no time left on the clock, runs into the Baylor end zone for the winning score.

This incident really happened during the 1999 college football season. It cannot be explained . . . or can it? Could a coach or quarterback be so foolish as to try to score points after the game is all wrapped up in their favor? What would be the benefit? Perhaps the following could have happened. Could Baylor being favored by 9 or 10 points represent enough motivation to try to score not just a victory, but a victory of 11 or 12 points—not 5 points? Could a team risk victory in order to win by a large enough margin to satisfy everyone (specifically fans and alumni) that might have bet on the game?

But the biggest fear created by sports wagering is that games are "fixed" or that the outcome has been predetermined by influences inside (players, coaches) and outside (bookmakers, organized crime) the game. Equally worrisome is the notion that players could try to manipulate the score (called shaving points) so that professional gamblers could be assured of winning their bets while at the same time the players' team could still win the game. These fears are not only felt by teams and governing bodies, such as the NFL, NBA, MLB, NHL, and NCAA, but also by casinos and bookmakers because dishonest games damage the ability to make money for all involved. Fans won't watch television or buy tickets, concessions, and merchandise if they think games are corrupt, and gamblers won't bet on them either. It is precisely this kind of rationale that is used by college athletics and professional sports leagues when they urge that there be no legalized betting on their games.

Point shaving and game fixing are not new to sports, as gambling scandals have followed athletic contests throughout the past century. The scandals are single episodes, but they are also ongoing, dating back to the first decade of the 20th century. These scandals have, in almost all cases, involved some form of illegal wagering on sports. For example, early boxing matches of the 20th century were held in Nevada towns, such as Goldfield, as the contests were illegal in most states. The matches were used to draw players to casinos, but betting was also very heavy on the contests. Boxing promoters such as Tex Rickard had close ties with members of organized crime, and it was generally accepted that matches were often rigged in order to favor certain gamblers. At the end of the century, the reputation of the sport had not been fully cleansed, as promoters such as Don King and fighters such as Mike Tyson have had long records of legal problems.

Gambling Problems in Baseball

Early baseball leagues also had problems with gambling. The National League began in 1876, and attempts to control bribery and gambling passed to team owners. The owners instituted the "reserve clause" that prohibited players from freely leaving one team and negotiating to play for another team. In turn, the owners lowered salaries for players and made many working conditions intolerable. Players responded by selling favors to gamblers—favors that included fixing game results. There were attempts to fix games in both the 1903 and 1904 World Series, and rumors spread that the 1912 and 1914 World Series were "thrown" by the losing teams. The game was put into major disrepute when it was revealed in 1920 that eight members of the Chicago White Sox team had accepted bribes given by professional gambler Arnold Rothstein (who controlled bookies in many major cities) through an intermediary and had purposely lost the 1919 World Series to the Cincinnati Reds. Their purported motivation was a salary dispute with an owner reputed to be "one of baseball's biggest skinflints," Charles Comiskey (Sifakis 1990, 32–33).

As a reaction to this "Black Sox" scandal of 1919, the eight players implicated were banned for life from the sport, although no legal action was ever taken against Rothstein and his organized crime cohorts. A new commissioner of baseball was appointed and given extreme powers to clean up the image of baseball. He was a federal judge named Kenesaw Mountain Landis. Landis proclaimed that "no player that throws a game, no player that entertains proposals or promises to throw a game, no player that sits in a conference with a bunch of crooks where the ways and means of throwing games are discussed, and does not promptly tell his club about it, will ever play professional baseball" (quoted in Moldea 1979, 43).

Gambling and baseball were never far apart. Landis came down hard on players who were accused of fixing games, but he was also strict with others who merely gambled on games. In the 1940s Brooklyn Dodger manager Leo Durocher was a close friend of gambling gangster Bugsy Seigel and was perhaps a compulsive gambler. Durocher was suspended from the game for the 1947 season for activities related to his gambling. As late as 1969, there were suggestions that he may have manipulated games while he was the manager of the league-leading Chicago Cubs as they let an almost certain National League pennant slip out of their hands with a major end-of-the-season losing streak. In 1943, Landis also ordered Philadelphia Phillies owner William Cox to sell the team after he admitted to placing a small number of $20 to $100 bets during the early stages of the 1943 season.

In 1970, a leading pitcher, Denny McClain, who had led the Detroit Tigers to a World Series championship in 1968, was suspended from the league for his own gambling and bookmaking activities and for his associations with mobsters during 1967. Contemporaneously, two of the most outstanding players of the century—Mickey Mantle and Willie Mays—were banned from having official associations with baseball for a period of time in the late 1970s because of their employment by Atlantic City casinos in public relations positions. The ban was lifted when the stars ended their casino employment.

Probably the most notable gambling scandal in sports history became public in 1989, and its effects have carried over well into the 21st century. Pete Rose, one of the greatest players of all time, was accused of betting on his own team while he served as the manager of the Cincinnati Reds and received a lifetime ban from baseball. As a player, Rose set the major league all-time hits record, led the league in hitting three times, had the longest hitting streak in the National League history (44 games), was a perennial All-Star, and had won a World Series. Rose admitted that he had been a relatively heavy gambler, but also insisted that he had never bet on baseball games as a player or manager.

Because Rose had many of his winning bets recorded, but did not keep recorded proof of his losing, the Internal Revenue Bureau made a claim that he had not paid sufficient income taxes. He was without a defense, and because of his losses, he was without the funds necessary to pay the back taxes, penalties, and fines. He was sentenced to federal prison and served a six-month sentence. In 1992 and then again in 1997, Rose applied for reinstatement but his appeals were not acted on by the commissioner's office. Finally, in his 2004 autobiography *My Prison Without Bars,* Rose "came clean" and admitted to betting on baseball and many other sports while both a player and manager of the Reds. He continued to state that he only bet on his team to win. He has been banned from consideration for membership in the Hall of Fame, a body filled with many old-time players and managers who regularly gambled—even on their own teams.

Gambling Scandals Reach College and Professional Basketball

Basketball scandals have touched both college and professional basketball, although the latter cases did not receive close public attention until the 2007 scandal involving former NBA official Tim Donaghy. Professional basketball did not have a widespread public following until race barriers were totally broken down in the 1970s and the tempo of the games increased, making them more exciting. The one key event which fostered the growth of the National Basketball Association was the 1979 NCAA Championship game, which pitted Michigan State University and its superstar, African American Earvin "Magic" Johnson, against undefeated Indiana State University, featuring the white Larry Bird. This one game captured the consciousness of the American sporting public, and the two players went on to superstardom on opposite coasts (Johnson to the fast-paced Los Angeles Lakers and Bird to the tradition-rich Boston Celtics) as the bookends to the foundation of the NBA as we now know it. Professional league expansion (to both Canada and smaller U.S. markets), additional highly marketable superstars such as Michael Jordan, and increased television exposure via national and regional cable contracts also increased interest.

As previously mentioned, very high salaries have made the prospects of bribing players unlikely, but left underpaid officials vulnerable. In 2008, Tim Donaghy, a 13-year veteran NBA referee, was sentenced to 15 months in federal prison due to his involvement in sports gambling. Donaghy was convicted of conspiracy to engage in wire fraud and transmitting wagering information through interstate commerce for passing betting on games in which he officiated and for passing information about games to other gamblers, including two high school friends.

Conversely, many college players often have financial "needs" due to upbringings in low socioeconomic areas and the restricted ability to work because of school and practice obligations. Bribes are always available to key players if they leave themselves open to the possibility, that is, if they do not purposefully decide to avoid certain contacts who may be asking them to fix games, shave points, or provide important information about their teams and teammates.

In 1951, everything "hit the fan" with revelations that more than 30 players on seven top national college teams had shaved points in exchange for money from gamblers. It was suggested that 86 games had been influenced and that in some, players threw victories. As the result of this major scandal, colleges such as Columbia, City College of New York, Manhattan, and Long Island University were never able to regain their reputations as nationally competitive teams. In 1952, the University of Kentucky, the 1951 NCAA champions, had their basketball program suspended for the 1952–53 season as a result of the scandal and other point shaving issues in the late 1940s involving All-Americans Ralph Beard and Alex Groza.

In the late 1970s and early 1980s, gambling issues again returned to college basketball, as Rick Kuhn, a Boston College player, along with two teammates, admitted to taking bribes to fix nine games. In 1985, John "Hot Rod" Williams and four other Tulane players were accused of shaving points in two games, resulting in the cancellation of the basketball program until the 1989–90 season. More recently, Stevin Smith, an Arizona State University guard, pled guilty to shaving points in four games in 1997 (the story was made into the movie *Big Shot: Confessions of a Campus Bookie*) and two Northwestern players, Dion Lee and Dewey Williams, admitted to attempting to fix games in 1995. In 2008, both basketball and football athletes at the University of Toledo faced point shaving allegations.

Scandals in Football

In December 1998, a former quarterback at Northwestern University pleaded guilty to lying to a grand jury about his role in betting on college games and his involvement in bookmaking operations at Northwestern and the University of Colorado. Ten other players on the football and basketball teams at Northwestern had already been charged, and all had pleaded guilty to offenses related to betting and point shaving activities. In 1996, 13 football players from Boston College were suspended for wagering on a variety of sports, including two players who admitted to betting against their own team in a game against Syracuse. As a result of these scandals, the century ended with a cloud hanging over football—much as the century had begun.

Early professional and collegiate football games must have been important for someone beyond local fans and college campuses, as games became very violent and quite often "ringers" (noneligible players) were put into lineups. This additional attention can probably be attributed to the interest of professional gamblers. The initial owners of professional football teams in the 1920s had ties to organized crime confidants. George Halas, founder of the Chicago Bears, was backed by a crony of Al Capone, while Tim Mara started in the bookmaking business as a teenaged runner between the bookies on his paper route. Art Rooney was a prominent Pittsburgh gambler before he was owner of the Steelers, and Baltimore Colts (later Los Angeles Rams and eventually the St. Louis Rams) owner Carroll Rosenbloom was also a high stakes gambler in the 1950s. In fact, he was close to mob leader Meyer Lansky and others who owned Cuban, and later, Bahamian casinos. In the mid-1980s, Philadelphia Eagles owner Leonard Tose lost the team because of his compulsive gambling activity.

The famous 1958 championship game was celebrated for making football the number one spectator sport in the United States, but the game was never officially investigated for obvious manipulations. Baltimore Colts owner Carroll Rosenbloom reportedly had made a very large wager on his own team. In fact, his betting caused the original line (the Colts favored by 3½) to move up two points, to 5½. The game ended with a tie score of 17 to 17 and was decided by sudden-death overtime. After holding the Giants on their first series, the Colts marched 80 yards down the field toward the Giants' goal line. With a second down on the 8-yard line, they did not try a "sure thing" field goal, but rather tried a dangerous pass. With a stroke of luck, the ball was caught and run to the 1-yard line. On third down, they again did not try a field goal, but instead, halfback Alan Ameche ran the ball over the goal line. It was a risky way to win the game, but then it was the only strategy to follow if you had to win by more than a 3½ or 5½ point spread and cover the owner's bets. According to Dan Moldea, rumors circulated around the National Football League that the Colts were playing to make sure they covered the point spread.

During the 1980s there was a league investigation of Leonard Tose's gambling problem. Officials found that as long as he had the money to make his wagers, there was no problem. The difficulty was that he was a compulsive gambler, and at times he did not have enough money to cover his losses. He supposedly would bet as much as $70,000 a hand at blackjack. The league had a policy against owners borrowing money from each other, but Tose was allowed to break the rule.

There is a reason why the league had a rule against inside financial deals among owners. Tose turned to William Clay Ford (of the Ford Motor Company family), who owned the Detroit Lions, to assist with covering a gambling debt. Ford arranged for a bank he controlled to make more loans to Tose. One of the consequences of the Ford-arranged loan to Tose was that Tose—who had a winning personality, a common trait among many compulsive gamblers—lobbied hard among all the owners to have the 1985 Super Bowl game played in January 1985 in the frozen tundra of Pontiac, Michigan (albeit inside the Silverdome), which obviously financially benefited the Detroit Lions organization and the Ford family. Moldea writes that the owner of the Tampa Bay Buccaneers also loaned Tose $400,000 so he could pay off casino debts. The league's commissioner Pete Rozelle commented that he would be "a hell of a lot more concerned if he knew that a player had bet at the casinos."

Players were in a different situation. Two New York Giant players, Merle Hapes and Frank Filchock, were approached by gamblers prior to the 1946 championship game and offered $2,500 bribes to shave points. Hapes came clean before the game and was suspended from the championship game by commissioner Bert Bell. In 1963, Detroit Lions star Alex Karras and the Green Bay Packers' Paul Hornung were suspended indefinitely because they placed bets on their own teams and were linked with known gamblers (they were reinstated after one year). The NFL suspended Art Schlichter, a quarterback with the Colts, in 1983 when the league discovered he had gambling debts that had reached more than $150,000. After numerous stints in prison related to his compulsive gambling, Schlichter was released in 2006 and founded Gambling Prevention Awareness, an organization dedicated to educating people about the dangers of compulsive gambling, which includes programs for NCAA and NFL players.

Other Sports Hit By Scandals

Other sports, both team and individual, have also been impacted by gambling scandals. The National Hockey League (NHL), had two players (Don Gallinger and Billy Taylor) receive a lifetime ban for gambling in 1947. More recently, Rich Tocchet, a former NHL player who was an assistant coach with the Phoenix Coyotes, pleaded guilty in 2007 to conspiracy and promoting gambling as the result of his financial backing of a gambling ring in New Jersey. Tocchet took a leave of absence from his coaching position and returned to coaching in 2008.

Lesser known international sports have also felt the sting of scandal related to game fixing, point shaving, and abnormal betting patterns. Between 2000 and 2004, the most popular worldwide sport, soccer, saw match fixing by players in the Italian Football Federation and the UEFA Cup, while in 2005 two instances of referees linked to gambling were uncovered in the German Football Association and the Brazilian National Championships. Scandals also involved cricket (match fixing by Hansie Cronje, the captain of the South African team in 2000) and tennis (irregular betting patterns causing online sites to cancel wagers and allegations of the extortion of international players by organized crime).

THE INVOLVEMENT OF GOVERNING BODIES

The National Collegiate Athletic Association (NCAA), along with many other professional leagues, has long been a critic of betting on sporting contests. In the late 1990s, the NCAA lobbied Congress for a national law that would ban all legal betting on college sports contests. Bills were introduced in Congress in both 2000 and 2001 to effectuate the ban. This national governing body of intercollegiate athletics cautioned that gambling activities were widespread on campuses throughout the country. Cedric Dempsey, former executive director of the NCAA, asserted that "every campus has student bookies. We are also seeing an increase in the involvement of organized crime on sports wagering" (National Gambling Impact Study Commission 1999, 2–15).

The concern of the NCAA was based on gambling rings that were exposed during the 1990s at many colleges, including Michigan State University, Boston College, University of Maine, and the University of Rhode Island. The betting was not confined to local bookies, but had expanded to wagers via online sites. According to Christiansen Capital Advisors, a firm that monitors

Internet gambling, there are more than 2,000 sports betting services on the Web. Most of these online sites operate illegally, but some are sanctioned and licensed by foreign governments.

Gambling on college campuses was not restricted to the general student body, but also included betting by student-athletes, in addition to point shaving and fixing of games. All of these college scandals involved illegal gambling, but in some cases, college gambling rings used Las Vegas sportsbooks to lay off money when they found that their student gamblers were betting too heavily for one team against another. In many cases, Las Vegas casinos helped the Federal Bureau of Investigation (FBI) and the NCAA in exposing the sports betting scandals as they discovered unusual betting patterns. The American Gaming Association, representing Nevada casinos and sportsbooks, accepts that the integrity of games is extremely important. Indeed, they realize that without honest games, the sportsbook function of casinos would collapse. On the other hand, they question whether making sports gambling in Las Vegas illegal would markedly improve the integrity of games. It would take the eyes of the Las Vegas establishment—including those of the Nevada Gaming Control Board—off the intricacies of play inside each game covered on the betting boards of the casinos. For example, because gambling on teams based in Nevada was not permitted at the time, there was no Las Vegas betting on the UNLV-Baylor football game discussed earlier in this entry. There was no central betting place where wagers could be monitored to observe if the play on the field was just "stupid" play or if it was motivated by something more dishonest.

Because the NCAA holds student-athletes to a higher standard than the "normal" college student, student-athletes are held not only to federal and state laws and policies of their educational institution, but also to NCAA Bylaw 10.3. NCAA Bylaw 10.3 prohibits any student-athlete from gambling on sports involving any team, professional or collegiate. According to *Don't Bet On It,* produced by the NCAA, all student-athletes are forbidden from betting on sports, participating in sports pools and squares, taking part in Internet gambling, using "800" sports information numbers, playing fantasy sports, and exchanging any gambling information. Examples of gambling information include updates on injuries, strategy, and personnel moves. Take into account the following example when considering how valuable this type of information can be to the sports gambler:

> *During the 2008 season, Central Michigan University (CMU) was the home team and opened on Tuesday as a three-point favorite against their hated conference rival, Western Michigan University (WMU). By Wednesday evening, CMU went from being a three-point favorite to being a two-point underdog for a game scheduled to be played on Saturday afternoon. Why? The forecast was for perfect weather, both teams were undefeated in conference play, and all key players were expected to play. Ninety minutes before the game it was announced that CMU's starting quarterback, the reigning conference MVP, was not going to play due to an ankle injury. While this was unexpected and shocking information to CMU fans as they enjoyed their tailgating festivities, it was obviously old news to the*

gambling public. They "somehow" knew by Tuesday afternoon, and the change in the point spread reflected their knowledge.

The penalty for the violation of Bylaw 10.3 is expulsion from the team and other potential sanctions such as suspension or dismissal from school and criminal charges. The biggest punishment may be the elimination of any professional aspirations due to the stigma attached to individuals engaging in gambling behavior jeopardizing the integrity of the sport. Past history has shown that individuals who have wagered on sports as players, coaches, or referees have become pariahs within sports.

Professional sports have also begun to take a tougher stance on sports gambling. Major League Baseball and the NFL have antigambling signs posted in their locker rooms and, as a result of the recent Tim Donaghy scandal, the NBA has instituted a comprehensive gambling education program for players, coaches, administration, and referees. As the result of recent scandals in their sports, the National Hockey League (NHL) and the governing bodies of tennis are also reevaluating their policies and making recommendations regarding sports gambling regulations and enforcement.

The reevaluation of these policies and subsequent enforcement techniques is not only rooted in past scandals, but by recent research conducted by the NCAA and its member schools. A University of Michigan study conducted in 1999 and reported by the National Gambling Impact Study Commission indicated that 45 percent of male college athletes admitted to betting on sports events. Five percent indicated that they furnished information about team activities to others for gambling purposes and also may have gambled on games in which they participated. Another study, conducted by the University of Michigan in 2000, found that 40 percent of officials wagered on sports, 2 percent bet using illegal bookmakers, and 12 percent knew of other officials not calling a game correctly due to gambling influences. In 2003, the NCAA finished a comprehensive study of over 21,000 male and female athletes. This study uncovered that 35 percent of males and 10 percent of females wagered on sports, and 20 percent of males and 5 percent of females specifically bet on college athletics. Two percent of football and basketball players had been asked to affect the outcome of a game.

While on the surface it appears that sports organizations and governing bodies want to restrict or stop wagering on sports for altruistic reasons, when intercollegiate sports and professional leagues oppose legal betting on games, questions have to be raised about possible hypocrisy. Every league works with media (television, radio, newspapers, magazines, Internet) that give the public betting information such as the publication of point spreads, injury reports, weather conditions, and expert analysis. Every league also recognizes that the betting public adds increased interest in sports, resulting in revenues that come to the teams and leagues through television and radio contracts.

Coauthored by Tim Otteman

References

American Gaming Association. 2008. *State of States: The AGA Survey of Casino Entertainment.* Washington, DC: A.G.A.

Christiansen, Eugene Martin. 1999. "The 1998 Gross Annual Wager." *International Gaming and Wagering Business* (August): 20ff.

Commission on the Review of the National Policy toward Gambling. 1976. *Gambling in America: Final Report.* Washington, DC: Government Printing Office.

Klein, Howard J., and Gary Selesner. 1982. "Results of the First Gallup Organization Study of Public Attitudes toward Legalized Gambling." *Gaming Business Magazine* (November): 5–7, 48–49.

Moldea, Dan E. 1979. *Interference: How Organized Crime Influences Professional Football.* New York: William Morrow.

National Collegiate Athletic Association [NCAA]. 1999. *Don't Bet on It: Don't Gamble on Your Future.* Indianapolis: NCAA.

National Gambling Impact Study Commission [NGISC]. 1999. *Final Report.* Washington, DC: NGISC.

Nevada Gaming Control Board. 2007. Nevada Gaming Abstract.

Oregon Lottery. 2008. Annual Report.

Rose, Pete, and Roger Kahn. 1989. *Pete Rose: My Story.* New York: Macmillan.

Sifakis, Carl. 1990. *The Encyclopedia of Gambling.* New York: Facts on File.

Vollano, A. G., & Gregg, D. L. 2000. *NCAA Division I Officials: Gambling with the Integrity of College Sports?* Ann Arbor: University of Michigan Department of Athletics.

THE STOCK MARKET

Proponents of legalized gambling of one form or another are wont to call "the law" a hypocrite by pointing to the fact that governments that proscribe gambling in casinos, at racetracks, or in private homes are the same governments that endorse the existence of stock markets. Indeed, they are the same governments that invest pension funds in the markets, the same governments that go to the markets for bonds to use for various public projects. If it is good enough for the government, why will the government not allow others to play games of chance as well?

There can be little debate about whether stock market and bond market trading (stocks and bonds are referred to as securities) involves some of the elements of gambling: Persons put up something of value for consideration—that is, they advance money into the market—and they do so with the hopes of achieving a prize—that is, a financial gain. And, as with gambling, there is some risk involved. Although all of these elements of gambling may be found in the market, and although some people who enter the market do so with the same inclinations as people who wager on the green felt tables of Las Vegas, there are material differences between betting at a casino, at a racetrack, or on a lottery, on the one hand, and putting your money down on a commodity—bond or stock—in the market, on the other hand. The differences are so substantial in a material way that it is not possible to give any in-depth treatment to stock markets here. Nonetheless, a clear delineation between market investments and wagers at games of chance should be offered.

Those who would think of Wall Street as a casino must also think that any business venture is gambling. Yet stock investments, bond investments, and other commodity transactions are vehicles for the creation of wealth. By investing, the stock-purchasing public is saying that it has confidence that certain products and services will be desired by others and will serve to meet the demands of the public. A bond purchase or the purchase of an initial public offering (IPO; the first sale of a stock by a company) does indeed transfer money from individuals to entrepreneurs. Most stock purchases, however, are on a secondary market, such as the New York Stock Exchange; that is, people buy and sell stocks, and money is transferred back and forth between the buyer and seller without any money going to the company. Nonetheless, if the stock performs well, it benefits the entrepreneurs in many ways. First of all, such a performance creates an incentive for recruiting talent, as companies invariably give stock options to top managers and perhaps to other employees as well. A company may take some stock and hold it in reserve, putting a current price on it as of the time it was put into the reserves. The company then tells employees that if they stay with the company for some period of time, they may buy the stock from the company at that predetermined price. If the value of the stock goes up, the employees of the company gain wealth, and their loyalty to the company is enhanced. New employees can more easily be recruited if the stock values are rising. A second benefit of a successful stock, in terms of its market price, is that it makes it much easier for a company to issue new shares, through an IPO, and hence recruit more capital for corporate projects.

But let us go back to the individual investor. The investor may or may not give close study and scrutiny to the purchase of a stock. After all, not all of us have the time, energy, or financial acumen to make the best choices on the market. For a fee, however, we can find persons with expertise. On the other hand, we may want to play a hunch. Or we may just wish to take a dart and throw it at the New York Stock Exchange or National Association of Securities Dealers Automated Quotations (NASDAQ) listings in the *Wall Street Journal*. Is this not just like going to Las Vegas and betting on a red seven on the roulette wheel? The answer is, "No, it is not." The roulette wheel, the craps table, the blackjack game, the lottery, and the horse race are all zero-sum games. For each set of winning numbers, there is more than that number of losing numbers. Indeed, the casino game is not a zero-sum game, but by necessity must be a negative-sum game that casts the players as a collective into a losing position over any period of time except a very short run.

Although the stock player going through a broker must give a commission for a sale, that commission can be considerably less than 1 percent of the value of the purchase. This compares favorably to the best odds one can get at a craps table and is substantially better than the casino's brokerage fee of 2 to 20 percent on other games. It is far better than the predetermined house edge of 20 percent on the typical horse or dog race and much better than the 40 to 50 percent commission the lottery player pays the government for the right to enter that market. Casino games are rigged against the players as a whole, and this can be justified only on the basis that they are selling an entertainment value for the play experience. Wall Street does not exist to sell entertainment value in trading.

The stock market can very well be a positive-sum game in which every player can be a winner. Indeed, through the 1990s the substantial majority—perhaps 90 percent or more—of the investors were winners. They did not take their winnings away from anyone; they did not win against other stock owners; they did not win against the companies in which they invested. They won because the companies in which they invested created wealth through their entrepreneurial activities. They made products out of raw materials and labor and ingenuity, and when the products were sold, the public bought them at a price considerably higher than that of the sum of the input investments into the products. In turn, this gave greater value to their shares. But it is also true that everyone can lose. Witness the sad days of October 1929, or October 1987, or, more recently, the stock crashes of April 2000 and autumn 2008. Here then is another difference between the casino and Wall Street. In the casino, the roulette wheel stops, the dice stop, the reels of the slot machine stop, the Ping-Pong balls of the bingo or lottery game quit floating to the surface, and the horses cross the finish line. The game in terms of time is finite. It ends, and someone has to pay the piper right then and there. But until a company goes fully bankrupt—the bankruptcy laws, with their chapters 9 and 11 and in the worst cases, chapter 7, use the lucky numbers of gambling to indicate the status of a company that has failed—the stockholder can hold on and wait for a better day. The stock market may be a game, but if it is, the game is continuous, and it need end only when the investor decides to make his or her final sale.

Who knows what tomorrow may bring? If we look at history, we can see only good results. The cumulative stock exchange has never gone downward for a full decade. Indeed, for a 10-year span, the stock market since its beginnings in the 19th century has never moved upward less than 10.5 percent. That was the gain during the Depression years of 1929 to 1939. There is no secret to success on the market. To be on the safe side, however, one could suggest that investors purchase index funds that go up and down with the full market—for instance, a fund consisting of all the stocks on the New York Stock Exchange or one of the 500 funds—or the 30 leading stocks upon which the Dow Jones average is based. There is a fund (with the symbol QQQ fund) that includes the top 100 NASDAQ stocks (newer stocks that have become identified with technologies of the computer age).

If one gets in the mood to throw darts and really feels like taking a risk, however, one can buy options. These are purchases of the right to buy or sell a stock at a certain value at a time 30, 60, or 90 days in the future. Here, unlike other stock investments, there is a particular time when a transaction must be completed, and although the options may promise great rewards, they also carry great risk—such as the loss of the total investment, a risk that is very rare for a stock purchase. Even more risky is a practice that has become more popular in recent years as computers have allowed investors to have immediate information on the movement of stock prices. It is called day trading.

Day trading is the act of quickly buying and selling stocks and bonds throughout the day. At the end of the day, the day trader usually owns no securities. Indeed, when he or she places an order to buy, there is a period of time (usually three business days if he or she has an account with the broker) to complete the purchase by providing funds for the security, during which time the investor eagerly seeks to make a sale of the security, because it is unlikely that he or she has the actual funds to cover the initial purchase. The day trader is not a professional and typically has little or no formal training in the financial markets. He or she is an amateur, usually working without any supervision and using his or her own money to buy and sell the stocks, futures, and options. The day trader may sit in front of a computer screen, watching the price movements of the stocks he or she is trading, hoping to make a quick "killing" with the slightest movement upward of the stock during the day.

As an example, consider that AT&T stock is selling for $60 a share. The trader places an order for 1,000 shares, hoping to sell it for $60.10 if it moves. This very small movement is the smallest movement publicly listed on the exchange. If the investor sells the stock, the quick profit is $100. By making similar moves throughout the day, the day trader can achieve some very nice gains.

Several factors work against repeated success on these ventures, however, and make day trading quite similar to gambling. For one thing, there are commissions that must be paid when purchases and sales of stock are executed. Even at a low rate of $8.95 from a broker who will handle the transaction without offering advice, the buy and sell will cost $17.90. This commission is paid, win or lose, whether the stock goes up, stays at $60, or descends in value. For each dollar the stock goes down, the trader loses $1,000 plus the commission. Another

psychological factor against repeated success is that the trader has to hold his or her breath waiting to see whether he or she makes a sale before the payment is due—it is unlikely the day trader actually has the $60,000 for the purchase.

Another cost to day traders, who may gather at a broker's office, is a fee to use computers there. Also, under the arrangement, the broker is not selling advice but rather only a space to work. A broker who works with an ordinary investor seeks to find value in the market, because he or she too will be receiving a commission—a little higher than the $8.95 charged by the passive broker—and wants a lot of repeat business. The broker has an incentive for performing well. On the other hand, a day trader and a gambler are both alone with their money and the roll of the dice on the computer screen. Each day the gambler trader must prove his worth by successfully trading to make a profit or by getting out of the deal with as little a loss as possible.

Often if losses begin to accumulate, the day trader's money reserve begins to dwindle. Possessing some of the same traits as a pathological gambler, the losing day trader will seek funds from every possible source for his trades. A brokerage firm, like a casino, may actually loan the day trader money for transactions and, in a sense, help him or her string out the losing experience. The loans have to be secured with the day trader's stock account assets. Losing these, the trader turns to his or her home mortgage and other hard assets to bail himself or herself out. Often day traders do not get out in time, and they start downward on the same slippery slope as the problem gambler.

Over the course of time, the stock market performs quite rationally. Long-term trends have been solid. In the short run, however, the market can do many irrational things. Stocks of established companies could be expected to increase in the long run if the company has a record of successful performance and has value behind the price of the stock. In the short run, however, prices can take quick dips and rises that may be totally unexpected. The inability to live with these wild short-term swings in price has ruined many a day trader. The market can be beaten, but it takes patience, and actually there is no one to beat—as there is with the casino.

Spurred on by greed and promises of great riches, day trading has become the modern-day California gold rush. Unfortunately, very few day traders make money—or perhaps this is fortunate, because day traders are not playing the game the way it is supposed to be played. They are not investors. Still, no one really likes to lose money, and fewer accept losses when they realize that their own bad judgment caused them. Consequently, day traders have been known to irrationally blame others for losses. This happened in Atlanta, Georgia, during the summer of 1999. A day trader faced with losing everything, including his business and his house, blamed the manager of a brokerage house where he did his trading. He felt that the manager of the firm that specialized in giving services to day traders should have warned him to be more vigilant. He also was angry with other day traders for not sympathizing with his plight. He went to the firm's office and began shooting people. After a murdering rampage, he committed suicide.

A long-term, patient investor should be secure in feeling that the stock market will be kind to him or her. A short-term day trader may make a killing, but it is just like the pathological gambler's first big win. Losses are sure to catch up and overtake wins, if he or she does not get out quickly. There is only one difference between day trading and gambling: in Las Vegas the gamblers get free drinks.

Coauthored by Bonnie Galloway

References

Know, Harvey A. 1969. *Stock Market Behavior.* New York: Random House.

Mallios, William S. 2000. *Modeling Parallels between Sports Gambling and Financial Markets.* Boston: Kluwer Academic Publishers.

Mayer, Martin. 1988. *Markets: Who Plays, Who Risks, Who Gains, Who Loses.* New York: W. W. Norton.

Shelton, Ronald B. 1997. *Gaming the Market.* New York: Wiley and Sons.

TAXES, GAMBLING

A primary rationale for the legalization of almost any form of gambling has been the anticipation of government revenues derived from special taxation on the gambling activities. Proponents of gambling often argue that "since people gamble anyway," the activity should be legalized so that it can be taxed. Persons opposed to gambling might dispute the premise that there is "gambling anyway," and they claim that even where there is legalization, the amount of tax revenue gained is in most cases only a small part of a government's budget. It is also argued that legalization efforts will result in increased gambling, as government actors will begin to rely upon gambling revenues, whatever their amount, and will therefore encourage the activity. This is especially the case where the gambling is conducted as a government enterprise (e.g., state and provincial lotteries). Increased gambling can have a depressing effect upon other tax revenues when the gambling products are substitute purchases replacing the sale of other goods, which would also be taxed. Mindful of these arguments, when Great Britain legalized commercial casinos in 1968, the nation purposely provided that there would be no special casino taxes. The government simply did not want government officials to have an incentive for allowing the activity to increase.

Additional issues concerning the taxation of gambling revolve around the "fairness" of the taxes. Critics ask, "Do the taxes fall most heavily upon poor people, or upon people who can afford to pay more taxes?" Of course, proponents of gambling emphasize that taxation in this case is voluntary.

RATES OF TAXATION

Lotteries

A typical lottery ticket may sell for $1. Of this amount, half may be designated for prizes to be returned to players. Fifteen percent of the ticket price is often directed toward expenses (advertising, ticket distribution and sales commissions, printing tickets, managing funds). About 35 percent is reserved for government treasuries,

either for a specific use or for general uses. If we consider that a ticket purchase results in a value of $.50 going to the player, we can assume that the player has purchased a product worth $.50. At the point of purchase, however, the price was $1, or $.50 more. If the lottery purchase was considered to be the purchase of any other product, we could say that it carried a 100 percent sales tax. If we see the extra $.50 as a profit margin, we could say that the seller was paying a tax of 70 percent on the gross profit—that is, $.35 on $.50. Or we might simply say that the government tax is 35 percent of the gross sales, and all other costs are costs of doing business. However we conceive the rate of taxation, we can see that lottery operations carry the highest taxation rates of any gambling products. Also it can be claimed that the use of a lottery to raise money for government activities is very expensive. It costs $.15 in expenses to raise $.35 for government use.

Pari-mutuel Racing

In pari-mutuel wagering, players typically make all their bets, and these are placed into a common pool (e.g., $1,000). A set amount of the pool is then given back to the winning players (about $800). As a sales tax, we can say that the tax on the player is 25 percent ($20 on $80). Expenses and shares given to the track and animal owners constitute most of the $200, however. The government would typically keep only $60 or $70. It might then be said that the government tax is 30 percent (or 35 percent of the profits from the wagering), or 6 percent (or 7 percent of the gross sale price of the betting tickets). As the government incurs only a very small part of the cost of race betting operations (having a state racing commission), the cost of raising the $60 or $70 is very small, perhaps less than 10 percent of the amount raised.

Casinos

Typically casinos pay many kinds of fees as well as taxes on their gambling winnings. Fees are charged for licensing activities and also for having individual numbers of machines or gambling tables. Taxes on the winnings are assessed on the gross gambling win—that is, the amount of money the casino retains after all prizes are given to the players. The rates of the casino win taxes vary considerably among the commercial casino jurisdictions of the United States. Nevada has the lowest rate—6.75 percent of the win—followed by a rate of 8 percent in New Jersey, Mississippi, and South Dakota. In Michigan, the state tax on wins is 18 percent, and Louisiana has an 18.5 percent win tax. Several states have taxes of 20 percent (Iowa, Indiana, and Missouri). The highest rate is found in Illinois, where a graduated tax has climbed to as high as 70 percent of the casino win. These taxes are generally more efficient than those for lotteries and pari-mutuel racing. The government collection costs are consumed by state regulatory commissions and are normally less than 5 percent of the revenues collected.

TAX INCIDENCE AND EQUITY

The questions of who pays the gambling tax and its impact upon society are important policy questions. The answer is that the gambler pays the taxes, as the gambler is the source of the tax money—

no matter how many hands it is processed through before it reaches a state treasury. When gambling opponents proclaim that we should "tax the casinos" more or that the "casinos must pay their fair share," false notions are being generated. All taxes come from people, and that is especially the case with gambling taxes. The proper question to ask is, "Which people?" For sure they are volunteer gamblers. But are they local residents? Or are they tourist visitors who would not otherwise be spending money in the community? More important, are they affluent people who can afford the recreational activity of gambling, or are they poor people who must divert funds from family needs in order to gamble?

Studies of lotteries have suggested that the burden of taxation from sales of tickets falls most heavily upon lower-income people. Their purchases of tickets constitute a higher proportion of their income and resources than do purchases of tickets made by more affluent persons. Moreover, many have suggested with empirical studies that governments purposely put lottery ticket sales outlets in poorer residential areas in higher proportion than they do in other neighborhoods. They also direct their advertisement messages toward poorer people. These people are considered their best potential customers in terms of volumes of sales. The National Gambling Impact Study Commission was very critical of lottery advertising. Lottery taxes are considered to be regressive (National Gambling Impact Study Commission 1999, 3–17).

Pari-mutuel racing locations are such that betting on races is not as convenient as buying lottery tickets. Hence, fewer poor people are attracted to this kind of gambling. Also, the process of selecting probable winners of races is much more difficult than buying a lottery ticket. Nonetheless, many of the regular racetrack bettors are poorer people—perhaps because they are regular bettors.

Casino taxes may be regressive or progressive. Casino betting may be convenient, or it may require such major investments of time, energy, and travel money that poorer persons avoid the gambling. For instance, in Las Vegas, taxes on casino gambling can be considered both regressive and progressive. Slot machines are permitted in bars, convenience stores, and grocery stores within walking distance of almost all the residents of Las Vegas. Tourists do not play at these machines. Nor do affluent persons. Many of the bars and 7–11–type stores are established for the primary purpose of offering machine gambling. The grocery stores of Las Vegas stay open 24 hours a day in order to service gamblers. A high proportion of the grocery store and 7–11 players are probably problem gamblers. Taxation of their gambling exploits the conditions of these players and must be considered regressive (Thompson 1998, 459–461).

On the other hand, the Las Vegas Strip casinos attract tourists. Over half of the casino visitors arrive in Las Vegas by air. They stay at the hotels for an average of four days, but they gamble only four hours each day. Their gambling dollars are from their recreational budgets. They can afford to gamble; hence, taxes on their activity tend to be progressive taxes (Las Vegas Convention and Visitors Authority 1999).

VOLUME OF GAMBLING TAXATION

Special gambling taxes provide large amounts of revenues to many of the jurisdictions with legalized gambling. In the state of Nevada, casino taxes provide the largest share of public revenues from any tax source. In 2003, more than $776 million was generated by the 6.75 percent gross win tax, plus various fees on licensing, machines, and table games. Additional revenues go to local governments in the form of fees as well as property taxes. That year more than 42 percent of the state's internal source funding came from the casino sector of the economy. More revenues flow to the state treasury as a result of the nongambling activities of tourists who are drawn to the state because of its casinos. These taxes take the form of room taxes, entertainment taxes, and general sales taxes. No other state or provincial jurisdiction in North America receives as high a proportion of its revenues through gambling activities.

In a recent year, South Dakota received $112 million from casino taxes, amounting to 12.8 percent of its budget, while the state of Mississippi received $325 million from casino taxes, or just over nine percent of its internally generated revenues. No other state receives as much as 9 percent of its revenues from casino taxes. Lotteries yield low portions of state budgets as well. At the low end, New Mexico's lottery gives the state only 0.4 percent of its budget; at the high end, Georgia receives 4.1 percent of its state revenues from its lottery (Christiansen 1999).

Although Nevada is the state that is most dependent upon gambling revenues, many other states receive more dollars from gambling sources. Nevada ranks only 13th among all states in taxes and other gambling revenues. New York leads the list. Governments of the Empire State, Texas, Florida, and California each receive more than $1 billion a year from lottery operations. Illinois and New Jersey each receive well over a billion dollars from a combination of lottery revenues and casino taxes. Lottery receipts in Pennsylvania, Massachusetts, and Georgia also exceed Nevada gambling tax revenues, as do the combined lottery revenues and casino taxes of Indiana and Michigan. Quebec and Ontario, the two largest Canadian provinces, also receive more government funds from gambling sources than does the state of Nevada. Both provinces have large lotteries. Quebec has three government-owned casinos, which provide all their profits to the government. In Ontario, the government is the casino owner, but there are private operators. The operators pay a 20 percent gross win tax, then they take 5 percent as their share of the profits. After other casino expenses are paid, the province is given the remainder of the revenues.

EARMARKING GAMBLING TAXES

Many jurisdictions with gambling operations earmark tax revenues for certain functions. In Canada, governments devote some gambling revenues to private charities, and in the United States, a variety of activities is selected to be beneficiaries of revenues. Most of the 43 lotteries (42 states plus the District of Columbia) earmark some funds to specific functions of government. Most of the funds are designated for educational activities; others send funds to senior citizen programs, parks and recreation programs, or public safety. Casino taxes are often earmarked as well. Special slot machine taxes in Nevada are designated for education, as are a portion of the casino taxes in Illinois, Michigan, Mississippi, and Missouri. Colorado and South Dakota use casino taxes

for tourism and historical preservation. Indiana uses casino taxes for economic development, Iowa for infrastructure and local governments, Missouri for public safety, and New Jersey for senior citizens and urban redevelopment.

Earmarking is not necessarily the most efficient way to distribute public funds. The process removes a certain amount of flexibility from legislators who may be trying to set priorities for the state on the basis of current needs. By designating a specific function to receive gambling taxes, however, proponents of casinos, lotteries, or other forms of gambling can win critical support from important groups in their campaigns for legalization. Proponents of the lottery in Georgia won such critical support by offering lottery money for college scholarships for all Georgia high school graduates who received B averages.

After a gambling operation begins, the objectives of the earmarking process are often difficult to maintain. If the functions supported by earmarking are old activities, legislators are prone to reduce previous funding of the activities from other taxes and merely replace the funding with gambling revenues. The activity receives the same funding as it did before. Also, when earmarking provisions are established, legislators seek to broaden definitions of the activities. As mentioned, Nevada uses special slot machine taxes to fund education. One year the state wished to build a basketball arena for the Running Rebel basketball team of the University of Nevada, Las Vegas, and the state was short of general fund monies for the project. With some minor redesign, the basketball facility ended up with some meeting rooms, which were sometimes scheduled to hold classes. Hence, the basketball arena became an educational facility and gambling revenues could be used to fund the construction.

FEDERAL GAMBLING EXCISE TAXES

The first federal excise tax on gambling devices was passed as part of the Revenue Act of 1941. A stamp act of $10 was levied on pinball and similar amusement machines and $50 on slot machines—meaning machines that operate by means of insertion of a coin or token and that "by application of the element of chance may deliver . . . cash premiums, merchandise or tokens." Ordinary vending machines were excluded from the tax.

The Revenue Act of 1951 raised the stamp act to $250 for slot machines. The amusement machine and slot taxes were repealed in 1978. The state of Nevada took over the tax, however, and has dedicated the receipts to educational programs. The 1951 Revenue Act also imposed a 10 percent fee on the amount of money wagered on a sports event or on a lottery conducted for private profit. This tax was lowered to 2 percent in the 1970s and to 0.25 percent in 1982. (The tax remains at 2 percent if the gambling is illegal.) In addition, the 1951 law created an occupational tax of $50 for each person working for a gambling establishment. Later the tax was raised to $500. Today it remains $500 for illegal gamblers but is only $50 for those engaged in legal wagering. Those involved with lotteries, pari-mutuel gambling, slot machine games, and casino table games (not considered wagering) are exempt from the occupational tax.

In 1994, President Clinton proposed a 4 percent tax for all gambling profits realized by commercial operations. The proposal died in Congress amidst a flurry of opposition from casino interests.

The federal gambling taxes have produced only a minuscule amount of revenue for the national budget. The real purpose of the taxes seemed to be to discourage gambling and also to delineate a separate criminal offense for persons not paying the taxes. Illegal gamblers were obligated to pay the tax, and of course, most did not. In 1968, however, the U.S. Supreme Court ruled that the government could not require illegal operations to pay the taxes, as such payment would constitute a forced self-incrimination in violation of the Fifth Amendment of the U.S. Constitution.

References

Christiansen, Eugene Martin. 1999. "The 1998 Gross Annual Wager." *International Gaming and Wagering Business* (August): 20ff.

Las Vegas Convention and Visitors Authority [LVCVA]. 1999. *Las Vegas Visitors Profile.* Las Vegas: LVCVA.

McQueen, Patricia. 2008. "$17.5 billion in revenues." *International Gaming and Wagering Business* (April): 1, 29–30.

National Gambling Impact Study Commission [NGISC]. 1999. *Final Report.* Washington, DC: NGISC.

Revenue Act of 1941 (Public Law 77–250, signed into law September 20, 1941).

Revenue Act of 1951 (Public Law 82–183, signed into law October 20, 1951).

Thompson, William N., and Christopher Stream. 2005. "Casino Taxation and Revenue Sharing: A Budget Game, or a Game for Economic Development?" 22, no. 3: 556–567.

Thompson, William N. 1994. *Taxation and Casino Gambling.* Las Vegas: Mirage

Thompson, William N. 1998. "Not Exactly the Best Gaming Venue: The Nevada Grocery Store Casino." *Gaming Law Review* 2, no. 5 (October): 459–461.

THE TRAVEL ACT OF 1961

The Travel Act of 1961 was designed to target members of organized crime. It was part of Attorney General Robert F. Kennedy's package of crime-fighting legislation. The law was written in very general terms and could be applied to myriad situations involving individuals or criminal groups. A person could be punished with a fine of $10,000 or a prison sentence of five years for traveling "in interstate commerce" or using any facility of interstate commerce (including the mail) with an intent to commit a "crime of violence" or to "otherwise promote, manage, establish," or carry out any unlawful activity. "Any unlawful activity" included gambling.

The broad sweep of the language in the act means that it could apply to a wide variety of methods of "transportation," possibly even the Internet and credit card machines. Courts have even held that intrastate mails are covered by the act, as they are part of an interstate mail system.

Reference

The Travel Act of 1961 (Public Law 87–228, signed September 13, 1961).

Unlawful Internet Gambling Enforcement Act of 2006. *See* Internet Gambling.

THE WAGERING PARAPHERNALIA ACT OF 1961

The Wagering Paraphernalia Act of 1961 was part of Attorney General Robert F. Kennedy's crime-fighting legislation package. The act authorized fines up to $10,000 and prison sentences up to five years for any person who "knowingly carries or sends" in any interstate commerce any information that is conveyed as writing, paper, token, slip, bills, certificates, tickets, record, paraphernalia, or "devices used" for the purpose of "bookmaking," "wagering pools with respect to a sporting event," or lotteries and numbers games. The law did not apply where the wagers were legal in the state to which they were sent.

The purpose of the act seemed to be to cut off supplies to illegal gamers, especially those in numbers games and illegal lotteries that were dependent upon paper products. The act did not apply to materials carried by common carriers as a normal part of their business, to pari-mutuel materials sent to tracks where wagering was legal, to newspaper publications, or to materials used in legal lotteries.

In 1993, the penalty provisions were amended to authorize fines from $3,000 to $30,000, with maximum prison time remaining at five years.

Reference

The Wagering Paraphernalia Act of 1961 (Public Law 87–218, signed into law September 13, 1961).

Section Two
GAMES

BACCARA, CHEMIN DE FER, AND BACCARAT-TYPE GAMES

There are several variations of a game called baccara. The word *baccara* means "zero" in Italian. The game originated in Italy and developed during the Middle Ages. The game was exported to France, where it became known as *baccarat* and also as *chemin de fer*. The latter term means "railroad" and refers to the fact that the bank for the traditional game was passed around the table from player to player. Other variations of the game are called *punto banco* and mini-baccarat.

Although the manner of play in the different types of games varies, the strategy is quite similar. The goal in all the games is to get a series of two or three cards that total 9 in value or as close to 9 as possible. The side that is closer to 9 wins the game. Cards are typically drawn from a six-deck shoe. Cards are alternately given face down to one side, called the "bank," and to the other side, called the "player." The cards are then turned over—first the player's cards, then the bank's cards. The ace is counted as 1; each numbered card is counted as its value, except for the 10, which is counted as 0; the face cards are counted as 0. When the numbers are added up, 10 (or 20) is subtracted from any number over 9 (or 19). If the player's first two cards add up to 8 or 9, it is considered a "natural," and no more cards are drawn for either side. The bank's cards are revealed, and the winner is determined. If both hands

have the same number, it is a tie. If the player's hand is not a natural, the bank hand is examined to be sure it is not a natural. If it is a natural, there is no draw for the player's hand. The player's hand draws another card if the hand adds up to 0, 1, 2, 3, 4, or 5. If the player's hand adds up to 6 or 7, it gets no more cards. Whatever the player's hand has, the bank must draw if it has a 0, 1, or 2. It stands on a 7, and of course on a natural 8 or 9. If the bank has a 3, 4, 5, or 6, it takes cards depending upon the cards of the player. In the baccarat game played in most casinos today, there are absolutely no possibilities for deviating from these rules. In some variations of the game, there is an option of drawing or standing when the player's hand is 5.

The games now played find all players betting against the house—against the casino. The players may bet either that the bank hand wins or that the player hand wins. Players receive even-money payoffs if their bets are correct. If there is a tie, neither hand wins or loses. The players may also wager on a tie, however, and they are paid 8 to 1 if the game is a tie.

In some European casinos, now as well as traditionally, there may be a double table for baccarat. This game gives the casino dealer a degree of discretion. Three hands are dealt. One hand, the bank hand, is the casino's hand. Two hands—one for each side of

Frank Sinatra dealing baccarat at the Sands, 1959.

the table—are designated as player's hands. The casino (bank) competes one-on-one against each of the player's hands. In this game, the casino patron may bet only on the player's hand at his side of the table. As the player's hands are revealed (both before the bank's hand is revealed—except to check for naturals), the casino dealer must then within strict limits decide whether to play in a way to maximize winning against one or the other side of the table. The dealer considers the amounts wagered at each end of the table if choices are possible to draw or stand.

Casinos in the United States use only a single-table baccarat table for games, although players are spread all around the table. In this commonly played game (which is universally played in the United States), the players who bet on the bank and win must pay a 5 percent commission fee on the amount of their winnings. With this commission, the casino maintains a 1.17 percent advantage over the players who bet on the bank and a 1.36 percent advantage over players betting on the player hand. In the European chemin de fer game, the advantage actually belongs to one of the patrons at the table. He or she bets against all other players, who must bet on the player's hand. That patron keeps the bank as long as the bank hand wins. On each such bank win, however, he or she must give the casino a 5 percent commission on all winnings. It is in this game that the player hand (actually played by the largest bettor against the bank) has the option of standing or playing on a five.

There is also a popular variation of the baccarat game that is played at a small table (the size of a blackjack table). All players face the dealer, who handles all the cards, dealing both hands, turning over the cards of each hand, and making set bets without any options. A minibaccarat game typically allows low-stakes bets, whereas the casino baccarat game has gained a reputation for being the casino's most elegant game, as it has the highest table limits permitted in the casino.

Except when played at the minitable, there is great ritual at the baccarat game. Cards are turned over by the player (one player in turn represents the player's hand) with great suspense. The casino's dealers mimic this style as they reveal the bank's hand and then draw new cards. Casinos find the highest bets at these tables. The highest rollers to be found in the world gravitate to the baccarat tables of the leading casinos. They may play several hundreds of thousands of dollars per hand. The games are favored especially by the wealthiest Asian and European players wherever they may be found. The games may be separated from other tables by ropes. Dealers wear tuxedos at baccarat tables, but only standard casino uniforms at others. In European casinos where drinks and food are not allowed on casino floors, exceptions are made for the baccarat players.

System players using simple methods, ranging from the Martingale strategy to much more elaborate schemes, also seek out the baccarat tables for their even-money bets, as these tables offer the best odds to players on even-money choices. Casinos compete with each other to win the loyalty of the baccarat high rollers. Gifts of every type imaginable are offered to these special players. From month to month, Las Vegas Strip casinos see their bottom-line revenues go up and down considerably, depending upon how much is played at the baccarat tables and whether or not one or several of the richest players hit a prolonged winning streak. Occasionally, a casino will experience a monthly loss because of a run of player luck at baccarat. This cannot be said of any other game (unless there is cheating). Another attraction of the baccarat table is that the players can act as a social group and bet together—whether on the bank or player—and can cheer and console each other, as the case may be.

References

Miller, Len. 1983. *Gambling Times Guide to Casino Games.* Secaucus, NJ: Lyle Stuart, 157–160.

Scarne, John. 1986. *Scarne's New Complete Guide to Gambling.* New York: Simon and Schuster, 459–489.

Sifakis, Carl. 1990. *Encyclopedia of Gambling.* New York: Facts on File, 10–15.

Big Wheel (Wheel of Fortune or Big Six). *See* Roulette and Wheels of Fortune.

BINGO

Bingo has been the quintessential charity game in the United States for most of a century. Expansion of the game (in terms of hours played and prize amounts) led to the court cases culminating in decisions that generated the initiation and widespread proliferation of Native American gambling in the United States. Bingo is also played in many commercial casinos. The game demands vigilance and attention from the players, who may form a collective audience of a dozen or several thousands (or more with satellite connections among several bingo halls).

Bingo is played on two basic styles of cards. A bingo card in the United States has 25 spaces arranged in 5 rows and 5 columns. Numbers are on 24 spaces; the center space has a star or another mark, designating it as a "free space." The columns are designated as B, I, N, G, and O. Under the respective letters are numbers between 1 and 15, 16 and 30, 31 and 45, 46 and 60, and 61 and 75. In simple games, the object is to get 4 or 5 numbers called to fill a column, a row, or a diagonal line through the center, or to fill in each corner of a card. More complex games may require filling in a pattern (for example, a letter T—top row and center N column—or filling the outer edge—top and bottom rows and B and O columns) or covering all 24 numbers on the card.

The second type of bingo card, popular in Europe, is called a tombola. The card has 3 lines and 5 columns. Each individual card has 5 numbers on a line, for 15 numbers in all. Eighty-one numbers are used in the game. Each game has 2 winners. The first winner is the one who first calls "bingo" when all 5 numbers of any one line are filled. The second winner is one who gets all 15 numbers on the card filled.

Although casinos and bingo halls may offer guaranteed prizes for winners of certain games, traditionally the prize pool has been taken from player purchases of cards, making the game a pari-mutuel player-banked exercise in gambling. If two or more persons win at the same time, the prize is divided. On big cover-all games, a bingo hall may offer a big prize if the cover-all is reached within a certain number of calls, for instance, 45 numbers. If it is not, a part of the prize pool may be carried over to another day, and the big prize increased in a progressive manner.

In many Las Vegas casinos that cater to senior citizens, bingo offers a large return to the players. That practice is used as an incentive to draw in customers who are expected to play slot machines and other games between and after the bingo games.

The numbers called at the bingo game usually appear on Ping-Pong balls that blow about in a sealed cage. When a small tunnel to the cage is opened, one ball is sucked up into an area where a caller can take it. The number on the ball is called and then recorded on a board that all can see. The ball is usually held up so that it can be physically seen as well. If a player has a win, he (or, more appropriately, she, as more players of bingo are women than men—quite different than almost all other games) must call out "bingo" before the next number is called. The bingo card is then verified to assure that all numbers are on it and that it contains the last number called.

The percentage payout varies considerably, depending upon the desires for an operator to get a certain return from the players by setting prizes at a certain level. The bingo game utilized today is an outgrowth of a private Italian game called *lotto*. This in turn was derived from a national lottery game that began in the 16th century. Forms of bingo (called by other names) were played in the United States in the mid-19th century. The popularity of the game was developed in the 1920s, when movie halls used it for raffle prizes given to those attending shows.

The American card used today in bingo is traced to the 1920s. The name *bingo* had been used as a reference to beans that players used to mark winning numbers.

Bingo has maintained a widespread popularity due to its simplicity, its almost "pure luck" form, and the fact that it is a very social game that can be easily set up for commercial or charitable functions.

Reference

Scarne, John. 1986. *Scarne's New Complete Guide to Gambling*. New York: Simon and Schuster, 205–223.

BLACKJACK

Blackjack is the most popular card game in casinos throughout the world. The game is an American creation in its present form, although it has origins in European games such as the French *vingt-un* (translated as "21") and the game *trente et quarante* (or "31") as well as the English game of pontoon. The form of 21 used in the United States was modified in 1912 when play at some card rooms in Indiana added an additional 3-to-2 payoff for winners who had a "natural 21," that is, a 21 count on their first two cards.

The popularity of the game was greatly enhanced by the publication of Edward O. Thorpe's book *Beat the Dealer* in 1962 (*see* Annotated Bibliography). The book presented solid evidence that with proper playing techniques and structures, the odds for this game can actually change and favor the player.

Blackjack is a house-banked game in which a house dealer seeks to have cards valuing 21 or a number closer to 21 (without being over 21), but higher than the values of cards held by players. The player makes an initial bet according to the house limits. A dealer gives two cards (one at a time) to each player and also takes two cards himself or herself. The blackjack table may accommodate up to seven players, each of whom individually competes with the dealer. The object of the game is to get cards totaling 21. The cards from 2 through 10 count as their number value. The jack, queen, and king each count as 10 points. An ace may count as 1 or as 11. If a hand has a value of 22 or more it is a "bust," a losing hand for a player, and in most cases for the dealer as well. Although there are variations, in general the two player cards are dealt face up, whereas one dealer card is dealt down and one face up. The player may ask for additional cards in hopes of getting a 21, or closer to 21 than the dealer's hand. If an extra card makes the player's hand go to 22 or over, however, the player immediately loses the hand, regardless of what happens to the dealer's hand. A player who is satisfied with the hand's value and has not "busted" indicates that he or she wants no more cards. After all players are done taking cards, the dealer exposes the face-down (or hole) card. He or she takes extra cards if that total is 16 or less but stands (that is, takes no more cards) if the value of the cards is 17 or more. In some casinos, a dealer will take more cards when he or she has a value of 17, which includes an ace that is counted as an 11. (This is called hitting a soft 17.)

Winners are paid at even money; if they bet $5, they win $5, a return of $10. If both the player and the dealer have hands with the same value, it is a tie, and the player's bet is returned to him or her. A player who busts loses even if the dealer later busts in the same hand.

The situation is altered if the player or the dealer has a natural blackjack. A natural blackjack consists of an ace and a card valued at 10 (10, jack, queen, or king). If the player's first two cards are a blackjack, he or she wins and is paid 3 to 2; that is, a win of $7.50 plus $5, or a return of $12.50. This win is negated if the dealer also has a two-card blackjack, in which case the play is a tie. If the dealer has a blackjack, he or she beats all players who do not also have a

blackjack. In the case of a dealer showing an ace or a 10-value card, the dealer looks at his other card; if it makes a blackjack, he or she reveals it and collects the bets from the losing players without giving them the opportunity to draw cards. If the dealer is showing an ace, however, he or she first offers all players a chance to make insurance bets, which are described later.

Certain special plays and bets are allowed to the players. For instance, if both of the player's first two cards are the same, he or she may split them into two hands by making an equal bet on the second hand. Some casinos also allow resplitting. New Jersey casinos and many in other jurisdictions, Nevada excluded, allow the player to make a "surrender" play. After the player looks at the dealer's one card and his or her own two cards, the player may forfeit the hand immediately for only half of the original bet. The player may also like the situation so much that he or she doubles the bet. After "doubling down," the player may be given only one more card—if he or she desires more cards. Some casinos allow a player to double down if showing cards with values of 10 or 11. Other casinos allow any player to double down.

If the dealer is showing an ace, the player may make a bet called "insurance." This is a side bet that does not affect the main bet on the value of the player's and dealer's hands. The player bets up to half of his or her original bet and wins a 2 to 1 payoff if the dealer reveals that he or she has a natural blackjack. With this side bet, the casino has an 8 percent edge over the player, as there are 16 10-valued cards (which can make the insurance bet a winner) and 36 other cards.

The casinos may use from one to eight decks of cards for play at blackjack. As players use strategies that may depend in part upon the cards that have already been bet (counting strategies), some players like single-deck blackjack. This is a game dealt from the dealer's hand with both of the player's cards being dealt face down. Most casinos shy away from single-deck games as hand dealing introduces opportunities for cheating and hence requires more monitoring. In multideck games, the cards are dealt from a shoe. A shoe is a box, usually plastic, into which the shuffled decks of cards are placed. They are dealt as the dealer slides cards from one end of the box through an opening. Shoes are also used with baccarat games and other card games.

The popularity of blackjack derives from the fact that, in addition to allowing a strategy that can give the player the edge, the game is simple in concept but also allows for very personal strategies. As a variety of strategies and playing styles is used by players, it is not possible to assess the odds-advantage possessed by the house (casino). In one strategy, the player seeks simply never to bust. Hence, he or she stands on any cards giving him or her a value of 12 or more, regardless of the card shown by the dealer. Under this strategy, the casino has a 6.35 percent edge over the player. If the player instead mimics the rules followed by the dealer—taking cards when he or she has a 16 or less and holding on 17 or more, then the casino's edge is reduced to 5.90 percent. A more complicated, but more effective, strategy called "basic blackjack strategy" can reduce the house edge to below 1 percent, and to even, or a slight player edge, with a single-deck game. With properly executed card counting (the Thorpe strategy), the player can gain a 1 or 2 percent edge over the house.

References

Miller, Len. 1983. *Gambling Times Guide to Casino Games*. Secaucus, NJ: Lyle Stuart, 25–39.

Scarne, John. 1986. *Scarne's New Complete Guide to Gambling*. New York: Simon and Schuster, 342–392.

Sifakis, Carl. 1990. *Encyclopedia of Gambling*. New York: Facts on File, 33–39.

Thorpe, Edward O. 1962. *Beat the Dealer*. New York: Random House.

CRAPS AND OTHER DICE GAMES

Dice (plural for di) have been used in games for 5,000 years or more. Anthropologists discovered four-sided objects in the form of pyramids and marked with numbers on their sides (called pips) in tombs in Mesopotamia that were carbon dated back to 3000 BCE. Other dice from the ancient eras were found in India. Many took other shapes and were five or six sided, and some were formed from the knuckle bones of animals. Accordingly, in popular parlance dice are known as "bones." Many different games use dice.

CRAPS

In modern times, craps has been the most popular dice game. It may be played among players (as few as two), or in a casino with bank odds. Among players it was the most widely played game during war times, because all players needed for "action" was a pair of dice in order to wager on a very basic game. The game has been less popular in casinos because it usually requires four employees for supervision and there are security issues as it is the only casino game where players actually hold and manipulate the tools of the game. The game is very fast and in casinos involves a multitude of bets requiring constant monitoring, with game supervisors watching each other as well as the players.

The basic game is played with two di, or a pair of dice. A player rolls the pair of dice across the table (or maybe just the ground if it is a game outside of a casino). For security reasons, in a casino the dice must be held in one hand only, and when rolled they must hit the table side before they come to rest. There is a first roll and everyone must bet either "pass" (that the roller wins) or "don't pass" (that the roller loses). If the first roll results in a 7 or an 11 it is a "pass." If the roll is a 2 or 3 or 11 "pass" loses, and with a 2 or 3 "don't pass" wins. However, if the first roll is another number—4, 5, 6, 8, 9, 10—then this number becomes "the point." In continuing rolls, if the point comes up before another 7 is rolled "pass" wins, but if a 7 comes up before the point, then "don't pass" wins. In casino games there are many other bet combinations. A popular one finds a player (who has bet either "pass" or "don't pass") making a separate bet that the specific "point" number will emerge before a 7, and on this bet the player gets natural odds—there is no house advantage. Players may also bet on having a specific number or one of a combination of numbers come up on a single roll; however, house odds always favor the casino in these cases.

HAZARD

Hazard is an old English dice game that contains elements of today's craps game. Knights played hazard as early as the 12th century during the crusades to Arabia and the Middle East. It was not until the 17th and 18th centuries, however, that hazard became the most popular English casino game.

In basic hazard, a shooter throws two dice. He throws and rethrows until he gets a 5, 6, 7, 8, or 9. This number then becomes his "point." He rolls again (and again), until a game-ending number comes up. He wins if he makes the point and also if he rolls an 11 or 12 (with some exceptions). He loses if he rolls a 2 or 3 (called a crabs). With a 4 or 10, he rolls again. If he rolls a 5, 6, 7, 8, or 9 that is not his point, it now becomes his "chance," and he loses if he rolls it again (which means he rolls it before he rolls his point or a 2, 3, 11, or 12).

For a player making rolls over and over, the game was not difficult to understand, although it certainly seems to be a complicated game. To make matters more confusing, many variations were added to the game over time. When the game was brought to the North American colonies, the craps version was introduced, and this version was accepted as the standard two-dice game in North America. A three-dice game called grand hazard was also widely played in the colonies. The games of chuck-a-luck and sic bo became a variation of grand hazard.

CHUCK-A-LUCK

Chuck-a-luck is a three-dice game also known as "bird cage." Three dice are placed into a large cage shaped like an hourglass. The cage is on an axis, and it is rotated several times by a dealer. The dice fall, and their numbers total from 3 to 18 (each die showing a 1 to 6). A player may bet that a certain number (1 to 6) will show on at least one die. If it does, he or she receives an even-money payoff; if the number appears on two dice, the payoff is 2 to 1; if all three dice show the number, the payoff is 3 to 1. Although the bet appears to most casual observers to favor the player, the house actually has a 7.87 percent advantage.

Other bets can also be made. For instance, a player could wager that there would be a three of a kind on a particular number, or any three of a kind. A player could also bet on a high series of numbers or a low series of numbers.

SIC BO AND CUSSEC

Sic bo and cussec are two variations of chuck-a-luck. Sic bo is popular in Canada; cussec is played in many Asian countries, as well as in Portugal. Until 1999, no dice were allowed in Canadian games. Sic bo was played in some rather unique ways. A casino in Vancouver had players roll three small balls into a roulette wheel marked with the faces of two dice on each number area (36 markings). At the charity casino in Winnipeg's Convention Centre (open for a few years during the 1980s), there

was an actual slot machine that had three reels. On each reel was the face of a die. The three die faces became the player's "roll."

FRENCH BANK

French bank is a very fast three-dice game played in Portugal. It is one of the most popular games in Portuguese casinos. The three dice are thrown rapidly until a low series (5, 6, or 7) or a high series (14, 15, and 16) comes up. Players wager even money on low or high. If three aces (1–1–1) come up, all players lose, except those betting on the three aces—they win a 60 to 1 payoff.

BACKGAMMON

Backgammon is a game played with two dice and a board. It involves moving tiles around a playing surface and also blocking movements made by one's opponents. The game is considered by some to be the oldest board game, as it dates back to Roman times. In the 18th and 19th centuries, it was very popular with English nobility and involved very high gambling stakes.

References

Scarne, John. 1986. *Scarne's New Complete Guide to Gambling.* New York: Simon and Schuster, 259–330.

Schwartz, David G. 2006. *Roll the Bones.* New York: Gotham, 9–16.

Sifakis, Carl. 1990. *Encyclopedia of Gambling.* New York: Facts on File, 15, 65–66, 77–82.

Silberstang, Edwin. 1980. *Playboy's Guide to Casino Gambling.* Chicago: Playboy Press, 19–123.

Draw Poker. *See* Poker.

FARO

The game of faro was played in France as early as the 17th century. The game came to North America through the colonial port of New Orleans. As Louisiana was transferred to the new nation, the game became very popular on Mississippi riverboats and on the western frontier. The game survived late into the 20th century in Nevada casinos. Its slow action combined with its low return for the casinos, however, caused houses to drop faro in favor of games such as the increasingly popular blackjack.

The word *faro* was derived from the word *pharaoh,* as the winning card was seen as the "king." The rather simple luck game is played on a layout called a faro bank. The table has pictures of cards on two sides, the ace through six on one side, the seven at the end in the center, and the eight through the king on the other side. There is also an area marked as "high" on one side. Cards are dealt from a 52-card deck. Suits are not considered, only the card values. After a first card is exposed and discarded, 25 two-card pairs are dealt, leaving one remaining card that is not played. The pairs are dealt one card at a time. The first card is a losing card, the second one a winning card. Basically, the players bet that a certain numbered card will appear as the winning or losing card in a pair when the card is next exposed. Correct bets are paid even money. If the card comes up and the other card of the pair is the same, the house wins half of the bet. If a pair does not contain the card, the bet remains until the card comes up in a future pair. For instance, if the bet is that a six will lose, cards are dealt in

A faro game at the Old Las Vegas Club in Las Vegas.

pairs until a six comes up, either as a winning or losing part of the pair. If two sixes come up, the player loses half the bet. The dealer records which numbers have been played, and the player can make subsequent bets with a knowledge about chances that a pair will be dealt with that number. The house edge starts at about 2.94 percent when the first pair is dealt and increases against players betting on subsequent pairs if the card bet upon (for example, a six) has not yet appeared. If three of the four sixes have appeared, however, the house edge is gone if the player bets the six will either be a winner or loser when it comes up the fourth time. Players betting on the high can bet that the winning or the losing card will be a higher-valued card.

There is also a variety of combination bets, many of which give the player a very bad disadvantage. The changing odds structures of the game can be calculated as play progresses, giving the game many strategies. The game attracted many systems players, and their many deliberations caused play to be slow compared to other casino games. In early times, systems were probably to no avail as games at the mining camps and on the riverboats were known to often be run by cheaters and sharps.

References

Lemmel, Maurice. 1966. *Gambling: Nevada Style*. Garden City, NY: Dolphin Books, 105–124.

Scarne, John. 1986. *Scarne's New Complete Guide to Gambling*. New York: Simon and Schuster, 234–235.

Sifakis, Carl. 1990. *Encyclopedia of Gambling*. New York: Facts on File, 113–115.

HOUSE-BANKED GAMES

A house-banked game is conducted by a gambling enterprise such as a casino, a lottery, a bingo hall, or an organized charity. The game is one in which the player opposes the gambling enterprise, and either the player or the enterprise wins the bet (unless there is a tie). There may be many players (thousands, as in a lottery) or a single player (e.g., one player at a blackjack table), but there is only one house—one gambling enterprise. The house (enterprise) runs the game and puts its resources (money) against the resources (money) of all of the players.

Most, but not all, casino games are housed-banked games. These include blackjack, craps, roulette, baccarat, *punto banco* (minibaccarat), and the big wheel. Las Vegas sports betting on football, basketball, baseball, and hockey games is also house banked. In all of these games, each player at the game is individually wagering money against the house. Most commercial (and Native American) bingo games are house banked, although the players are pitted against each other to see which one (or several) is the first to fill a card or line full of numbers. The game is banked if the house guarantees a specific winning prize to the players regardless of how many players are playing or how much money the players have wagered. If there is a predetermined prize, the house is engaging in gambling, as it is putting its resources at risk—it may lose money if too few players are in the game or if it has a high prize for a player covering a card in so many calls of numbers, and a player does so. The house would not have to give out the prize if no players accomplished that goal, however, and its winnings would be higher than otherwise.

Some charity bingo games are not house banked. In these the house awards a prize based upon the money that is actually wagered by the players when they purchase cards. The house may take out a percentage of the money as its share and then divide the rest of the money among the winners (or winner) of the bingo game. In this case the game is player banked, and the house is merely an agent managing the players' money for a fee.

In most lottery games, a player is guaranteed a prize of a certain amount of money if the player has a winning number. In the case of instant tickets, a finite number of tickets are sold. If all of a batch are sold, the lottery is like the bingo organization, as it merely manages the players' money, shifting it from losers to winners and taking out a fee. Instant ticket games are not house-banked games. On the other hand, if the player (or a random number generator) picks a number that is played (for instance, in a pick-3, pick-4, or pick–5 game), and a winner is guaranteed an individual prize that is given regardless of the actual number of players or winners in the game, then the game is house banked. The lottery is risking its money against the play of each individual player. The house-banked nature of the pick-3 game was highlighted in 1999 when the Pennsylvania lottery attempted to close

down play on certain popular numbers (777, 333, 666) in order to avoid high financial losses if the popular numbers were selected. The lottery knew it was in a risky house-banked situation, and it wished to minimize its risk. Indeed, the lottery officials knew what they were doing. In 1979 one game was rigged by a contract employee of the lottery who controlled the number-generating machine. The number 666 was chosen as the winner. Not only did an inside group of cheaters win a lot of money, but so did regular players who always played the popular 666—known as the devil's number because of references in the Bible's Book of Revelation. The state of Pennsylvania took a severe loss on that day (*see* Crime and Gambling).

Lotto games have giant prizes that are based upon amounts of money that have been wagered by the players. There is a superprize that is usually awarded to a player (or all players in a shared basis) who selects all six winning numbers (numbers may include 1 through 50). If no player selects all the winning numbers, a pool of money is gathered from ticket sales and transferred to the superprize for a subsequent game the next week. In a way, the giant lotto prize can be considered a player-banked game, but this is not truly the case. Only if the money played in the single drawing contributed to the giant prize would the game really be player banked. No lotto game is played this way. The starting game after a giant prize has been given away the previous week offers a guaranteed superjackpot prize, regardless of how much is wagered during that first game. In Texas, the state sets the superprize for the starting week at $4 million. If a player selects all the winning numbers in the first drawing, the state is definitely a loser. The lottery organization is banking the game. The fact that superprizes are shared does not change the house-banked nature of the game. Also, there is no legal requirement that the government continue to have new games after superprizes reach multi-million-dollar levels, although so far no major games have been discontinued. Moreover, each lotto game has guaranteed prizes for players who correctly pick only some of the winning numbers, again making the game essentially a house-banked game.

Often a lottery will put a cap (ceiling) on the amount it gives to big winners without changing smaller prizes and without guaranteeing that there will be a superwinner at all. These are house-banked games, as the lottery is risking its money against the wagers of the players. The lottery is either a small winner, a big winner, or occasionally a loser. An example of such a game is run in Texas. There the Texas Millionaire Game asks players to pick four numbers between 0 and 99. Guaranteed prizes of specific dollar amounts are given to players who select either two or three correct numbers. Players matching all four numbers win $1 million. If no one correctly picks the four numbers, the lottery is the winner pure and simple. If more than 10 people pick the correct four numbers, they must collectively share a prize of $10 million. The lottery caps its losses, but the game is still a house-banked game, just the same as a blackjack game in a casino.

The most typical games that are player banked rather than house banked include live games of poker, pari-mutuel games on activities such as horse and dog races, jai alai games, and lottery instant ticket games—when all tickets in a batch of tickets are sold (*see* Pari-mutuel Wagering Systems; Player-banked Games).

Reference

Thompson, William N. 1997. *Legalized Gambling: A Reference Handbook*. 2nd ed. Santa Barbara, CA: ABC-CLIO.

Jai Alai

Jai alai is a game that is played on the basic principles used for handball and racquetball games. Jai alai contests have been used for pari-mutuel betting in Florida, Connecticut, and Rhode Island and for almost a decade were featured in the MGM casinos of Las Vegas and Reno, Nevada.

The game is considered the oldest ball game played today; it is also considered the fastest game played. Players either compete as individuals or in teams of two.

The game is played on a very large court, 177 feet long, 55 feet wide, and 55 feet high. The playing facility is called a fronton. The ball is very hard—harder than a golf ball—and is about three-fourths the size of a baseball. The ball, called a *pelota,* is propelled by the players toward the front wall of the court. The players hold a *cesta,* which is a curved basket that extends from one of their arms. They catch the ball in the basket device and then without letting it settle, they propel it back to the front wall. They must retrieve and return the ball before it hits the floor two times. The balls may move as fast as 150 miles per hour in the games, faster than any other ball in any game.

The game of jai alai may have had ancient predecessors, as the origins of handball have been found in many prehistoric societies. In its present form, however, the game is traced to Basque villages in the Pyrenees of France and Spain. The origins of the game may go back to the 15th century. Mythmakers suggest that the game may have been the invention of St. Ignatius of Loyola, who—like his compatriot St. Francis Xavier—was Basque. What is less mythical is the fact that the game was played during religious festival occasions in the Catholic region. The words *jai alai* mean "merry festival." The game has also been known as *pelota vasca* or Basque ball. The game is celebrated in the classic art of Spain. Francisco Goya created a tapestry called *Game of Pelota* for the Prado in Madrid. Many mythical heroic characters of Basque tradition were pelota players.

As the Basques and persons from the surrounding regions migrated to the Western Hemisphere, they brought the game with them. It came to Cuba by the beginning of the 20th century, although Castro closed down games in 1960 as he closed the Cuban casinos, and it was showcased at the St. Louis World's Fair of 1904. It came to Florida in 1924. Although the game enjoyed some natural popularity for its basic excitement, it did not draw large crowds until 1937, when the Florida legislature authorized pari-mutuel betting on the winners of the games.

In the jai alai game there are eight players (or eight teams of two players each). They play round robin matches. A player (team) who wins a point remains in the game; the loser is replaced with another player (team). They keep playing until one player (team) has scored seven points. In a sweep, one player could score seven straight points but would have to do so by scoring against every other team in the contest. The contests result in one winner with seven points and second- and third-place players (teams) with the next highest number of points. If there is a tie, the tying teams play off for their position. Those making wagers can bet the basic win, place, and show as in horse racing. Jai alai contests also were innovative because they created the quinella, perfecta, and exacta bets. A trifecta bet is also used.

Florida developed many frontons, but play levels pale in comparison with other betting venues such as bingo halls, horse tracks, and Native American casinos. The MGM Grand Hotels of Las Vegas and Reno had frontons until the mid-1980s. Connecticut authorized jai alai betting in the early 1970s, as did Rhode Island in 1976. However, both have since closed there frontons, as Rhode Island has also made the live game illegal. Efforts to get the sport accepted elsewhere in North America for pari-mutuel wagering have not been successful.

References

Keever, William R. 1984. *The Gambling Times Guide to Jai Alai.* Hollywood: Gambling Times.

Scarne, John. 1986. *Scarne's New Complete Guide to Gambling.* New York: Simon and Schuster, 135–136.

Sifakis, Carl. 1990. *Encyclopedia of Gambling.* New York: Facts on File, 167–168.

KENO

Keno is a game that enjoyed great popularity in Nevada casinos in the mid-20th century. Its use is now waning, as serious players realize that it does not offer a good expected return. Casinos also realize that it requires much labor and also considerable security to ensure that all play is honest. The game that is now played can be traced back to Chinese games two millennia ago. The Chinese used boards with 90 (or more) characters. They brought the game to the United States as they emigrated to the West Coast for jobs on the railroads and in the mines.

Americans modified the game so that numbers replaced characters. When casinos reopened in Nevada in the 1930s, an 80-number game became standard, and it is still in use. The player is given a sheet of paper with 10 columns and 8 rows of numbers. He or she may bet on from 1 to 15 numbers. Numbered balls (or a computer number generator) are then retrieved from a randomizer, and 20 numbers are called. Hence, for a 1-number pick, there is a 1 in 4 chance to have it called. The payoff is even money. In addition to picking one set of numbers (up to 15 of them), the player may use his card for making several combination bets. After marking the card, the player gives it to a casino official (or keno runner) who verifies it and gives him a receipt.

The convenient feature of keno in a casino is that players can wager and play the game while dining, watching entertainers, or playing other games. The winning numbers are posted on boards throughout the casino facility. Games are separated by 15 or 20 minutes, and winners usually have several hours to turn in cards for payoffs. The house edge is determined by payoff schedules. Typical Nevada payoffs to players range from about 75 percent to about 65 percent (a house edge of 35 percent) depending upon how many numbers are bet. When more than three numbers are bet, there are prizes for having some (but not all) of the numbers called.

Although the game is considered by most experts to be a "sucker's bet," many persons like the fantasy of being able to play a $1 game and win $25,000 or $50,000 for hitting 14 of 15 numbers. The casino, however, guards itself from extraordinary risks by limiting all prizes on a game to an arbitrary figure, such as $50,000. If there are multiple big winners on the game, they have to divide the prize.

References

Lemmel, Maurice. 1966. *Gambling Nevada Style.* Garden City, NY: Dolphin Books, 95–104.

Miller, Len. 1983. *Gambling Times Guide to Casino Games.* Secaucus, NY: Lyle Stuart, 75–95.

Scarne, John. 1986. *Scarne's New Complete Guide to Gambling.* New York: Simon and Schuster, 490–499.

Sifakis, Carl. 1990. *Encyclopedia of Gambling.* New York: Facts on File, 173–174.

LOTTERIES

The drawing of lots probably constitutes the oldest form of gambling, and in modern times these games are the most prevalent form of gambling. Public opinion polls also show that the public approves of legalization of lotteries more than any other form of gambling.

HISTORY AND DEVELOPMENT

There is evidence that lottery games were played in ancient China, India, and Greece. The "drawing of lots" constitutes most of the references to "gambling" in the Holy Bible. The technical elements of gambling may not necessarily have been present, however, in all the biblical situations, as lots were used mostly for decision making.

Lotteries were part of Roman celebrations. They were used at Roman parties to present gifts to guests, much as door prizes are given at parties and events today. Lotteries were also found in the Middle Ages, as merchants used drawings to dispose of items that could not otherwise be sold.

The first lottery game based upon purchases of tickets and awards of money prizes was instituted in the Italian city-state of Florence in 1530. Word of its success spread quickly, as France had a lottery drawing in 1533. The English monarch authorized a lottery that began operations in 1569. The English lotteries were licensed by the crown, but they were operated by private interests. One of the first lotteries held was for the benefit of the struggling Virginia Colony in North America. The 1612 drawing was held in London. Lotteries were soon being conducted in Virginia and the other colonies. It cannot be known for certain when the first lottery occurred in North America, as Spanish royalty had also approved of lotteries and may have held drawings in their colonial possessions. And, of course, Native Americans had games that encompassed the attributes of lotteries.

Lotteries were very popular throughout the 17th and 18th centuries in North America, and they were utilized both by governments and private parties. As in the Middle Ages, merchants used lotteries to empty shelves of undesired or very high-priced goods. Individuals would do the same when they wished to sell estates, and no persons had sufficient capital to purchase large holdings. Institutions used lotteries to fund many building projects—both for public and private use. Canals, bridges, and roads were funded through lotteries, as banking institutions and bonding mechanisms were not yet developed in the colonies.

The reconstruction of Boston's Faneuil Hall in 1762 was accomplished through the sale of lottery tickets. So, too, were construction projects for many colleges, including Harvard, Yale, Princeton, Dartmouth, Brown, and William and Mary. Colonial churches were not universally opposed to lotteries, as they also used ticket sales to build structures. Only the early Puritans and the Quakers voiced opposition.

Generally, governments did not use lotteries except for specific building projects. They did, however, institute laws to license as well as govern operations of lotteries; many lotteries were outside of government supervision. Most uses of lotteries had a noble or charitable purpose. Several entities, first as colonies and then as states, used lotteries for the support of military activities during both the French and Indian Wars of the 1750s and the Revolutionary War two decades later. The Continental Congress authorized four lotteries in support of George Washington's troops.

As the new nation began and a new century opened, lotteries remained very popular. Thomas Jefferson, who had earlier (in 1810) indicated that he would never participate in a lottery "however laudable or desirable its object may be" (Clotfelter and Cook 1989, 299), changed his outlook in 1826, as he was financially short and desperately needed money to manage his estate. He asked the Virginia legislature to allow him to operate a lottery. In his later years he had mellowed on the subject of lotteries, as he described the lottery as a "painless tax, paid only by the willing" (quoted in Clotfelter and Cook 1989, 298; Thompson 1997, 8–9).

Lotteries proliferated in the early decades of the 19th century. In 1832 there were 420 drawings in the United States. The price of all the tickets combined constituted 3 percent of the national income and exceeded by several times the budget of the federal government. Soon the lottery was on a downhill slide, however, as the reform movement led by President Andrew Jackson coalesced opposition to the drawings. Loose regulations and controls had permitted many scandals to surround the games. In one case a bogus lottery sold $400,000 worth of tickets but awarded no prizes. A Maine lottery director was discovered to have personally kept $10 million as expenses for a lottery that sold $16 million in tickets. In 1833, states started passing laws abolishing lotteries. First, Pennsylvania, Massachusetts, and New York prohibited the games, then all other states followed suit. As new states wrote their constitutions, the prohibitions were locked into basic laws. By the start of the Civil War only the border states of Delaware, Missouri, and Kentucky allowed lotteries. At the end of the war there were no lotteries.

The Civil War brought devastation to the American South, and several states looked toward lotteries for help. Most of the attempts to raise money with this kind of gambling were short lived, however. Only the notorious Louisiana Lottery persisted into the 1890s. The Louisiana Lottery was conducted by private parties under a license from the state. Considerable corruption and bribery generated by the operation led the citizens of the state to ban the lottery in a public referendum. Legal lotteries ceased to exist in the United States until New Hampshire authorized a state-run sweepstakes in 1963.

Although legal lotteries remained dormant for nearly seven decades, illegal operations flourished in many parts of the country. In the 19th century, side lotteries had developed, and private syndicates, for a few pennies, would allow a person to "insure" that a number would not be selected. This game became known as policy, and was the forerunner of the numbers game. By the early decades of the 20th century, the numbers game was well entrenched as an organized crime enterprise.

Lotteries returned to the legal scene with the passage of the New Hampshire Sweepstakes Law in 1963. Ticket sales began days after local communities approved their sale. Each ticket cost $3, and buyers registered their names and addresses. The new lottery was based upon results of a horse race. First, 48 winning tickets were picked and each assigned to a horse in a special race. Depending on how the horse ran, the winners received from $200 to $100,000. The results were not an overwhelming success, but they generated substantial interest in the lottery idea. In 1967 New York State instituted a state-run lottery with monthly drawings. Tickets were purchased at banks where the buyers registered their names as in New Hampshire. In 1969 New Jersey followed. New Jersey was the first state to achieve desired levels of sales, as they used a weekly game and attracted customers with mass-marketing techniques. New Jersey also appealed to customers by selling tickets for 50 cents each, and players did not have to declare their names. New Jersey also utilized computers to track sales.

New Hampshire, New York, and New Jersey were not the first North American or Caribbean jurisdictions to have lotteries in the 20th century. Mexico had established a game in the 1770s while it was still governed from Madrid, and the game persisted as the country gained its independence. Puerto Rico started its lottery in 1932. Canada, however, was influenced by the activity in the United States, as the national Parliament approved lottery schemes under provincial control in 1969. The first provincial lotteries appeared in Quebec in 1970. The spread of lotteries was quite rapid after the 1970s. All Canadian provinces

as well as the Yukon Territory and Northwest Territories instituted games, as did most of the states. By the end of the century, lotteries were in 37 states plus the District of Columbia. Politically, the lotteries have commanded public favor, as many states adopted lotteries through popular referenda votes that amended state constitutions. Of all the states only two, North Dakota and Alabama, have ever rejected lottery propositions.

Lottery revenues constitute over one-third of all the gambling revenues in North America. State and provincial governments have come to rely on the revenue, although in most cases it constitutes 3 percent or less of the budgets of the jurisdiction. The revenues fluctuate from year to year, but over the past several decades they have provided a constant steady flow of money to public treasuries. The certainty of that steady flow is dependent upon governments' adjusting to changing market desires of players and to advertising efforts. Game formats have changed considerably since New Hampshire first used its horse race sweepstakes drawings. When one state offered an innovation—as New Jersey did in 1969—other lottery states and provinces often followed with imitations. In 1974 Massachusetts began an instant lottery game using a scratch-off ticket that is preprogrammed to be a winner or loser. In 1975 New Jersey started a numbers game with the specific goal of competing with (and hopefully destroying) the prevalent illegal numbers game. New Jersey also installed an online system for tracking numbers at the same time.

Massachusetts tried a lotto game temporarily in 1977; then Ontario instituted the first permanent lotto game in 1978.

Players choose six numbers from 1 to 40, and if no player has all six winning numbers, part of the money played is carried over into a future drawing with new sales of fresh tickets and a new drawing of winning numbers. Massachusetts allowed telephone accounts for lottery sales in 1980. South Dakota introduced the video lottery in 1989 with state-owned gambling machines that operate not unlike slot machines—albeit winning players receive tickets they must redeem for cash. The state of Oregon introduced its sports lottery also in 1989. Players pick four teams on a parlay card and if all the teams win, they receive a prize awarded on a pari-mutuel basis. In the 1970s Delaware had tried a sports lottery based upon individual National Football League games, but dropped the experiment after it suffered significant financial losses. Sports lotteries did not spread to other states, as Congress passed a law banning sports betting in all but Nevada, Oregon, Delaware, and Montana. Canadian provinces have sports lotteries.

With the beginnings of lotto games, lottery operations all went online; all the gaming sales outlets in the jurisdiction were linked together with a computer network. The next stage of lottery gaming could consist of games linked to individual home computers. Several European jurisdictions and Australian states offer these games. The Coeur d'Alene Indian tribe of Idaho had such a game for a brief time. Political opposition to Internet gambling, as well as attempts to enforce existing laws against transmitting bets over state lines, have precluded lotteries from venturing more into Internet gambling.

Several small states have banded together in order to offer bigger prizes and thereby compete with the bigger states. The first multistate lottery began in 1985 and involved New Hampshire, Maine, and Vermont. This was but a precursor of the Powerball game that started in the mid-1990s with the participation of 21 state lotteries. Another latter-day innovation for lotteries has been the use of instant ticket vending machines. It is estimated that there are 30,000 of the machines in operation in 30 states today.

DEFINITION

In a generic sense, the word *lottery* can cover almost any form of gambling. The word has been applied to any game that offers prizes on the basis of an element of luck or chance in exchange for consideration, that is, something of value. In Canada, the term *lottery scheme* has come to include all casino games. The term as used in Wisconsin law similarly encompassed casino games, and as a result Native Americans were permitted to have casinos because the state had a lottery.

Thomas Clark's definition in *The Dictionary of Gambling and Gaming* is typical (Clark 1987). He views a lottery as "a scheme for raising money by selling lots or chances, to share in the distribution of prizes, now usually money, through numbered tickets selected as winners" (122).

THE VARIETY OF GAMES

Passive Games

The first lottery games set up in the 1960s and 1970s were what are called passive games, in which the buyer is given a ticket with a number preprinted on it. At a later date—perhaps as much as a week (but originally even months)—the lottery organization selects the winning number in some random manner. Usually the organization will use a Ping-Pong ball machine that is mechanical and can be easily observed by viewers. Computers might do a better job in the selection process, but ticket buyers seem to like to see the process of numbers being selected. The ordinary games involved numbers with three, four, five, six, or more digits. Passive games have been operated on monthly, weekly, biweekly, or even daily schedules. These games are described as passive because the player's role is limited to buying a ticket; the player does not select the number on the ticket. Also, the player must wait for a drawing; the player cannot affect the timing of the drawing.

Instant Games

In the case of instant tickets, a finite number of tickets are sold. The state contracts to have all the tickets printed. A number or symbol indicates that the player wins or loses. The symbol is covered by a substance that can be rubbed off by the player; however, the substance guarantees that the symbol cannot be viewed in any way before it is rubbed off. If all of a batch are sold, the lottery is like a bingo organization, as it merely manages the players' money, shifting it from losers to winners and taking out a fee. The lottery organization is the winner. Unlike passive games, in instant games the player determines the speed of the game; the player activates the game at any time by rubbing off the covering substance.

Numbers Games

In numbers games, players are permitted to actively select their own numbers, which are then matched against numbers selected by the lottery at some later time. Many numbers games are played on a daily cycle. Usually the lottery will have a three-digit number game and a four-digit number game. A pick-three game allows the player to pick three digits, which may be bet as a single three-digit number or in other combinations. A machine may also pick the number or digits for the player. However the number is picked and bet, the player is guaranteed a fixed prize if the number is a winning number. For instance, if it is bet as a single number, such as 234, and number 234 is selected by a randomizer as the winning number, the player receives a fixed prize of $500 for a $1 play. For a pick-four game the prize typically would be $5,000 for a winning number bet "straight-up."

In these games, there can be no doubt but that the lottery organization is a player betting against the ticket purchaser. These are in effect house-banked games. Some states have sought to improve their odds (even though their payoffs give them a theoretical 50 percent edge over the player) by limiting play on certain numbers or by seeking to adjust the prize according to how many winners there are for the number picked.

Lotto Games

There is a variety of lotto games. In Texas there is a pick-six game. The lotto player selects six numbers or lets a computer pick six numbers from a field of numbers 1 through 50. A ticket costs $1. A random generator picks six winning numbers. A fourth prize guarantees the ticket holder

$3 for having three numbers. A pool amount for third prize is divided among players who have four numbers selected. A second-place pool is divided among players who have five numbers, and a grand prize pool is reserved for players with all six winning numbers. If no player has six winning numbers, the grand prize pool is placed into the grand prize pool for a subsequent game played at a later time. The lotto games gain great attention owing to superprizes that often exceed $100 million—the biggest prize was over twice that much. On April 26, 1989, the Pennsylvania lottery gave a prize in excess of $100 million for the first time (NBC's *Today Show,* April 26, 1989). In the early 1990s a multistate lottery awarded a prize of about $250 million, and since then many other huge prizes have been given.

Video Lottery Terminals

Video lottery terminals are played very much like slot machines. They are authorized to be run by lotteries in several states, including South Dakota, Oregon, and Montana, in bars and taverns. In Louisiana the machines also are permitted but are operated by the state police. Racetracks operate machines under government control in 9 states. Seven of the Canadian provinces have lottery-controlled machines in bars. They are also at racetracks in Alberta, Saskatchewan, Manitoba, and Ontario. Where the machines are operating in large numbers, they usually dwarf other revenues of the lottery.

LOTTERY REVENUES

An overview of lotteries shows that in 2007 traditional (nonlottery machines) ticket sales amounted to nearly $52.7 billion. Of this amount, $31.9 billion (60.5 percent) was returned to players as prizes, and $20.7 billion (39.5 percent) was winnings for the lottery. Each resident in the lottery states spent an average of $186.17 on ticket purchases. This represented 0.5 percent of the personal income in the states. Governments retained $15.3 billion (29.2 percent) of the money spent on tickets after all expenses were paid. Lottery efficiency analysis shows that overall it cost 37.5 cents for each dollar raised for government programs by the lotteries. The efficiency of raising money ranged from New Jersey, where it cost 25.7 cents, to Montana, where it cost 78.8 cents in expenses to raise the dollar for government programs via lotteries.

CRITICISMS

Criticisms of lotteries come from several sources. With information such as that in the preceding section, many have suggested that lotteries are an inefficient way to raise money for government. Lotteries are also open to the charge of being regressive taxes, albeit "voluntary" ones, as Thomas Jefferson suggested. The National Gambling Impact Study Commission reserved many of its harshest criticisms for state lotteries. (It should be added that lottery organizations were not represented in the membership of the commission.) The commission was strong in protesting against lottery advertising, both for being misleading and for encouraging people to participate in irresponsible gambling. The commission also concluded that lotteries did not produce good jobs (National Gambling Impact Study Commission 1999, 3–4, 3–5). Special criticism was reserved for convenience gambling involving lotteries, as the commission recommended that instant tickets be banned and that machine gaming outside of casinos—such as video lottery terminals at racetracks—be abolished (3–18).

Some also criticize lotteries as inappropriate enterprises that redistribute income by taking money from the poor and making millionaires, suggesting that some of these new millionaires are unprepared for their wealth and do not use it responsibly. This criticism is dealt with at length in H. Roy Kaplan's *Lottery Winners* (1978), discussed in the Annotated Bibliography.

References

Clark, Thomas L. 1987. *The Dictionary of Gambling and Gaming.* Cold Spring, NY: Lexik House Publishers, 122–123.

Clotfelter, Charles T., and Philip J. Cook. 1989. *Selling Hope: State Lotteries in America.* Cambridge, MA: Harvard University Press.

McQueen, Patricia A. "Lotteries Bring in $17.5 billion," *International Gaming and Wagering Business Magazine,* April 2008, 1: 29–30.

National Gambling Impact Study Commission [NGISC]. 1999. *Final Report.* Washington, DC: NGISC.

See also Economics and Gambling; Louisiana Lottery Company (in Venues and Places section).

Lottery Laws, Federal. *See* Federal Lottery Laws (in Venues and Places section).

Lotto Games. *See* Lotteries.

Mah Jong. *See* Pai Gow.

PAI GOW AND GAMES WITH DOMINOS

Pai gow is a popular casino game played with dominos. A variation of the game, pai gow poker, is also played with cards.

Dominos are flat tile objects that are twice as long as they are wide. They are marked with a number of dots (pips) on each end (each tile is divided into two squares). Sets of dominos are utilized in a wide variety of games. They have their origins in India and China, and date back many thousands of years. In pai gow, the players are at a table with 32 domino tiles placed face down. The player and dealer each draw four tiles. These are then arranged by each into two hands—a high hand and a low hand. The player's and dealer's high hands are matched against each others, as are their low hands. The winning hand in each match has a number of pips closest to nine, as in a game of baccarat. If the number of pips is more than nine, ten is subtracted to get the number value (ergo, pips totaling 13 are counted as 3). Tiles having the same number of pips at each end carry higher values in the game. There is also a system for breaking ties.

The very popular Asian game of mahjong, while engrained in cultures of Eastern peoples, is not often played in casinos. The sets of tiles are different than those used in pai gow. Eighty-four tiles are on a table and each of four players draws 13 of them. There are different suits of tiles and the game is played with rules similar to those in card games of rummy, as players discard tiles and draw new ones seeking to make winning hands.

References

Millington, A. D. 1993. *The Complete Book of Mah Jong.* London: Weidenfeld and Nicolson.

Morehead, Albert H., and Geoffrey Mott-Smith. 2001. *Hoyle's Rules of Games.* New York: Penguin USA.

Schwartz, David G. 2006. *Roll the Bones.* New York: Gotham, 16–17, 223–226.

PARI-MUTUEL GAMES AND WAGERING SYSTEMS

Pari-mutuel wagering systems are used for almost all horse race and dog race betting, as well as for betting on jai alai games in the United States. The system allows for player-banked betting with all bets pooled and prizes awarded from the pool. Winning bets on other racing events are also determined on a pari-mutuel basis. In Japan, the system is used to award prizes to winners of wagers on motorboat and bicycle races. In Oregon, sports betting card bets are distributed to winners on this basis also. The state permits players to pick four winners of football games on a single card. The state takes 50 percent of all the money played and then divides the remainder among those who picked four winners. The California lottery actually uses a pari-mutuel system for its pick-three numbers game in order to avoid exposure to high risks resulting from the fact that many players' have the same favorite numbers. Whenever there is a pari-mutuel system, the organization running the system takes a percentage of the pool before bets are redistributed from the losers to the winners.

Although the pari-mutuel system is built on quite a simple concept, it was not a part of the betting fabric until late in the 19th century. It was invented in Paris by Pierre Oller in 1865. John Scarne's *Guide to Casino Gambling* (1978) suggests that Oller acted in response to a bookie who quoted odds on each horse before a race, but was not very good at his trade and therefore often suffered losses because too many bettors placed their wagers on the winning horses. The bookie asked Oller if he could figure out a way in which the bookie could take bets without ever having to suffer losses—the gambler's eternal dream. Oller found a way: take bets but announce odds only after all bets were taken. Oller invented what became known as a totalizator. His tallying machine would add up all the bets on each horse, compare them, and then determine odds. All the odds could then be cut a set percentage to assure a profit for the bookie. Soon a ticket machine was added to a totalizator device, and with the passing of time, more advanced machines made the bet-taking process more efficient and allowed tracks to consider changing their betting structures to the pari-mutuel system. As they did so, the tracks themselves became the operators of the betting on horse racing.

It is suggested that the system became known as pari-mutuel as a shorter reference to Paris Mutuel. The totalizator was first used at North American tracks in 1933; as horse race betting was revived in more and more jurisdictions during the 1930s and afterwards, the pari-mutuel system totally displaced other betting systems.

A simple example of how a pari-mutuel wager works might find that all bettors wagered $100,000 on a race. Let's say that Horse Surething attracted $30,000 of the bets in the eight-horse field. The track calculated all bets, totaled them, and then subtracted 18 percent as its fee. Actually this 18 percent, or $18,000, was divided three ways—$6,000 to the government as a tax, $6,000 to the track owners, and $6,000 as a prize for the winning horse. Sure enough it was Surething. All the people who bet on Surething were winners. Together they shared the $82,000 that was left in the pool of betting money. For example, if 500 people bet $100,000 on the race, and of these 50 bet on Surething to win, the 50 would share the $82,000 prize. They would share it in proportion to the amount they had bet. If

collectively the 50 persons had bet $50,000 on Surething to win, each $1 they had bet would be rewarded with a prize of $1.64. A typical $2 bet would receive a return of $3.68, and a person who made a $1,000 bet would receive $1,640 in return. In actuality the $2 bettor would receive $3.60, because the track always rounds down to the nearest ten cents. The eight cents is called the breakage. Money from breakage is usually assigned to some party that takes money from the 18 percent (the track, horse owners, government).

In racing there are many kinds of bets (*see* Horse Racing). There are the straight bets—betting that the horse will come in first (win), first or second (place), or first, second, or third (show). There are also exotic bets, such as the daily double (winners of the two designated races) or the exacta (picking the first-place and second-place winners in a race). For each kind of bet—show, exacta, daily double—there is a separate pool, and winners are paid from that pool alone. The betting arrangements can get very complicated, but modern computers can calculate results instantaneously, whereas in the past, several minutes would pass before a winner would know how much the winning prize was.

In the past, off-track betting houses—such as the casinos in Las Vegas—would not participate in the pari-mutuel pools. Rather, they would simply pay the track odds and keep the takeout percentage (18 percent). In doing so they would put themselves at risk, as they were running a banking game. Now all participate with the tracks in the pari-mutuel system, as the off-track bets are thrown into the same pool as the track bets. In exchange for being able to avoid the risk of being a house banker, however, the off-track facility, such as the Las Vegas casino, gets to receive only a very small portion of the action wagered at their facility— 5 or 6 percent rather than the theoretical 18 percent they would have received if their bettors made wagers in the same proportion as those at the track.

References

Scarne, John. 1978. *Scarne's Guide to Casino Gambling.* New York: Simon and Schuster.

Thompson, William N. 1997. *Legalized Gambling: A Reference Handbook.* 2nd ed. Santa Barbara, CA: ABC-CLIO.

See also Horse Racing; House-banked Games; Player-banked Games.

PLAYER-BANKED GAMES

In a player-banked game, the money wagered by the players is either put against the funds of one other single player who acts as "the bank" (much as in a house-banked game), or it is put into a common pool of funds that is then distributed to the winner (or winners) when the game is over. Player-banked games include many variations of live poker games, special variations of blackjack such as California Aces, and pari-mutuel games in which wagers are placed on results of horse or dog races and jai alai games in the United States and Canada.

In poker games that are played socially—poker is probably the most prevalent social game in North America—players usually make an ante bet, that is, a wager before any cards are dealt. The ante is thrown into the middle of the table area. Then either as successive cards are dealt or as individual players are asked to state what they are willing to risk if the game continues, extra money is thrown into the center area by all players wishing to remain in the game. When the betting is done (according to the rules of the game), the winner is determined, and all the money is given to the winner.

When such games are played in casinos or poker rooms (as in California), the house provides a neutral dealer who oversees and monitors the game to assure that it is honest and that specific rules of the game and rules on betting procedures (antes, raises, limits) are followed. For this service, the house charges either a per-hand price to each player in the game, a fee based upon the time the player is at the table (usually collected each half hour, as in California), or a percentage of the money that is played in the game (the practice in Las Vegas casinos).

The players in the player-banked game are seeking to win money from each other and not from the casino or the poker room organization. In traditional baccara, players rotate the bank, holding it as long as the "bank" position in the game is a winner, then when losing passing it on to an adjacent player. The bank therefore passes around the table as if it were a train moving on a track. The game is also known as *chemin de fer,* a French expression meaning *railroad.* In charitable bingo games, the organization running the game sells cards for play. After all cards are sold, the organization totals up the sales (money that comes from the players), takes out its share (usually 20 to 40 percent), and then announces the amount of money that will be given to the winner(s).

Several Native American tribal casinos use player-banked systems for games that are normally house banked. For instance, in both California and Texas, tribal casinos offer a standard blackjack game with extra opportunities for player wins. The casino still wins money from the actual game, however. This money is then placed into a pool, and players are given chances to win the pooled money by spinning a wheel or playing another chance game. In this way, 100 percent of the money played is returned to the players, so in a very real sense, their play is merely a redistribution of money among themselves. Another player-banked version of blackjack is called California Aces. Cards are dealt in a standard fashion, but there is no dealer hand. Also there is no busting (losing) for going over 21. Actually 22 is the best hand, and other hands are ranked according to how close to 22 they are, with lower numbers being superior to numbers over 22. (For example, the order of best to worst hands is 22, 21, 23, 20, 24, 19, 25, 18, and so on.) All money played goes to the player with the best hand. The casino does not collect any money from the game; however, the players in all these games pay the casino a fee for each hand they play. (After Proposition 1A passed in California in 2000, the Native American casinos there made compacts that allow them to offer house-banked games.)

Reference

Thompson, William N. 1997. *Legalized Gambling: A Reference Handbook.* 2nd ed. Santa Barbara, CA: ABC-CLIO.

See also California (in Venues and Places section); House-banked Games; Parimutuel Games and Wagering System.

POKER

Poker is the most widely known card game. In one or another of its many formats, it is played more often than any other game. Live poker games are typically player-banked games that involve not only the luck of drawing certain cards but also much skill in determining how the cards should be played in order to defeat the hands held by other players. Some forms of the game, typically those played with machines (video poker), are house-banked games in which the player seeks to achieve hands of certain values in isolation of any other hand, whether held by a person or by a machine. (As the preponderance of poker players are male, this entry will use male gender forms to refer to players.)

THE POKER HAND

All poker games are based upon the value of a five-card hand. The 10 best hands are listed here in descending order. (1) A royal flush consists of an ace, king, queen, jack, and 10, all of the same suit (e.g., all hearts or all spades). (2) The straight flush also consists of five cards in the same suit and also in order. Next to the royal flush, the best straight flush would be king, queen, jack, 10, and 9 of the same suit. (3) Four of a kind consists of four aces, four kings, four 2s, and so on. (4) A full house consists of three of a kind and two of a kind (a pair). The highest-ranking full houses have the top three of a kind (three aces and another pair). (5) A flush consists of five cards all of the same suit but not necessarily in any order or sequence. (6) A straight is a consecutive sequence of cards that are not necessarily of the same suit, for instance, a 3, 4, 5, 6, and 7 of varying suits. (7) In a three of a kind, the cards are of the same rank (three 4s, etc.), along with any two other cards. (8) Next is the combination of two pairs of cards and one other card. The highest pair would decide the value of the hands if two players had two pairs each. (9) The next combination is one pair. (10) Last is a hand valued by the highest card in a hand without at least a pair. (In pai gow and pai gow poker, two-card hands are ranked according to the highest pair [the best hand is two aces] or the highest card if there is no pair.)

DRAW AND STUD POKER

Two styles of poker games are draw poker and stud poker. In draw poker, the several players are each dealt (in turn) five cards. They may then request up to three new cards (more in some games) and throw away up to three cards. In the other form, stud poker, there is no draw. The player must utilize the cards that are dealt the first time. Stud poker games may involve more than five cards. In seven-card stud, the player is asked to make the best five-card hand possible from the seven cards.

The sequence of betting is tied to the rules of particular games. For two examples, consider five-card draw and a seven-card stud game called hold 'em, a game popular in Las Vegas. In a five-card draw game, all players at a table make an initial bet (called an ante). Then five cards are dealt to each player, all face down, for only the one player to see. Usually there must be at least one player with a minimum hand (for instance, a pair of jacks or better) in order to start the next round of betting. Such a player may open with another bet, and other players decide to either stay in the game and match the bet or drop out. Other players also may raise the bet, requiring all others to meet the raise or drop out. (Rules of the particular game put limits on the amount of bets and raises. If there are no limits, a person is entitled to stay in a game by placing all his money into the game pot. His winnings are confined to moneys equal to his bet from each other player. If he loses he is out of the game.) The players then throw away cards they do not want and draw new replacement cards. They then engage in another round of bets and raises according to rules (some games limit the number of raises to three). The final player to call or raise then must show his cards; others may drop out without showing cards. Of course the player who wins must show his cards. All cards are secret until the final play is made.

In variations of stud poker, cards are dealt face up as well as face down, so that all players can know partial values of their opponents' hands. In seven-card hold 'em, there is an ante bet, and then initially two cards are dealt face down to each player. There is then another round of betting that is followed by a dealing of an additional three face-up cards that are placed in the center of the table. These are common cards. Each player now can make a five-card hand. Then another round of betting ensues in which players match each others' bets or drop out. A fourth common card (one that may be used by any or all players in their hands) is dealt for all to see, and there is a final round of betting. Finally, the fifth common card is placed upon the table, and each remaining player puts forth his best five-card hand using his own two cards and three of the five cards from the common pool of cards on the table.

Each of these poker games involves many calculations of which cards are likely to be dealt from the remainder of the single deck that is used for the games, as do the many variations, including low ball, in which bettors seek to have the lowest hand at the table. There are also great psychological skills used to seek how to discover signs that will reveal what an opponent may be holding. The main questions asked about the heavy bettor in a game are, "Is he bluffing?" and "Does he really have a good hand, or is he just trying to scare others out of the game?" If all others drop out, he can win without having to show his hand. As suggested by Kenny Rogers's famous gambling song, each hand can win, and each hand can lose, depending upon how it is played and on how the player is able to "read" other players. Even a royal flush can be misplayed in such a way that the one holding it can really be a "loser." If the player cannot conceal his joy at such a good hand, the other players will drop out, and all he will win is their ante. If

played properly, the hand can be used to draw out big bets from the other players. Players seek to find characteristics called "tells" that will reveal an opponent's holdings.

The live-card poker game among players is extremely exciting. The game is one that, more than any other, attracts professional players. Some of them actually make a living with their skills, although there are not many examples of biographies revealing players who kept their fortunes well into old age.

CARIBBEAN STUD POKER

Other forms of poker games do not have the suspense and psychology of the live player-banked game, but they do involve the poker hand. In Caribbean stud poker (a house-banked game), the player puts his five-card stud hand against a dealer's hand.

First the player makes an ante bet. Then the dealer gives him five cards and also takes five cards. Four of the dealer's cards are down, and one is up for the player to see. The player looks at his cards and then either drops out or bets an amount double his ante. The dealer does not look at his cards until the players' bets are finished. When he looks at them, he determines if he has a "qualifying hand." The qualifying hand has at least an ace and king cards high or one pair. If the hand does not qualify, the dealer folds and pays the remaining players a win equal only to their ante bet. The second bet they made is simply returned.

If the dealer's hand is qualified, however, the player either loses or wins an amount equal to the ante and the second bet. He also is eligible to win a bonus depending upon the value of his hand.

For instance, a straight gets a 4 to 1 bonus (on the second bet amount); a flush, 5 to 1; four of a kind, 20 to 1; and a royal flush, 100 to 1.

There is also another side bet that the player makes at the beginning. He may bet $1 on the value of his hand, and he can win a special payoff if he stays in the betting, even if the dealer's hand is not qualified. The casino will have a progressive jackpot for this bet. A flush will get $50, a full house $100, a straight flush 10 percent of the progressive jackpot, and a royal flush the full jackpot. The progressive meter displayed above the Caribbean stud tables attracts players with the notion that they can win six figures on a $1 bet. Experts who study the game find that this extra $1 bet favors the house until the progressive jackpot grows beyond $200,000, which is rather rare.

LET IT RIDE

The game of let it ride poker was introduced to Las Vegas casinos in 1993 and has gained some popularity with casinos in many jurisdictions. Like Caribbean stud, it is a five-card stud poker game that is house banked. In this game the player hopes to get a hand with a good value. There is no dealer's hand. The player lays three equal bets on the table. Each player then receives three cards face down. At that time he may let his first bet stay on the table, or he may withdraw it. A fourth community card is dealt (to be used by all players), and he then can make another decision to withdraw his second bet, or "let it ride." His third bet must stay. Then a final card, also a community card, is revealed. He now has his hand. The hand is paid off according to a schedule. If the player

does not have at least a pair of 10s, he loses. The one pair of 10s gets the bettor's wagers returned to him. Two pairs give him a 2 to 1 return; a flush, 8 to 1; a royal flush, 1,000 to 1. Like Caribbean stud, there is also an opportunity to make a $1 bonus bet that pays off $20,000 for a royal flush and less for other good hands. On this bonus bet payoff, the expected return to the player is less than 80 percent, whereas the basic game pays back over 96 percent.

PAI GOW POKER

Pai gow poker is a house-banked even-payout game. The player is given seven cards, as is the dealer. Each then makes his best two-card and five-card hand. If both of the player's hands are better than the dealer's two hands, the player wins but pays a 5 percent commission on the winnings. If both of the dealer's hands are better, the dealer wins; if one is and one is not, it is a tie. One 52-card deck is used along with a joker, which may be used as an ace or as a card to complete a straight or a flush. The best possible hand is five aces.

SOCIAL HISTORY OF POKER

Poker achieved instant popularity among 19th-century gamblers in New Orleans where the game began, and also among Mississippi river boat gamblers. In early forms poker was known as "the cheating game," because gamblers could control cards by false shuffling and dealing from the bottom of the deck. When the Civil War years came, riverboat commerce waned and action shifted west to the mining camps. The Texas oil boom brought poker to the southwest in the early 20th century, and Texas hold 'em games were created and became popular.

For most of the 20th century, poker was a game played socially in private homes, and its commercial appeal was found in illegal games. Until recent years the appeal of the game was directed at older players. Now it is a game that has appeal to the old as well as the young. The new popularity of the game is driven by television, tournaments and Internet play, and by widespread publicity given to celebrities as they compete in games. It remains a game mostly played by males, and there is a distinct aura of machismo in today's play.

One tournament stands above all others—the World Series of Poker (WSOP). The WSOP has its origins in a 1949 series of games between Texan Johnny Moss and the leading card personality of the time, "Nick the Greek" Dandolos, held at Benny Binion's Horseshoe casino in Las Vegas. The idea of a big game with the best players remained in Binion's mind for two decades. Then a year after celebrating a reunion of Texas poker players in Reno, he decided to invite the best players to Las Vegas for what he called "The World Series of Poker." The initial game in 1970 involved six players who each paid a $5,000 entry fee. Slowly the tournament grew as everyone was invited to play, and anyone could put forth $10,000 and sit with the best players in the world. Now nearly 10,000 compete each year. Several categories of winners take home millions of dollars in prizes. Tournament games are shown on the ESPN television network. The WSOP has also been the inspiration for many other large tournaments. Additionally, Internet poker games may be found on hundreds of sites. On-demand tournaments are single table events that begin anytime, 24 hours a day, everyday as soon as a sufficient number of players come together to play a type of game with the desired limits.

References

Jensen, Martin. 2000. *Secrets of the New Casinos Games.* New York: Cardoza, 14–105.

Miller, Len. 1983. *Gambling Times Guide to Casino Games.* Secaucus, NJ: Lyle Stuart, 97–108.

Scarne, John. 1986. *Scarne's New Complete Guide to Gambling.* New York: Simon and Schuster, 670–671.

RED DOG

Red Dog is a casino card game (as well as a private game) in which a player is dealt a total of three cards from a standard deck. The player makes an opening bet, and then the first two cards are dealt face up. The player may then double the bet or let stand the original bet. The player wagers that the third card, which is then dealt, will fall between the first two cards. (An ace is considered the highest card.) If the first two cards are consecutive (e.g., a 6 and a 7), the play is considered a draw, and no third card is given. If both cards are the same (e.g., a 3 and a 3), a third card is given to the player. If it is the same (another 3), the player wins an 11 to 1 payoff. If it is different, the game is a draw. For other cards, the player wins if the third card falls between the first two. The payoff is even money if the first two cards have at least a four-card spread between them. If the spread is three cards in between, and the third card comes between the first two, the payoff is 2 to 1; if the spread is only two cards, and the player wins, the payoff is 4 to 1; but if there is only one card in between the first two, and that

card is played for the player, the payoff is 5 to 1.

Because a table indicates all play and payoff possibilities, Red Dog is a very simple game to understand, and as such it has some popularity. It is not found in many U.S. casinos, however, as it provides the house a substantial advantage of nearly 10 percent.

References

Jensen, Marten. 2000. *Secrets of the New Casino Games.* New York: Cardoza Publishing, 125–126.

Sifakis, Carl. 1990. *Encyclopedia of Gambling.* New York: Facts on File, 249.

ROULETTE, WHEELS OF FORTUNE, AND OTHER WHEEL GAMES

The notion that fortune is tied to cycles and the turning of wheels is buried in deep antiquity. The wheel itself was developed about 5,000 years ago. During the time of Christ, the Roman emperor Caesar Augustus had a rotating horizontal chariot wheel fixed with numbers around its circumference and used it in games of chance. The Zodiac wheel was also conceived of more than 2,000 years ago and forms the basis for horoscopes that predict a person's fortune based upon cycles of movements of the stars and planets. Wheels or other objects were spun in various ways for games in primitive societies. Despite this long history, the origins of the wheels used in casinos today came much later in European history.

E-O AND HOCA

Carl Sifakis suggests that today's roulette wheel may have had its origins in wheels called E-O and hoca that appeared in the early 1600s in central Europe. E-O stands for even-odd. The game was played using a circular table that had 40 gouges, or pockets, carved into it around the edge. The table had 20 pockets marked as even and 20 as odd. Two pockets (1 odd and 1 even) had Xs marked on them as well. If a player bet on even, and an even number received the ball that was rolled around the table, the player won. The game paid even money to a winner. If the ball fell into an even pocket marked with an X, it was a tie. If the ball fell in any of the 20 odd pockets, the player lost. This gave the house a 2.5 percent advantage. The game of hoca also used a table with 40 pockets, but 3 were marked with zeros, and the even money payouts gave the house an advantage of 7.5 percent. These games ceased operation with the appearance of the French roulette wheel.

The French wheel was purportedly developed by French mathematician Blaise Pascal, who lived from 1623 to 1662. In his mathematics work he expounded at length on probability theory. His wheel was useful for explaining his theories. Legend has it that Pascal conceived of the wheel during a retreat at a religious monastery. Others perfected the wheel that is used in French roulette (also called European roulette) today. Given the early origins of the game, it can be suggested that roulette is the oldest casino game still in active play.

FRENCH (EUROPEAN) AND AMERICAN ROULETTE

There are two basic styles of roulette games—French (European) roulette and American roulette. There are other variations of the games, with different sets of numbers, including the big wheel, boule, golden ten, and *espherodromo,* which are discussed later in this entry.

Both the French and American wheels have numbers from 1 to 36 on parts of the inner circle, each separated by frets. The French wheel also includes a zero, and the American wheel has a zero and a double zero. The croupiers rotate the wheel, and as it spins in one direction, he or she rolls the ball (plastic

A roulette class at St. Clair College, Windsor, Ontario.

or ivory) in the opposite direction in a circular groove at the top of the wheel. Soon the ball slows down and falls toward the numbers in the inner circle. As it does, it hits small metal bumps on the surface of the wheel that cause the ball to bounce in ways that make its path random as it lands on a number or the zero or double zero. This number is the winner.

The player makes bets on a layout showing the 36 numbers in 3 columns and 12 rows. The zero (and double zero) are placed at the top of the columns. On the sides of the columns are places for bets on odd or even numbers, red or black, and low or high numbers.

The French wheel has a different distribution of numbers around the wheel than does the American wheel. On both, red and black numbers alternate, but not even-odd or high and low numbers. The logic of the number arrangement seeks to enhance making the number selection random.

The French game is worked by several dealers who are called croupiers. The main croupier controls the wheel.

Others help by making bets for players by placing their chips on the layout. The players all use casino value chips, so it is important that the croupiers keep a close track on just who is making each bet, as all the chips are the same. Another croupier places a marker on the winning number and separates the winning bet chips from other chips that he rakes in. All bets are paid out with wins that allow the casino to have a 2.7 percent edge. The bets on the individual numbers are paid at 35 to 1 even though the true odds are 36 to 1. Even payouts are given for odd-even, red-black, and high-low, and the chance of each bet winning is 18 in 37. Bets may also be made on columns, rows, adjacent numbers on the layout, four numbers on the layout, and special combinations of numbers that appear near other numbers. A *voisins* bet (meaning "neighbors") is placed on the four numbers that surround the last winning number. A *les voisins du zero* bet covers the numbers surrounding the zero. A finals bet can be placed on all numbers ending in the same digit (for example, 6, 16, 26, and 36), and a *les tiers* bet covering one-third of the wheel is also available. *Les orphelins* is a bet covering numbers not in *les tiers* or *les voisins du zero*.

Because the croupiers place bets and deliver payouts for the players and all the chips look the same, the playing process is slow. Each game involving the spinning of the wheel takes two minutes or more if there are several players. This contrasts with the American wheel game, where a play usually occurs more than once a minute, and even as often as 100 times an hour.

The American game offers worse odds for the player, as the wheel has two zeros along with the 36 numbers. The odds against the player hitting a single number are therefore 37 to 1, but the payoff is the same as with the French game, 35 to 1. This gives the house an edge of 5.26 percent. Red-black, even-odd, and high-low bets are paid even money, but the player's chances of success are 18 in 38, for the same 5.26 percent house advantage. The player could do worse yet. He or she could bet on a series of five numbers at the end of the table—the 0, 00, 1, 2, and 3, with a payoff possibility of 6 to 1, whereas the true chances are 33 to 1, for a house advantage of 7.89 percent. In some casinos with American roulette (e.g., Atlantic City casinos), a bettor on even payout bets (odd-even, red-black, high-low) loses only half of his or her bet if the zero or double zero comes up. This rule, called *en prison* (because half of the bet remains on the table unless it is withdrawn), reduces the house edge to 2.70 percent on this bet.

In American roulette, only one dealer is needed to spin the wheel and to handle all wagers. The players purchase (with cash or casino value chips) individual colored chips that are distinguished from those of all the other players. The players place their own chips. All the dealer must do is make sure there are no bets placed after the ball descends into the winning number's space.

The English variation of roulette offers the player the best odds. A French wheel is used with its single zero, but players have their individualized American chips. The house edge of 2.7 percent is in contrast to French roulette because of another difference. In French roulette the player is obligated to tip the dealer with each win. If the player wins 35 chips, he or she "must" pay one to the croupiers as a tip. *Must* is a strong word, but if the tip is not paid, the croupier just might lose track of that player's future bets if they are winners (after all, the chips are all the same for all the players). In England this is not a major problem—first, because the players have individualized chips, and second, because tipping of dealers is prohibited in the casinos. Hence in effect, the true edge in England is 2.7 percent, whereas in France it is closer to the American edge of 5.26 percent.

Because of the odds disadvantage, the game of American roulette is not popular. Indeed, roulette action in Las Vegas casinos is close to zero, certainly less than 1 percent of the action. Yet the game of roulette has qualities that make it attractive worldwide. Roulette is the premier table game at most European casinos. Roulette is a simple game that is easily understood even by the most novice gambler. Also with but a few exceptions (the *en prison* rule and the five-series bet in American roulette), all bets on the roulette table have the same expected payout—94.74 percent for American roulette and 97.3 percent for French roulette—whether the player bets on one number, two, a column, or odds or even, red or black, or high or low numbers. It is a democratic game; all the players, amateur and professional, get the same chances. Unlike blackjack or craps, there is no "stupid" bet—that is, once one decides to start playing.

Roulette is a game that permits players to try a wide variety of systems. Many casinos encourage systems by keeping boards that display the last 20 numbers that have come up on the wheel. Also some casinos publish books showing the actual numbers that came up on individual wheels over weeks, months, and even years. Whatever system a player may conjure up, the player can pretest it by applying it to real numbers and sequences of numbers that have come up on actual wheels.

BOULE

Boule is quite similar to roulette. A stationary rounded table has 18 pockets, two for each number from 1 to 9. A ball is rolled into the table, which is essentially a cone in shape. The ball bounces around and falls into one of the numbers—the winning number. Players betting on the number are paid off at 7 to 1, although true chances are 8 to 1, for a house advantage of 11.11 percent. Players can also bet on red and black, odds or evens, high or low, for an even payoff. They lose on even bets when a 5 appears, making the true chances of winning only 4 to 9, for the same house advantage of 11.11 percent. The game was very popular in France prior to the introduction of slot machines in the late 1980s. Slot rooms and boule rooms in France do not have admission charges. The game was also played at the Crystal Casino in Winnipeg, Manitoba, through the 1990s. Until recently, it was the only game allowed in Switzerland, where the payout was only 6 to 1 for a single-number play, for a house edge of 22.22 percent.

BIG WHEEL (WHEEL OF FORTUNE OR BIG SIX)

A big vertical wheel of fortune is a common sight at carnivals and charity casino events. The wheel of fortune is also popular in U.S. casinos but less prevalent in casinos in other jurisdictions. The mechanical wheel is spun by a dealer, who also supervises betting activity on a table in front of the wheel. The wheel's simplicity and exposure to a gambling crowd makes it susceptible to cheating, so it would be advisable not to play the game except in a regulated atmosphere. Casinos must be vigilant to assure that the wheel is not compromised by players.

The wheel is about five feet across from top to bottom. It has 54 equally spaced sections that are separated by nails that are near the rim of the wheel. A strap of leather is mounted above the wheel, and it hits the nails as the wheel spins around. The friction of contact slows the wheel and it stops with the leather strap settling on one of the 54 spaces—the winning space.

The spaces are designated by denominations of dollar bills. There are 23 sections that are marked with a $1 bill, 15 with $2 bills, 8 with $5 bills, 4 with $10 bills, and two with $20 bills. Two others are marked with a joker and a flag marking. The player bets on the category of bill he or she expects the wheel to hit. He or she receives an even money payout for a successful bet on the $1 bill, although the chances of success are only 23 of 54. This gives the house a 14.8 percent edge. A bet on $5 pays 2 to 1 for a casino advantage of 16.6 percent; other bets give the house an edge of from 14.8 percent to 22.2 percent. A bet on the joker or the flag is paid at 45 to 1. These odds advantages for the house make the big wheel a bad bet for the player. The simple nature of the activity and the symbolism of the wheel of fortune have sustained a modicum of popularity of the wheel among amateur players.

ESPHERODROMO

Legal restrictions on gambling are not often followed to the letter. In addition to those who would confront the law with blatant illegality, there are those who seek to find nonconfrontational ways around the law. The roulette form of gambling is quite popular, so where roulette is in itself illegal, there are those who will seek to find other games like roulette that might survive legal challenges. Two of those games are *espherodromo* and golden ten. Espherodromo appeared in the city of Bogota, Colombia, where casinos were always on the edge of the law. Therefore entrepreneurs came up with a game that certainly did not look like roulette, but in format was a roulette-style game. (*See* description of the game in the Colombia entry.)

GOLDEN TEN

The golden ten game was offered to players in nonauthorized settings; however, its operators were quite successful in avoiding prosecution on the basis that their game was not a gambling game. The golden ten wheel game was instead advanced as a skill game. The game gained an especially viable hold in the Netherlands in the 1980s after the government tried a crackdown on patently illegal casino gaming. Operators came up with this new game, although some suggest it was invented by Germans. The game is called golden ten because it uses a wheel with numbers in the center around a circle; one of the numbers is marked zero, and the other is marked with a big golden X. There are 24 numbers on the wheel, so if it were a random-ordered game, the house would have an advantage of about 8 percent, as payoffs on single numbers are 23 to 1, whereas the expectation should require a payoff of 25 to 1. But those running the wheel claimed that the numbers, although falling randomly, could be predicted by the players. Indeed, the game was also called "observation roulette."

The circular bowl for the game is stationary. A ball rolled into the smooth metal bowl makes slow, descending spirals downward until it hits the center area, where it bounces into one of the numbered areas, or the area marked zero or X. The metal bowl contains two concentric circles on its sides, about one-third and two-thirds of the way down the sides. The circles are simply markings on the bowl that do not affect the roll of the ball. The player makes his or her bet after the ball has passed the first circle but before it crosses the lower circle. The player can watch the ball come out of the dealer's hand and watch it cross the first circle line. By observing the rolls over and over, the player is supposed to be in a good position to "predict" where the ball will likely land. With successful predictions, the player becomes a skillful winner, not a gambler at all. Gambling demands that chance be a material part of the play on at least a meaningful part of the play. The casinos with golden tens provided lists of rules requiring players to make many observations before they tried playing. They wanted the players to be skillful. When legal authorities claimed it was a gambling game, the defenders of the game asked the government to prove that players were not using skill. One judge suggested that prosecuting officials would have to show that the players did not do better, or could not do better, than achieving the 92 percent

expected payout. As the golden ten games closed down whenever police or government officials came into the premises, it was difficult to acquire such proof. For over a dozen years, court officials allowed the game to be played and not harassed by the law. In the mid-1990s, judicial policies allowed a more effective enforcement of the law, and most of the games closed down permanently.

Was golden ten a skill game? When the editor interviewed one operator in Rotterdam on July 20, 1986, and asked whether indeed a skillful player could "beat the casino," he was assured that one could. Truly, one could use skill and predict where the ball would fall. When asked what would happen if a player came in and did predict over and over where the ball would fall, the operator paused a bit before replying slowly, "Well, we would have to throw him out." (An option always open to illegal casinos.) In truth, they never had to do so, because no player could pick a winner by any other force than the force of luck.

References

Cabot, Anthony N., William N. Thompson, Andrew Tottenham, and Carl Braunlich, eds. 1999. *International Casino Law*. 3rd ed. Reno: Institute for the Study of Gambling, University of Nevada, Reno, 446–451.

Sifakis, Carl. 1990. *Encyclopedia of Gambling*. New York: Facts on File, 30, 44–45, 252–256.

Silberstang, Edwin. 1980. *Playboy's Guide to Casino Gambling*. Chicago: Playboy Press, 245–348.

Thompson, William N., and J. Kent Pinney. 1990. "The Mismarketing of Dutch Casinos." *Journal of Gambling Behavior* 6: 205–221.

SLOT MACHINES AND MACHINE GAMBLING

THE VALUE OF THE MACHINES

Slot machines are very attractive. They are the devices that usually get amateurs started gambling. They move very fast and they can be quite captivating. This can be quite all right if the gambling is responsible. Certainly, machines add a lot to the entertainment value of many lives. They also shift revenues to employees, as well as to government coffers. Individual slot machines make considerable sums of money for their owners, ranging from about $50 a day ($18,000 plus a year) to more than ten

---

A PERSONAL STORY FROM THE EDITOR

Let me tell you about my introduction to slot machines, an introduction that taught me about beginner's luck. That is what I had the first time I went to a casino in Las Vegas. I was on my job interview at the University of Nevada, Las Vegas, in 1980. The department chairman recruiting me suggested that we go to the Hilton. There I saw bank after bank of slot machines and tables. I indicated a hesitation to play the table games, as I did not know the rules, and they seemed somewhat complicated. Moreover, the games moved very fast, and the players at the tables really looked as if they knew what they were doing. Like other slot machine players, I felt intimidated by the table play. So we found some empty machines. I thought I would just have to put in the coins, so I bought $10 worth of quarters.

The machine asked me a question, however: Did I want to play one, two, or three coins? I had to think about that for a while (something a player cannot do when he sits down at a table game—take a little time to think things over). The machine indicated that with one coin I could win only with cherries; with two, I could win with cherries and other fruit and bells; with three coins, I could win any time the machine showed a winning combination—cherries, fruit, bells, and the jackpot bars. Well, we were educated, smart people (we both had PhDs, and those are not easy to come by). So we figured the jackpot ($100) was just a bit too much to hope for, too much of a "long shot." I would play two coins.

I played the two coins the first time and lost. I played two coins again, the reels spun, and what do you know, one, two, then three bars—jackpot! Bells and whistles, lights, the $100 jackpot sign flashed. The trouble was that no money flowed from the machine. I had not won the jackpot that the machine so proudly proclaimed for the world to see, because I had only put two coins into the machines.

(Continued on next page)

A PERSONAL STORY FROM THE EDITOR, *Continued*

This was bad enough, but soon other people around me were telling me, "Why, you didn't win because you have to put three coins in for a jackpot." I was quite aware of what had happened (PhDs have some intelligence). Then someone else would tell me the same thing. I also heard side comments about that "stupid tourist" who does not know you always put in the maximum number of coins. I had most of my roll of quarters left, so I played on, but with very little enthusiasm. When the coins were gone, I left as quietly as I could.

Beginner's luck? Some might not think so. I certainly did not feel "lucky" at the moment. After I began to study gambling, however, I became quite convinced that that is precisely what I had experienced — beginner's luck.

Just think, within five minutes of my first exposure to slot machines, I had learned that machines were not easy things that could be played without some thought. Indeed, since 1980 the slots have increased in variety and in complexity. I learned that the gambling devices were smarter than I was and that that might have something to do with the fact that they seemed to be taking over the casinos and winning so much money away from the players. I also learned the best lesson any new resident of Las Vegas can ever learn — that the player has to be a loser, or to put it in personal terms, this player (I) was a loser. The lesson has not stopped me from gambling, but it sure has slowed me down. Imagine my potential gambling history had I won $100 after playing $1 in quarters. I shudder to think about it. I have to live in Las Vegas, a city with nearly 200,000 slot machines, and they are everywhere — on the Strip, in locals' casinos, in bars and taverns, restaurants, car washes, liquor stores, convenience stores, drug stores, and supermarkets.

times that much ($200,000 plus a year), depending on where they are found. Yet each machine usually represents an investment of less than $4,000 or $5,000 a year. A machine and related equipment cost from $10,000 to $15,000, and labor and energy costs to operate the machine are minimal, perhaps an equal amount of dollars (supervisors can watch 10 to 20 machines, and a service person can handle 100 machines). These are lifetime costs. The costs can then be divided by a three- to five-year annual cycle. For example, the typical Las Vegas casino machine might cost the operator $5,000 a year to maintain (including all overhead), whereas it produces $35,000 in revenue — that is, it takes $35,000

a year away from the players (even the "smart" ones who know they should put in the maximum three coins each time they play).

In the early days of Las Vegas casinos (the 1930s into the 1970s), slot machines were an extra among the gambling products. The really serious gambling was at the tables, and the machines produced only a small part of the house revenues. Casino owners would say such things as, "They pay the electric bills," or, in a sexist phrase, "They keep the women busy while their men are doing the real gambling at the tables." Now this casual attitude about machines is gone. One discussion of Las Vegas games published in the 1960s told how machines made

Megabucks slot machines feature multi-million dollar jackpots.

about 15 percent of the revenues of the big Strip casinos. Now many Nevada casinos, especially those such as Texas Station that serve local residents or casinos appealing to drive-in gamblers from Phoenix or southern California (e.g., those in Laughlin), bring in over 80 percent of their revenues from machines. Over the past two decades, the machines have also become much more generous to the players, often giving respectable returns of over 95 percent—a gamble as good as that offered at many table games. The higher returns are essential for the success of the machines, as the players of machines are now much more sophisticated—in terms of searching for best payout schedules.

The value of slot machines for the casinos is reflected in the fact that almost all the casino properties in any competitive jurisdiction will give free services (complimentaries) to slot machine players, something they did only for table high rollers in the recent past. Since the mid-1980s, the casinos have instituted "slot clubs," and through magnetic cards they record the amount of play an individual has, then award extra prizes—free meals, free casino stays, free shows, merchandise, and even cash bonuses—based on the player's patronage. In the Harrah's chain of casinos with dozens of locations, there is a single slot club, and players can use their card in any of the casinos to accumulate points for prizes.

If there is a Gresham's law in gambling, it would simply be that slot (and other) machines for gambling will, where permitted, eventually drive out all other forms of gambling. In Europe over the past three decades, country after country has seriously deliberated over issues such as whether the casinos could serve drinks on their gambling floors, whether local residents could enter the casinos, whether casinos could advertise and have signage, and whether the casinos could cash patron's personal checks. Although public officials oversaw such earthshaking measures in order to properly protect the public from this "sin" industry, the same governments with very little deliberation decided that slot machines could go almost anywhere—in taverns, in children's arcades, in seaside recreation halls. Even though Spanish casinos were being "taxed to death" (they pay a gross win tax averaging over 50 percent), more than 500,000 slots filled Spanish restaurants and bars, paying scant taxes. British authorities delayed for years a decision to allow casinos to expand their offerings of two machines to four, while at the same time giving no attention to the fact that gambling halls throughout the urban areas and recreational communities were able to have hundreds of machines. The issue in European gambling is no longer how to apply intricate, detailed regulation to casinos, but just how wide open noncasino machine gambling can become. Or in the case of France, the issue is to what extent will machine gambling be allowed to go within casinos that were prohibited from having them until the late 1980s. In several U.S., Canadian, and other Western Hemisphere jurisdictions, lotteries are finding that their best revenues come from slot machines dispersed throughout their territories and called video lottery terminals. In many of these places, horse and dog racetracks have turned to machines to boost their revenues and have found that slot machines have become their essential business product. More and more, all over the world, the expansion of gambling has become essentially an expansion of machine gambling.

The era of machine gambling seems to have arrived with the 21st century, but the ride of machine gambling from the latest years of the 19th century has been an uneven and rocky journey.

THE HISTORY OF SLOT MACHINES

The notion of using a machine for gambling bounced around in many inventors' heads during the last decade of the 19th century. It was the era of inventions, after all. Gambling contraptions of one sort or another proliferated around San Francisco. There, in 1893, Gustav Frederick Wilhelm Schultze registered a patent for a wheel machine. This gave the

inspiration for Charles August Fey to make a machine with spinning reels. Three years later he put together his final version of a machine that bears a resemblance to today's machine. Fey called his machine the Liberty Bell. It had three reels with bells, hearts, diamonds, spades, and horseshoes. Three bells paid off 10-for-1 in drinks. Schultze challenged Fey's and others' rights to make machines, but he was unsuccessful in having his patent stand up in court, as the validity of gambling machines was questionable.

Fey did not seek to win a patent for his machine. Instead, he sought to guard it by maintaining ownership over each unit he produced. He arranged to place the machines in establishments around San Francisco and other nearby areas, with an arrangement that he would take 50 percent of the revenues from the machine and let the owner of the premises have 50 percent. The process was effective for several years, but according to Fey's grandson, Marshall Fey, in 1905 someone from the Mill's Novelty Company of Chicago secured a machine through unauthorized means and used it as a model for their own machine (Fey 1983). Soon the Mill's company was making a wide line of machines. In 1906 it developed the first machine that stood upright on its own and did not have to be placed on a stand. This machine, called the Kalamazoo, and all others came under the scrutiny of legal enforcement against gambling.

Back in San Francisco, the police chief arrested several owners who had machines on the premises. One was fined but appealed. He won the appeal in the Superior Court, which ruled that the machine games were not lotteries. Police actions were also frustrated by defense allegations that enforcement was hypocritical in that California permitted poker card clubs. Nonetheless, the machine makers were wary of legal crackdowns, and they made several adjustments to try to defend their products. Some adjustments and subterfuges used by the manufacturers over the early days of machines included the following (many of these ruses are still attempted in various places):

- Machines indicated that prizes were paid off as cigars or drinks or other merchandise rather than cash.

- Signs on machines indicated that the machines were *not* gambling machines.

- The machines played music as the coins entered them, and they had signs saying that any coins coming out had to be reinserted to play more music.

- Buttons were placed on the machines, and reels could be stopped from spinning when the buttons were pushed. In this way a skillful player could always win, hence the element of chance was removed and the machines were not gambling machines.

- The machines portrayed game symbols from games that were legal. For instance, they used poker hands in California.

- One of the most ingenuous attempts at seeking to avoid the tag of being a "gambling" machine came early, as machines were developed that would tell the player *exactly* what they would win when they put the next coin in. There was no chance.

Of course, what the player was seeking was a chance to play in order to find out what would come after that. Courts wrestled with definitions of gambling on these kinds of machines for many decades.

- Machines also were configured so that a player would actually get a piece of gum or some other novelty prize with each play, under the ruse that they were buying merchandise from the machine.

Throughout the 20th century, cat-and-mouse games were played among machine owners, operators, police, and the courts. But these games were often quite secondary to the fact that machines were illegal and yet were operating. Public acceptance along with patterns of public bribery and lax law enforcement allowed the machines to proliferate in most locales of the United States. During the years of national prohibition of alcoholic beverages, mobsters gained control over the placement of many machines, and accordingly, the machines became associated with organized crime in the minds of many law enforcement people. As gambling became legalized in many forms, such an association caused policymakers to leave machines out of the mix of legalized gambling products. Even down to the current day, the biggest battles over the scope of Native American gambling permitted under the Indian Gaming Regulatory Act of 1988 has focused upon whether a state has to allow a tribe to have slot machines (or other gambling machines).

Over the years since Fey's first Liberty Bell, the machines did not change much in basic appearance. Although their facades contained many variations, they all had spinning reels. Growth in the number of machines was constant into mid-century. In 1931, a new company in Chicago developed the Ballyhoo pinball machine. Bally's placed more than 50,000 such "skill" machines in bars and restaurants during their first year of operation. The machines allowed players to win more games but not money. In fact, winners could be paid for the number of games they won. Bally's concentrated on these "novelty" machines as its corporate strength grew.

In 1951, the federal government passed the Johnson Act in an attempt to stop illegal gambling machines. The law exempted machines from prosecution if they were in legal jurisdictions, and as a result, many operators moved their businesses to Nevada. The law also caused Bally's to lobby Illinois for permission to make machines. In 1963, Illinois repealed the state prohibition on manufacturing machines. At this time the Mill's company and two others (including Jennings, a spin-off from Mill's), dominated the gambling machine business. This was soon to change, as Bally's entered the field with a new knowledge base about recreational machines and their players. Within 20 years Bally's took over three-quarters of the machine business in the United States.

THE ERA OF BALLY'S, IGT, AND THEIR COMPETITORS

Bally's was the worldwide innovator. It moved machines from being mere mechanical devices activated by pulling a handle to being electromechanical devices. The handle pull was now just an alternative way to push a button to make the machine run. Bally's first machine was the Money Honey, which contained a much larger capacity to store coins, making bigger payoffs more possible. In 1964, Bally's developed a progressive machine, which permitted a jackpot amount to grow each time the player made a losing play. The possibility of winning thousands of dollars on machine play was opened up. Also, the machines could accumulate jackpots large enough that the expected payoff return for a player could become positive (over 100 percent). Soon the company made multipliers, that is, machines that accepted up to five coins; with each additional coin put in, the prizes would multiply. Bally's added reels to some models. In 1968, it marketed a machine that had three play lines on it. In the late 1970s, it developed low-boy machines that had flat horizontal playing surfaces, over which the player could lean. Eventually, this style of machine was adjusted to be operational on a bar surface. Bally's also developed the popular Big Bertha, an extremely large machine (six to eight feet across) that would dominate a casino floor, drawing attention to slot machine play. In 1980, Bally's engineered another breakthrough. It linked machines together so that several could offer one very big progressive jackpot. The Hilton casinos of Las Vegas used these networks of machines to offer million-dollar guaranteed Pot of Gold jackpots.

The 1980s were not kind to Bally's. It entered the casino business as an owner of an Atlantic City casino and then several casinos in Nevada. Other casinos became somewhat reluctant to buy Bally's products and thereby display the name of a competitor of their gambling floors. But more importantly, the computer age had descended, and Bally's was hesitant to make the leap. One of Bally's sales executives, Si Redd, worked on the development of a video gambling device with a cathode-ray tube. Poker could be played on his device. He wanted Bally's to market the machine and give him the appropriate credit. Bally's higher executives, however, did not want to stray from their "winning formula" from the 1960s and 1970s. They struck a deal: Si Redd would leave the company and promise not to make any machines that would compete with the Bally's models nor to use knowledge he had gained at Bally's. In return, Redd would be given a five-year exclusive right to develop his poker machine. Redd became instrumental in starting International Gaming Technologies (IGT), which manufactured and sold video poker machines. Five years was all he needed. By the mid-1980s, IGT surpassed Bally's in machine sales, and after IGT won the right to make reel machines as well, it thoroughly dominated the market, with over 75 percent of the sales of machines in the United States and Canada. IGT now stands as perhaps the largest slot machine company in the world, sharing that world market stage with Aristocrat and Sigma.

Computer technologies and cathode-ray tube video screens have changed the look and operations of machines in many ways. When California authorized a state lottery in 1984, Nevada casinos were worried. They could not compete with a multi-million-dollar jackpot; IGT came to the rescue. The company developed Megabucks, a statewide network of machines offering one progressive jackpot. Although the jackpot has never risen to the levels of some lottery jackpots, it has gone over $20 million several times, and it keeps many Nevada regulars from running to the state line to buy California tickets—at least until the California jackpots get really high. The Megabucks network includes upward of 1,000 machines. Within casinos there are many other linked networks of machines.

Modern machines developed by IGT, Sigma, Bally's, Anchor, Mikohn, and other companies have also incorporated additional features. One machine has holograms in its displays. One blackjack machine features a three-dimensional dealer who appears to actually deal out cards as he talks to the players, wishing them good luck, congratulating them on wins, consoling them on losses, and urging them to try again. Sigma has simulated a racetrack and horse races. The games have also taken on names of popular nongambling games. Mikohn has a Yahtzee machine. Anchor developed a Wheel of Fortune game involving reel play; when a certain winning combination appears, a wheel above the machine spins for the superjackpot as noises from the television *Wheel of Fortune* game show are heard. There is also a monopoly game. Several casinos have banks of Elvis machines. Although all the machines offer gambling games, with their variety has come a variety of rules, making the machines much more sophisticated than the ones that just asked the player to pull a handle—or decide how many coins to play and then pull a handle.

TABLE 1. Machine Gaming Revenue 1999 (hold %)

	Jan	Feb	Mar	April	May	June	July	Aug	Sept	Oct	Nov	Dec	Ave	Medn	Std Dev
Illinois															
Alton Belle	5.31	5.48	5.43	5.49	5.39	5.66	5.52	5.43	5.16	5.39	5.39	5.25	5.41	5.41	0.13
Par-A-Dice	6.51	6.60	6.49	6.61	6.54	6.61	6.55	6.31	6.79	6.60	6.44	6.24	6.52	6.55	0.15
Rock Island	7.44	7.24	7.46	6.98	6.81	6.84	6.40	6.68	6.22	6.36	6.25	6.65	6.78	6.75	0.44
Empress Joliet	5.60	5.74	6.01	6.12	5.85	5.84	6.04	5.84	5.90	5.75	5.59	5.59	5.82	5.84	0.18
Harrah's Joliet	5.72	5.99	5.77	5.88	5.83	5.80	5.73	5.86	5.97	5.77	5.94	5.91	5.85	5.85	0.09
Players Metropolis	6.77	6.69	6.70	6.44	6.34	5.85	5.70	5.95	5.96	6.06	6.00	6.25	6.23	6.16	0.36
Hollywood Casino	5.50	5.77	5.77	5.70	5.94	5.85	5.89	5.69	5.94	5.86	5.79	5.90	5.80	5.82	0.13
Casino Queen	4.98	4.89	5.01	4.82	4.85	4.82	5.29	5.08	5.19	5.11	5.04	5.03	5.01	5.02	0.15
Grand Victoria	5.22	5.30	5.42	5.46	5.18	5.26	5.29	5.26	5.17	5.30	5.46	5.12	5.29	5.28	0.11
*Total ave. for Illinois	**5.89**	**5.96**	**6.01**	**5.92**	**5.87**	**5.89**	**5.84**	**5.76**	**5.81**	**5.79**	**5.77**	**5.74**	**5.86**	**5.85**	**0.19**
Indiana															
Casino Aztar	8.10	8.60	7.90	7.70	8.04	8.38	8.14	8.00	8.59	8.00	8.00	7.99	8.12	8.02	0.27
Empress Hammond	6.74	6.80	6.80	6.90	6.83	6.80	6.92	6.70	6.74	6.96	6.96	7.13	6.86	6.82	0.12
Grand Victoria	6.01	6.30	6.60	6.20	6.49	6.30	6.58	6.20	6.21	6.46	6.46	6.55	6.36	6.38	0.19
Majestic Star	7.07	7.30	7.00	7.00	6.58	7.10	6.71	6.90	6.91	7.12	7.12	7.08	6.99	7.04	0.19
Trump Casino	6.00	6.30	6.20	6.50	6.65	6.60	6.78	6.60	6.82	6.58	6.58	6.36	6.50	6.58	0.24
Argosy Casino	6.21	6.10	6.00	5.90	6.07	6.00	5.97	5.90	6.01	5.71	5.71	5.64	5.94	5.99	0.17
Blue Chip Casino	6.20	6.30	6.10	6.25	6.20	6.43	6.30	6.12	6.24	6.24	6.11	6.21	6.22	5.99	0.12
Caesars	6.32	6.60	6.80	7.00	6.90	6.60	7.10	6.90	6.96	6.97	5.97	6.79	6.74	6.85	0.33
Harrah's	6.37	6.60	6.70	6.10	6.40	7.00	6.95	6.90	6.83	6.97	5.97	6.70	6.62	6.70	0.35
*Total ave. for Indiana	**6.53**	**6.76**	**6.71**	**6.59**	**6.69**	**6.78**	**6.84**	**6.71**	**6.80**	**6.78**	**6.56**	**6.71**	**6.70**	**6.73**	**0.22**
Iowa															
Ameristar Casino	5.69	5.60	5.87	5.90	6.12	6.43	6.45	6.10	5.90	5.85	5.79	5.92	5.89	5.33	0.32
Catfish Bend	7.68	7.67	7.60	7.53	7.68	7.84	8.06	7.63	7.62	7.37	7.95	6.78	7.62	7.65	0.32
Dubuque Diamond Jo	6.40	6.72	6.40	6.64	6.10	6.24	6.25	6.47	6.25	6.03	6.11	6.41	6.34	6.33	0.21
Harvey's Iowa	5.86	5.80	5.74	5.84	5.72	5.88	5.99	5.61	5.76	5.86	5.84	5.98	5.82	5.84	0.11

Casino	1	2	3	4	5	6	7	8	9	10	11	12	13	Average*	Std. Dev.**
Lady Luck Casino	6.11	6.31	6.23	6.21	5.95	6.19	6.21	6.19	6.25	6.17	6.26	6.06	6.18	6.20	0.36
Miss Marquette	6.32	6.84	6.89	6.64	5.74	5.86	6.59	6.35	6.76	6.53	6.53	6.41	6.46	6.53	0.18
Mississippi Belle 2	7.03	7.33	7.07	6.76	7.12	6.95	7.21	7.21	7.40	7.01	7.19	7.32	7.13	7.16	0.17
President Casino	6.38	6.60	6.56	6.34	6.46	6.47	6.62	6.17	6.32	6.38	6.51	6.07	6.41	6.42	0.17
Belle of Sioux City	6.83	7.50	7.10	7.27	6.34	6.84	6.94	6.80	6.84	6.78	6.51	6.91	6.89	6.84	0.31
*Total ave. for Iowa	**6.44**	**6.72**	**6.58**	**6.57**	**6.33**	**6.49**	**6.70**	**6.54**	**6.59**	**6.45**	**6.53**	**6.41**	**6.53**	**6.54**	**0.23**
New Jersey															
Hilton	7.60	7.70	8.20	8.10	8.10	8.40	8.40	8.10	8.10	8.70	8.30	8.00	8.14	8.10	0.30
Park Place	8.30	8.50	8.40	8.50	8.20	8.10	8.10	8.00	8.30	8.20	8.10	7.90	8.22	8.20	0.19
Caesars Casino	7.80	8.20	8.00	7.80	8.50	8.40	8.00	8.50	8.30	7.90	7.90	8.80	8.18	8.10	0.33
Claridge Casino	8.70	8.70	9.20	8.50	8.00	9.70	8.00	9.20	9.80	10.00	8.60	8.50	8.91	8.70	0.67
Harrah's Casino	7.40	7.50	7.40	7.90	7.30	7.70	7.50	7.70	7.70	7.60	7.70	7.60	7.58	7.60	0.17
Resorts Casino	9.20	9.40	9.60	10.01	9.70	9.60	9.30	9.30	9.30	9.20	8.90	8.60	9.34	9.30	0.37
Sands Casino	8.00	8.30	8.10	8.40	8.20	7.90	8.20	8.80	7.90	8.00	8.00	7.90	8.14	8.05	0.26
Showboat Casino	9.00	8.90	8.80	8.80	8.90	9.00	9.10	9.30	9.20	9.20	9.10	8.70	9.00	9.00	0.19
Tropicana Casino	7.30	7.60	8.10	8.10	8.00	8.10	8.00	7.90	7.80	7.90	8.00	7.80	7.88	7.95	0.24
Trump Plaza	7.80	8.10	8.10	8.20	8.10	8.00	8.20	8.10	7.90	8.00	7.90	7.70	8.01	8.05	0.16
Taj Mahal Casino	7.90	8.30	8.20	8.30	8.40	8.30	8.10	8.60	8.50	8.20	8.10	8.00	8.24	8.25	0.20
Trump Marina	n/a	8.50	8.30	8.20	7.90	7.90	7.90	8.00	8.00	7.80	8.00	8.00	8.05	8.00	0.21
*Total ave. for New Jersey	**8.09**	**8.31**	**8.37**	**8.40**	**8.28**	**8.43**	**8.23**	**8.46**	**8.40**	**8.39**	**8.22**	**8.13**	**8.31**	**8.28**	**0.27**
Averages four states	**6.74**	**6.94**	**6.92**	**6.87**	**6.79**	**6.90**	**6.89**	**6.90**	**6.87**	**6.85**	**6.77**	**6.75**	**6.85**	**6.85**	**0.23****

*These are averages of the monthly average for each casino.

**The standard deviation represents 3.35% of the total averages.

Source: Based on information in various issues of *Casino Journal*.

CHARACTERISTICS OF MACHINE GAMBLING

Machine gambling is essentially a house-banked gambling operation. Certainly the player is wagering against a machine. As many states have lotteries or allow only games such as bingo that are played among players, the states have sought to keep Native American tribes from having slot machines of the type that are found in casinos. For instance, in California, the state spent a decade fighting the tribes, insisting that the tribes had to have only machines that were linked together so that players had to electronically pool their money, from which 95 percent—or some percent— could be awarded as prizes. Only the voters who passed Proposition 1A in March 2000 were able to change the situation, and now by popular approval the tribes have slot machines. In the state of Washington many tribes agreed to have these pooled arrangements for their machines. Although the state may seek some legal technicality that makes pools acceptable and regular slot play unacceptable, the players will have a hard time telling the difference. Moreover, the state is doing a major disservice to the notion that the player should be given an equal chance to make the big win on every play as he is in Las Vegas, rather than having a list of winning prizes that diminishes every time a player takes a win. In Las Vegas and other places with regular slot machines, the machines have random number generators that are activated with each play. The player has the same chance of winning a jackpot, a line of bells, bars, or other prizes with every single pull, and the casinos could conceivably lose on every single pull. It is called gambling, after all.

The reality is, however, that the law of large numbers applies to slot machine play, and the payout rates are very consistent over time. Table 1 shows the rates of returns for each of the casinos in New Jersey, Illinois, Indiana, and Iowa over each month of 1999. Even if the state mandated a specific return, as it does for a lottery or for a bingo game, the returns could not be much more consistent. Note that some states and casinos have better returns than others—actually Las Vegas casinos offer the best returns—consistently over 95 percent. In no way does the different return amount come from any manipulation of the computer randomizer chip in the machines. Quite simply it comes from the payoff schedule. Two machines can have exactly the same play dimensions, but payout percentage returns to the player can differ greatly simply by setting the win for a certain configuration (say three bells) at 18 rather than 20, or on a poker machine making the wins for flush and full house 5 and 8 instead of 6 and 9. Sophisticated players know the machines, and they can discern the best payout machines by simply looking at the prizes listed on the front of the machines. For obvious reasons, payoffs are better at the higher-denomination machines. A five-cents machine may cost as much to buy as a dollar machine; therefore the casino expects that it needs to hold a higher percentage of the money played on the nickel machines. Actually today all the big casinos have very high denomination machines; indeed, several have machines that take $500 tokens in play—and to win the best prizes on these machines, the player has to play three coins a pull.

Machines have appeal to both the player and the operator. In most cases they can be played alone. The player can study the machine before playing it. It is unusual that a player will criticize the way another person plays, and with a little study machine playing is easy to learn. Operators like machines because they do not involve much labor, they are very secure (although cheating has been a historical problem), and they can be left alone to do their job without complaining.

Machine play is the bread and butter for most casinos around the world. Machine gambling offers opportunities pursued by many lotteries and offers the golden hope (or silver bullet) that many feel can save the horseracing industry. Machines have also crawled into Nevada convenience and grocery stores, and if policymakers allow them, they will be in bars and taverns across the country, all across the globe. It could easily be predicted that machine gambling is the wave of gambling in the future, but now the Internet has come onto the scene, and perhaps it is that machine that will soon be the most lucrative and alluring gambling device.

The assistance of William Holmes in providing resources and advice on this section is appreciated.

References

Fey, Marshall. 1983. *Slot Machines: An Illustrated History of America's Most Popular Coin-Operated Device.* Las Vegas: Nevada Publications.

Holmes, William L. 1987. "Effect of Gambling Device Laws: Foreign and United States." Paper presented to the Seventh International Conference on Gambling and Risk Taking, August 23, Reno, Nevada.

Scarne, John. 1986. *Scarne's New Complete Guide to Gambling.* New York: Simon and Schuster, 430–458.

TRENTE ET QUARANTE (30 AND 40)

Trente et quarante has been a very popular game in Continental European casinos, especially in France, where the game was developed. It is a simple luck game that gives the player a very good expected return of more than 98 percent. All the bets are even-money bets. The dealer uses a six-deck shoe. Cards are given their number value; aces count as 1, and face cards count as 10. The dealer deals out two rows of cards. The first row is called *noir* (black); the second row is called *rouge* (red). Cards are dealt until each row has a collective card value between 31 and 40. For instance, the dealer deals a 6 of hearts, 10, queen, 3, and 8 for a total of 37 for the first (noir) row. Then he or she deals a 9, jack, ace, 5, and 7 for a total of 32 on the second (rouge) row. The row with the lower number (closest to 31) wins. In this example, the rouge row wins. Players betting on rouge win even money; for example. $100 on a $100 bet. The players may also make an even-money bet on whether or not the first card dealt (the 6 of hearts) has the same color as the winning line (rouge). As the heart is red, and the winning line is red, those betting "color" (yes) win. Those betting "inverse" (no) lose that bet. If the two lines tie, there is no bet, unless there is a tie on the number 31. Then the house takes half of all bets, giving the house a small edge of about 1.1 percent.

A side bet of 1 percent of the original stake (ergo, $1) may be made to ensure that the 31 tie situation does not arise. If this insurance bet is placed and there is a 31 tie, the player does not lose half of his or her bet and keeps his or her insurance bet. If there is no 31 tie, the player loses the insurance bet, but the other bets are paid as if there were no insurance side bet. The insurance bet reduces the house edge to 0.9 percent. (If the casino requires an insurance bet in excess of 1 percent, it increases its edge, and players are wise to avoid the bet). There is a 2.19 percent chance that there will be a 31 tie.

Being a simple game with easily tracked results, trente et quarante attracts system bettors. The low house edge also makes the game very desirable for high rollers. It is also a fast game, making the table one of the most exciting places in the staid European casino halls.

References

Scarne, John. 1986. *Scarne's New Complete Guide to Gambling.* New York: Simon and Schuster, 515–518.

Sifakis, Carl. 1990. *Encyclopedia of Gambling.* New York: Facts on File, 295–296.

TWO UP

Two up is a popular game in Australia. It was played briefly at the Main Street Station casino in downtown Las Vegas during the 1990s. It is a very simple game that involves tossing two coins in the air and watching them make their random falls to the floor. Its social setting provides the action in the game. A group of players surrounds a person who is selected to toss the coins using a special stick. Players can bet that two heads or two tails will come up. If the two coins are different—odds—there is no decision, and they are tossed again.

When two heads or two tails are the correct bet, the payoff is even money. If five odds come up in a row, however, all players lose. All persons in the circle around the coin tosser may make bets. The players may bet that heads or tails will come up three times in a row, and if they do, players are paid off at 7.5 to 1, for a 6.25 percent house advantage (odds are ignored in the sequence).

Reference

Schwartz, David G. 2006. *Roll the Bones.* New York: Gotham, 233–234.

Section Three

BIOGRAPHIES OF LEADING FIGURES IN GAMBLING

ADELSON, SHELDON

During the 1990s, Sheldon Adelson became one of the leading entrepreneurs in the gambling industry as the primary developer and owner of the Venetian Casino resort on the Las Vegas Strip.

Adelson was born in 1933 in Boston, the son of a cab driver. He worked hard and studied hard as a youth. He received a bachelor's degree in real estate and corporate finance from the City University of New York. After a period of service in the United States Army, Adelson set upon a plan to make himself fabulously rich. He succeeded more than one time. As a venture capitalist in the 1960s, he acquired scores of companies, only to see his budding financial empire fall as the stock market took a plunge in 1969. He came back by developing a series of trade shows, the most important of which was COMDEX, a popular computer dealers' exposition, which by the 1980s became the leading annual convention in Las Vegas each year. The success of the show led to other ventures such as developing airlines. That success also focused his attention upon Las Vegas. The convention was a gold mine for Adelson, but even Las Vegas did not have enough convention space. He privately built a facility next to the Las Vegas Convention Center and gave it to the county, realizing that the revenues from his big show would cover his capital costs in a few years. But he wanted more—his own convention center.

In the late 1980s, Sheldon Adelson was able to finance the purchase of the Sands Casino Hotel from its owner,

Kirk Kerkorian. In 1989, it was licensed by the Nevada Gaming Commission, and Adelson became a casino magnate. Actually he was just holding on to the property waiting for something bigger. In 1993, he built the Sands Exposition Center, a one-million-square-foot convention facility on the Sands property. But he was still waiting for something bigger. His chance to "do something" with the Sands came in 1995 when he was able to sell the COMDEX show and 16 other trade shows for $860 million. The next year he imploded (blew-up) the Sands, and he devoted his new resources to the construction of the Venetian Hotel. The Venetian opened in April 1999, with a 113,000-square-foot casino, a shopping mall set alongside canals with gondolas, and 500,000 feet of new convention space. The hotel's 33-story tower and 3,000 rooms featured luxuries not found elsewhere. The basic room was over 700 square feet, making it the largest standard room for a hotel anywhere. The total square footage of the rooms actually exceeded that of the MGM Grand, with its 5,009 rooms. The facility had a first-phase price tag of $1.5 billion "plus." The "plus" was the result of the fact that others paid the price. Adelson leased all the space for shops and restaurants, keeping only the casino, hotel, and meeting areas under his financial control.

As the new century began, the revenues for the casino were meeting all expectations and then some, and

Adelson planned a phase-two construction that included a museum and a new casino and hotel tower with 3,036 rooms, located next to the Venetian. The new tower, called the Palazzo, opened in 2007, while the museum came and went. The early decade of the 21st century started very well for Adelson as he won one of three licenses to develop casinos in Macau. In 2004, he opened the first American-owned casino on the Chinese enclave. A second casino was opened in 2007. In 2006, Adelson was granted a license for a new casino in Singapore, scheduled to open in 2009. The casino magnate also has opened a casino in Bethlehem, Pennsylvania.

Adelson made a public offering of stock in his company in 2004, and quickly emerged as one of the richest men in the world—the third wealthiest in the United States. In the latter part of the decade, however, the heavy debt load of his new projects accompanied by the global economic depression led to discussions about possible bankruptcy for his company, and reduced his standing to number 73 on the list of America's most wealthy.

BENAZET, JACQUES, AND EDWARD BENAZET

The father and son team of Jacques and Edward Benazet are prominent in world gambling history for overseeing the Baden-Baden casino during its most glorious years in the mid-19th century.

The careers of the Benazet family—like those of many giants in the casino industry—were tied to politics and the legal decrees of governments. Jacques Benazet was born in Foix, France, in 1778. In his early life he was a clerk in the commercial court. Later he was a lawyer. He used his position as counsel in a dispute to seize the opportunity to purchase a casino at the Palais Royal in Paris in 1827. There he thrived until the French Chamber of Deputies decided to close all the country's casinos at the end of 1837. As the closing date became eminent, Jacques and his son Edward were made aware that a German casino in Baden-Baden was not performing well. They knew that its fate was about to turn around as wealthy French gamers would be anxious to find a location for their habits. They jumped at the chance to purchase the property at a low price. They took over Baden-Baden and began making improvements and expanding its rooms. They developed the facility into the finest casino of its era. Even today, Baden-Baden may claim to be the most elegant casino anywhere.

In 1848, Jacques died and his son became the head of operations. A decade later he opened a racetrack in Baden-Baden. The casino and location remained a top tourist location in Europe until it was closed by the Bismarck government in 1872.

BENNETT, BILL, AND BILL PENNINGTON

Bill Bennett and Bill Pennington purchased the Circus Circus casino from Jay Sarno in 1974. They immediately transformed a losing property into a "winner," as they parlayed the investment into one of the most successful casino companies in the world.

Bennett was born in Glendale, Arizona, on November 26, 1924. Following his service in World War II as a pilot, he returned to Phoenix to run a furniture store. Soon, however, a friend coaxed him into investing in a financial firm. The firm went broke and so did Bennett. Luck was on his side, however, as his friend L. C. Jacobsen was president of the Del Webb Construction Company. Jacobsen was looking for personnel who could help in the company's newly acquired casino properties. Bennett signed on and worked his way up to a top management post with the Mint Hotel in Las Vegas. In 1971, he cashed in his stock options with Webb and entered into a partnership with Bill Pennington. The two established a company that distributed gaming machines to casinos. In 1974, they found Jay Sarno in deep financial trouble, and they helped bail him out by taking over the Circus Circus casino in a lease option deal.

Bennett and Pennington liked the Circus Circus idea, but the two believed that the property needed changes. They first made plans for a tower of hotel rooms and cleaned up many carnival games that at best would be considered "sleazy." Circus acts were moved away from the gambling tables. They marketed the property heavily through radio advertisements and dropped Sarno's notion that Circus Circus could appeal to high rollers. Instead, they nurtured and developed the idea of marketing the property to middle-class patrons—lots of them. The new owners placed a much greater emphasis on their slot machine department than it had received previously. The property also began sponsoring many sporting events. Bennett was a stunt pilot, and he rode motorcycles and speedboats. Soon Circus Circus had a hydroplane boat on the professional racing circuit.

Bennett and Pennington also reached out to develop new properties. They built Circus Circus–Reno in 1978, and they purchased the Edgewater Casino in Laughlin, Nevada, in 1983. Later they added the Colorado Belle. In 1983, Circus Circus became a public company. Over the next 10 years, the stock outperformed all others in the casino gambling field. Values of shares increased 1,400 percent. Pennington retired in 1988.

The 1990s were good to Circus Circus, although the company was not always good to Bill Bennett. At the beginning of the decade, the company opened the largest hotel casino in the world. The Excalibur featured a medieval court with the knights of the round table. The facility had 4,000 rooms and was built at a cost exceeding $250 million. In 1993, the Luxor, a pyramid-shaped casino hotel with 2,500 rooms, opened, and the next year a Circus Circus casino opened in Tunica, Mississippi. In 1994, several management changes accompanied lower-than-anticipated revenues at the upscale Luxor property, and Bennett was roundly criticized by an organized opposition at an annual stockholders' meeting. He decided to step down as chairman of the board, ultimately leaving the company completely. He sold his stock for $230 million and promptly purchased the Sahara Hotel for $193 million. He knew the Sahara, as it had originally been a Del Webb casino. Now it was aging and in bad repair. Bennett invested millions more in improvements and in the construction of a new tower of hotel rooms. Working to the end, he died on December 22, 2002, in Las Vegas.

Of course Las Vegas needs dreamers and builders like Jay Sarno, and it needs people like Howard Hughes, who will purchase properties others wish to get rid of. But it especially needs persons who will take others' dreams and convert them into reality for stockholders and customers. In the gambling industry, Bennett was not just a dreamer—he was one who made dreams come true.

Bennett, William J.

William J. Bennett (1943–) has been an outspoken champion of virtues in our society. At the same time he has displayed a severe human weakness: he has been an excessive casino gambler. Many may suggest that he was a problem gambler, a pathological gambler, or a compulsive gambler. The efficacy of using these terms should be open for discussion. That his gambling was excessive, however, and that it has exposed him, rightly or wrongly, to being labeled a hypocrite is not debatable.

Bennett was born into a Roman Catholic family in Brooklyn and moved to Washington, D.C., during his childhood. He attended Catholic schools growing up and later received his undergraduate education at Williams College. He went on to receive a doctorate in philosophy from the University of Texas and later earned a law degree from Harvard. He taught philosophy at the University of Southern Mississippi and was on the faculty of Boston University. He is married and has two sons.

In his public career, Bennett has held positions as the director of the National Endowment for the Humanities and Secretary of Education. He also served as the head of President George H. W. Bush's program on drug policy ("The Drug Czar"). After this service he became a commentator on national radio and television, sharing his views on a variety of public events. He strongly advocates personal responsibility, as well as the need to hold people accountable for breaches of high moral standards. He was one of President Bill Clinton's strongest critics during the president's impeachment trial and in the ensuing controversy over his moral lapses.

In 1988, Bennett wrote *The Death of Outrage: Bill Clinton and the Assault on American Morals*. He has written more than 10 other books, most notably *The Book of Virtues: A Treasury of Great Moral Stories* (1993), a collection of stories about people performing virtuous acts. His book lists 10 major virtues: self-discipline, compassion, responsibility, friendship, work, courage, perseverance, honesty, loyalty, and faith. Within the pages, however, he has but one collateral reference to gambling. Surprisingly, it is not a negative reference. Indeed it is a positive one. He quotes Rudyard Kipling's poem "If," offering that the losing gambler is demonstrating good virtues by accepting the results without complaint or remorse.

After being exposed in 2003 for losing as much as $8 million at video poker machines in Atlantic City and Las Vegas, Bennett exercised model behavior in the context offered by Kipling. He did not complain. He showed little remorse as he indicated that he had met all his obligations to his family and society. He was a rich man. He wasn't betting "the milk money." His behavior had been consistent with the moral outlook of his religion, Catholicism (*see* Religion and Gambling). Although he has been called "The Bookie of Virtue," he has shunned the label of "hypocrite." He did admit that his play was excessive, and he indicated that he would seek help for his problem gambling. For a short period, William Bennett's commentary was not heard on national radio and television, but he eventually returned to offer his message that public policy makers should be virtuous.

Reference

Bennett, William J. 2003. *The Book of Virtues: A Treasury of Great Moral Stories.* New York: Simon and Schuster.

BINION, BENNY, AND JACK BINION

For over four decades, Benny Binion was a local hero in Las Vegas; actually, he was a hero among the gambling community worldwide. He was known as the "Cowboy Gambler," who—like his image in bronze on a horse at Second and Ogden streets in downtown Las Vegas—always rode "high in the saddle." His casino, Binion's Horseshoe, gained the reputation for being the "gamblers' casino" in Las Vegas. His casino started the World Series of Poker, and his casino was the only one that would take a "hit" for any amount of money. A hit is a single bet on a single play (*see* Glossary). It is a bet where both sides let it all ride, one time, one spin of the wheel, and one whirl of the dice—no next time, one time. Most casinos will limit hits to the normal table limits—several thousands of dollars. Binion's had no limit. The limit was what the player was willing to lay down on the table in hard cash. Hits are risky business, because the laws of probability are based upon large numbers—large numbers of bets. One time a gambler came into Binion's Horseshoe with a suitcase of money. He opened the suitcase and poured $777,000 onto the table. He bet on "don't pass" on the craps table. The dice rolled a few times, and the boxman called out "don't pass wins." The cage prepared a stack of cash worth $1,554,000, and the gambler took the money and left. If a casino that was owned by a publicly traded corporation did something so risky, a stockowner lawsuit might just be successful. But Binion's was privately held by the Binion family so they were able to offer such bets. And maybe they were not being too risky, because the publicity they received for paying off the bet was also worth a whole lot of money. The same man came back and later bet $1,000,000 and lost. So in the long run, it actually had been good business. (Three months later the man committed suicide. He was broke, but the police said he had romantic problems, too.)

The editor of these volumes did a few shots for the PBS show *Going Places: Las Vegas*. When he and Al Roker went into a casino on the Strip, people were crowding the cameras, waving their hands and calling out "Hi, mom" and the like. But when they went into the Horseshoe, they shot an interview with the poker pit directly behind us. The producers did not have to make a double take, nor did they have to wait for the place to be quiet or for a distracting guest to move on. They shot the interview and not one single bettor even lifted his eyes to observe the network cameras. The bettors were more interested in the action on the table. On the Strip, the action might have been a television camera; in the Horseshoe, the action was the next card being dealt.

Over the decades that Benny Binion reigned as the cowboy gambler, and when he and his wife and sons ran the casino, other gambling entrepreneurs came to Binion's when they wanted to gamble. It was their local casino. Called the "most popular gambler" in the United States, Binion was especially popular with his fellow casino owners. He did not cater to tourists, except the hard-core gambling kind. He had no show, no music, and no two-for-one "fun book." He did not have people out in the streets hawking the wares, trying to get the sucker in the door. His players were not suckers. He gave the best odds on the table games, offering all the options in blackjack and giving ten times odds for even bets at craps. His machines were programmed to give the largest payouts in Las Vegas—and Las Vegas gives the best payouts of any gambling city in the world.

Benny Binion's one concession to the tourists was a plastic-covered horseshoe display of $1 million dollars in cash: he had mounted 100 ten-thousand-dollar bills. He invited the public to come in and look and to have their picture taken with the money at no cost. When the editor saw that, his head began to spin numbers around, figuring that Binion was losing a couple hundred dollars a day just in the interest the money could be earning in a bank. But then, maybe the money was in a bank, and maybe he could not be earning the interest. The Nevada gambling regulators demand that large casinos have several millions of dollars on hand at all times in order to cover any large win that a player (perhaps with a suitcase) may have at any moment. Las Vegas builds its reputation on paying off, and the reputation could disappear quickly if there was a pattern of casinos making players wait until the "other" banks opened before they got their money. After all, when the player loses, the casino takes the money right away (well, there are credit gamblers too). The million on display may just have been part of the cage requirement, and Binion would also have been out the interest if he had had the money locked in a vault. Moreover, with the extra security (and the money was well guarded) of having the displayed million dollars, other casinos could always count on Binion's having surplus funds. When other casinos hit a run of bad luck and their reserves fell below what the law requires, very often they would send a special security detail up to the Horseshoe to borrow a million or two, just to tide them over until the other banks opened. Rumor has it that Steve Wynn, as the executive of the Golden Nugget across the street from the Horseshoe, had to do just that.

Benny Binion was born in Pilot Point, Grayson County, Texas, in 1904. When he was 15 years old, he dropped out of school and ran away, first to El Paso and then to Dallas. He got a job in the St. George Hotel, and there he learned about gambling. When in his later years he was asked if he would do it again, he said yes, he would have had to become a gambler: "What else could an uneducated person do?" Dallas was a wide-open town, a place of opportunity. At age 22, Benny opened a casino game at the Southland Hotel, and two years later he established a leadership role in the Dallas numbers games. Things in Dallas were rough, and the competition could be tough. Although the government tolerated games for a price (he paid $10 a gambler to the politicians in order to stay open), others wanted him closed. In two separate instances he was in gun battles over just who would stay open; he survived. Two others died and were never able to spin the wheels of fortune again. One of those times Binion received a suspended sentence; he was acquitted on grounds of self-defense the other time. During World War II he bought a casino in Fort Worth, but its time was limited. There was a crackdown on Texas gambling after the war. There had been 27 casinos in the Dallas area during the war, and some felt they could stay and try to ride it out until another election could bring the right people to office. Binion did not; he packed up his family in 1946 and went to Las Vegas.

In Las Vegas, Benny Binion opened a casino on Fremont Street along with Kell Houssels, a man who was actively involved in many casinos. As time went on, however, Binion felt that he was being restricted on doing things the way he wanted to do things. Houssels did not like the idea of allowing the players to have high limits. Some professional operators figure that with high limits, the players can use a system called the Martingale, which allows them to keep doubling their bets when they lose, and eventually they will win. But Binion knew (and it was a risk as to when) that streaks or runs of a wheel on black or red, odd or even very often can go five, six, seven, or more in length. Increasing the odds only allows one or two more bets against a fate of losing.

Binion broke up the partnership, and in 1951 he bought the Apache Hotel, renaming it Binion's Horseshoe. His limits became the highest limits in town. On one occasion the Mob leaders at the Flamingo did persuade Binion that he should not try to compete with them too vigorously, and Binion lowered his keno limit for a while.

Binion's problems with the law did not end when he came to Las Vegas. In the mid-1950s, he was convicted of income tax evasion and served 42 months in a federal prison. When he was released in 1957, the state of Nevada suspended his casino license, and management of the Horseshoe was given to his wife and his son Jack. Jack carried on the tradition of Benny Binion when he established the World Series of Poker in 1970. The tournament has grown considerably since that time. All players must put up $10,000 to enter. The winner collects a million dollars. Amateurs from every corner of the globe come to compete with the most professional of all gamblers. The editor of these volumes was in Birmingham, England, touring casinos, when he came upon the Rainbow, which displayed a big sign and a program for Binion's World Series. The casino ran the British Poker Championship, and the first prize was an all-expense paid trip to Las Vegas with the stakes to enter Binion's World Series.

On June 1, 1988, the Horseshoe empire spread out a bit, and the Binion family purchased the next-door Mint Casino from the Del Webb estate for $27 million. The Horseshoe Casino expanded its gambling area and also gained 300 hotel rooms. Previously, the Horseshoe had fewer than 100 rooms. The Horseshoe also took over the restaurant at the top of the Mint, and it became the Steakhouse. There the finest beef, nurtured on Binion's Montana ranch, was served. The casino was also able to expand its complimentary services with the larger facility. Over $1 million worth of free food was given to selected players each month. Rarely did the casino charge a full price room rate. Most rooms were frequently occupied by very good players.

On Christmas Day 1989, Benny Binion went on to "cowboy heaven," and he left his family in charge of the gambling on Fremont Street. Jack Binion, who was born in 1937, carried on. He also branched out, establishing the number-one riverboat casino in Louisiana and then the number-one revenue-producing casino in Tunica, Mississippi. He also become a partner in an Illinois riverboat. Family fights interrupted the business after Benny's wife, Teddy, died in 1994. Jack's brother, Ted, was involved with substance abuse problems and lost his casino license. He later died suspiciously. It was charged that he was murdered by a former girlfriend and her new boyfriend, who were seeking Ted's wealth. One criminal trial resulted in their conviction, but in a retrial they were found "not guilty." Two sisters fought Jack over control of the casino, and finally Jack sold the downtown Las Vegas property to one of his sisters and devoted his full attention to gambling interests in the Mississippi Valley. That property was subsequently sold to Harrah's. Harrah's also took over Jack's riverboat interests in 2003 in exchange for $1.45 billion.

BLANC, FRANCOIS, AND LOUIS BLANC

Twin brothers Francois and Louis Blanc were born on December 12, 1806, in Copurtezon, France. Like the celebrated Benazet family, who owned casinos in France and later in Germany, the Blancs were influenced by political forces in France and Germany. They were driven out of the banking industry in Bordeaux as a result of a criminal conviction in 1837. The brothers had used bribery to gain the cooperation of operators of a government communication system in order to get advanced information from Paris on securities prices. After avoiding prison and paying a fine for bribery and corruption, they ventured to Paris. There they met up with the Benazets and became sensitized to the opportunities available in casino gambling—first in the gambling booths of the Palais Royal, and then outside of France. In 1838 they took control of a gambling hall in Luxembourg, and two years later they jumped at a chance to set up shop in Homburg, a small town near Frankfort, Germany. They opened a casino in 1841, and over the next two decades Louis and Francois Blanc developed the gaming rooms into some of the most appealing ones in Europe, even competing with the elegant tables at Baden-Baden for patronage of the most wealthy players. Louis died in 1852, leaving Francois and later his son Camille to take over the legacy.

The Blancs developed the hot springs of Homburg, and they built a theater, restaurants, luxurious hotels, and a ballroom that could hold over a thousand revelers. The games were made more competitive by policies allowing virtually unlimited bets. The casinos also opened all year round. An innovation of the time, their roulette wheels had only one zero, cutting in half their margins of chance over the players.

Because parts of Germany—notably Prussia, which did not yet control Homburg—were banning gambling, Francois Blanc thought it best to seek greater opportunities elsewhere. He recognized that even though his tables were open all year, his patrons left for the warmer shores of the Mediterranean in wintertime. Gambling was banned in France and Italy on the sea coast; however, in the tiny, remote, rocky principality of Monaco it was legal—if players could get there. The impoverished government of Monaco needed something, and its ruler Prince Charles III wanted a casino. Until he met Francois Blanc in 1856, Charles could not find an investor who had sufficient funds to do the job. A deal was struck between the two.

Blanc gave Charles an upfront sum of 1.7 million francs (worth about $15 million U.S. today), a promise to build facilities, and a promise of 10 percent of all profits over the course of a 50-year concession. In 1866, the grand casino building was finished, and soon afterwards the new Hotel de Paris and the Café de Paris. However, the key element in the investment was the completion of a railway from Monaco to Nice in 1868, linking the casino to all of Europe.

Following the closure of the main German casinos in 1872 (and all German casinos in 1877), Monaco had a monopoly over all European casino gambling until 1907, when limited gambling was authorized once more for France (but not Paris). Francois Blanc died in 1872, and all operations were transferred into the hands of his son Camille. In the 15 years that he ran the show, Francois Blanc amassed a fortune of what would be equal to a half billion U.S. dollars today—all from the gambling activity of Monaco.

BOYD, SAM, AND WILLIAM BOYD

Las Vegas casino owner John Wolfram once told this editor how he sat in a car way out of town, on the Boulder Highway where Flamingo Road began. He was with Sam Boyd, and Sam asked him to look at the cars and count them. Sam told John that each of those cars was worth a dollar, or some such number, that a certain number of cars would pull into a casino if it were located right there. Wolfram said that he was not into that kind of speculation and that he would pass on the offer to buy a piece of the action. Wolfram has been successful in his own smaller casinos; in later years, he owned the Klondike at the far south end of the Strip. Sam Boyd was not only successful: he became a phenomenon in Las Vegas gambling. But it did not start when Sam's Town Hotel and Casino opened at the corners of Nellis, Flamingo, and the Boulder Highway; the seeds of success were planted decades before.

Sam Boyd was born in Enid, Oklahoma, in 1910. His father did well as the owner of a small-town taxicab company, but he died when Sam was only nine years old. Sam's mother was a nurse, who felt that to support her family, she needed a job in a more prosperous location. Eventually, the family relocated to Long Beach, California. Not only did Long Beach have better jobs for those in the medical fields, but it also offered opportunities for other people who liked to "hustle." And as a teenager Sam Boyd came to like hustling a lot. He worked as a barker and a carnival games operator on the Pike. The lessons he learned on how to draw people into games were lessons he would use throughout his lifetime. He came to use "fun books," flags, balloons, parties, anything to make the player feel the game was exciting. He also learned that the operator could make a lot of money if he went after the masses—a few dollars from everyone was worth the same as many dollars from a single player. After the carnival gaming experience, Sam Boyd learned all about casino games on one of the gambling ships that operated out of southern California. He dealt each game. He also became a bingo game operator.

He married Mary Neuman in 1931, and the following year their only child, Bill, was born. Sam always emphasized to Bill that his career would be much better if he received a formal college education. Bill got an undergraduate education, and then he earned a law degree. His "enhanced" career began in a law office, but he soon found that he could be helpful as the attorney for his father's casino interests. He later realized that he could be even more helpful as a casino executive himself. He eventually helped the Boyd organization make the transition to a corporate property with interests in many locations in addition to Las Vegas.

In the late 1930s, Sam Boyd spent five years in Hawaii involved with a variety of bingo establishments. In those short years he came to appreciate the Hawaiian population, with its Asian heritage and love for gambling. This appreciation became the nexus of his marketing efforts when he set up operations in Las Vegas several years later.

Sam came to Las Vegas in 1941, in response to a federal crackdown on gambling in California. His first jobs were in small casinos on Fremont Street. He went on to work at the El Rancho Vegas, the first casino on the Las Vegas Strip. After a tour of duty with the army in World War II, he was employed at the Flamingo, after "Bugsy" Siegel. He also worked in northern Nevada at Lake Tahoe. His son, while a student at the University of Nevada in Reno, worked with him during summers. Sam also held positions at the Sahara and the Thunderbird. Sam Boyd loved working, and he was very diligent about saving as much of his salary as possible. In 1952, he had a chance to buy 1 percent of the Sahara. Hard work habits now became a compulsion. Sam purchased more shares when the Sahara developed the Mint downtown. He kept working and saving. In 1962, Sam, his son, and two others purchased the casino that became the El Dorado in downtown Henderson. In 1971, he became a partner in the Union Plaza casino at the end of Fremont Street. There he was innovative, as he used women as dealers at blackjack games. His goal was to build a player base. He also brought musical plays onto the property.

Sam Boyd took his money out of the Plaza so that he could become the major investor in the California Hotel just off Fremont Street. Quickly the California Hotel became the venue for Hawaiian players. His controlling interests in the California and the property in Henderson necessitated that he drive the 13 miles that separated the two properties each day. (This distance is significant to the editor, after participating in an official mini-marathon race sponsored by the Boyds, which stretched between the doors of the two hotels.) It was on one of these drives that he realized there might be a market among the many cars that were on Boulder Highway each day.

Realtor Chuck Ruthe was on the board of directors of Boyd Casinos and used his expertise to put together the land deal that allowed the construction of Sam's Town and its opening in 1979. Many establishments had previously tried to target local gamblers for their market—most were on Fremont Street, but there was also the Showboat, at the top of Boulder Highway. The Sam Boyd touch, however, made his efforts to get the local gamblers especially lucrative. His Sam's Town ushered in a new genre of Las Vegas casino—the locals' casino. Without Sam's Town showing the way, it is unlikely there would have been an Arizona Charlie's, Santa Fe, Texas, Boulder Station, Fiesta, or Sunset Station. As the 1980s went on, however, Sam Boyd realized that the old management styles would not be totally effective if Boyd's were to expand into a public company and expand into new jurisdictions. He yielded corporate power to his son and enjoyed his final years as an elder statesman representing the days of the personal touch in Las Vegas. He was able to see his company set higher goals under Bill's leadership. Sam Boyd died in 1993, before

the company entered the Tunica, Mississippi, market with the largest hotel in the state, established a riverboat in Missouri, and made a management agreement with a large casino for the Choctaw tribe in Mississippi. In the same year, his son, Bill Boyd, took control of operations and converted the company into a publicly traded entity. Under Bill's leadership the company grew into a national leader with 16 properties in six states and 25,000 employees. Bill Boyd also established himself as a major community leader in Las Vegas with his work for many charities and especially as the moving force financially and otherwise in the creation of the William Boyd School of Law at the University of Nevada, Las Vegas.

CANFIELD, RICHARD

Richard Canfield (1855–1914) rose out of poverty in New Bedford, Massachusetts, to become the leading gambling entrepreneur in the United States at the turn of the 20th century. He was the leading casino owner in New York City, and in 1902 he purchased and rebuilt the Saratoga Club House in Saratoga, New York, bringing it back to the elegance it had displayed when it was the private preserve of Jack Morrissey. As an operator, Canfield never gambled; instead, he enjoyed the finer things of life—wine, art, and fashionable clothing and carriages. He did gamble in his youth, and although the activity helped him economically and gave him a

social standing, it also earned him a short stay in prison as a result of operating a poker joint in Providence, Rhode Island.

Canfield was a student of many things, and when he decided that casino gambling would be a business pursuit, he decided to study gambling in its finest settings. He actually took a year to travel to Europe and examine the many elegant gambling halls in England and on the continent. He was able to utilize his new knowledge when he moved the venue of his operations to New York City. New York was friendlier than Providence, as the police seemed to make their system of noninterference more regularized and reliable.

In New York, Canfield determined that the best gambling money to be made would be money spent by wealthy players, not money spent by immigrants in dives. He offered games to the upper classes, and he was able to woo this clientele with his fine tastes and intellectual banter. Canfield was self-educated and extremely well read, could converse with the most renowned scholars of the day, and certainly was a welcomed host by the best business minds. He gathered partners, and they financed the most exclusive rooms in New York City for gambling. After a decade of operations, however, reformers Charles Parkhurst and Anthony Comstock pressured the city to close down Canfield's casinos.

Rather than resist the police action of 1901 and 1902, Canfield shifted his sights to Saratoga. There he acquired a stable of the finest racehorses, and he stood above all the local casino operators by running the finest casino—the Saratoga Club House. A feature of his house was the cuisine: the best offered in the United States. He discovered the value of loss leaders. Each summer he would lose $70,000 on food operations, much of it going for "comps" to high rollers, but he more than made up for the losses at his tables.

The Saratoga Club House remained in operation as a gambling hall par excellence for only five more years, as the reform movement reached into northern New York in 1907. This time Richard Canfield did not fight history. Rather, he retreated to a life as a Wall Street investor and a collector of fine art works. He was a friend of James Whistler, and the famous artist did Canfield's portrait. Canfield's collection of Whistler and other well-known artists was often displayed in major museums. A man of distinction and fine taste, he died in 1914 in a rather mundane manner, after falling on the steps leading to the New York subway.

CARDANO, GAROLAMO, AND BLAISE PASCAL

Two leading mathematicians and scholars of the 16th and 17th centuries are considered together in one entry because it was their collective (but separately completed) work that impacted greatly on gambling activity, moving it from private pursuits toward much wider commercial activities. Both were statisticians whose revelations about probabilities have been incorporated into the entrepreneurial mindset of gaming industry captains for over three centuries.

Gerolamo Cardano was born in Pavia (Lombardi), Italy, on September 24, 1501. He studied medicine and as a physician is credited as the first man to describe typhoid fever. He was also an astrologer, mathematician, and an avid gambler. Because of a combative personality and quarrels with professional colleagues and often authorities, he found he could not sell his services to clients; ergo, he was often broke. At these times, he turned to gambling. Surprisingly, although he became an astute scholar regarding the chances in front of him, he was invariably a loser.

In 1560, he wrote *Liber de Ludo Aleae* (although it was not published until 1663), a book about games of chance. The book contained a systematic analysis of probability, the first of its kind. The book applied probability to gambling games and also included a chapter on cheating.

As an astrologer, he lost favor with church authorities for using a horoscope to chart the activities of Christ's earthly life. He also followed the stars and correctly predicted the date of his own death—September 21, 1576. (Some, however, claim that he committed suicide in order for his prediction to be true.)

Blaise Pascal was born on June 19, 1623, in France. He was a child prodigy, as he had to be in order to make the massive contributions to science that he made—for he only lived (most of the time in pain) to age 39, dying on August 19, 1662. While Pascal was also a physicist and a religious philosopher, mathematics was his central love. His studies of probability had a very strong influence on modern economics and social science.

In 1654, at the insistence of a friend who was consumed by gambling, he collaborated with another scholar in giving birth to the mathematical theory of probability (in a sense, but unbeknownst to him, repeating much of the work done by Cardano). He used a basic bit of information—the number of outcomes (chances) presented with a game. From this he exposed the proper betting stakes for the game. He also solved a problem involving what each player should receive if a game was to be suspended before it finished. His research expounded on the notion of "expected value" for the first time.

Pascal's failing health turned him toward religion, where he also applied his mathematical understandings. Given the basic question, "Should one believe in God?" he argued thusly: If one believes in God, and there is no God, the end game is simple. No harm is done. However, if there is a God, the person's belief is rewarded with eternal salvation. On the other hand, if one determines not to believe in God, and there is no God, there is also no harm done. However, if there is a God, and one chooses not to believe, that person risks eternal damnation. The odds favor believing.

The efforts of Cardano and Pascal helped move gambling out of its place as merely a realm for certain rich persons to contest with their peers. This old realm found all sharing the same risks, but also subjecting themselves to victimization at the hands of cheaters. However, armed with the correct probabilities of each game and a full knowledge of correct odds on each outcome, independent gambling operators could conduct games (as a "house") for masses of people with an assurance that in the long run, they could not lose. Most importantly, they could operate games honestly. Honesty was their friend.

Today's casino industry owes its success to the foundations put into place by Gerolamo Cardano and Blaise Pascal.

CHUN RAK-WON

Chun Rak-Won, "The Godfather" of South Korean casinos, was born in 1927. While a very successful entrepreneur, Rak-Won was also an avid patron of the arts. He established the Kaywon School of Art and Design, and he directly participated in casino design as well as design of promotional materials for casinos.

In 1973, Chun Rak-Won acquired Korea's premier casino, located at the Walker Hill Sheraton Hotel in Seoul. It had previously been owned by the government. It was renamed the Paradise Casino. Its purchase was followed with the purchases of the Paradise brand casinos in Incheon, Busan, and on Cheju Island. Chun Rak-Won also established the Paradise Safari Park Casino in Kenya. At the time of his death in 2004, the Paradise group employed 3,000 people and earned annual gaming revenues of $540 million.

COMSTOCK, ANTHONY

Anthony Comstock was one of the most prominent reformers in the Victorian era of the later 19th century. Other biographies included in this encyclopedia look at the leading gamblers, certainly rogues of the time, but some attention should be given to one who might be truly considered the greatest rogue of all. Comstock did not cheat the innocent, naive, and greedy out of their money. Rather, he purposely cheated society out of personal freedoms, and his vehicle for doing so was government policy and police enforcement powers. His target was immoral activity—of all types, especially those activities of a sexual nature, but also drinking alcohol and gambling. The impact of the laws he pushed toward passage is still felt today.

On March 7, 1844, Anthony Comstock was born in the small town of New Canaan, Connecticut. He was raised in a very religious family, and he had a disciplined childhood shielded from sinful activities. He came out of this cocoon in 1863, when he joined the 17th Connecticut Company for service in the Civil War. He felt an obligation to serve in place of his brother, who had fallen in battle. The 17th Company saw firefights in South Carolina before it withdrew for passive duty in St. Augustine, Florida. Comstock's real battles began there. He confronted the foul language and base habits of his fellow soldiers, and he resolved that he would have to change their behaviors. He found the means to change other people in the Army's Christian Commission and the Young Men's Christian Association (YMCA). After the war he moved to New York City and found that once again he was surrounded by sins of all kinds. He actively involved his YMCA comrades in harassing the sinners at every opportunity. He pressured police forces to enforce laws against prostitution and wide-open drinking and gambling.

His politics of enforcement put him in direct opposition to feminist groups. He gained considerable attention in seeking to win a prosecution against Victoria Claffin Woodhall, a free-love advocate who ran for president in 1872. As the result of the following he gained in the battle, he went to Washington, D.C., and secured passage of what became known as the Comstock Obscenity Law. The law prohibited the mailing of any materials with a sexual message of any type. In 1873, he secured a position as the chief inspector of the Postal Service, so the enforcement of the law was in his hands. He performed the job with vigor.

Soon afterwards he persuaded the New York legislature to charter the New York Society to Suppress Vice. The charter act gave officials of the society "arrest" powers as if they were police officers. Comstock won support from several leading entrepreneurs who wanted to root out the influence of sin over their workforce. Among his supporters was J. P. Morgan. Comstock pushed the New York legislature to act as well. In 1882, state laws were recodified, and all gambling except for horse racing was made illegal. Anthony Comstock went to work against gambling. He harassed the police into some prosecutions against casinos that operated openly in New York City. In this fight he was not successful until 1900 and 1901, when he forced Richard Canfield to close down his city casino, the most glamorous in the country at the time. Comstock was less successful in closing down the Canfield casino in Saratoga.

During Comstock's later career, he did not emphasize his disdain for gambling, but he pushed where he could. He rivaled, but also allied, Reverend Charles Parkhurst and the Society for the Prevention of Crime in his fights. He was with Parkhurst in 1890 as the reformers persuaded Congress to pass the law banning the use of the U.S. mails by lotteries and other gambling interests. Comstock's activities were also blended into those of the Progressive movement, and he was aboard the ride that found all gambling, except horse racing, banned everywhere. Soon after his death in 1915, all alcoholic beverages were banned throughout the United States as well.

See also Canfield, Richard.

COOLIDGE, CASSIUS MARCELLUS, AND THOSE "POKER PLAYING DOGS"

Cassius Marcellus Coolidge is perhaps the most famous "unknown" artist in American history. We might not know the artist, but we certainly know his work. Of all the paintings of gambling activity none are as popular as Cassius

Marcellus Coolidge's 16 pieces showing dogs playing poker. Well over a million prints of the paintings hang around the world in pool halls, saloons, and gambling halls. In 2004, one of his originals sold at auction for $590,000.

The paintings put the dogs in various card playing postures showing impending victory, busting, and serious contemplation. A favorite is called "A Friend in Need," as it shows one dog passing a card to another with his foot. Two popular paintings show examples of gambling's "bad beat." In one, a dog is holding four aces during a game on a train. The conductor announces that it is his station and he must get off. In the other a dog again holds a certain winning hand just as the police come in to break up the illegal game. Coolidge's work drew inspiration from the style of the Dutch Masters who preceded him by a century, and also depicted a surrealism that was not popular for another half century

Coolidge was born in upstate New York in 1844. As a young man in the 1860s, he attempted many different careers as he was always looking for a way to make money. He tried his hand at being a druggist, a street sign painter, an art teacher, a music composer, and a cartoonist. He also founded a bank and started a newspaper. His initial interest in painting dogs came with an opportunity to do art work for a cigar company. In 1903, an advertising company commissioned him to do a set of dog paintings for a calendar. It was then that he came up with his famous paintings. Coolidge died in 1934 before fame had discovered his work Nonetheless, he was given his "15 minutes" in a private limelight as his paintings were considered influential to the work of Andy Warhol. The current wave of popularity for "the dogs" came after 1973 when an issue of Antiques Magazine used them in advertisements that caught the public's attention. A craze began, and today one can not only buy reprints of the dog paintings, but also many other items displaying the dogs: wall clocks, coffee mugs, salt and pepper shakers, ashtrays, playing cards, calendars, tee shirts, and toilet seat covers.

DALITZ, MORRIS

Moe Dalitz started his career in the shadows of the law, but as that career unraveled in Las Vegas, his life became one involving community development and philanthropy. More than any other of the "founding fathers" of Las Vegas, Moe Dalitz converted a questionable past into honored status as a community icon.

Morris "Moe" Barney Dalitz was born on December 24, 1899, in Boston, Massachusetts. When Moe was very young, his family moved to Michigan. There his father started Varsity Laundry near the University of Michigan campus. The laundry business expanded, and soon the Michigan Industrial

Laundry in Detroit was in son Moe Dalitz's control. The laundry had certain symbiotic relationships that opened doors for Dalitz's new business interests. When Prohibition descended upon the nation, bootleggers needed delivery mechanisms. Dalitz had trucks. The laundry trucks served customers at hotels and could also be put onto barges that could be transported across the waters of the Detroit River, Lake St. Clair, Lake Huron, and Lake Erie from Canada. One of the favorite points of entry for liquor as it came from Canada to the bootleggers in the United States was the point where Mayfield Road near Cleveland ended at the shores of Lake Erie. Dalitz became the leader of a group called the Mayfield Road Gang, which operated in Cleveland, Detroit, and Ann Arbor.

From the earliest days, Moe Dalitz took the profits from his bootlegging activities and converted them into legitimate businesses: more laundry businesses, the Detroit Steel Company, and even a railroad. He also had his eye out for what his liquor customers wanted, especially when Prohibition ended. He concluded that gambling was a natural business for a follow-up. Dalitz became a principal owner of several illegal casinos throughout the Midwest, including several in Cleveland and northern Kentucky.

Moe Dalitz was too old to be drafted when the United States entered World War II. He had a strong sense of obligation, however, and he enlisted as a private. His business acumen landed him in the quartermaster corps, when he received a commission. He served stateside running army laundry services. His assignment allowed him to keep in touch with his private investments.

Moe Dalitz remained active in the Detroit laundry business into the 1950s. Inevitably, he came face to face with Jimmy Hoffa during negotiations with the International Brotherhood of Teamsters (the Teamsters union). At first it appeared that there would be a monumental confrontation, with both sides calling out their "muscle" to make their position stronger. But cooler heads prevailed as they found that mutual benefits could flow from friendly relationships. Later, Hoffa negotiated major loans for several Dalitz gambling projects and for other things as well. The first Teamsters loan to Las Vegas went to Dalitz so that he could finance Sunrise Hospital. Later loans also financed the Winterwood Golf Course, the Las Vegas Country Club, and Boulevard Mall—the largest shopping center in Nevada, even today.

Dalitz had come to Las Vegas in the aftermath of the crackdowns on illegal gambling that had been prompted by the Kefauver investigations. Dalitz himself was a witness in front of the Kefauver Committee. When asked if he had made money bootlegging, he told Senator Kefauver that he had not inherited his money. He added that if the committee members and other fine people had not drunk the whiskey, he would not have bootlegged it.

In the 1950s, Dalitz had had to choose between Las Vegas and Havana, and after trying Cuba, he decided to leave that territory to his friend Meyer Lansky. In actuality Fidel Castro's takeover of the island ended Dalitz's thoughts about Havana casinos. If he had pursued the Havana idea, the Nevada gambling regulators would have informed him that no Nevada casino license holder could have a casino interest elsewhere.

The leaders of organized crime families in the United States had declared Las Vegas an "open city" after Benjamin Siegel finished his Flamingo in 1946. This meant that groups of entrepreneurs, such as those with whom Dalitz was associated, were welcome to come into Las Vegas and compete alongside Meyer Lansky, Lucky Luciano, Frank Costello, and other eastern Mob leaders. The Dalitz group found its opportunity on the Strip with Wilbur Clark's Desert Inn Resort project. Clark had gathered resources to build his dream in 1947, but he was way short of what he needed. Dalitz and his Cleveland group made Clark an offer he "couldn't refuse." Clark gave up 74 percent of the ownership (that is, majority control) in return for seeing the project with his name still on it. Later the name was dropped. Dalitz added a special touch that changed marketing approaches for casinos in the future. He added a championship golf course next to the Desert Inn. Then he created a major tournament on the Professional Golf Association's tour: the Tournament of Champions, in which only winners of other tour events could compete.

In 1955, West Coast crime figure Tony Cornero died. Cornero had made his name running casino ships off the coast of California until authorities such as Governor Earl Warren closed down the gambling. Cornero moved to Las Vegas and started the Stardust. When he died, the remaining ownership group was very scattered and lacked the funds to complete the project. Dalitz moved in and secured a loan from Jimmy Hoffa's Teamsters union and finished the job. He took control of management when the property opened in 1958. The Stardust added a golf course with another champions tournament. The casinos increased the glitz level of the Las Vegas Strip by having the largest and most noticeable sign. The Stardust also brought in the Lido Show from Paris, which featured a chorus line of 50 well-costumed but still topless showgirls.

Moe Dalitz's interests also went to downtown Las Vegas, where he bought and sold the Fremont and also constructed the Sundance (now the Fitzgerald), which was the tallest building in the state for many years. His investment in a California resort called Rancho La Costa brought a lot of attention, as he again used Teamsters loans and his partners were people with questionable backgrounds. Dalitz sued *Penthouse* magazine for writing a very critical article about his participation with mobsters. He lost the suit, and the Nevada Gaming Commission began to examine the question of whether or not he should hold casino licenses. He had by this time already sold the Desert Inn, and he sold other casino interests as well, keeping the properties and leasing them to the holders of the gambling licenses. He became content to be an elder statesman for Las Vegas. Other business interests satisfied all his financial needs, and his many charities made him a leading citizen.

Moe Dalitz had organized a group of casino owners in the mid-1960s to develop a strategy to make casinos more legitimate in the eyes of the power holders in the state. The Nevada Resorts Association was established as a lobbying arm of the casinos. One of their first projects was to support the creation of a hotel school at the new University of Nevada, Las Vegas. Dalitz gave additional contributions to the new university to furnish its first building—Maude Frazier Hall. He was also a major contributor to many charities. His money was instrumental in starting a major temple for his faith. He was named Humanitarian of the Year by the American Cancer Society and in 1982 received an award from the Anti Defamation League of B'nai B'rith. When he died on August 31, 1989, he had completed the transition from being an outlaw businessman to being the most respected citizen of his city.

Dalitz's career had a personal impact on the editor of this encyclopedia, who grew up in Ann Arbor, Michigan, where his family patronized the Varsity Laundry started by Moe Dalitz's father. Neighbors' houses were sold by Dalitz Realty. When the editor's father visited him in Las Vegas, he asked if there was a Moe Dalitz in the city. The editor offered that Mr. Dalitz was one of the founders of the Las Vegas Strip. The editor's father then related that he had played cards with Moe's father, Barney, in the 1920s and that they had lived just two blocks away from us on Granger Street.

In the late 1980s the editor went to Ohio to study a campaign for casinos in Lorain, near Cleveland. As he drove off the interstate highway into town, he noticed the name of the road was Mayfield Road, famous from Prohibition days. He had come to another spot in Moe Dalitz's career. Now in Las Vegas the editor shops at the Boulevard Mall; one year his boys went to the school at Temple Beth Shalom; he has also visited the emergency room at Sunrise Hospital when his kids needed a stitch or two. At one time he walked by Frazier Hall on the University of Nevada, Las Vegas, campus five days a week (until the building was razed for another structure)—all these places were associated with Dalitz. His university office has been in the building that houses the Hotel College. On occasion he has had the pleasure of dining at the Las Vegas Country Club as a guest of one "important" person or another. The editor feels that the shadow of Moe Dalitz has covered many of his footsteps.

DANDOLOS, NICK

"Nick the Greek" Dandolos was born in Crete in 1893. Over a career of great renown, he secured the reputation as the last of the gentlemen gamblers and a man of great personal integrity, although some suggest the latter honor was not entirely deserved. Nick was the son of a rug merchant and the grandson of a ship owner. His grandfather sponsored Nick's coming to the United States, and he became a citizen in 1902, when he was 18 years

old. His grandfather also gave Nick an allowance of $150 a week. Although he also gained a job selling figs, with his guaranteed stake he quickly moved to gambling action wherever he could find it. First he followed the horses and then turned to cards and dice.

During a career that made him one of the major celebrities of Las Vegas, Dandolos often gave his assessment of the gambling life: "The greatest pleasure in my life is gambling and winning. The next greatest pleasure is gambling and losing" (Alvarez 1983, 115). He might have added the rest of the compulsive gambler's mantra: "Whatever is in third place ain't even close." Over his career he won and lost over $50 million—actually he lost quite a bit more than he won.

Nick the Greek won his reputation as the greatest player of his day and as a gentleman from the fact that he would play for the highest stakes available anywhere. When he came to Las Vegas, he gained a cult following among Greek Americans with his big bets. He was a gentleman because he always showed grace when he lost, whether it was a few hundred dollars or several hundreds of thousands of dollars. He could afford to be graceful, because for most games he was staked— he was playing with other people's money. Many times it was money given to him by compatriots of Greek heritage. Some writers have suggested that his frequent losses, for which his Greek sponsors would forgive him because he was one of them, were caused because he made arrangements with his adversaries across the tables. It has been alleged that he would lose on purpose and receive a kickback after play was over.

Dandolos came to Las Vegas before the Mob had taken over the Strip. He played at the Flamingo when Bugsy Siegel was still alive. A few years later he became a national figure when Benny Binion of the Horseshoe invited Dandolos to play in a poker game against Johnny Moss. Moss and Dandolos went at it one-on-one in the front window of the Horseshoe. The game, or series of games, lasted five months and was a precursor to the establishment of the World Championship of Poker. The lead went back and forth, but in the end Moss, 14 years the Greek's junior, outlasted Dandolos.

Although his reputation remained for another decade, Nick the Greek began slipping in the 1950s. He started borrowing heavily, and his losing continued. A collection had to be taken to pay his funeral costs after he died on Christmas Day in 1966. To the end he was a gambler in his heart. When he was asked why people gambled, he responded, "Why? Because they find ordinary life a swindle, a sellout, a ripoff. It's just eating, working, dying. The nose to the ground and the boss chewing out your ass. Attached to one woman, she growing wrinkled and mean before your eyes. Okay, okay; most people accept it. Most people accept anything and do not balk. But the few who don't accept, that's your lifelong gambler."

Reference

Longstreet, Stephen. 1977. *Win or Lose: A Social History of Gambling.* Indianapolis, IN: Bobbs-Merrill.

DAVIS, JOHN

John Davis is considered to be the first casino entrepreneur in the United States. But gambling was not the essential part of his life, as he was a patron of the arts. He was born in Santo Domingo (his date of birth is not known) and educated in

French colleges, studying music and art. When he came to New Orleans his attention was on the arts. He gained much social prestige as he built the Theatre d'Orleans where operatic performances were given. He also opened an exclusive ballroom. John Davis gave the raucous frontier community its culture.

John Davis associated with the "best" people of New Orleans, and when the opportunity to have a gambling hall arose, he sensed that his group of friends would not want to be playing games among the street hoi polloi in saloons and brothels. Therefore in 1827 he applied for a license for a different style of gambling hall, one that was not just an annex to a saloon. His emporium of games was located beside his ballroom on Orleans near Bourbon Street. Perhaps he anticipated the style of Steve Wynn's Bellagio in Las Vegas, as Davis's casino was carpeted; featured fine furniture, fine food, and the best of liquid refreshments; and was adorned with fine music and its walls lined with art works. The amenities—all the food, drink, and entertainment—were free to his valued customers. Perhaps he can be credited with inventing the "comp" (complimentary), at least in the United States. In a sense his casino was comparable to the best in Las Vegas, without the slot machines and without the masses of people wandering in and out. When he was given his license, his was the only exclusive hall for games. He only had to compete with the dives of New Orleans, that seem even today not to have gone away—surviving everything including Hurricane Katrina. As his upmarket clientele kept growing, he branched out and started a second casino in suburban Bayou St. John.

During the early 1830s, others attempted to imitate his establishments, but they fell short of his standards. His offerings were the most elegant of any gambling facility for decades to come. His "run," however, was not a long one. In 1835, a reform movement—perhaps taking its cues from the antigambling mobs upriver in Vicksburg—pressured the city government to rescind all of the gambling licenses. Davis's reaction was not to try to operate underground, nor was it to run off to another jurisdiction where he could seek accommodations with legal authorities. He was a social leader in New Orleans, and he was an operator of integrity. The classy John Davis was also a man of wealth. He merely closed the doors to his gambling operations, and he returned to a full-time pursuit as the city's primary patron of the opera and the arts. For Davis gambling had always been the amenity.

EADINGTON, WILLIAM R.

William R. Eadington may be called "the father of modern gaming research." He is a professor of economics at the University of Nevada, Reno, and the director of its Institute for the Study of Gambling and Commercial Gaming. His institute has been directly responsible for launching similar institutes in many other venues including East Asia, Europe, the United Kingdom, and

Australia. Eadington was the founder of the International Conference on Gambling and Risk Taking, which had its first meeting in 1974. Since then, the conference has met 14 times, bringing together researchers on gaming from throughout the world. Indeed the existence of the conference as a forum has stimulated hundreds of research papers and publications. Eadington himself has served as an editor for many collections, including *Gambling and Society* (1976), *The Gambling Papers* (1982), *The Gambling Studies* (1985), *Gambling Research* (1988), *Indian Gaming and the Law* (1990), *Gambling and Public Policy* (1991), and *Gambling Behavior and Problem Gambing* (1993). He has been the co-editor of a special edition of the *Annals of the American Academy of Political Science* (1984) that was dedicated to gambling issues, and also the *Annals of Tourism Research* and the *Journal of Gambling Studies*. He has been a visiting professor at the Harvard Medical School, the London School of Economics, and the University of Salford in England. He has consulted with many governments and gaming organizations on questions of gambling law and public policy and gambling. Eadington received his undergraduate education at Santa Clara University with a degree in mathematics. He earned an MA and a PhD in economics from the Claremont Graduate College.

FAHRENKOPF, FRANK JR.

Frank Fahrenkopf is the president and chief executive of the American Gaming Association, which he helped found in 1994. The AGA is the chief lobbying group for the American casino industry. Fahrenkopf was born in Brooklyn, New York, on August 28, 1939. He was raised in Reno, Nevada. There he attended the University of Nevada (BA, 1962), later receiving a law degree (1965) from the University of California—Berkeley. He practiced law in Reno for 17 years, specializing in gaming law. He was always very active in Republican politics, and in 1983 he was elected as chairman of the Republican National Committee, a position he held until 1989. Since the mid-1980s, he has also served as the vice chair of the Commission on Presidential Debates. Subsequent to being national party chairman, he joined a Washington, D.C., law firm and specialized in international trade matters until he began service with the AGA. As leader of the AGA, he has defended the casino industry from its opponents with testimony to legislative groups throughout the country and to the National Gambling Impact Study Commission. He has also directed campaign funds to supporters of the industry. Under his effective watch, the industry has seen considerable growth as it has also resisted attacks and many pleas for increased taxation. He has also conducted public relations efforts that have included sponsorship and guidance for programs on responsible gambling.

GATES, JOHN W.

John W. "Bet a Million" Gates, who was born in 1855, became a fabulously wealthy man as a producer of barbed wire as the West was opening up for farmers and ranchers. He was also a big player and winner on the stock market, controlling the flow of wheat in the economy. Gates was not happy just being a businessman, however; he wanted more action. He found it in gambling activity. During the Gay Nineties and the few years afterwards, he became known as the biggest player anywhere. Gates would bet on anything: the flip of a coin, which piece of sugar would draw the most flies, which raindrop on a window pane would fall to the bottom first. He would bet up to a dollar a point at bridge. Although he probably never bet a million dollars on a single play, he certainly won and lost hundreds of thousands of dollars at a single sitting. A 1902 game of faro at Richard Canfield's Saratoga Casino cost Gates $400,000 one afternoon. The same evening he won back $150,000.

Gates dressed like the millionaire he was (until his later years), wearing several diamonds on his shirt. He played with other millionaires, such as Cornelius Vanderbilt and Diamond Jim Brady, usually on a cross-country train or in exclusive hotel rooms. He also loved the horses.

Gates was very philosophical about his play. He explained why he had to wager such large amounts of money: "For me there's no fun in betting just a few thousand. I want to bet enough to hurt the other fellow if he loses, and enough to hurt me if I lose" (Chafetz, 363). A lot of people got hurt when he played. He hurt the most. Like the other "big players," he lost more than he won, and he often was "the sucker." He played the stock market heavily until he lost most of his fortune in the panic of 1907. Soon afterwards, he swore off all gambling, suggesting of the stock market that "sometimes the bulls win, sometimes the bears win, but the hogs never win" (Longstreet, 166). In 1909, he testified to a group of Methodist ministers in Texas, pleading: "Don't gamble, play cards, bet on horses, speculate on wheat or the stock exchange, and don't shirk honest labor. Don't be a gambler, once a gambler, always a gambler" (Asbury, 451). Preaching to the choir, Tom Grey, of the National Coalition against Legalized Gambling, could not have expressed it any clearer. "Bet a Million" Gates died a humble man at the age of 56 in 1911.

References

Asbury, Herbert. 1938. *Sucker's Progress: An Informal History of Gambling in America from the Colonies to Canfield.* New York: Dodd, Mead.

Chafetz, Henry. 1960. *Play the Devil: A History of Gambling in the United States from 1492 to 1955.* New York: Potter Publishers.

Longstreet, Stephen. 1977. *Win or Lose: A Social History of Gambling.* Indianapolis, IN: Bobbs-Merrill.

GAUGHAN, JACKIE, AND MICHAEL GAUGHAN

For nearly six decades, Jackie Gaughan held the reputation of being "Mr. Downtown Las Vegas." He was the principal owner of two anchor properties at the ends of the Fremont Street Experience: the Jackie Gaughan Plaza (formerly called the Union Plaza before he bought out his partners), located where Fremont Street ends at Main Street, and the El Cortez, a property built in 1941 and the oldest property in Las Vegas still bearing its original name. In between these gambling halls he owned the Western, the Gold Spike, and the Las Vegas Club. He operated only in downtown Las Vegas, where his five properties once had 37 percent of all the slot machines, 36 percent of the casino floor space, and 24 percent of the hotel rooms. He was a hands-on manager, walking through each property every day, and he even lived in the penthouse of one of his casino-hotels—the El Cortez. The key to his success was customer service.

Jackie Gaughan was born in Nebraska on October 20, 1920. He learned to gamble in the Midwest, and catered to middle-class players from that region. He is considered the biggest Nebraska Cornhusker football fan in Las Vegas. His grandfather had been a policeman who grew up in Ireland. His father strayed a bit from the line of law-abiding behavior—just a bit. He owned racehorses, and he was a bookmaker. One of Jackie's brothers was a bootlegger. When Jackie was only 16 years old and working as a messenger for other bookies, he started to take action on his own. He has been in the gambling business ever since. Soon he owned two bookie shops in Omaha. He also participated in casino gaming in the area. A change in the course of the Missouri River had left an enclave of Iowa on the Omaha side of the river. Therefore, the Iowa authorities had to travel an inconvenient distance to patrol the area. There a wise entrepreneur established the Chez Paris—an illegal casino. It was run by Jackie's uncle. Jackie participated in the business.

Jackie Gaughan attended Creighton University before he joined the Air Corp in World War II. His gambling activity did not skip a beat, as he was soon running his games on a base near Tonopah, Nevada. That assignment brought him close to Las Vegas, and in 1943 he visited the city, stayed at the El Cortez, and established some lifelong contacts. By 1943, he was married; his son Michael was born the same year. In 1946, after the war ended, he borrowed money from his mother to purchase a small stake in a little Fremont Street casino called the Boulder Club. He remained in Omaha, keeping his fingers in the business there until 1951. When he came back to Las Vegas, he purchased a small piece of the Flamingo, which he held until 1968.

His tale became one of working incredibly long hours at several properties and slowly acquiring shares of the businesses where he worked. He especially liked sports betting, and he started the first exclusive sports and race book in the downtown area. Sports betting was always a part of each of his ventures.

In 1959, he bought the Las Vegas Club, and in 1963 he acquired the El Cortez. In 1971 he joined with several other local interests—Sam Boyd, Frank Scott, Kell Houssels, and Walter Zick—to create the Union Plaza casino. This was the most expensive new property at that time in downtown—costing $20 million. It was also the largest, with more than 500 rooms and a 66,000-square-foot gaming floor. It was themed as a railroad casino, because it actually was (and still is) the station for the railroad that ran through Las Vegas. In the early 1980s, the property added a second tower with a convention center and another 500-plus rooms. Until the Golden Nugget added two towers and a convention center, the Union Plaza was the only convention property downtown. In 1990, Gaughan acquired full control of the Union Plaza and changed its name. By then he also had the Western and Gold Spike—two smaller downtown casino hotels.

As a hands-on customer-oriented casino owner-operator, Jackie Gaughan has been an innovator. If he did not invent the Las Vegas Fun Book (a coupon book with bargains such as low-cost meals, free souvenirs, and chances for double money bets), he certainly perfected it and made it a basic tool for promotions in the community. He also started a constant line of promotional giveaways. He discovered that there were "professional" contest players who seemed to win most of the prizes while his out-of-town players and other regulars were left out. So he devised a special contest that has become synonymous with the El Cortez—the Social Security number drawing. No player could have more than one entry in the contest, and the players would have to come in every day to check the prize list. He also developed what he calls the Season Pass for players who win jackpots on his machines. The pass holders are given three weeknights free at one of his hotels quarterly for the next 12 months. It keeps 'em coming back.

Jackie Gaughan is one of the "old-timers" of Las Vegas. His methods are tried and true, and they still work in the market he goes after. The new breed of corporate gamers looks at operations a little differently. Michael Gaughan, Jackie's son, has moved his attention to the Strip and also to the edges of town, where he appeals to a new kind of "local" gambler and tourist. He has partnered in Coast Casino's operations. He also has a major riverboat in the St. Louis market. Michael Gaughan is college educated, holding a master's degree in business administration from the University of Southern California, where he also studied computers. Computers drive Michael's operations, but perhaps he is the bridge to the future, as he has not abandoned the basic lessons his father taught him—Michael talks the corporate game, but he walks the old-timer walk with hands-on management. Despite the difference in their education, there is little doubt that Michael is his father's son.

Some time ago when the editor encountered Michael Gaughan at the Barbary Coast Casino in order to interview him for a customer service book, Michael was breathing hard and speaking rapidly in stop-and-go phrases. He had just completed his daily walk-through of the casino, and he was reviewing and explaining the daily computerized report on each of his slot machines. He was indicating how each part of his property contributed to the bottom line, but mostly he was telling about the individual players he had just greeted by name. He told how he was striving to keep them happy and to keep them coming back time and time again.

It was the kind of personalized service that one would not expect at a casino on the Las Vegas Strip, let alone a casino on the major corner of the Strip—Flamingo Road and Las Vegas Boulevard South.

Michael developed a separate company called Coast Casinos, building the Gold Coast, Orleans, Sun Coast, and South Coast properties. In 2002, he sold his interest in all but the South Coast to Boyd Properties. He renamed his remaining property South Point. Jackie Gaughan sold his downtown interests in 2004.

GREY, THOMAS A.

Tom Grey emerged in the 1990s as the leading advocate against gambling in U.S. society. Although he has not held any official government position, his role has paralleled that of Anthony Comstock (see the Anthony Comstock entry) one hundred years prior. Grey was born in 1941. In his twenties he served in Viet Nam as an infantry man. He claims to use tactics he learned in combat against the forces promoting the expansion of gambling. After his military service he studied theology and was ordained as a minister in the United Methodist Church. Serving in that capacity in Galena, Illinois, he was confronted by the downside of gambling when several parishioners succumbed to the travails of problem gambling while patronizing a local riverboat casino. In 1992, he began organizing opposition forces determined to limit the spread of gambling. Soon he formed the National

Coalition Against Legalized Gambling (*see* National Coalition Against Legalized Gambling entry). On a very limited salary and a small budget he has taken on the very well financed interests in favor of gambling, and he has won more fights than he has lost, defeating campaigns to expand legalized gambling in more than 20 states. Associated Press writer John Curran writes of the "Gospel According to Grey": "Casinos have failed as economic development tools and are instead driving America to bankruptcy, suicide, and divorce. And governments, by approving casino gambling and promoting their own state-run lotteries, share in the blame."

Reference

Curren, John. 1998. "No Dice." *South Coast Today.* http://archive.southcoasttoday.com/daily/01-98/01-31-98/b021i81.htm.

HARRAH, WILLIAM F.

Harrah's Casino Corporation has more gambling facilities across the United States than any other casino company. There is a Harrah's casino in each major casino jurisdiction and in many other places as well—Atlantic City, Laughlin, Lake Tahoe, Las Vegas, Reno; the states of Mississippi, Louisiana, Missouri, and Colorado; and New Zealand. Harrah's operates many Native American casinos as well. Until the Hilton casino group (Park Place Gaming) and Caesars Casinos merged in 1999, Harrah's was the biggest gambling company in the world. Harrah's gambling revenues are well over $1 billion a year. Harrah's markets to middle America and features many tour packages for its customers.

The founding father of Harrah's casinos started his gambling activities in Venice Beach, California. William F. Harrah was born in southern California in 1911. His father ran bingo halls and carnival gambling games in Venice Beach. Father and son discovered that gambling activities in a jurisdiction that really did not want gambling could be rather tenuous. The Depression years were also hard on them. They sought to practice their business activities elsewhere. When Nevada legalized casino gambling in 1931, it certainly appeared to be the place to go. Both Harrahs came to Reno in 1937, but by the time they did, young Bill had bought out his father's interest in the business. Bill Harrah first opened a bingo parlor, but then turned to casinos.

Bill Harrah had learned lessons in California that he applied in Reno, lessons that the rest of the casino industry had to also learn if survival in a competitive world was desired. When others were operating down-market "joints" that sought to extract money from players any way they could, including cheating, Harrah made customer service a top priority. He also was the first to put carpets on the casino floors. He sought to make casinos more respectable by having windows to the outside and by having women dealers. He also took new measures to control all flows of money at a time when other properties were victims of skimming by employees and others.

In 1955, Bill Harrah built a casino on the south shores of Lake Tahoe. He was warned that the location was too remote, but he took the chance that people would enjoy staying near the most beautiful lake in the Sierras. Harrah did find that the casino had a seasonal problem, as winter could restrict travel for all but those coming to the area to ski. In response to the problem, Bill Harrah developed a busing system to bring in players from all over California. This was an innovation that has now been imitated in almost all other U.S. jurisdictions.

Bill Harrah was the sole owner of his property, and he mixed his private life into the business. He had been indulged by his father from the time he was a small child, and with the casino profits he continued to indulge himself. He was a playboy (he was married seven times), he built personal retreats, and he developed an exquisite collection of automobiles that he maintained as business expenses. As he became older, he neglected his properties, and his excesses affected his bottom-line profits. In desperate need for funds, in 1971 he converted his personal empire into one of the first publicly traded corporate gambling properties. This gave him the funds to develop a high-rise tower at his Lake Tahoe casino. Every room in his tower had windows facing the lake and its surrounding mountains.

His personal excesses hurt his company through the 1970s, however. Harrah's associates tried to persuade him that he should sell his assets, but he steadfastly refused. Months after he died in 1979, his executive attorney, Mead Dixon, negotiated a deal to sell all of Harrah's properties to Holiday Inn for $300 million. Much of the money was used to pay estate taxes. Although the price was considered excessive at the time, Holiday Inn was able to realize over $100 million from selling Harrah's car collection. A new management team led by Holiday Inn's Michael Rose and Dixon introduced management controls and policies that emphasized both financial responsibility and property upgrades. Existing casinos in Las Vegas and Atlantic City that carried the Holiday Inn name changed their signs to carry the Harrah name, and the empire began to move into every major casino jurisdiction in the United States and many beyond the borders of the country. The Harrah's Company became the largest gaming enterprise in the world at the beginning of the 21st century as the organization purchased the former properties of the Caesars empire.

HO, STANLEY

Stanley Ho's casinos account for one-third of the gross domestic product of Macau and provide 30 percent of the taxes to the former Portuguese colony.

Ho was born on November 25, 1921, in Hong Kong. He was educated at the University of Hong Kong and afterwards joined a Japanese import-export firm when he was 22. He soon amassed a fortune by smuggling goods into Macau during World War II. After the War, Ho and his partners began acquiring businesses in Macau. In 1962, they were able to make a successful bid for the concession to run the casinos in Macau. The casino operations began to expand rapidly, growing from just one casino to six. Their company STDM soon took over other betting activities, including horse racing, dog racing, jai alai, lotteries, and sports betting. By the time the Portuguese colony was transferred to China in 1999, Ho's gaming businesses were responsible for 80 percent of the tax revenues.

Under China, Ho was forced to bid again to have his casinos. He did so successfully, but his monopoly was broken as three concessions were shared with other investors, including Sheldon Adelson and Steven Wynn of Las Vegas. Ho also has controlled casinos in Portugal and North Korea. His son Lawrence and daughter Pansy are also active casino entrepreneurs, the latter partnering with MGM-Mirage in a new Macau casino.

HOFFA, JIMMY

James Riddle Hoffa became an essential part of the Las Vegas casino industry when he arranged the financing of several new properties in the late 1950s and early 1960s with the use of pension funds of the International Brotherhood of Teamsters.

Hoffa was born in Brazil, Indiana, on Valentine's Day in 1913. He was the son of a coal driller who died when Jimmy was seven years old. His mother soon moved the family to Detroit, where she secured employment in an automobile factory. Jimmy got his first job when he was eleven years old. Life was tough, and Hoffa responded to it with his fists, fighting and scrapping all the way. Through experiences in many hard jobs, Hoffa was drawn into the union movement. He organized a strike at a Kroger's grocery store where he worked in the stockroom. That successful effort resulted in his first affiliation with the International Brotherhood of Teamsters (often referred to as the Teamsters union). He went on to work for the union, first in 1932 as a recruiter, then as a business agent, and soon as a leading organizer. In the mid-1930s, he became the president of Detroit Local 299. Hoffa rose in the Teamsters' ranks, and in 1952 he became the chairman of the Michigan Conference of Teamsters. He joined in the efforts to help make David Beck the Teamsters' president, and Hoffa got the vice presidency of the union as a result.

David Beck was the first victim of the U.S. Senate's McClellan Committee hearings on union corruption. It was revealed that Beck had misused the Teamsters' pension funds, and he had to step down from the presidency in 1957.

Hoffa became union president. The McClellan Committee, with its counsel Robert Kennedy, never ceased its attacks on the Teamsters union, now making Hoffa its target of choice. An ongoing battle between Kennedy and Hoffa ensued, lasting for almost a decade.

During his union presidency, the Teamsters union's Central States Pension Fund became the leading source of funds for capital financing of Las Vegas casinos. Moe Dalitz turned to Hoffa for the money needed to build La Costa Country Club in California, the Sunrise Hospital in Las Vegas, and the Stardust Casino in Las Vegas. Hoffa financed the Dunes Casino through his personal attorney, Morris Shenker, and also the Landmark, the Four Queens, Aladdin, Circus Circus, and Caesars Palace. Caesars received the biggest Teamsters' loans, over $20 million. The money was critical, as it came into Las Vegas at a time when organized crime interests tied to Meyer Lansky were pulling back from investments because they were coming under more and more scrutiny from federal investigators. The Hoffa pension fund money provided an interlude between Lansky capital and Howard Hughes capital financing. The Teamsters' loans came at a price, even though interest rates were not high—actually quite the opposite. Through a variety of means, however, Hoffa reportedly received kickbacks and also access to casino operations. He could place his people in the casino, and he also could demand a piece of the action through different skimming-type mechanisms.

Although Hoffa lived a very modest middle-class lifestyle, the charges of corruption and misuse of funds came to rest at his doorstep. Robert Kennedy pursued a prosecution of Hoffa with a vigor that probably transcended notions of due process or adherence to constitutional liberties or values. After one unsuccessful prosecution in 1962, Hoffa was finally nailed with a conviction for tampering with the jury. In 1964, he was convicted again of misappropriating union funds. His appeals ran out, and in 1967 he stepped down from union office and went to prison for 58 months.

President Nixon commuted Hoffa's sentence in 1971 with a pardon decreeing that he could not hold union office again until 1980. In 1975, Hoffa was purportedly cooperating with federal authorities who were still investigating the misuse of Teamsters' pension funds. Perhaps he was seeking to have his pardon changed so that he could reclaim the union presidency. That was not to be. On July 31, 1975, he disappeared. The presumption is that he was murdered, although his body was never recovered, and the crime has never been solved.

In 1936, Hoffa married Josephine Poszywak. They had a daughter, born in 1938, and a son, James Hoffa Jr., in 1941. The son is now the president of the Teamsters union.

HUGHES, HOWARD

More than any other individual, Howard Robard Hughes stamped the seal of legitimacy upon a Las Vegas casino industry that had been labeled as corrupt and Mob-invested in the general public mind. Hughes paved the way for corporate America to invest in gambling properties that had previously been controlled to a large degree by pension funds of the International Brotherhood of Teamsters and assorted underworld characters. Hughes did not necessarily transform Las Vegas from a profit center for organized crime into the favorite resort in the United States on purpose. Moreover, there were many unanticipated consequences of his drive to dominate Las Vegas gambling, not the least of which was the scandal that will go down in the history books as Watergate.

Hughes was born in Houston, Texas, in 1905. Four years later his father, Howard Hughes Sr., helped develop a drilling bit that could penetrate hard rocks with ease. The tool revolutionized oil drilling and made the Hughes family wealthy. At age 18, the younger Hughes became the majority stockholder of Hughes Tool Company when his father died in 1924. Having been warned by his father never to have partners, he immediately set plans into motion for acquiring all the stock in the company from his relatives. He also began to diversify his interests. He maintained a stake in mineral extraction in addition to developing experimental aircraft, producing movies, and designing military hardware. Very soon he became a multimillionaire and also a playboy working the Hollywood scene. For excitement he flew many of his experimental aircraft. In 1938, he flew around the world, setting various speed records. The downside of his flying came with several crashes. Perhaps the most serious one was in 1946, after which doctors expected him to die. They gave him excessive dosages of morphine to kill his pain, not thinking of consequences if he lived. He lived and developed a lifetime addiction to drugs. It is also suggested that his plane crashes caused many head injuries that left a mark on later behavior that would have to be called "bizarre," to say the least.

During the 1940s Hughes was a frequent visitor to Las Vegas, and several times prior to 1966 he had attempted to move his corporate interests to the desert. He purchased 28,000 acres of land on the west side of the city with the notion that the land would be used for aircraft development and testing. It remained undeveloped until the 1980s, when it became the essence of Summerlin, a residential expanse that filled as Las Vegas became the fastest-growing city in the United States. During the 1950s Hughes's fortune approached $2 billion, and he became the principal owner of Trans-World-Airlines (TWA). Hughes hired Robert Maheu, a former Federal Bureau of Investigation agent, to be his chief business agent, and from 1957 on, Hughes became a recluse unwilling to meet any business associate on a face-to-face basis. All his contacts with Maheu from 1957 to 1970 were by telephone or on note pads. In the early 1960s, Hughes relocated his operations to the Bahamas, but he still yearned to be in Las Vegas. On Thanksgiving Day 1966, he moved to town. Soon he was buying casinos.

The 1960s had been hard on Las Vegas. Bobby Kennedy had pushed the McClellan Committee of the U.S. Senate in its investigation of Teamsters union money in Las Vegas. As attorney general, Kennedy carried on ongoing probes into Mob activity in Las Vegas. No new casinos were being built because the Mob was fearful that the federal government might shut down gambling. Public corporations were precluded from owning casinos (unless every single stockholder was licensed), and legitimate lenders—banks and other institutional financial houses—would not touch the industry. Las Vegas was looking for a miracle, and here came Howard Robard Hughes—with money to spend. In May 1966, Hughes refused to appear before a congressional committee investigating aspects of the operations of TWA. To avoid having to appear in public, he willingly agreed to divest himself of all his holdings in the company—78 percent of the stock. He received $546.5 million for an investment that had originally cost him $80. For purposes of avoiding excessive taxation, he had to quickly reinvest the money. Las Vegas was waiting.

Fiction and fact become mingled and confused as the story of Howard Hughes unwrapped in Las Vegas. Some say events just occurred; others see a masterful plan behind Hughes's entry into the gambling community. In November 1966, Maheu rented the top two floors of the Desert Inn for Hughes's living quarters. He was supposed to stay for 10 days, but after he entered his hotel suite, he stayed there for almost four years—until November 5, 1970. He may have been secretly taken out of the room on a few occasions, but no one outside a very small group of personal attendants saw him over these four years. A whole litany of strange behaviors, manias, phobias, delusions, and obsessions afflicted

Hughes during his Las Vegas stay, but crazy or not, he made an impact on the town.

When Hughes refused to leave the Desert Inn after his 10-day stay, Maheu began to negotiate a deal with Moe Dalitz and the other owners of the property. On March 22, 1967, the parties agreed that Hughes would purchase the Desert Inn for $13.2 million. The licensing process for casino ownership entailed many hurdles. These included financial statements, personal statements, fingerprints, photographs, fees, and a personal appearance in front of the Gaming Control Board and the Nevada Gaming Commission. There was no way that Howard Hughes was going to endure such procedures. On the other hand, there was no way Nevada was going to allow Hughes to slip away. Governor Paul Laxalt and the gaming officials waived many requirements and allowed Maheu to appear on behalf of Hughes in the licensing hearing. The license was not opposed by anyone. Said board chairman Alan Arber, "After all, Mr. Hughes' life and background are well known to this Board and he is considered highly qualified" (Garrison, 52–53). The truth was quite different. Neither Hughes nor anyone in his organization had any experience managing a gambling facility.

Safely brought into the business, Hughes and the state of Nevada wanted more. In July 1967, Hughes purchased the Sands Hotel and Casino and 183 acres of land beside it for $14.6 million, and in September he acquired the Frontier. He quickly followed this with purchases of the smaller Castaways and Silver Slipper casinos. He also bought Harold's Club in Reno. Then he set his sights on the Stardust and the Landmark. But by then, the federal government had set its sights on Hughes as well.

U.S. attorney general Ramsey Clark thought Hughes had bought enough. Clark contended that any further purchases would make Hughes a monopolistic owner on the Las Vegas Strip. Hughes did not like to be told no. Clark and U.S. President Lyndon Johnson were due to leave office soon, and so Hughes maneuvered to control the next president's capacity to refuse his desires. In 1968, Hughes hired Larry O'Brien, a family friend and political confidant of the Kennedy family, to be on his legal team. O'Brien had also been in the Kennedy cabinet. Then Hughes gave Richard Nixon, Republican candidate for the presidency, a $100,000 campaign "contribution." Some thought that the contribution could be considered a bribe. Hughes also gave Democratic candidate Hubert Humphrey a $50,000 "contribution" (Drosnin, 250). In 1960, Hughes had given Nixon's brother a large loan that remained unpaid, and Nixon's opponents had used the loan as a major campaign issue against Nixon. In 1968, Nixon was elected, and he promptly removed objections to Hughes's purchases of more casinos. Hughes gave up his desire to purchase the Stardust, but he did finalize the purchase of the Landmark. In 1972, Nixon declared himself to be a candidate for reelection, except there was a little bug in his plans. Larry O'Brien was now the chairman of the Democratic National Committee. Nixon strongly suspected that O'Brien had information about the 1968 contribution (the alleged bribe)—as he was working for Hughes when it was made—and might use that information against Nixon. Nixon told his aides to find out what O'Brien knew and what his campaign plans were. The aides began to gather information from many sources. They decided to break into O'Brien's office in the Watergate Hotel in

Washington, D.C. The irony is that O'Brien could not raise the issue of the money, because Democratic candidate Humphrey had accepted a similar contribution. But Nixon did not know that—not in time. Hughes had brought down a president.

It has been suggested that Hughes purchased the hotels he did because they surrounded the Desert Inn, and he wished to own every hotel he could see from his 10th-floor suite. Maheu suggested that the casinos purchased were on a list of casinos that Robert Kennedy suspected of being Mob establishments. The practical effect of the purchases was to give the United States the impression that Las Vegas was being cleaned up and that the organized crime elements were leaving town. That was not exactly true. A major change was in order, however. Even though Hughes had brought capital to the Las Vegas Strip, he had invested in existing properties; he did not build new ones, nor did he remodel and improve those he purchased. The Strip needed infusions of new capital for new casinos. The activity of Hughes had given the legitimate investment community a new perspective on Las Vegas. It could be a good place. Before Hughes left town for the Bahamas with his entourage on November 5, 1970 (firing Maheu in the process), the state of Nevada had passed (in 1969) the Corporate Gaming Act, which allowed publicly traded corporations to have Nevada subsidiaries that could be licensed for casino ownership in the name of the principal stockholders— not all of the stockholders. As Hughes exited the state, Hilton came in—what Hughes started, others would finish. As Hughes was an absentee owner while living in his secluded 10th-floor suite, he was the same while he was in the Bahamas and elsewhere. His sanity was severely questioned, as he remained in seclusion for the rest of his life. Only once did he agree to meet with Nevada officials. That was in 1972 when rumors of his death caused concern. He agreed to meet the governor—Mike O'Callaghan—in London for a very brief session just to verify that he was alive. That he was, but not really very alive. He was in miserable physical shape; nonetheless his life continued until he was defeated by kidney failure in April 1976.

References

Drosnin, Michael. 1985. *Citizen Hughes*. New York: Holt, Rinehart, and Winston.

Garrison, Omar. 1970. *Howard Hughes in Las Vegas*. New York: *Las Vegas*. Las Vegas: Huntington Press.

Maheu, Robert. Personal interview in Las Vegas, June 7, 2007.

JONES, "CANADA BILL"

"Canada Bill" Jones (1820–1877) was the master of three-card monte in the middle years of the 19th century. Stories are told about characters in the gambling world, and some of the best are told about Canada Bill. When he was circulating throughout the South during the post–Civil War years conning people with his monte games and looking for any action, he found a poker game. As he entered the game he was warned that it was a crooked game. He responded simply, "I know, but it is the only game in town." Certainly the same story has been told about other gamblers. It was quite likely to be true about Canada Bill, however, who in his lifetime won millions of dollars on his own specialty game. He then turned around and lost the money gambling in other games, usually poker and faro games.

Bill Jones was born in Yorkshire, England, to a family of gypsies. He was raised among fortunetellers and horse traders and thieves. He learned that the secret of living involved using con jobs. In his early twenties he moved to Canada, where he got his nickname. There he met his gambling mentor, Dick Cady, who taught him the sleight-of-hand operations of three-card monte, a card game that worked like the proverbial shell game. When Jones heard about the riverboats, he left the frozen tundra behind, becoming a man of the South.

During the 1850s, he traveled the Mississippi River with his monte operation in a partnership with George Devol (*see* George Devol entry in Annotated Bibliography). Devol was a fighter. But Canada Bill was only 130 pounds and afraid of a fight. He knew how to get Devol to make a defensive stand as he led the escape from the "tight" situations. After touring the river for several years, he worked his scams on the new railroads in the United States. He actually proposed to one line that he be given a monopoly concession for the train. He was denied the exclusive opportunity and had to travel with other gamblers—probably guaranteeing that he would not keep his winnings. Canada Bill was the best at three-card monte, as he could almost change a card as he was throwing it down to the table. In his later years he worked county fairs and the world fair, and also racetracks. He was unlike other professional gamblers of the era, as he did not dress to impress. Quite the opposite, he always appeared as the rube, unshaven, in rumpled oversized clothes, looking like a sucker ready to be taken. He often said that "suckers had no business with money, anyway" (Chafetz, 73). He was what he appeared to be. He died a pauper.

After his funeral in Reading, Pennsylvania, in 1877, it was reported that while two gamblers were lowering the coffin into the ground, one said, "I'll bet you my hundred against your fifty." "On what?" said the other. "I'll bet that he isn't in the coffin." He then related that Canada Bill had squeezed out of tighter boxes in his lifetime (Chafetz, 103). Indeed, he had gotten out of town ahead of his victims on more than several occasions.

Reference

Chafetz, Henry. 1960. *Play the Devil: A History of Gambling in the United States from 1492 to 1955.* New York: Potter Publishers.

KENNEDY, ROBERT F.

Robert F. Kennedy was a U.S. senator and attorney general. Robert Francis Kennedy, known as Bobby, was born on November 20, 1925, in Massachusetts. He was the son of Ambassador Joseph Kennedy and the brother of President

John F. Kennedy and U.S. Senator Edward Kennedy. Robert Kennedy graduated from Harvard University with a BA in 1948 and received his legal education at the University of Virginia, earning an LL B degree in 1951. After graduation he worked briefly in the U.S. Department of Justice before becoming a counsel in 1953 with a Senate committee investigating internal security, chaired by Senator Joseph McCarthy (R-Wisconsin).

After the Democratic party secured the Senate majority in 1955, Kennedy became chief counsel of the Investigations Committee under the chairmanship of Senator John McClellan (D-Arkansas). In 1957, the committee became known as the Rackets Committee as it focused its attention on organized crime and illegal activity in labor unions. The first target of the investigations was the International Brotherhood of Teamsters (often referred to as the Teamsters union). Union president Dave Beck was implicated in personal corruption; he was subsequently tried, convicted, removed from office, and imprisoned. Then Kennedy went after Beck's replacement, James Riddle ("Jimmy") Hoffa. Kennedy was able to demonstrate Hoffa's interactions with organized crime figures and illicit gambling activity. Kennedy's work with the committee led to the 1959 passage of the Landrum-Griffin Act, which regulated financial activities of labor unions. The committee action also established Robert Kennedy's reputation as a fighter against organized crime. That reputation was enhanced when he authored the best-selling book *The Enemy Within* (1960).

In 1960, Kennedy demonstrated his political expertise as he managed John F. Kennedy's successful campaign for the presidency of the United States. Bobby

Kennedy's reward was his appointment to the office of attorney general in January 1961. He held the office until September 1964. He concentrated the energies of his office and his Department of Justice on civil rights issues and on organized crime. He continued his quest to bring down James Hoffa; however, he was frustrated in these endeavors. It was left to his successors to finally guide the prosecutions that resulted in the imprisonment of Hoffa.

Attorney General Kennedy established an organized crime task force, and he pursued his objectives with prosecutions as well as with an agenda of new legislation. Three major bills dealing with illegal gambling were passed into law as a result of his efforts. These included the Federal Wire Act of 1961, the Travel Act of 1961, and the 1962 amendments to the Johnson Act (Gambling Devices Act), which expanded the prohibition of transportation of slot machines across state lines to include all gambling equipment. Congress also passed the Racketeer Influenced Corrupt Organizations Act (RICO) in 1961.

Kennedy maintained his steady attacks on organized crime until late 1963 when his brother, President John Kennedy, was assassinated. There has been more than one set of rumors suggesting an organized crime connection to the assassination. One account (Davis 1988) suggests that organized crime had been quite influential in the president's election and that crime figures maintained close relationships with the president and his father (who had been involved in bootlegging businesses decades before). Some feel that the attorney general's vigorous attacks on Mob activity somehow represented a double cross by the president.

After John Kennedy's assassination, Robert Kennedy turned his energies toward passage of civil rights legislation. In 1964, he resigned the office of attorney general in order to successfully run for a U.S. Senate seat from New York State. In 1968, while he was running for the presidency, Robert F. Kennedy was assassinated in Los Angeles.

References

Davis, John. 1988. *Mafia Kingfish: Carlos Marcellos and the Assassination of John F. Kennedy.* New York: McGraw-Hill.

Hersh, Seymour. 1997. *The Darker Side of Camelot.* Boston: Little, Brown.

Kennedy, Robert. 1960. *The Enemy Within.* New York: Harper.

KERKORIAN, KIRK

Three times one man built the largest hotel in the world. First it was the 1,512-room International Hotel on Paradise Road in Las Vegas in 1969. (This is now the Las Vegas Hilton.) Next it was the 2,084-room MGM Grand on Flamingo Road at the Las Vegas Strip in 1973. (This is now Bally's, which is also part of the Harrah's Casino Group.) Then, in 1993, it was the second Las Vegas MGM Grand Hotel and casino—with theme park. This facility, at Tropicana and the Strip, with 5,009 rooms, was the first billion-dollar casino project in Las Vegas. These achievements alone would merit mention of the man behind the projects—Kirk Kerkorian—in any encyclopedia of gambling, but his story is more interesting than that of simply being a builder. Parts of his story make him sound like Howard Hughes, other parts like Steve Wynn, but he was really neither. He is unique in the annals of casino personalities.

Kirk Kerkorian was born in Fresno, California, on June 6, 1917. His family moved to Los Angeles, where he had to contribute to their finances by selling newspapers at the age of nine and performing whatever other work he could find. He had spoken only the Armenian language of his forefathers until he reached the streets of Los Angeles. Los Angeles taught him that life was to be a struggle, and he willing jumped into the flow of the activity. He drove trucks to carry produce from the San Joaquin Valley, he worked with logging operations in Sequoia National Park, and he was an amateur boxer who won 29 of his 33 fights.

In 1939, he fell in love with flying, and within two years he had a commercial pilot's license. He soon became a flight instructor, and at the first chance he joined the British Royal Air Force. He ferried bombers from Canada to England on one very dangerous mission after another. In one flight he set a speed record for his aircraft. After the war, his interest remained in the air. In 1945, he visited Las Vegas, bought a single-engine Cessna, and went into the charter business. He would fly into Las Vegas almost daily. In 1947, he purchased the Los Angeles Air Service. Soon he went into the business of refurbishing planes and reselling them. He renamed his company Trans International Airlines and went into the passenger service business in 1959. His business continued to expand, and he would spend much of his free time in Las Vegas at the casinos.

Kerkorian always kept his eyes open for deals. In 1962, he was able to purchase the 80 acres across from the Flamingo on the Las Vegas Strip. By consolidating other pieces of land, he was able to create the parcel of property that Jay Sarno purchased in order to build Caesars Palace. Kerkorian also bought 82 acres of land on Paradise Road in 1967. The same year he was able to purchase the Flamingo Hotel for $12.5 million. In 1968, he sold Trans International Airlines for $104 million. The sale gave him the resources for his first major project, the International. He invested $16.6 million of his own money in the $80 million facility. He took the properties public in 1969 when the International opened, featuring performers such as Barbra Streisand, Ike and Tina Turner, and Elvis Presley. Yet the Securities and Exchange Commission did not allow him to sell sufficient shares of stock to pay off debts on this and other projects in which he was involved. He felt that he had to sell the Flamingo and International in order to satisfy his business obligations. Hilton took over the two hotel casinos in 1970 and 1971, but Kerkorian was not out of town for long.

He started out by buying a controlling interest in Western Airlines, and he began buying stock in a failing movie company called MGM Grand. He pushed the company toward diversifying into resort hotels. Their first project was the MGM Grand Hotel Casino in Las Vegas, named after the 1932 film *Grand Hotel*. The hotel opened on July 5, 1973, with a 1,200-seat show room, a shopping arcade, a movie theater featuring classic MGM films, and a jai alai fronton. In 1976, Kerkorian sold a large block of Western Airlines stock and began a new hotel-casino in Reno. In 1978, the $131 million MGM Grand–Reno opened, with the largest casino floor in the world and a 2,000-room tower—making it Reno's largest hotel.

Disaster struck the MGM Grand in Las Vegas on November 20, 1980. A fire that started in an electrical panel in a kitchen quickly shot through the casino area, killing a score of players and employees. When the fire reached the hotel lobby, it was knocked down by the sprinkler system. A massive smoke cloud was able to rise up stairwell and elevator shafts, however, before it was trapped on the upper floors. There the smoke penetrated guest rooms, killing dozens more. In all, 87 persons perished. Although the tragedy was devastating, Kerkorian quickly decided he would rebuild. By the end of 1981, the MGM was operating at full force. In 1986, however, Kerkorian walked away from his two properties, the Las Vegas MGM and the Reno MGM, selling them to Bally's for $594 million. Subsequently Bally's Reno was sold to Hilton, and in turn Hilton bought all of Bally's, so both properties—like the International before—have become part of Hilton's, now part of Harrah's.

Kirk Kerkorian could not stay away from Las Vegas gambling for long. Once again, he began to plan. One plan to take control of Chrysler Corporation fell short of its goal, although Kerkorian became the largest stockholder in the automotive giant. His other plan led to the creation of the world's largest hotel and casino floor (at the time). His 5,009-room colossus, also called MGM Grand (he had held on to the right to the name), featured a 330-acre theme park, a health club, eight restaurants, and a 15,000-seat arena where boxer Mike Tyson performed on many occasions (some notable, some infamous). Barbra Streisand came out of a 20-year moratorium on personal concerts to perform there as well for the grand opening in 1993.

When Kerkorian opened the International, he included a youth hostel in the facility. Later the Hilton had a youth recreation area in the facility. His 1993 MGM Grand was heralded as a casino for families with children. It had a Dorothy and the Wizard of Oz theme, with an Emerald City and a Yellow Brick Road. The word went out that Las Vegas was a place to bring children. Within a very short time, Kerkorian and the MGM management realized that children want two things from their parents—time and money. Both ways the casino loses. Kerkorian has backed off the family theme, and so has Las Vegas. The theme park at the MGM Grand has been consistently downsized, and plans have been made for expanding convention space and also for developing more rooms for prosperous gambling patrons.

Kerkorian, in the meantime, keeps moving forward, always seeking new business deals. In 2000, he failed in an effort to take over Chrysler Motors, but he did succeed in a takeover of Steve Wynn's Mirage Resorts, with a stock purchase for $6.6 billion. In the first decade of the new century, as majority owner of the new MGM-Mirage company, Kerkorian kept his eye on expansion. In 2004, the company purchased Mandalay Resorts (formerly Circus Circus) and thus acquired a majority of the hotel rooms on the Las Vegas Strip. These were added to their holdings in Atlantic City, Detroit, Mississippi, and Illinois. MGM-Mirage also won permission to build a casino in Macau, opening their property there in December 2007. Their biggest venture was the CityCenter project for the Las Vegas Strip. The first parts of the project were due to open in late 2009. CityCenter involves six entities, including hotels, casinos, condo facilities, entertainment and shopping centers. The $10 billion building complex is the largest private building project in the world. It is being financed as a joint venture with a government corporation from Dubai.

KERZNER, SOL

Solomon Kerzner, a.k.a. "The Sun King," was born in Johannesburg, South Africa, on August 23, 1935. While still in his twenties he built his first hotel in Durbin. He then took advantage of two South African laws. The first law banned all gambling. The second one, passed in 1976, created four "homelands" for the indigenous Black population. The homelands were given a degree of independence, which included the power to allow casino gambling. Kerzner jumped at a chance to gain a monopoly hold on casinos in the homelands. In 1977, he built his first casinos in Mmabatho, the capital city of Bophuthatswana. In 1979, he followed with his massive Sun City resort complex, built on the model of a Las Vegas resort and located only 100 miles from Johannesburg. The resort complex offered restaurants, disco nightclubs, boxing matches, and top entertainers. He continued to expand his line of casinos, and by the time South Africa reformed its government and instituted integration and abolished the homelands, Kerzner controlled 19 casinos in southern Africa.

However, Kerzner saw the "writing on the wall," as he knew the new South Africa would have competing casinos in urban areas. Therefore he divested himself of his southern Africa holdings and relocated his interests to the Bahamas. In 1994, he acquired Merv Griffin's Resorts International in the Bahamas. He soon built the new Atlantis, and later took over Griffin's Atlantic City casino. He sold the Atlantic City property in 2001. Before that, in 1996, Kerzner built the Native American Mohegan Sun casino in Connecticut.

In 2004, Kerzner transferred control over all his casinos to his son Butch. The same year he was named corporate Hotelier of the Year by *Hotels Magazine*.

LANSKY, MEYER

In 1902, Meyer Lansky was born Meyer Suchowljansky in Grodno, a small city in a region that has been—at different times—part of Russia, Poland, and Germany. The mostly Jewish community was confronted by pogroms conducted by Czarist Russia, and Meyer's father fled to the United States in 1909. When Meyer was about 10 years old, he came to the United States with the rest of his family. They all settled in a low-rent neighborhood in Brooklyn, New York. From these humble beginnings in the tenements, Meyer Lansky rose to become the "godfather" of a national crime syndicate, a principal in an organization called "Murder, Incorporated," and the person recognized as the financial director of Mob activity in the Western Hemisphere.

Much of the financial activity conducted by Lansky concerned money used for the establishment of casinos—both legal and illegal—and also money taken out of the profits of these casinos. Meyer and his brother, Jake, who became involved in many of Meyer's activities, learned about crime on the streets of Brooklyn. Lansky was also an excellent student, with a mind finely tuned for mathematical skills. He took a liking to the gambling rackets he observed on his neighborhood streets, because the games and scams conducted by various sharps and gangsters had a certain mathematical quality at their core. He also learned about the psychology of gambling and how the activity could prey upon the gullibility of players. Lansky also learned that street life had its violent side. While still a teenager, he intervened to stop another boy he had never met from shooting a fellow craps player. The aggressive boy was Benjamin Siegel. There on the streets, in the middle of what could have been a violent episode that could have ended what became a violent career, Lansky and Siegel (later to be known as "Bugsy") became very close friends. They became partners in crime until the end—that is, Siegel's end. Lansky was able to control Siegel's temper as no one else could, and he was also able to direct Siegel's penchant for violence. The two shared a similar background on the streets. When Prohibition began in 1921, they were prepared to be business partners.

Together Lansky and Siegel operated bootlegging activities. Bootlegging also brought Lansky into contact with Charlie "Lucky" Luciano. As their imbibing customers also craved gambling, their businesses were expanded. Liquor, betting, and wagering went together. With regard to gambling, Lansky was different from other mobsters running gambling joints. The others had proclivities to cheat customers, but Lansky knew the nature of the games. You did not have to cheat to make money. The odds favored the house, and all the operator needed was to have a certain volume of activity and to make sure that players were not cheating the house. Lansky could handle the numbers of customers he needed, and the numbers involved in determining the odds of each game. His mind was a calculator that allowed him to play it straight with the customers—and with his partners. But his operations also had rivals, and he cooperated with Luciano, Siegel, and others in consolidating control over their business enterprises by using violence.

When Prohibition ended on December 5, 1933, gambling became the major business interest for Lansky and many of his associates. Lansky became involved with gambling facilities in Saratoga Springs, New York; New York City; New Orleans; Omaha; and Miami. He also formed alliances with operations in Arkansas and Texas. In 1938, Cuban dictator Fulgencio Batista begged Lansky to come to the island and establish some honesty in their gambling casinos. The dealers were cheating the customers, and they were also robbing the dictator blind. He wanted his share. Lansky agreed to give him $3 million plus 50 percent of the profits from the casino. True to his word, Lansky cleaned up the operations. Later he took his skills for running an "honest" game for illicit operators to Haiti, the Bahamas, and London's Colony Club.

Perhaps Meyer Lansky's greatest legacy in gaming was found in Las Vegas. There he established the Mob's reputation for running honest games—albeit on behalf of mobsters. Lansky became a silent partner in the El Cortez in 1945. Soon his syndicate sold the property for a profit (they demonstrated it could make a profit), and they reinvested the money in the construction of the Flamingo Hotel and Casino on the Las Vegas Strip, six miles from the established casino area in downtown Las Vegas on Fremont Street. Bugsy Siegel was given the primary responsibilities for finishing the project. Siegel completed the job on time but not on budget. When the Flamingo opened in December 1946, it began to lose money. Lansky and his partners felt that Siegel had siphoned off much of the construction overruns as well as the operating revenues and put them into his own pockets—or into Swiss bank accounts. In June 1947, Siegel was murdered (by person or persons unknown) in the Beverly Hills apartment of his girlfriend. Soon afterwards the Flamingo was returning good profits under the operating hands of other Lansky associates.

Lansky's presence in Las Vegas persisted through the 1960s, as he was a silent partner in many gambling houses. It was said that he developed and perfected the art of skimming in order to get his share of the profits into his own pockets. A typical skimming device was to give large amounts of credit to players on gambling junkets. The players would then repay their loans to Lansky's associates, and not the casino, which would write them off as bad debts. It was alleged that Meyer Lansky skimmed $36 million from the Flamingo over an eight-year period. He was also alleged to have taken portions of the profits from the Sands, Fremont, Horseshoe, Desert Inn, and Stardust through similar skimming scams. Lansky also availed himself of large sums of money by taking a finder's fee when the Flamingo Casino Hotel was sold to Kirk Kerkorian in 1968.

In 1970, Lansky started an abortive campaign to legalize casinos in Miami Beach, where he had a residence. The year was not a good one for Lansky, as he was charged with tax evasion in federal court. He escaped prosecution by fleeing to Israel. There he sought citizenship under the Law of Return, which offered asylum to any person with a Jewish mother. As a result of considerable international as well as domestic pressure, he was denied Israeli citizenship and was exiled from Israel in November 1972. Back in the United States, he had to face tax charges and skimming charges, as well as contempt of court charges for fleeing prosecution. He dodged these charges at first because the court recognized he was in ailing health. Then, in 1974, after he had undergone heart surgery, his case was brought before federal judge Roger Foley in Las Vegas. Foley dismissed all charges. The U.S. Justice Department appealed the judge's action but could not get it overturned.

Lansky was free and in the United States. But he was old and in ill health, and his family was in considerable turmoil. Although some sources suggested that he was a wealthy man—with resources between $100 and $300 million—he was not. His resources were depleted as he lived out his last years alone and with very few assets. He was estranged from his daughter, and one handicapped son died in abject poverty. Perhaps the longest reign of an American "godfather" ended with little notice when he died in 1983.

LAUGHLIN, DON, AND LAUGHLIN, NEVADA

The post office said if he wanted delivery service he had to give a name to the town. And so in 1970, Laughlin, Nevada, was added to the map. Don Laughlin had moved to the "community," if it could be called that, four years before. He had been looking for a place to put a gambling hall, and he found a patch of land at the extreme south end of the state, near Davis Dam and across the Colorado River from a small town called Bullhead City, Arizona. Laughlin had run a small casino called the 101 Club in North Las Vegas for five years before he sold it in 1964 for $165,000. That was his stake as he entered the barren desert 100 miles south of Las Vegas.

Don Laughlin did not come to Nevada as an amateur in the gambling business. He was born and raised in Owatonna, Minnesota, where he lived throughout the 1930s and 1940s. There he saw gambling machines and other paraphernalia and instantly found them fascinating. As a teenager just beginning high school, he somehow ordered a slot machine from a mail-order catalog and was able to place it in a local club. Using profits from the machine, he bought more machines, and soon he ran a route of machines, punchboards, and pull tabs. Of course, all of this was illegal. He was forced to leave school because of his activity, but he did not mind, as he was making very good money for the time. It was not until 1952, following the work of the Kefauver Committee, that Minnesota cracked down on this illegal activity. With the passage of the Gambling Devices Act of 1951 (the Johnson Act), manufacturers could not easily ship gambling machines into the state. Laughlin knew there had to be better places to ply his trade. He vacationed in Las Vegas and upon seeing the city he quickly repeated the words of Brigham Young: "This is the place." In his twenties he worked in casinos and bars and then purchased his own beer and wine house. He added slot machines. His modest success allowed him to have funds to buy the 101 Club.

In Laughlin, Don Laughlin acquired an eight-room motel, which became the basis for expansion. He called his resort the Riverside. By 1972, it had 48 rooms and a casino. Eventually the Riverside grew to 1,400 rooms and included a recreational vehicle (RV) park with 800 spaces.

Today, the Riverside is but one of 10 casino hotels in a community having 11,000 rooms. Certainly Laughlin was gambling's boomtown of the 1980s as Harrah's, the Hilton, Circus Circus, Ramada (Tropicana), and the Golden Nugget all built there. In the 1990s business fell off as Native American casinos in both California and Arizona picked off customers on their way to the river resort. Laughlin has also been hurt by large casinos in Las Vegas and by the fact that commercial air travel to the town is very limited. The essential market for the town is drive-in traffic from southern California and the Phoenix area as well as a steady stream of senior citizens from all over the United States and Canada. Laughlin features many RV parks near all of its resorts as well as the most inexpensive hotel rooms in a gambling resort in North America. The casinos of Laughlin, Nevada, employ 9,677 people. In 2007, they achieved gaming revenues of $625 million, and other revenues of $325 million.

Don Laughlin continues to be a booster for the gambling town, seeking to have events that will attract both younger and older patrons. Country music artists and motorcycle rallies are always part of the fare.

MALOOF, GEORGE

Over the past decade, George Maloof has emerged as the leading new entrepreneur in the Las Vegas casino industry. He has given Las Vegas a fresh energy with a casino property, the Palms Resort, which appeals to young players from professional sports and the entertainment industry. He has also demonstrated a spirit of looking to the future and building even when others are mired in doubts and regrets about hard economic times. After the 9-11 disasters severely affected Las Vegas tourism, he gave the order to keep building the Palms. In 2008, as the U.S. economy hit new lows and other corporations began to scrap plans for future projects, he gave the orders to continue work on a new tower at the Palms. With established entrepreneur Steve Wynn as a Las Vegas soul mate of sorts, the two kept faith with the spirit of "the gambler" as they looked only to the future and their "next bet."

George Maloof was born in Albuquerque, New Mexico, in 1964. His father, Lebanese-born George Sr., operated the Coors beer distributorship for the state. The Maloof family soon branched out with new investments in both hotel and gaming. With his brothers and his mother, George Jr. turned his eyes to Las Vegas. George attended the University of Nevada, Las Vegas, majoring in hotel management and participating on the Running Rebels football team. It was off-campus Las Vegas that gave George his real education. He constantly studied the operations of the casinos while he was a student. After graduation in 1987, he persuaded his family to invest in their first casino in Central City, Colorado. Soon afterwards, he returned to Las Vegas and in 1994 purchased the land to build the Fiesta Casino in northwest Las Vegas. A small 35,000-square-foot casino facility constantly expanded after the doors opened. The Fiesta Casino became the top casino revenue producer on a per-square-foot basis in the state of Nevada. By 2000, it offered 75,000 square feet of gaming space.

The Fiesta was then sold, and the funds thus secured (more than $185 million) became the basic investment for construction of the Palms. That property was completed at the end of 2001. It was an instant winner as celebrities flocked to the casino. The Maloof family also ventured into other entertainment venues, one of which was pro basketball. They purchased the Sacramento Kings and Monarchs basketball teams of the NBA and WNBA. Because of this ownership, the Las Vegas casino was not allowed to take wagers on pro basketball games. For this reason the Palm became a big draw for professional basketball players, who could freely gamble at the resort with no fear of league officials or others worrying that they were betting on their own games. The Maloofs have also invested heavily in the music and motion picture business, giving them access to the stars of these industries. Maloof was able to establish several clubs in his facility, one of which is the Playboy Club—the first Playboy Club to open in two decades.

MORRISSEY, JACK

Jack Morrissey (1831–1878) was born in Ireland. His family moved to Troy, New York, when he was three years old. It was not long before the small boy became a man larger than life. In Troy he was a gang fighter, gaining the nickname "Old Smoke" from a barroom brawl in which he and his adversary knocked over a stove. They finished their "match" on the floor among burning coals. When Morrissey rose up as the winner, his hair and clothing were on fire. Soon afterward, "Old Smoke" was fighting according to the rules of professional boxing.

Morrissey sought a fortune by heading West during the California Gold Rush in the 1840s. The nuggets he got, however, were the result of an arranged prizefight. He performed so well that he was recruited back to the East Coast, where he participated in and won a heavyweight championship match. There is no record of a defense, so he probably retired as the undefeated champ. He was only 22 at the time, but there was real money to be made, in politics, in the saloon business, and in gambling. He opened a dancing and gambling joint in New York in 1852, and he used it as a staging point for political activity.

In New York, he became an important player in the Tammany political machine, as the organization needed tough characters to monitor their ballot-stuffing activities and to keep opponents at bay. Although an Irishman, Morrissey was their man, and he often led fights against immigrant opponents—often other Irishmen. Through his alliances in politics, Morrissey served two terms in the U.S. House of Representatives. He is the only heavyweight boxing champion to have served in the U.S. Congress. While not exactly a legislative leader, he would occasionally make a fiery speech on the House floor. There he would rant and rave and challenge any 10 of his political opponents to fight him at a single time.

In the meantime, Morrissey was attracted to the racing scene. In the 1860s, he organized the first thoroughbred races at Saratoga, New York, and he built the track that is still in use today. Morrissey wanted to achieve the high social status of those he saw in Saratoga, and he went after it. He upgraded the quality of gambling action at the resort by building the Saratoga Club House, the plushest casino in the United States at the time. He had only two rules for his house: no residents of Saratoga could gamble, and no women were permitted in the gambling saloons. Women, however, could come to the restaurants and the other entertainment areas. It is reported that more than 25,000 women came into the Saratoga Club House each season (Chafetz, 285–286). For a dozen years the Saratoga Club House was the national champion casino. Through it all Morrissey smoked 20 cigars a day and led a very fast, tough life to the end. In 1878, at the age of 47, he had worn his body out, and when he was hit by a heavy cold, the champ was out for the count.

Reference

Chafetz, Henry. 1960. *Play the Devil: A History of Gambling in the United States from 1492 to 1955.* New York: Potter Publishers, 271–296.

MOSS, JOHNNY

Johnny Moss, superb gamester, gambler, and world champion of poker, was born in 1907 in a poor Texas town. Eventually his family drifted into Dallas when their economic condition did not improve much. At eight years old Johnny quit school and began selling newspapers. At this time he also met his lifelong friend, Benny Binion. Together they learned games, and they began their careers as players. By the time Johnny Moss was 15, he was making a living at dice.

Soon he was wandering around Texas playing games and learning games. In West Texas he also worked on a ranch. One day he rode his horse by a golf course and saw two hackers betting as they played. He figured, "What folks are betting on, you learn to play, that's all." So he learned to play golf. He learned so well that years later he played a round of golf at the Desert Inn for a $100,000 stake. He beat 80, shooting 79, with irons only. At an earlier time, he had won a $5,000 bet that he could shoot 9 below 45 with only a four iron. Johnny also learned to bowl. But these were really just side games. An automobile accident left him unable to compete in physical activities at the level that a hustler must perform in order to win. He turned to his real game—poker.

But still there were physical dangers. "To be a professional gambler," he related, not only means "you have to know how to play the games, [but also] you have to keep your eyes open for two dangers, the hijackers and the law" (Bradshaw, 165). But that was before the big action moved to Las Vegas and was held under the big tops of the legal casinos. In 1949, Nick the Greek Dandolos came to Las Vegas looking for a game. Benny Binion, of the Horseshoe casino, called his friend Johnny Moss in Texas and suggested they have a one-on-one match in his casino. It was the first world championship poker match, and it lasted five months before Nick the Greek threw in his cards and walked away.

Twenty-one years later, the formal World Series of Poker began. Johnny Moss won it three times in the 1970s. Moss won the first tournament and played in every one until 1995. In his later years, he played regularly, but not for the big stakes that had previously driven him. For a while, he was the poker room manager at the Aladdin Hotel. But mostly he traveled back and forth between Las Vegas and his home in Odessa, Texas. He died there at the age of 88, in 1995.

Reference

Bradshaw, Joe. 1975. *Fast Company.* New York: Harper Magazine Press.

PENDLETON, EDWARD

Edward Pendleton was a 19th-century gambling service provider for political leaders in the United States. To get an idea of what he provided, just suppose that the mid-1990s proposal for a legalized casino within the jurisdiction of the District of Columbia had passed. Imagine that congressmen, cabinet members, Supreme Court justices, maybe the president himself, could come to the casino and be wined and dined, then offered credit for gambling at the tables. Imagine lobbyists circulating within the facility the day before a major vote in Congress or a major decision by the court. Imagine the opportunities to buy favors, to line the pockets of the mighty in exchange for policy outcomes.

Well, it is not necessary to imagine. You need only read a history of Edward Pendleton and his Palace of Fortune located within walking distance of the houses of government in the District of Columbia through the 1830s, 1840s, and 1850s. The facility at 14th and Pennsylvania Avenue, two blocks from the White House, became the favorite of the ruling classes. The president of the United States, James Buchanan, was a regular at the faro bank. The nation's most important policymakers would wager at Pendleton's faro bank and inevitably lose. They would then become indebted to the casino owner. He, of course, was a lobbyist. Actually, win or lose, he came out ahead. It is reported that in the 26 years that Pendleton ran the Palace of Fortune he was responsible for the passage of hundreds of bills, most of which were private bills providing favors for selected citizens. The casino was extremely luxurious, as the owner became a very rich man.

The casino was also the meeting place where abolitionists and slave-owning senators could come together on neutral ground. Many of the compromises that kept the Civil War from erupting until 1861 may have been reached over the tables of the Palace.

Pendleton married the daughter of one of the leading architects of the District of Columbia. The couple became a dominant part of the social scene, well respected as many other gamblers in other venues were not. When Edward Pendleton died in 1858 at the age of 68, his funeral was attended by the president and most leaders of Congress.

ROSE, I. NELSON

Professor I. Nelson Rose is internationally recognized as a leading scholar of gambling law. He is a Distinguished Senior Professor at Whittier Law School in California and a Visiting Professor at the University of Macau. He completed his undergraduate education at UCLA, and he received his law degree from Harvard. In 1979, Rose published a major article in the *Fordham Law Review* that traced American gambling policy through three waves: the Colonial and Revolutionary era, the Post–Civil War era, and the Modern era, commencing with the establishment of the New Hampshire lottery in 1964. In 1986, he published the book *Gambling and the Law.* He has also coauthored *Blackjack and the Law* (1998), *Internet Gaming Law* (1st edition, 2005; 2nd edition, 2009), and *Gaming Law: Cases and Materials* (2003). He shares his expertise through an internationally syndicated column with his trademarked title, "Gambling and the Law." He is co-editor-in-chief of the *Gaming Law Review.*

Rose has been a consultant to industry and governments, including international corporations; players; major law firms; licensed casinos; lotteries; Indian tribes; the city of Windsor, Ontario; the states of Arizona, California, Delaware, Florida, Illinois, Michigan, New Jersey, Texas; and, the federal governments of Canada, Mexico, and the United States. He has testified as an expert witness in administrative, civil, and criminal cases throughout the United States and in Australia and New Zealand, including the first tribunal on gaming issues held under the North American Free Trade Agreement (NAFTA). He has taught classes on gaming law to the FBI, at the University of Ljubljana in Slovenia, Sun Yat-sen University in China, the Universidad de Cantabria in Spain, Université de Toulouse in France, and as a Visiting Scholar for the University of Nevada–Reno's Institute for the Study of Gambling and Commercial Gaming.

ROTHSTEIN, ARNOLD

Arnold Rothstein (1882–1928) represents a great transition in the history of gambling in the United States. He took gambling enterprise from being an entrepreneurial activity of individuals operating at the edge of the law to becoming a major industry centrally controlled by criminal elements. In the process, he established a reputation for being a man of his word and a dominant high-stakes player. He defeated Nick the Greek Dandolos in a dice game with stakes of $600,000. Rothstein owned several casinos, and he was the financial linchpin who held together the ring that fixed the 1919 World Series. He also developed the layoff system for bookies across the country. His transitional role coincided with the coming of national Prohibition, which, of course, provided great incentives for centralized Mob activities.

Arnold Rothstein was born in 1882, the son of Arthur Rothstein. His father was a successful merchant. Although he wanted Arnold to follow in his footsteps, it was not to be. Arnold loved games, and he also loved to play. In 1909, Arnold got married in Saratoga, New York, during the racing season. He actually used his ring and his wife's jewelry as collateral for his bets on his wedding night. Compulsive gamblers say that gambling is the most powerful of life's urges, and whatever is in second place cannot even compete. Rothstein coveted the lifestyle he found at Saratoga, and he vowed (some vows are taken seriously) that he would come back in a role other than a tourist player.

Rothstein started playing harder and harder in New York City and also on ocean liners. Then he started running the games. Before he was 30, he had gambling halls in the city, and soon he was planning his return to Saratoga.

In Saratoga he created and opened the Brook, a nightclub with gambling. He began to restore an aura that Richard Canfield had established in the first decade of the century. Rothstein later acquired the Spa casino, and he invited Meyer Lansky and Lucky Luciano to be operators of his games. Other figures who emerged as leading mobsters and propelled the Mob's gambling activity toward the Las Vegas Strip were his friends—Frank Costello, Dutch Schultz, Waxey Gordon, and Jack "Legs" Diamond.

Rothstein had a stable of horses, and he became very active in bookmaking—for races and other sports events. At a casual meeting of other bookies, one remarked that he had passed up a lot of action recently because too many bets were on one side of the proposition, and he had to control his risks. Rothstein told him if that happened again to call him, and he would cover the action and thereby help the bookie balance his books—for a small percentage. Rothstein's headquarters suddenly became the center of sports and race betting in the United States. Layoffs came from Rothstein. (Layoffs occur when the clients of minor bookies bet too heavily in favor of one team. The minor bookies seek out major players, such as the Rothsteins, in order to spread out their risk—that is, lay off some of their bets with a bigger bookie.) The central headquarters also became the source of odds for sports gambling.

From such a position of power and influence in sports betting, Rothstein became involved in the most notorious sports scandal of the 20th century. A Boston bookie called him because some players on the Chicago White Sox had requested $80,000 to throw the 1919 World Series in which they were playing the underdog Cincinnati Reds. Definitive facts do not exist to say for sure if Rothstein provided all or part of the $80,000. Many writers think he did. For sure he gambled heavily that the Cincinnati team would win. He took hundreds of thousands of dollars in gambling wins on the series. The fix held. Revelations of the fix were not made public for a year. The subsequent response was for major leagues (especially the baseball leagues) to establish strict rules governing betting by players. Owners were treated differently. Neither players nor owners, however, were ever to bet on games involving their own teams. Rape, drug sales, and even murder were lesser crimes compared to this serious matter. Players involved in the 1919 scandal were banned forever from baseball, just as has been Pete Rose for his alleged bets that his team would win games in the 1980s. (The name of the greatest hitter in the history of the sport is not found in the Hall of Fame because of transgressions that violate the rules that arose from the 1919 scandal.)

Rothstein's days as a leading hitter came early in his life. Actually, there were not many days later in his life. Although he had been considered a man of integrity, he welshed on gambling debts stemming from a game in 1928 in which he lost $340,000. He refused to pay because he thought the game had been rigged. A few weeks after refusing to pay, he was found with a bullet in his side. He knew enough of the code of honor not to squeal on his assailant in the day or so he lingered before he died. He was only 46.

SAWYER, GRANT

Grant Sawyer came to the governorship of the state of Nevada somewhat accidentally, but once in office he set about his job with defined purpose. During his eight years in office, Sawyer directed the restructuring of gambling regulation in the state, defended the sovereignty of the state against an abusive federal Justice Department, championed integration of gambling casinos, and championed civil liberties for Nevada citizens.

On December 14, 1918, Grant Sawyer was born in Twin Falls, Idaho. His parents were doctors, but they divorced when he was very young. He remained with his mother and a stepfather in Idaho. The home was staunchly Baptist, and young Grant was encouraged to go to Linfield College in Oregon. At the Baptist college he gained a love for history and political science. He felt that the social rules imposed by the school were too strict for his tastes, however, so he moved to Nevada where he could be near his father (who had moved to Fallon) and attend the University of Nevada campus at Reno. In Reno he became plugged into Nevada politics. After graduation he won the sponsorship of U.S. Senator Pat McCarran and went to Washington, D.C., with a job at the U.S. Capitol. He also attained a spot at the George Washington University Law School. His stint in law school was interrupted by World War II service in the Pacific. He finished legal studies at Georgetown Law School and then returned to Nevada and politics.

Although he was certainly expected to be a McCarran loyalist, McCarran's very conservative politics did not suit Sawyer—just as a Baptist college that banned dancing had not suited him. McCarran was allied with Senator Joseph McCarthy and his communist witch hunts, and Sawyer simply disagreed with those politics. But national policy was not that important to his first political jobs. He moved to Elko, Nevada, where political opportunities were open. He became active in the Democratic party and was elected to the post of district attorney. In 1956, he sought a post on the University of Nevada Board of Regents. Although he was not successful in the election, he received an appointment when the size of the board was increased. In 1958, he decided to seek statewide office. His father urged him to seek the attorney general post, as the position was being vacated by the incumbent, who was planning to run for governor. That man was the very conservative Harvey Dickerson, a protégé of the late Senator McCarran. On an impulse, however, Sawyer filed to be a candidate for governor. His political sense was right. The Democratic Party in the state had turned away from McCarran conservatism, and Sawyer was a much more dynamic candidate than Dickerson could hope to be. Sawyer won the primary and then faced the very popular Republican Governor Charles Russell. Russell was finishing his second term in office, however, and Nevada had never elected a governor to serve three terms. Besides, 1958 was a good year for Democrats everywhere. Sawyer was elected governor by a small margin.

Sawyer immediately put together a legislative package for reforms in gambling. His bill called for the creation of a Nevada Gaming Commission to replace the state taxation commission as the "supreme" gaming regulatory agency. The Gaming Control Board would then report to the commission. Members of both the commission and the board had to be nonpartisan and not involved in any politics. The legislation passed. At Sawyer's direction the commission created a black book, officially called the Book of Excluded Persons. Sawyer was very aware of the work of the McClellan Senate committee and its attacks on racketeering in gambling. He knew that federal officials were looking at Nevada, and he wanted to make sure that the federal government knew that state officials did not want organized crime interests to play an active role in casino gambling. The black book included a list of notori-

ous persons who would not be allowed to set foot in any casino property in the state.

Sawyer was a strong supporter of Senator John F. Kennedy in the nomination campaign and in the presidential election of 1960. He was excited to see Kennedy inaugurated and was happy to see Robert (Bobby) Kennedy selected as attorney general. Sawyer had reason to believe that they understood Nevada and that they would support his efforts to keep the state's gambling industry clean. It was not very long, however, before Robert Kennedy put Nevada in his sights and aimed to destroy gambling. Robert Kennedy revealed to the state attorney general a plan to deputize all 56 assistant attorneys general in Nevada as federal assistant attorneys general. Then Kennedy was going to conduct a simultaneous raid on the cages of all the casinos in the state. Enraged by what he saw as a violation of civil liberties, Sawyer was on the next plane to Washington, D.C., as soon as the Nevada attorney general reported the plan to him. There Sawyer confronted Bobby Kennedy at his office in socks and a tennis sweater. He found Bobby to be condescending and extremely arrogant. There was no resolution of anything, and Grant Sawyer simply went to the White House and demanded an audience with the president. The president listened seriously and promised nothing, but Sawyer felt he had made his point. In a symbolic gesture one Nevada assistant attorney general was deputized by Bobby Kennedy, and there was no raid.

Sawyer did not contend that all was well with Nevada gambling. He knew that the commission and the board would have to be tough. He backed them to the hilt when they disciplined casinos for improper activities. He supported them when they revoked Frank Sinatra's casino license because he had hosted a member of the black book at his casino and then refused to cooperate with the board when he was called to appear to be disciplined.

Nevada was selectively segregated all through its early casino era. Sawyer recognized that this was wrong, bad for business, and certainly adverse to the interests of the gambling industry in Washington, D.C. In 1963 he supported civil rights leaders in their effort to integrate the casinos. He brokered the deal that precluded a march on the casinos by African American activists, in return for the immediate opening of all casino resort facilities to persons of all races without discrimination. When it appeared that there might be race riots in Las Vegas two years later, Sawyer personally drove into the westside neighborhoods of Las Vegas and met the residents one on one. The residents knew where he stood on civil rights matters, and they supported him in keeping the community peaceful during a troubled time.

Sawyer was also instrumental in beginning the interstate cooperation with California that led to growth limits and environmental protection policies for the Lake Tahoe Basin.

During Sawyer's second four-year term in office, the state had a popular new lieutenant governor named Paul Laxalt. When Sawyer sought a third term in 1966, he had several disadvantages: he was running against Laxalt, and he had made important enemies due to tough policies on civil rights, gambling, and other issues. Ironically, his opposition to Bobby Kennedy spilled over into opposition to J. Edgar Hoover and the Federal Bureau of Investigation's attempt to tap telephone lines in the casinos searching for evidence of organized crime involvement. After Sawyer condemned the actions, Hoover let key people in the state know that Sawyer was being soft on criminals. Laxalt won a close victory.

Sawyer retired from public office. He founded the world's largest law firm specializing in gambling law—Lionel, Sawyer, and Collins—in Las Vegas. He also became the chair of the Nevada chapter of the American Civil Liberties Union. Sawyer died in Las Vegas on February 24, 1996.

SIEGEL, BENJAMIN

It has been said that it is an ill wind that blows no good. When this editor heard of such an occasion on a visit to Puerto Rico, it reminded him of a similar situation in Las Vegas. On a visit to Puerto Rico a year or so after a tragic fire had killed scores of patrons at the Du Pont Plaza Hotel and Casino on New Year's Eve in 1986, the editor asked a manager of another hotel about the effects of the disaster on casino business in San Juan, expecting to hear that revenues had gone down. To his surprise, the manager said, "I can't say this too loudly, but you know, that fire really helped our business." He added, "Before the disaster nobody knew that Puerto Rico had casinos; now the story about one of our casinos was on the front page of every newspaper in the world." The story can be applied to Las Vegas as well. Years before the tragedy in Puerto Rico, Las Vegas had been just a cowboy town with a few casino joints, hardly in the minds of anyone far away. Then on June 20, 1947, a bullet rushed through the handsome head of Benjamin Siegel, a mobster who had orchestrated the construction and the opening of the most glamorous casino of the day. The next day his murder was headline material for newspapers everywhere. Part of the story focused upon the property he had developed and the many glamorous people—mainly movie stars—who frequented his Flamingo Hotel Casino resort. Las Vegas was on the map!

In death, Benjamin Siegel, also known as "Bugsy" (although no one dared to call him that), became an indelible part of the history of Las Vegas, credited in large part for developing the Las Vegas Strip. The reality diverges somewhat from the myth. Siegel did not start the Strip, he did not own the Flamingo, and his role as the manager-builder of the property was secondary to his image as a handsome but nonetheless ruthless mobster who controlled rackets on the West Coast mainly through intimidation. But his death certainly was a bit of marketing genius for Las Vegas, although it can be certain that city promoters were not responsible for pulling the trigger on the army carbine that did the trick.

Benjamin Siegel was born in 1905 in Brooklyn. As a youngster he became a friend of Meyer Lansky, and the two drifted into rackets, including bootlegging and illegal gambling. The engendered fear that Siegel cast upon others as he walked through his shortened life was a product of the fact that the "Bugsy and Meyer" gang gained a reputation for doing contract work for other organized crime interests. But all need not have feared. As Siegel told builder Del Webb, who was constructing the Flamingo, "We only kill each other." Lansky and the other New York Mob leaders chose Siegel to be the chief of their West Coast operations, specifically the wire services that carried information on horse and dog races. In California, Siegel befriended the Hollywood movie crowd, and himself became something of a celebrity. He pushed himself into most local rackets. He took a piece of the action from gambling boats operating off the Pacific shore, he controlled action at dog tracks, and he had a piece of the Agua Caliente track and casino in Tijuana. Siegel also bought into several Las Vegas casinos, including the Golden Nugget and Frontier.

In 1945, Meyer Lansky and Siegel drove to Las Vegas together to check on their interests there—the casinos and the wire services—and they discussed the notion of having a new resort that could attract a real tourist crowd as opposed to the existing "sawdust" joints that thrived on local and drive-in trade. They found the Flamingo. It had been the dream of Billy Wilkerson, an owner of a nightclub in Hollywood. Wilkerson shared lots of friends with Lansky and Siegel, but he did not have access to their money. His dream was stymied by a lack of financial resources. Siegel and Lansky saw an opportunity, and they took over the project. The organized crime elements in New York and Chicago invested $1.5 million into the venture, and Siegel was given the task of getting it done and opening the doors.

Siegel, like Wilkerson, had financial problems with the property. World War II was ending, and materials were scarce. He paid Del Webb's construction firm top dollar for overtime to rush the construction schedule. Many suppliers found that Siegel did not have a business sense that allowed him to keep track of inventories, and they effectively cheated him out of many dollars worth of goods. Cost overruns followed cost overruns. At the same time, Siegel was carrying on a relationship with Hollywood actress Virginia Hill. That tempestuous affair caused him to neglect work duties as well. As the mobsters back East were being hit for more and more money for construction, they became suspicious that Siegel himself was stealing from the project. They became convinced when Virginia Hill started making trips to Europe and visited Swiss banks. By the end of the project, the price tag had risen from $1 million to $6 million, and conversations about changing management via assassination had arisen.

Siegel was allowed to survive to open the property, and he did so on December 26, 1946. The opening was another financial disaster, however. The hotel's rooms were not finished, so guests stayed elsewhere. Bad weather precluded many celebrities from flying in from Los Angeles for the opening. And the players had a run of luck beating the house. To stop the financial hemorrhaging, Siegel closed the Flamingo. He reopened it in March 1947 when the rooms were done and the weather was better. His luck was better, too, and soon the Flamingo was turning a profit. Unfortunately, it was not soon enough for Siegel. His mobster partners had entered the contract for his life. Virginia Hill was in Europe in June, but Bugsy decided that a trip to her apartment in Beverly Hills would beat staying in the Las Vegas heat. He was sitting in her living room reading the *Los Angeles Times* when three bullets flew into the window and changed the mythology and probably also the history of Las Vegas. The identity of the killer was never discovered.

THOMPSON, "TITANIC" (ALVIN CLARENCE THOMAS)

Alvin Clarence Thomas was one of the great gambling hustlers of the modern era. He was born in the Ozarks near Monnet, Missouri, on November 30, 1892. There are several different stories about why he was called "Titanic."

Some refer to the notion that he was unsinkable, unlike the ship. Others suggest that when he won a lot of money, he was on the top of the world, but that he would often sink rapidly if he continued to play. For many years he was "Titanic

Thomas," but once a newspaper mistakenly called him "Titanic Thompson," and he did not bother to make a correction, perhaps liking the sound of the name better. After all, he was not fond of being called Alvin Clarence either—why not change it all? Titanic was renowned for the proposition bet. He loved all games, and he loved to participate in physical games as well as to turn cards or roll dice. As a teenager, he trained his dog to dive into a 15-foot-deep pond to retrieve rocks he threw. One day he "chanced" upon a fisherman who had a modern rod and reel that the teenager coveted. He engaged in conversation with the fisherman, who said he sure liked the dog. Thompson made a wager: he bet the dog against the rod and reel that the dog could fetch a small pebble from the bottom of the pool if he threw it in. The bet was made, and to assure that all was on the up and up, Titanic marked the pebble with an X. He threw it in, the dog jumped after it, dived to the bottom of the pool, and brought up a pebble in his mouth. The pebble was marked with an X. Thompson won his first proposition. He neglected to tell the fisherman that he had spent the previous day marking pebbles with X's and lining the pool with them.

His talents as an athlete were renowned. Al Capone once wagered that Thompson could not throw an orange over a five-story building. Titanic extracted a good odds advantage and then indicated that he needed a harder orange. He returned from a fruit stand and threw the "orange" over the building. In fact, with sleight of hand he had changed the orange for a harder and smaller lemon. Capone just laughed and paid him off, not knowing he had been tricked.

Titanic Thompson was an accomplished golf player, and he hustled millions of dollars on various wagers on the golf course. He often won money from professional players from whom he would negotiate a handicap advantage—although he was capable of winning straight up. He was very adept at determining the changing odds as a poker game progressed. Had blackjack been popular, he would have been able to execute the card-counting strategies of Edward Thorpe with the best of them. Thompson could also work magic with his hands, dealing any card from the bottom or middle of a deck of cards. He could substitute crooked dice into a craps game. With his crowd and such advantage he could achieve what was always considered "fair game." The loser had only one option, pay up and play again, or pay up and not play again.

Titanic Thompson did not have a formal education, and he could not read or write for his entire life. But he could count, he could figure out numbers quickly in his head, and he could memorize words. He achieved great wealth during the course of his hustling days, and he used all the trappings of wealth in his games. He had a fine home in Beverly Hills, he drove the best cars, and he wore elaborate clothes. He also had beautiful wives—five of them at different times.

Thompson played with the most renowned gamblers of his time, from Al Capone to Johnny Moss. He also played with Arthur Rothstein. In 1928, he was in Rothstein's last card game. Rothstein, like other gamblers, had his favorite games, but there were also games where he was a sucker. In poker, Rothstein was a sucker. Leading players from all over the country descended upon his New York City apartment when he put out the word that he wanted to play. He liked

games with no limit, and he had a reputation of paying off. In this game, he lost
hundreds of thousands of dollars to
Thompson and others, and he gave his
word that he would make his payoff
later. He word was accepted, but he
welshed on his promise. After several
weeks passed and he kept avoiding his
obligation, he declared that the game had
been rigged and that he would not pay.
He was found in a hotel lobby with a bullet wound in his side. He refused to talk
from his hospital bed, where he died a
day later. Thompson was arrested along
with the other players in the big game.
He testified in the murder trial to the
integrity of his co-players, and the
charges were dropped for lack of evidence. Thompson was never considered

the triggerman, although in his hustling
career he had killed at least five men in
"self-defense" situations.

Titanic Thompson was in his heyday
through the 1950s when the big players
discovered Las Vegas and routinized their
play. They sought regular games with
rules. The big gambling scene for hustlers
was over. He suffered a major downfall
when he was jailed for several months in
1962 after a big party at his Phoenix
home. It was found that one of the "play-
mates" in his crowd of friends was underage. He dropped from the scene, although
for his remaining days he kept trying to
hustle—efforts that led to losses as often
as wins. In 1974, at the age of 81, he died
of a stroke in a rest home near Dallas. He
was broke and broken.

TRUMP, DONALD JOHN

Donald John Trump emerged as the
dominant personality of Atlantic City in
the 1980s as he developed three casinos
in the East Coast gambling center. He
was not yet in his forties when he won a
license in 1982, along with his younger
brother, Robert, to build and operate the
Trump Plaza. Soon he negotiated a
merger for the ownership of the property
with Holiday Inn. The finished property
opened in 1984 as the Harrah's at Trump
Plaza. In 1986, Trump bought out his
Holiday Inn partners and also purchased
a casino, which was being constructed
by the Hilton Corporation, after Hilton
was denied a license. The project
became known as the Trump Castle. In
1988, he acquired rights to the Taj Mahal

casino in a financial struggle with
Resorts International and directed the
completion of Atlantic City's largest
property, which at the time featured the
largest casino floor in the world. By the
time the Taj Mahal opened in 1989, it
carried a price tag of $1 billion, the high-
est price for any casino project in the
world at the time. High prices come at a
cost, however, and in the early 1990s, the
property went through a bankruptcy
action in order to survive. But as the
economy began to improve in the mid-
1990s, Trump's properties made money
again, or at least were able to satisfy
their creditors. That is, he did well
enough to be able to sell equity shares in
his properties and keep everything afloat.

Out of the debts he arose again as the champion of the Boardwalk. He also expanded to the Midwest by opening a large riverboat in Indiana on the shores of Lake Michigan. The self-proclaimed "master of the deal" even allowed his sights to scan the political landscape, as he publicly pondered a run for the presidency in year 2000 on the Reform Party ticket.

Donald Trump was raised in wealth. His father, Fred Trump, was a builder who beginning in the 1920s parlayed construction of individual housing into development of tracts and building of large apartment complexes, often with government subsidies. His father learned all about political connections and how they were necessary in his line of work. Donald was born in 1946 in the Jamaica Estates in Queens, a borough of New York City. His family lived in a 23-room mansion. As a youth, the younger Trump gained a taste for fancy cars, tailored clothes, and fancy women—what he would consider to be the most important things in life—possessions. He also showed a proclivity to follow in his father's footsteps as a builder.

He was sent to the New York Military Academy in Cornwell on the Hudson. He was a good student, and he demonstrated leadership qualities. After military academy Trump attended Fordham University and the Wharton School at the University of Pennsylvania. He graduated with a BA in economics in 1968. Trump expressed disappointment that the real estate courses at Penn emphasized single-family dwellings because he desired to build big things. Soon he was working with his father building bigger things. And soon after that, he left to go on his own because his father did not want to build big enough things. His father was somewhat content

to be rich building in the neighborhoods, but Donald Trump wanted Manhattan.

Trump saw his first big opportunity come when the Penn Central Railroad declared bankruptcy. He took options on some of their land alongside the Hudson River, and he also took an option on the 59-year-old Commodore Hotel. He persuaded the city to purchase the riverfront land for a major convention center. Trump cut a deal with the Hyatt Corporation to construct the Grand Hyatt on the Commodore location; the new hotel, with 1,400 rooms, was finished in 1990. Almost simultaneously, Trump started other hotel projects and also a high-rise apartment building called Trump Towers. He visited Atlantic City often and pondered casinos. He never gave them serious thought, however, until he saw reports indicating that Hilton's two Las Vegas hotel casinos made almost half the income of all Hilton properties in the United States. Suddenly he realized that even a mediocre hotel with a casino could be much more profitable that the most luxurious hotels of the world.

Trump took a long look at Atlantic City before jumping into that market. He wanted land near the center of the Boardwalk area. In 1980, some land investors came to him with a plan by which he could gain control over what he considered the most prime land in the city. In his book *The Art of the Deal,* Trump describes the intricacies of how to put many separately owned parcels of land together (Trump and Schwartz 1987). Every offer he made for a purchase was contingent upon all parcels being purchased. He also determined that he would not start to build a casino until he was fully licensed. In 1982, he and his younger brother, Robert, won casino licenses. After he began to construct his casino, he went into a partnership with Holiday Inn. When the casino hotel was finished in 1984, it was called Harrah's at Trump Plaza. He bought out his partner in 1986 and installed his brother as its manager. Later Steve Hyde took over control of the casino aspects of the operation. The property became the Trump Plaza. By then, Trump had taken over the Hilton's 614-room hotel casino complex in a deal that was necessitated by the fact that the New Jersey gambling authorities had denied Hilton a license in 1985.

When the complicated deal was completed, Trump chose his wife, Ivana, to be the property manager of the new Trump Castle. Ivana had absolutely no experience in gaming—and in fact, neither did Trump. She saw the Castle as a place of glamour that could attract high rollers, whereas Hilton had intended to have a slot-intensive facility that would cater to the masses. The Plaza was a place for high rollers. Rather than working with a strategy that tied the two properties together, Trump encouraged Hyde and Ivana to operate as competitors. Soon internal corporate battles turned vicious. Also, Trump had found a girlfriend, Marla Maples. In order to conceal his affair with Maples, Trump allied himself with Hyde in the battle between Hyde and Ivana. His tryst flowered in the Plaza. Finally, Trump felt it was necessary to remove Ivana from the Castle and get her out of town. He publicly humiliated her as he moved her into a management role in one of his New York City properties. An inevitable divorce was followed by a short marriage to Marla Maples.

The next casino opportunity came for Trump when Resorts International president James Crosby died on April 10, 1986, at the premature age of 58. In 1984, he had revealed plans for the largest casino attached to a hotel in the United States. The Taj Mahal was to have more than 120,000 feet of gambling space and over 1,000 rooms—the largest number in Atlantic City. Resorts International won all the approvals for construction, and the process of building began. The death of Crosby plunged Resorts into a fiscal crisis, however, and Trump made a move to buy out the company and hence acquire the rights to the "largest casino in America." As New Jersey law provided that a casino owner could have only three properties, Trump indicated that he would close the Resorts Casino as soon as the Taj Mahal opened. Trump did win a controlling position in Resorts with his stock purchases. He found, however, that he lacked the capital to finish the Taj Mahal. Television entertainer Merv Griffin in a sense bailed Trump out by purchasing all Resorts property except the Taj Mahal from Trump in 1988. In 1989, the project was completed. Trump, however, did not have the funds to properly open the facility. Legal troubles flowing from his divorce further complicated his already complex financial affairs. The property was also beset with a tragedy, as Steve Hyde, who was to become its manager, and two other top executives were killed in a helicopter accident on October 10, 1989. Only recourse to bankruptcy proceedings in 1992 and transfers of equity in the property to bond holders and other creditors saved the property.

In 1995, Trump completed an initial public offering on the New York Stock Exchange to sell more than $300 million of common stock and senior secured notes backed by his casino revenue flow. That same year he was named to be a member of the World Gaming Congress Hall of Fame. When his rival Stephen Wynn heard this, he asked the congress to remove his name from the Hall of Fame. A rivalry persists, but Trump is the one who can say he "turned things around." Showing that he has something like the proverbial nine lives of a cat, through the early years of the new century Trump has gone into and come out of bankruptcy several times, launched new hotel and condo projects in several venues, and also launched a career as a television star with his production of "The Apprentice." These accolades earned Trump a star on the Hollywood walk of fame. Today Trump remains a man always in search of the next big deal, wherever that deal might be found.

Reference

Trump, Donald, and Tony Schwartz. 1987. *Trump: The Art of the Deal.* New York: Random House.

WALLNER, LEO

Austrian Leo Wallner was born in Amstetten in 1935. He studied at the University of Vienna, and afterwards was an economic advisor to the prime minister of the country. In 1968, he became the general manager of Casinos Austria, a post he held until 2007. Subsequently he joined the supervisory board of the corporation as a vice president. Under his leadership Casinos Austria developed into an international giant in gaming, developing its subsidiary Casinos Austria International and eventually participating in the management of more than 70 casinos in 18 countries on every continent. Wallner also engineered the creation of the Austrian lottery and developed Internet and video lottery games in his country. Wallner has been the president of the Austrian Olympic Committee, and since 1998 he has served as a member of the International Olympic Committee.

WYNN, STEPHEN ALAN

Stephen Alan Wynn may be considered a modern day "savior" for Las Vegas. Even though the Las Vegas Strip had not exactly died in the 1980s, it was not healthy. Wynn may not have raised a Lazarus from the grave, but he certainly performed the role of "healer" for a moribund casino industry. He healed with the medicine the community vitally needed—a good dose of entrepreneurial risk taking and an infusion of new capital investment. Revenues for the Strip were flat in the 1980s. No new Las Vegas property had been constructed since the completion of the MGM Grand (now Bally's) in 1973.

Other investors had shunned the town. New Jersey casino magnate Donald Trump had rejected Las Vegas. Wynn, however, turned away from his Atlantic City ventures and came back to Las Vegas, the city of his corporate beginnings. He "put it all on the line," and he "rolled a seven" as he developed what was truly the first mega-resort for the Strip, the Mirage.

In its long history in Las Vegas, the casino industry has many times had to call on individuals to rescue it from pending crashes into oblivion. A post–World War II economic letdown threatened to suspend the flow of tourist dollars as well as local dollars that could go into casino coffers. Bugsy Siegel appeared on the scene with his vision of world-class tourist-destination casinos; he built the Flamingo, and the Las Vegas Strip was in business. In the 1960s, federal investigative authorities focused attention on organized crime investments in Las Vegas casinos. Mob-run properties fell into decay as their owners sought anonymity. Almost like a miracle, Howard Hughes, a "legitimate" multi-multi-millionaire, came to Las Vegas and began buying properties and giving the Strip a cleaner image. More recently, Steve Wynn established himself as "the" entrepreneurial personality of Las Vegas with the opening of the Mirage in November 1989. This bright star was then only 47 years old, but he had already accumulated many years of valuable experience in the gambling industry and even before that many years near the industry.

Several antecedent events might have suggested that Stephen Alan Wynn was going to be a strong individual, a leader with personal magnetism. He was born in Utica, New York, on January 27, 1942. His nuclear family was critical in his development. Stephen Alan Wynn was the grandson of a traveling vaudeville performer and the son of gambling entrepreneur Mike Wynn, who, due to the times, was required to operate on the margins of the law, if not the margins of society. Steve Wynn's mother, Zelma, commented, "If you ran a bingo parlor, some people looked at you as if you were a bookie." (Evidently being a "bookie" was not a good thing in her eyes.) Steve Wynn's inheritance from his grandfather and father suggests that the excitement of entertaining and gaming may have been ingrained in his genetic makeup. Wynn's tie to gaming was more than just genetic, however. He was also exposed to bingo facilities, other gaming, and the personalities of a marginal gaming industry early in his life.

The year 1952 was a time of importance that has been noted in many profiles of Wynn. Steve Wynn has also spoken of it in several personal interviews. When he was just 10 years old, his father, Mike, brought him to Las Vegas. There the father attempted to become established as a bingo operator in the gambling Mecca of the United States. Steve saw the desert and the mountains, and he rode horses. But most important, as a preteenager he saw the action of Las Vegas and it seemingly left an indelible imprint. While in college at the University of Pennsylvania he studied chemistry, gave serious thought to becoming a doctor, graduated with a degree in English literature, and even briefly pursued legal studies. Yet Steve was destined to seek a career in gaming.

Although Steve may have found his dream, his father did not have a winning experience in Las Vegas. His bingo establishment within the Silver Slipper Casino lost out to competition from the better-heeled Last Frontier next door. Mike Wynn also lost his gaming profits through personal gambling activity. Steve told one reporter, "My father made a nice living from bingo, but he'd lose all his money playing gin or betting on baseball. And God forbid if there was a crap game in the vicinity." (Thompson, 200). Mike was given further negative news when the Nevada Gaming Board denied him a gaming license in April 1953.

Michael Wynn's personal drive for the golden ring ended prematurely. Heart failure led to his death on an operating table in 1963, at the age of 55. A business opportunity, or perhaps necessity, was placed into the hands and on the shoulders of the 21-year-old Ivy League college graduate, Steve. The weight of necessity was heavier, too, as Wynn married Elaine Pascal two months after his father died. Someone had to manage a string of bingo halls. But more than an opportunity or a necessity, a rekindled dream was placed directly in front of Steve Wynn. He was not destined to be a chemist, a doctor, a literature teacher, or a lawyer. He was destined to chase his childhood dream and achieve a success that eluded his father. Perhaps now the mission was clear and dominant in his mind. He was going to go to Las Vegas. And he would not only make it in Las Vegas, he would make it big in Las Vegas.

Steve Wynn has been able to achieve his triumphs while somewhat confined in mobility by an incurable eye disease called retinitis pigmentosa. He is unable to drive a car by himself, as his range of vision is limited. The disease may progress, but it has not been accepted as a burden by Wynn. He does consciously seek to conceal its limiting effects from the public, and in some ways it might propel his desires to achieve. He certainly expresses a desire for visual perfection with his personal appearance and his properties. He is always impeccably dressed (even when purposely informal), and his properties rate kudos from architectural analysts and the public alike for their good taste and detailed fixtures and furnishings. Paint lines are exact in corners, and brass railings are always polished. Wynn is noted for having a temper, and invariably the story is told that he expresses loud verbal displeasure when he observes that one light bulb is burned out in a sign with perhaps hundreds of lights. As a blind person is often credited with having a sixth sense, Steve Wynn's limited range of vision seems to give him a heightened sense of detailed vision. The physical limitations of his eye disease are outwardly considered to be but an inconvenience.

Wynn brought his family—his wife, Elaine, and daughter Kevin (born in 1966; a second daughter, Gillian, was born in 1969)—to Las Vegas in 1967. Through contacts gained by work in his father's bingo halls, Wynn was given an opportunity to make a 3 percent investment in the Frontier Hotel and Casino. Subsequent investments brought that to 5 percent. The opportunity must have been especially sweet considering his father's sour experiences in 1952. With the investment came a job as a slot manager. His new associates, however, were not the best people in gaming. They were exposed in a cheating scheme and later subjected to a federal criminal indictment. As a result, the property was sold to the Hughes organization, and Wynn, untainted by the activities of his associates, had to move on.

But Wynn needed help. He found it with two very important friends who played extremely critical roles in his commercial activities: E. Parry Thomas, president of Valley Bank of Nevada, and investment mogul Michael Milkin. Thomas helped Wynn win a liquor distributorship after he left the Frontier. More important, Thomas helped Wynn make a critical connection with Howard Hughes, also a client of Valley Bank. Thomas found that Hughes was paying a high rent for a piece of property next to his Landmark Hotel and Casino. The property was used for parking space for Landmark patrons. Hughes owned a strip of property next to Caesars, however, and he was collecting a lower rate of rent from Caesars so that it too could be used for parking. Caesars had attempted unsuccessfully to buy it from Hughes for about $1 million. Wynn found the owner of the Landmark parking lot and executed an option to buy the land for about a million dollars. Wynn then approached the Hughes organization and suggested a land swap. Hughes went for the deal. The financing for Wynn's purchase was arranged by Thomas. Wynn then started to play high-stakes poker. He turned down a cash offer for the land from Caesars, which would have given him a modest profit. Instead, he initiated a process to win a license for a newly constructed casino that would abut Caesars. He filled out all the application materials and went through the full planning process to obtain all necessary building permits. He even had a contractor break ground, before he extracted the price he wanted for the land—over $2 million. Wynn's personal profit was in excess of $700,000. This money was then used to buy shares of the Golden Nugget Casino.

In 1971, Wynn purchased a large block of Golden Nugget stock, won a place on the corporate board, and in 1973 emerged as the new chief executive of the downtown Las Vegas property. He constructed a new hotel tower and transformed an ordinary property into the most fashionable downtown casino. From his position as chief executive officer of the Golden Nugget, he masterminded the construction and operations of the Golden Nugget in Atlantic City; by all measures the most successful casino on the East Coast. But Wynn was constrained by resource limitations. Then in 1986 he was given a golden opportunity, as Bally's perceived that the only way it could defend itself from a hostile takeover move by Donald Trump (owner of two Atlantic City casinos) was to purchase a second casino of its own. (Atlantic City restricts owners to holding only three licenses, so Trump could not complete the hostile takeover if Bally's had two licenses rather than one.) Bally's wanted the Golden Nugget and wanted it quickly. The company agreed to pay Wynn an exorbitant sum for the property—well above its appraised value—and did so.

Steve Wynn was then free to make his defining Las Vegas move. The move, of course, was the creation of his dream property—the Mirage. It was the first new casino property built in Las Vegas in 16 years when it opened in 1989. Almost instantly, the Las Vegas community was transformed in its self-image. Development money was flowing into the Strip, not only for a big new property (Circus was building the Excalibur, but that was just a bigger Circus Circus), but also for the world's premier gambling entertainment center. The Mirage brought a new popular (but still high-roller) casino into

Las Vegas along with the world's top magic team—Siegfried and Roy—in a new production considered the greatest stage extravaganza in entertainment history. The front exterior of the Mirage featured a waterfall with an "erupting volcano" shooting flames 50 feet into the air all hours of the evening. The back exterior included a dolphin tank and arena. Inside, behind the front desk there was a shark tank. The interior also featured a tiger cage adjacent to a shopping mall, along with top-grade restaurants and state-of-the-art convention facilities. A new standard was set for the Strip; a new psychology of pride and growth took over the town. Others jumped up to follow. The Flamingo expanded, Circus Circus grew some more, and Kirk Kerkorian set his sights on creating the world's largest hotel-casino complex. The new MGM Grand opened with 5,009 rooms, and, of course, Wynn followed with his own Treasure Island (which opened in 1993) and his next dream property, the Bellagio (which opened in 1999). The 1990s became a decade of growth, but the decade would not have happened without its catalyst—Steve Wynn.

The year 2000 brought many surprises, as Kirk Kerkorian of the MGM Grand launched a successful bid to buy a majority of the shares of the Mirage Company. He was thus able to secure control of Steve Wynn's empire in a $6.6 billion transaction. Undaunted, Wynn took his share of the proceeds—about $600 million—and looked over the landscape for his next move. For less than half that amount, he was able to take over 100 percent of the ownership of the classic Desert Inn property, the famous location of Hughes's campaign to control Las Vegas. Wynn now had one of the historically best high-roller properties, and the only golf course on the Las Vegas Strip—a wonderful launching pad for a fresh start, or, that is, another new start. He immediately launched plans for yet another casino, the Wynn Las Vegas. The $2 billion complex opened in April 2005. Wynn had also won one of three new concessions for casinos in Macau, and he opened Wynn Macau in 2006. In 2008, he almost doubled the size of the Wynn Las Vegas resort complex by adding the Encore casino just to its north.

Other industrial towns have found their economies transformed from ones of entrepreneurial dominance to ones of corporate dominance with the passing of generations. But in Las Vegas (and Nevada), until 1963 the law precluded public corporations from operating casinos. Although corporations have now built very large casinos, private groups still have a major presence in the industry—Binions, Engelstadt, the Boyd Group. Also, corporations within the industry are still open to personal leadership, as open competition still welcomes imagination even if Wall Street investors shy away from it. Nevertheless, the first wave of corporate leadership in the casino industry did seem to stifle that imagination by trying to impose values of Wall Street and the Harvard Business School onto the gambling floor. At first, the traditional thinking held gambling back from creativity. Wynn suggests that this made his task as an emerging leader so much easier. "There was this sameness . . . on the Strip. Las Vegas was like the portrait of Dorian Gray. The world had been moving by for 20 years, but everything here stayed the same. You didn't have to be a genius to be a top dog; all you had to do was walk into the present" (Hopkins and Evans, 256).

References

Hopkins, A. D., and K. J. Evans. 1999. *The First 100: Portraits of the Men and Women Who Shaped Las Vegas.* Las Vegas: Huntington Press.

Thompson, William N. 1999. "Steve Wynn: I Got the Message." In *The Maverick Spirit: Building the New Nevada,* edited by Richard O. Davies, 194–210. Reno: University of Nevada Press.

ZIEMBA, WILLIAM T.

William T. Ziemba is a renowned professor of economics and an analyst of horse race betting. He was born on August 30, 1941. He received his PhD from the University of California–Berkeley in 1969. He has been a member of the faculty at the University of British Columbia since that time. He has also taught at UCLA, MIT, Stanford, Oxford, and the University of Zurich.

In the realm of gambling research, Dr. Ziemba has studied sports and lottery investments. He coauthored with Donald B. Hausch two important books on horse race betting, *Beat the Racetrack* (1984) and *Efficiency of Racetrack Betting Markets* (1994).

From his writings, he has gained notoriety for developing "Dr. Z's" betting system. Ziemba has determined that horse race bettors do collectively create a correct market for their picks when they make "win" (first-place) wagers. Therefore, he closely follows how the win bets are made for a race. Waiting until just before the race begins, he looks at the "show" (third-place) bets on the favorite and second-favorite horses. If the show bets for the favorites are substantially less (for example one-half less) than the win bets, he rushes to make a show bet on the horse. He demonstrates the value of the system by tracking all bets made on major races over the last few decades. Using his system with a simple eyeball test of the midfield toteboard at Churchill Downs, this editor was able to cash-in seven of nine show bets one Saturday afternoon in Louisville.

References

Ziemba, William T., and Donald B. Hausch. 1994. *Efficiency of Racetrack Betting Markets.* New York: Academic Press.

Ziemba, William T., and Donald B. Hausch. 1984. *Beat the Racetrack.* New York: Harcourt Brace.

Index